The Day Lasts More
than a
Hundred Years

The Day Lasts More than a Hundred Years

CHINGIZ AITMATOV

TRANSLATED BY JOHN FRENCH
FOREWORD BY KATERINA CLARK

Indiana University Press
Bloomington

Library of Congress Cataloging in Publication Data
Aïtmatov, Chingiz.
    The day lasts more than a hundred years.
    I. Title.
PG3478.I8D613   1983   891.73'44   83-48135
ISBN 0-253-11595-7   1 2 3 4 5 87 86 85 84 83

Foreword
by Katerina Clark

Readers of Chingiz Aitmatov's *The Day Lasts More than a Hundred Years* might well wonder how this novel ever managed to get published in the Soviet Union. After all, its central plot focuses on Yedigei, a Kazakh worker whose heroic task is to bury an old friend according to the traditional Muslim rituals of the Kazakhs, not to build bigger and better tractors as one might expect. Moreover, this is only one of several themes in the novel that seemingly advocate a revival of national traditions dating from before Russian dominance of Central Asia. The science fiction sub-plot can be read as an allegory attacking the Iron Curtain or the Berlin Wall; the interconnected motifs linking the sub-plot to the main story line (a ring of rockets around the earth to keep out a higher civilization and caps that constrict the heads of captured slaves, depriving them of their memories and sense of identity) suggest Soviet mind control or the subjection of the Soviet ethnic minorities and their cultures to the Great Russians. Indeed, it should be remembered that the novel's setting is the republic of Kazakhstan in Soviet Central Asia, an area that borders Afghanistan, which the Soviets invaded in December 1979, less than a year before this novel appeared.

It is not surprising, then, that the novel created a sensation among the Soviet intelligentsia. Copies of the issue of the journal *Novyi mir* in which it first came out* quickly became so unobtainable in

Novyi mir, no. 11, 1980. The novel was republished in book form under the title *The Railway Siding Burannyi* in 1981.

Moscow that an American correspondent there had some run off in the United States to distribute to his Soviet friends.

We might speculate that this novel "slipped past the censor" because Aitmatov is himself on the editorial board of *Novyi mir*. In reality, however, this is not the "dissident" work that it might first appear. Rather, it is one of those rare instances of a Soviet work that excites simultaneously the imaginations of the literary powers-that-be, the intelligentsia, and Western commentators.

Actually, *The Day Lasts More than a Hundred Years* has been a favorite of the Soviet literary establishment ever since it came out. The head of the Writers' Union, Georgy Markov, singled it out in his speech to the Seventh Writers' Congress in 1981 as the most promising recent novel. Since then, the novel has been elevated to the status of a canonical exemplar of socialist realism, and Yedigei has been placed on the short list of model "positive heroes" of Soviet literature, usually the only character on that list to come from a work published in the three decades since Stalin's death.

There are two main reasons for this book's appeal to such a range of constituencies. First, it is highly ambivalent (deliberately so, no doubt). Second and above all, it is timely. The novel dramatizes many of the critical debates going on in the Soviet Union in the early 1980s. Moreover, these are times of change. Even before Brezhnev's death, a reevaluation of some of the basic values and literary patterns which prevailed under Brezhnev had begun. Aitmatov's novel takes account of these changes and poses some of the questions that most preoccupy Soviet Russians today.

In official Soviet literature, the most important single change in the late 1970s and early 1980s has been the reaction against "village prose," the movement which dominated literature for most of the Brezhnev years. As the name implies, "village prose" comprises largely works about rural life. It is not so much the setting or the subject matter which defines "village prose," however, as its ethos. In large measure the movement represents a reaction against such traditional characteristics of Soviet literature as the cult of the superhero who performs titanic economic or political feats. Instead, "village prose" writers favor as their heroes modest, inconsequential people who embody the old virtues. "Village prose" fiction generally shows a marked bias against modernity, technology, and urban life—even against the official Soviet ideal of material progress. Its writers are, to varying degrees, attracted by prerevolutionary, traditional Russian peasant life.

Since the late 1970s, Soviet critics have been attacking "village prose" as a literature of "nostalgia" and insisting that literature must give technology and progress their due. Aitmatov has adjusted his stance somewhat in response. In an earlier work, *The White Ship* (1970), which was set in a remote place high in the mountains of his native Kirghizia, he presented himself more or less as a fellow traveller of "village prose." This work, told from the perspective of an innocent boy, contrasted the goodness of the local Kirghiz who were close to nature and the old traditions with the cynicism, brutality, and lack of morality of those who identified with the modern urban, bureaucratic world. In the present novel, however, Aitmatov emphasizes that technological progress has improved the lives of his characters; he even gives a tractor and an excavator a place in his otherwise traditional funeral cortege. He also lays greater stress on the working lives of his protagonists and the moral uplift they gain from work.

One can see the novel's setting, a remote settlement lost in the Sarozek steppe, as a variant on the usual setting of "village prose." Yet, since it is actually a dormitory for those who work at a railway siding rather than an organic "village," it can be classified as a place of work, the favorite setting of Stalinist fiction. Similarly, some see Yedigei as continuing the tradition of the good but marginal figure who is the stock hero of "village prose," while several Soviet critics claim him to be another Pavel Korchagin (from N. Ostrovsky's *How the Steel Was Tempered* of 1934), one of the most famous superheroes of Soviet literature.

Aitmatov is a "fellow traveller" of "village prose," rather than an actual member of the school, because "village prose" has been part of a neo-Slavophile revival with which Aitmatov, as a Kirghiz, has not identified. Many "village prose" writers are Russian Orthodox by persuasion (indeed purists maintain that in order to be a "village prose" writer one must be Orthodox), and their works are often informed by a Great Russian chauvinism or anti-semitism.

It is not surprising that "village prose" has caused alarm in some official quarters. *Inter alia,* its blatant Russo-centrism is disturbing at a time when the Soviet Union's national minorities have become a critical issue.* As is well known, the high birthrate among certain minorities—and Muslims in particular—means that Great Russians will soon no longer constitute the majority in the country. Indeed, in the next generation Muslims are expected to account for a quarter to a third of the population. At the same time, the minority peoples have over time made up much of the educational gap between them-selves and the Great Russians and might well begin to demand greater power and self-determination than they have enjoyed hitherto. This seems all the more likely, given the increase in ethnic nationalism in the world generally, and among Muslims in particular.

In the many attacks on "village prose" that have appeared in the late 1970s and early 1980s, critics and officials have reminded writers that Soviet literature must be a "multinational" literature and must stress the theme of *unity* among all the Soviet peoples. Editors of literary journals have been instructed to include in their journals a higher proportion of works by authors from the minorities. Special attention has been given to works written by authors of *one* national-ity, but about people of *another* (of which this book—by a Kirghiz and about Kazakhs—is of course an example).

Indeed, "village prose" seems to have taken refuge in the fiction of the national minorities, which, shifting focus, has become obsessed with the past of the people in question. Whether Russians or non-Russians, authors do not so much look at the past with "nostalgia" as they search it for a sense of their own people's cultural heritage, history, and identity. Memory has become *the* theme of Soviet litera-ture today, and Aitmatov has been a leader in exploring this theme. In myriad interconnected motifs (such as Yedigei's concussion, the fate of the *mankurts,* Abutalip's repression for trying to record his

*In writing the sections on the Soviet nationalities problem as it relates to Kazakhstan, I have drawn on Martha Brill Olcott's excellent unpublished essay, "The Development of Nationalism in Kazakhstan."

past, and the cosmonauts' exile for contacting a superior civilization) Aitmatov explores the consequences of not knowing one's past and the danger that history might repeat itself—a theme, incidentally, which Marx himself stressed.

One would anticipate that the resurgence in literature of ethnic national consciousness would be at odds with official Soviet policy on the nationalities, especially now that the theme of unity is being stressed. Actually, however, official policy on the nationalities has itself changed in recent years: the goal is no longer that all the peoples should draw closer to one another *(sblizhenie)*, but rather that the peoples live together in harmony, with each individual people and its culture flourishing *(rastsvet)* in its own way under Communism. This scenario, however, raises some tricky questions, such as what happens in an atheistic state to the belief systems of each people, how does a people retain its individual identity in the face of the homogenizing force of modernization, and where to mark the trade-off between one people's culture and the Russian-cum-Soviet model. Aitmatov's novel explores precisely these questions.

Kazakhstan provides a particularly good setting for examining such problems. What happens in this vast republic (the second largest after the RSFSR) is not an indifferent matter since it is in the area of two countries of crucial importance in Soviet foreign policy, China and Afghanistan. Moreover, the Kazakhs are Muslims; indeed, in some areas of Kazakhstan up to 50 percent of the population are practicing Muslims (although the potential for religious nationalism in Kazakhstan should not be exaggerated since most Kazakhs are Muslims by tradition rather than by belief, there is little Muslim hierarchy in the Republic, and few people are versed in the teachings of Islam).

Even more significant is the fact that the russification-cum-sovietization of Kazakhstan has left the Kazakhs a minority in the Republic (it has over four million Kazakhs, as compared with over five-and-a-half million Russians and almost a million Ukrainians). The progressive settlement of Kazakhstan by Russians has been going on since at least the time of unification with Imperial Russia in 1858 but was stepped up under the Soviets. First, in the thirties, the drive to collectivize agriculture was particularly vicious in Kazakhstan, where there was strong resistance to breaking with the old ways. Many Kazakhs fled to resettle in China or Afghanistan. Then, in the fifties, came Khrushchev's ambitious Virgin Lands scheme, for which thousands of young "volunteers" were sent from European Russia. Russian and Soviet domination also led to the progressive eradication of the Kazakhs' traditional way of life as pastoral nomads who revered their ancestors, their elders, and the good herdsman.

In recent years, Kazakh writers have turned to literature to discuss the traditions of the past and the changes that have occurred. It has often been possible to introduce in literature historical material which could not be discussed in history books. An entire school of writers concerned with their Kazakh heritage has grown up around the literary periodical *Zhuldyz*, and the writers in this group acknowledge their debt to Chingiz Aitmatov.

Of course Aitmatov is a Kirghiz, not a Kazakh. Why should he be concerned about the past of the Kazakhs? An initial reason might be that Aitmatov has always identified himself not merely as a Kirghiz, but as a member of the Turkic peoples of the Soviet Union, or as a Central Asian, and Kazakhstan is a part of this "homeland." Kirghizia borders on Kazakhstan (in fact Aitmatov comes from an area close to the border), and the two Soviet Republics were one political unit until 1936. Also, although the two peoples have clashed at various points in their history, there is not the bitter rivalry between them that exists between other neighboring Soviet ethnic groups, such as the Armenians and the Georgians. There are, however, differences between the two peoples; for instance, each speaks a different Turkic language and is ethnically quite distinct. The Kirghiz culture is oriented more toward its mountainous terrain, the Kazakh, more to its steppes and arid regions.

Despite these differences, the Kazakhs and Kirghiz share some common experiences which are particularly relevant to Aitmatov's novel. In particular, their history of association with the Russians is comparable, both are traditionally Muslim, and the culture of both centers on man's relationship to animals and to his forebears (central themes, incidentally, in many of Aitmatov's works). Thus, it is possible that Aitmatov, wishing to make some points about his own people's relationship to their past, used the time-honored strategy of distancing the subject by locating it in a different but comparable setting. That the Kirghiz past is a point of reference in the novel is suggested in the small detail that, at the end of the book, Aitmatov names Cholpon-Ata as the place where he wrote the work; Cholpon-Ata is not his home town or his usual place of residence but rather a town most remarkable for the fact that settlements dating back to the ancient past were unearthed nearby.

The havoc that collectivization wreaked on the traditional way of life is hinted at in the novel, and the topic of Stalinist repression receives fairly extensive coverage. Otherwise, however, Aitmatov is quite circumspect about what sovietization and russification have done to his people. For instance, he has been careful to keep his account of Soviet life largely within a Kazakh context: the capital from which the orders flow is not Moscow but Alma-Ata, and the most negative characters (the Tansykbaevs) are Kazakhs, while the few Russians in the novel are positive characters. Also, for the Kazakhs in the novel, China looms as a more menacing and extremist alternative to Soviet power; *that* is the land of mind control.

In general, politically delicate themes, such as how the Kazakhs, in danger of losing their distinctive culture, are striving to maintain their creative independence, have been treated metaphorically. They are present, for instance, in the accounts of how Yedigei prizes his camel, one of the last of a great old local breed, and how he refuses to castrate him, even though this means enduring periods of uncontrollable revolt. Above all, however, such politically delicate themes are embedded in the material Aitmatov presents as folk legends of the local Kazakhs.

There has been a marked vogue in recent years to use folklore and legends in fiction as a means of elucidating the present and exploring continuities with the past. In the West, this has led to such curious works as John Calvin Batchelor's *The Birth of the People's Republic of Antarctica*. In the Soviet Union, Aitmatov (who prefers to cite the leftist Marquez as a model rather than any "capitalist" writer) has been a trendsetter in this respect, with his *The White Ship*, which was built around a story purported to be the origin myth of the Kirghiz. In the present novel, however, the element of political allegory in the folklore material is more pronounced than in Aitmatov's earlier works.

Several Soviet critics have claimed that Aitmatov has based the various folk legends he uses in this novel on parts of the great Kirghiz epic poem, *The Manas*. *The Manas*, which comprises over 250,000 verses and is thus sixteen times the length of *The Iliad*, functioned for the largely illiterate Kirghiz of pre-Soviet times as the chief repository of their past. As far as one can ascertain, however, Aitmatov has appropriated some of the clichés of Central Asian traditional literature generally but has not followed any specific text. This seems to be the case with the key "legend" of the novel, the story of the founding of the Ana-Beiit cemetery, where Aitmatov appears to have combined elements from outside the regional traditions (such as the torture used on the young warriors) with kaleidoscopically recreated elements from the Central Asian epic (such as the mother's risking her life trying to search out and save a captured son).

There are, of course, ample European and Russian precedents for the literary appropriation of elements from folk epic. And, indeed, although Aitmatov's indebtedness to Central Asian sources in this novel is immediately apparent, the more profound influences have been those of Western, or specifically Russian, literature. Readers of Russian literature will readily recognize in this novel the mark of such writers as Pushkin, Chernyshevsky, and Dostoevsky and several well-known Soviet Russian writers of the post-Stalin era.

Aitmatov, the seeker after a distinct ethnic identity, then, does so in large measure by paying tribute to the literary tradition of the culture dominating his own. This paradox illustrates a basic ambivalence characteristic of many writers from the ethnic minorities who are involved in the movement for greater ethnic consciousness. These writers, who are largely bilingual (with Russian), come from and, in their readership, cater to, the Russianized educated elite of their people. Members of this elite are indebted to the Russians for the position they enjoy locally and appreciate that the Russians have given them access to the "civilization" of the world at large. Aitmatov comes from this elite. He is bilingual and writes in both Kirghiz and Russian. Indeed, his biography is itself an advertisement for the opportunities for social mobility via identification with Soviet power.

Aitmatov was born in 1928 in the *ail* (mountain village) of Sheker in the Talas Valley of Kirghizia. He completed only six years of school, but during World War II, though he was then fourteen, he became secretary (head) of the Village Soviet (council) and a tax collector. He later trained to be a veterinarian, graduating in 1953, and worked on an experimental farm.

In 1952 Aitmatov branched out into literature. In January of that year he published an article in *Soviet Kirghizia*, "On the Terminology of the Kirghiz Language," in which he remarked on how much the Kirghiz language had been enriched by borrowing from Russian. He then published a few short stories. These publications helped him get into the Literary Institute in Moscow, from which he graduated in 1958. While studying, Aitmatov published several short works but without notable success. He was propelled into the limelight only after his novella "Dzhamilia" came out in 1958 ("Dzhamilia" treats the right of a young Kirghiz woman to "reject patriarchal norms" and leave the husband she was given in a traditional, arranged marriage to run off with her true love). The work was translated into many languages and was especially taken up by Louis Aragon, who both translated it into French and wrote a foreword for it.

Since the publication of "Dzhamilia," Aitmatov has emerged as a major Soviet writer and a figure of the intellectual establishment. He is on the governing board of many intellectual and cultural institutions (such as the *Literary Gazette* and the Writers' Union) and, for the past twenty years, he has been head of the Kirghiz Filmmakers' Union. Since 1961, he has been a roving correspondent for *Pravda* in Central Asia and Kazakhstan. He is a member of the Supreme Soviet, was a delegate to the last four Party Congresses, and has won many national honors, including a Lenin Prize and a State Prize (both for literature) and the Hero of Socialist Labor medal (awarded for his fiftieth birthday). Additionally, Aitmatov has been a frequent speaker both in the capital and abroad, especially to Third World delegations and audiences. Of particular relevance to this novel are his appearances at East Bloc–sponsored peace conferences.

Although he has been coopted into the establishment, Aitmatov has not ceased trying to be a serious writer. His most important works published after "Dzhamilia" include three others available in translation: *Farewell, Gul'sary!* (1966)—the plot centers on a man tending his dying horse and musing over his past, on how he was excluded from the Party under Stalin, and on whether he should rejoin it, *The White Ship* (1970), and the play *The Ascent of Mount Fuji* (1973). Written together with Kaltai Mukhamedzhanov, the play concerns a reunion of old schoolfriends which is overshadowed by their knowledge that the brightest member of their group was purged under Stalin and perished, and that one of their number must have betrayed him.

The one shadow in this otherwise impeccable biography is that Aitmatov's father, a Party member, was purged during Aitmatov's childhood. This fact did not prevent the son from joining the Party himself in 1959 but may account for the prominence of the themes of Stalinist abuses and a child's loss of his father in many of his writings, including the present novel.

The name we most associate with fiction about Stalinist repression is Solzhenitsyn, and this novel shows Solzhenitsyn's influence. In particular, Aitmatov seems to have borrowed the main technique Solzhenitsyn used in *One Day in the Life of Ivan Denisovich* for focusing a large amount of disparate material from different points in Soviet history and geography. Like Solzhenitsyn, Aitmatov presents this material as part of his central character's musings on the past and his conversations with those around him during a mere "day" spent in a small area (in this case the day or so it takes Yedigei to give his friend a proper burial in the desert near the railway junction). Aitmatov has, however, expanded the parameters of space and time much further than Solzhenitsyn to embrace East and West, and even the infinite time/space possibilities of intergalactic travel, as well as the timelessness of legend.

This extremely ambitious expansion of the novel's time and space is not necessarily Aitmatov's own invention. In recent years, and in reaction against the trend of "village prose" writers to set their works in tiny, out-of-the-way places, authoritative voices have been urging writers to produce works which use a "large scale" and are of "global scope." In fact, the particular time and place patterns of Aitmatov's novel (i.e., that it embraces the Soviet past and present, legendary times, the West, and even space exploration) are quite commonly found in Soviet fiction today, especially in science fiction. This emphasis on "global scope" reflects the critical importance that international relations have assumed for the Soviet Union of late. All too often, however, recent fiction of "global scope" has developed into Cold War tracts, in which the evils of life in the West and its basic militarism are exposed.

Aitmatov's novel is not a predictable encounter of East versus West. Nor is it just about Kazakhstan or Kirghizia. He wanted a work which was both specific to the experience of his people and universal in resonance. He sought to achieve this by organizing his novel around a pattern of binary contrasts analogous to the binary implicit in his title, *The Day Lasts More than a Hundred Years* (actually, an alternative translation, *The Day Longer than an Age Does Last,* brings out this contrast better): small units of time and place (the day of Kazangap's burial and a railway junction in the Kazakh steppe) are contrasted, and yet also interconnected, with ever vaster units, extending as far as the timelessness of legend and the infinity of space. In consequence, the novel conveys both the miniature quality and sense of locale to be found in "village prose" and the greater "scale" that writers are now expected to use in their works. The individual lives of minor figures who live on that tiniest speck of the universe which is the railway junction resonate with the fate of the Kazakhs (or the Kirghiz, or the Turkic peoples of the Soviet Union, or the Central Asians), which in turn resonates with the history of the Soviet Union, the lot of mankind, and the universe itself.

Preface

Everyone knows that diligence is one of the essential yardsticks by which one judges the virtues of a man, and Yedigei Zhangel'din, or Burannyi Yedigei, as people who know still call him, is indeed a highly diligent and industrious person. He is the salt of the earth. He is also in the strictest sense at one with the time in which he lives – as far as I can tell – and in that is his whole being. He is a child of his time. Because of this, it was important to me in considering the problems touched on in this story to see the world through his eyes – the eyes of a man who had been a soldier at the front and a worker on the railway. And I have tried to do this as best I can.

The main object of socialist realism, in my view, is to present the image of the working man. However, I am far from confining the meaning of 'hard worker' to one sort – the 'simple, natural person' who assiduously tills the land and tends the cattle. In the clash of the eternal and the present in life, a hard worker is interesting and important in so much as he is an individual in the dimension of his soul and in so far as he reflects the time in which he lives. So I have tried to put Burannyi Yedigei in the centre of things – that is, in the centre of the problems that concern me.

Burannyi Yedigei is not only a hard worker by nature and by virtue of the *kind* of work he performs. He is a person with a diligent spirit; a man who will always ask himself questions and never be satisfied with easy answers – unlike other men, who, although conscientious workers, are basically lazy and live by taking what they can get.

Diligent spirits such as Burannyi Yedigei seem to share a sort of brotherhood – they can always recognize one another and share their understanding; or, if they do not always understand, at least they think things over. And our times give them so much to think about – more than any previous century. Already the thread of Man's memory stretches out from the earth into space.

It must be the most tragic contradiction of the late twentieth century that although Man's genius is unlimited, it is constrained on all sides by political, ideological and racial barriers arising out of imperialism. Today, we have not only the technological capability for safe space travel but also an urgent economic and ecological necessity for it; surely, then, pointless conflicts between peoples and the waste of material resources and mental energy on the arms race are the most monstrous crimes against Mankind? Only the breaking down of international tensions can be considered a progressive policy today. There is no more important task on earth, for if Man cannot learn to live in peace, he will perish. The atmosphere of mutual distrust, of global tension, of confrontation, is one of the most potent threats to the future welfare of Mankind.

People can be patient with each other, but they cannot think the same, because they remain people, preserving their human characteristics. The wish to deprive Man of his individuality has from ancient times down to the present accompanied imperialist, imperial and hegemonic claims.

A man without a sense of history, without memory of the past, who is forced to reconsider his place in the world, a man deprived of the historic experience of his own and other peoples, lacks any perspective and can only live for the present, for the day. To prove this, one has only to recall the 'Cultural Revolution' in China, which manipulated the consciousness of the people and reduced the many complications of life to the level of quotations from the so-called little Red books of Mao. Here, the ancient traditions of the people clashed with the hegemonic policies of the then Chinese government. Paradoxically this denial or falsification of the past went hand in hand with a self-satisfied, boastful chauvinism. The result was isolation; for only behind a real or metaphorical Wall of China can one preserve the myth of the superiority of one people over all others.

As in previous works, here also I draw on legends and myths handed down to us from former generations; together with these, for the first time in my writing career I also use fantasy to form part of the story. But, for me, neither is an end in itself, simply a method of expressing thoughts, a means of identifying and interpreting realities.

Of course, the events described here – the contacts with a civilization beyond earth – have no basis in fact. The Sarozek and Nevada space centres do not really exist. This cosmological tale has been dreamed up with one intention only – to draw attention in a paradoxical hyperbolic fashion, to a situation full of potential danger for people on earth.

There is one strange paradox in this world: in ancient Greece, wars ceased during the Olympiad; but today the Olympiad has become, for some countries, an excuse for Cold War.

As far as the meaning of fantasy is concerned, Dostoevsky in his time wrote: 'The fantastic in art has its limits and laws. The fantastic must so merge with reality that you can almost believe it.' Indeed, the mythology of the ancient, the fantasy-realism of Gogol, Bulgakov or Marquez, science fiction – all of these are convincing in so far as they touch reality. Fantasy highlights certain aspects of reality and, when Dostoevsky's rules are followed, shows them philosophically generalized, developed to their ultimate logical conclusion.

Fantasy also involves the use of metaphor, thus allowing us to see life from a new and unexpected point of view. Metaphor has become especially vital in our time, not only because of the scientific and technological advances in the fields of what was yesterday's fantasy, but more so because the fantastic world in which we live is full of contrasts – economic, political, ideological and racial.

May the Sarozek metaphors of my novel remind the working man once more of his responsibility for the fate of our planet . . .

And this book is – instead of my body,
And this word is – instead of my soul.

Grigor Narekatsi,
The Book of Sorrow,
10th century

The Day Lasts More
than a
Hundred Years

CHAPTER ONE

The hungry vixen had to be patient as she searched for prey among the dried-out gullies and the bare ravines. Following along the intertwining, giddily wandering tracks of the small burrowing animals – now furiously digging out a marmot's lair, now waiting until a small jerboa which had been hiding in an underground storm channel jumped out into the open where he could be quickly despatched – she moved quietly as a mouse, slowly and purposefully working her way towards the distant railway.

This railway, with its dark and even track stretching far away into the steppe, both lured and frightened her. First in one direction and then in the other, the clattering trains thundered by, shaking the whole earth around and leaving behind smoke, heat, and powerful, irritating smells that were carried over towards her by the wind.

Towards evening, the vixen lay alongside the telegraph line in the bottom of a culvert, in a thick, tall patch of dried horse sorrel. She curled herself up into a reddish-yellow ball under the dark red, seed-laden stems, patiently waiting for nightfall, nervously twitching her ears, continually listening to the high whistle of the wind in the waving dry grass. The telegraph wires and poles droned dully, but she was not afraid of them. At least the poles always stayed where they were and could not follow her.

But the deafening noise of the trains made the vixen shiver and curl up more tightly each time they passed. As the ground thundered beneath her, she felt its convulsions in every fibre of her slender body; felt the violence, the furious movement, and recoiled with fear and revulsion at the strange smells. She did not leave the culvert, but waited for darkness, when the rails would become relatively quiet. She came here infrequently, only when hunger drove her to it.

In the gaps between the trains, a sudden silence, like that after a fall of big stones down a cliff, descended upon the steppe; and in that utter stillness the vixen detected in the air a certain high-pitched sound which put her instantly on her guard. It came over the evening-lit steppe, hardly audible and apparently belonging to no one. Either it was a play of air currents or it heralded some imminent change in the weather.

The animal felt it instantly and froze in her tracks, silent, although inwardly she longed to howl, to yelp at this clear premonition of danger. But hunger stilled even this warning from nature. As she licked the pads of her paws, tired from her running, the vixen just whined a little, quietly.

At this time, autumn was on its way and the evenings were already cold. At night the ground quickly cooled, and by dawn the steppe was covered with a rime of white, just like salt crystals – the touch of a soon-disappearing frost. The time of want, the cheerless time, was approaching for the animals of the steppe. Many of the wild creatures which had been around in the summer had now left – some to warmer lands, others settling down in their lairs in the sand for the winter. Now every fox was out hunting for its food alone, as if the rest of its species had vanished off the face of the earth. The year's young ones had grown up and scattered, and the mating time was still far ahead – that time in winter when the foxes begin to run together to meet from all points of the compass and the dog foxes fight with that same ferocity that they have possessed since the dawn of creation.

When night fell, the vixen came out of the ditch. She stopped, ears pricked, and padded softly over to the railway track, noiselessly running, now to this side, now to the other side of the rails in search of food thrown out of train windows by the passengers. After running a long way down the embankment, sniffing at all sorts of objects, some foul-smelling, she finally found something edible. The whole track was littered with torn papers and screwed-up newspapers, broken bottles, cigarette ends, twisted tins and other rubbish. The intoxicating smell from the unbroken bottles was especially foul. After the vixen had become dizzy once or twice, she tried to avoid breathing in the alcoholic vapours, coughed and immediately ran away from the bottle.

But there was no sign of what she was hoping to find, what she had long waited for, fighting back her fear. All the same, in the hope that she might still find something more to eat, she ran tirelessly down the railway track, every now and then moving from one side to the other.

Suddenly the vixen froze in her tracks once more, lifting one front paw as if caught off guard. In the dim light of the high, mist-obscured moon, she stood between the rails like a ghost. The distant rumbling which had put the animal on her guard could again be heard, but it was still coming from far off. The vixen shifted from one foot to the other, tail straight out, ready at any moment to run off. But instead she began to hurry on over the sleepers, still hoping to come upon something edible.

Now the relentless, threatening noise of straining iron and the thundering of hundreds of wheels was getting closer. The vixen paused for a fraction of a minute – and that was enough; suddenly around a bend came the near and far lights of a pair of engines in tandem, the powerful, dazzling lights whitening the steppe and pitilessly laying bare its dead aridity. The train was hurtling along the rails with a shattering roar, filling the air with a smell of burning and clouds of choking dust.

The vixen ran off, now and again looking over her shoulder, cringing close to the ground in fear. The monster, its lights ablaze, raced past and for a long while rattled and groaned away in the distance, its wheels still beating out their rhythm. The vixen jumped up and raced away, off at full speed.

Then the animal rested and was once more drawn back to the railway track, hoping to assuage its hunger. But now there were more lights: once more a pair of locomotives were dragging a long, laden freight train . . .

The vixen ran away in a great curve over the steppe. She would return to the line when the trains had gone.

*

11

Trains in these parts went from East to West, and from West to East . . .

On either side of the railway lines lay the great wide spaces of the desert – Sary-Ozeki, the Middle lands of the yellow steppes.

In these parts any distance was measured in relation to the railway, as if from the Greenwich meridian . . .

And the trains went from East to West, and from West to East . . .

At midnight he could make out someone determinedly but slowly making their way towards him in the signal box. At first, the figure kept close to the railway lines, then, with the approach of a train, went down the embankment and, as if caught in a blizzard, put up its hands to protect its face against the squall of wind and dust raised by the fast freight train. (It was a special train with a distinctive letter, using the clear line, then going off down the spur into the Sary-Ozek-1 closed area, where they had their own special control staff. Evidently it was on its way to the launching site; all its waggons were covered with tarpaulins and there were armed guards on each truck.)

Yedigei recognized the figure as that of his wife, and he could see that she was hurrying. She must have something special to tell him – something serious. However, he was not allowed to leave his post until the last waggon with its armed guard on the open platform had gone by. He and the guard exchanged signals with their lamps to indicate that all was in order on the line. Only then did Yedigei, deafened by the noise, turn to his wife as she hurried up,

'What are you doing here?'

She looked at him, worried, and her lips moved. Yedigei could not hear what she said, but understood – or thought he did.

'Come in out of the wind.' He led her into the box.

But before he could hear from her lips what he himself had already guessed, he felt a momentary stab of pity for his wife: she was out of breath from running, hoarse from exhaustion, there was a croaking sound in her chest, and her shoulders were heaving. The strong electric light in the small white signal box suddenly showed up lines which he had never noticed before on Ukubala's blueing, dark cheeks – in the past, her face had been a healthy wheat-brown colour and her eyes had always sparkled. Then there was the toothless state of her mouth. A woman, as she grew old, should never be toothless. He should have taken her to the town long ago to have some of those metal teeth fitted. Everyone wore them now, young and old. Added to which, her white hair now hung untidily over her face. Altogether, the sight of her cut into his very heart. *Oh, my dear one, how old you have become . . .*

As his heart pitied her, he felt an aching sense of guilt for it all. Yet at the same time a silent gratitude came upon him – gratitude for all that they had lived through together over so many years. Especially it touched him to think that she had come running out along the tracks in the middle of the night, to the most distant part of the junction, out of respect, out of her sense of duty to him, because she knew how important it was to her Yedigei. She had run to tell him of the death of the unhappy Kazangap, a lonely old man who had died alone in an empty mud-walled shack. She understood that Yedigei alone in the world would take to heart the death of this old man, deserted by everyone else – although the dead man had been neither brother nor father to him.

'Sit down and get your breath back!' said Yedigei, once they were inside the box.

'You sit down, too,' she said to her husband.

They sat down.

'What's happened?'

'Kazangap has died.'

'When?'

'Well, I just looked in to see how he was; I thought that perhaps he needed something. I went in; his light was on, he was lying on his bed with his beard somehow sticking up in the air . . . I went closer. I said to him, "Kazake, Kazake, perhaps you'd like some tea . . ." but he was already –'

Her voice broke. The tears welled up from her reddened, tired eyelids and, with a sob, Ukubala began quietly to cry.

13

'So that's how it was at the end. What a man he was! And he died with no one to close his eyes. Who would have thought a man could die like that . . . Like a –' She was about to say like a dog on the road, but she kept silent; there was no point in saying more. All was clear enough without that.

Burannyi Yedigei – so-called because he had worked at the Boranly-Burannyi junction ever since he had returned from the war – sat on the bench in gloomy silence with his great hands, like gnarled branches, resting on his knees. The peak of his railway cap, thoroughly oil-soaked and untidy, covered his eyes. What was he thinking about?

'What are we going to do now?' said his wife.

Yedigei lifted up his head, looked at her and smiled wryly.

'What are we going to do? Just what people always do! Bury him.' He got up like a man with everything decided. 'You, my wife – you'd better get home as soon as you can. But first listen to me.'

'Yes?'

'Wake Ospan. Never mind that he's in charge of this junction – when death comes, all men are equal. Tell him that Kazangap has died. He worked forty years in this one place. Ospan probably wasn't even born when Kazangap started work here, and in those days you couldn't drag a dog to the Sarozek. Think how many trains have passed through here in his time – no one has hairs enough to count them all. Let him think that over. And there's something more.'

'I'm listening.'

'Wake everyone. Knock on their windows. There are eight houses here. Get everyone up. No one should sleep today when such a man has died. Wake them all up!'

'And what if they start to swear at me?'

'Our duty is to let everyone know – let them swear. Tell them that I told you to wake them. One must have a conscience. Wait!'

'What else?'

'Go to the duty man – Shaimerden is the controller today; tell him what has happened, and tell him it's up to him to decide what to do. Perhaps this time he could find me a relief.

If he can, then he should take the necessary action. You've got that? Off you go, then, and tell them.'

'I'll tell them, I'll tell them,' answered Ukubala. Then she hesitated, as if she had suddenly remembered the most important thing, which unforgiveably she had forgotten.

'What about his children? That lot! Surely it's our first duty to send them the news – but how? Their father's dead . . .'

Yedigei frowned and looked even more serious, but said nothing.

'Whatever they may be, they *are* his children,' continued Ukubala, in a tone of self-justification, knowing that it would be unpleasant for Yedigei to hear the words.

'Yes, I know,' he waved his hand, 'do you think I don't understand? I suppose we can't stop them coming – but if I had my way, I wouldn't let them near here!'

'Yedigei, it's none of our business. Let them come and bury him. The talking can come later, you can't avoid it . . .'

'Am I stopping you? Let them come.'

'But will the son manage to get here in time from the town?'

'He'll get here, if he wants to . . . The day before yesterday when I was at the station, I sent him a telegram to say that his father was near death. What else could I do? He has such a high opinion of himself, he should understand where his duty lies.'

'Well, if you did that, then that's all right.' His wife saw at once the force of what Yedigei had said, but at the same time there was something else that was worrying her. 'But it would be good if his wife came as well. After all, it *is* her father-in-law who's being buried . . .'

'Let them decide for themselves. What can we do about it – they're not little children.'

'Yes, yes.' But Ukubala was still not entirely convinced.

They were silent.

'Well then, that's that; don't wait any longer – hurry along,' said Yedigei.

His wife, however, had something else to say.

'. . . And there's his daughter – that poor Aizada. She's at

15

the station with her lazy good-for-nothing husband, and her children; she should come to the funeral too.'

Yedigei smiled, then patted his wife on the shoulder.

'There you go, worrying about everyone. It's not far to reach her; someone's sure to be going to the station in the morning – they can tell her the news. She'll come, of course. Remember, it's not worth expecting much from either Aizada or from Sabitzhan, even if he's the son and a grown man. You see – they'll come, but they won't lift a finger; they'll stand there like guests, while we do all the work. That's how it'll be. Now hurry along and do as I say.'

His wife went off, then stopped as if still in doubt and came back. But Yedigei called to her, 'Don't forget – go first to see Shaimerden, on duty; let him send someone to take my place here. I'll pay them back later. The dead man is lying there alone in an empty house. That mustn't be. Tell him so.'

Off went his wife with a nod. Meanwhile, at the distant signal there was a whistle from an engine and the red light was winking. Another train was approaching Boranly–Burannyi junction. On the orders of the duty signalman, it had to be diverted to the reserve line in order to allow the train waiting at the other end of the junction to pass through. This was the normal procedure. While the trains were moving along their lines, Yedigei now and again looked at Ukubala as she walked away along the edge of the tracks. He felt as if there was something else that he had forgotten to tell. Of course, there were plenty of things to say and there would be plenty more before the funeral, but you can't remember everything at once. There was another reason why he was gazing after her; it was simply that he was noticing again how much older she seemed. She had even begun to stoop recently – it was more noticeable than ever under the yellow misty lighting from the lamps over the track.

'It seems as if old age has already overtaken us,' he thought. 'So this is what we've come to – an old man and an old woman.'

God had not treated him badly, though – at least, as far as health was concerned. He was still strong. Nevertheless, quite a few years of his life had passed; sixty – no, sixty-one now.

'You've hardly had time to look around, and yet in two years you'll be ready to put in for retirement,' said Yedigei to himself, almost with a laugh.

But he knew quite well that he would not be retiring so soon. It would not be easy for his superiors to find a person from hereabouts to replace him – he was a track inspector and repair worker; he also operated the signals from time to time when others were sick or on leave. Would they find a new man prepared to accept the extra pay in exchange for all the remoteness and the isolation of life in the Sarozek? Unlikely. The young people of today would not put up with it.

You must have the will to live on the Sarozek junctions – otherwise you perish. The steppe is vast and man is small. The steppe takes no sides; it doesn't care if you are in trouble or if all is well with you; you have to take the steppe as it is. But a man cannot remain indifferent to the world around him; it worries him and torments him to think that he could be happier somewhere else, and that he is where he is simply through a mistake of fate. Because of this he wears himself out before the great, pitiless steppe and loses his will, just as that accumulator on Shaimerden's three-wheel motor-bike loses its charge. The owner looks after it, but does not ride it or lend it to anyone else. So the machine stands idle – and that's all there is to it – soon it won't start up any more, its starting power is lost. It is the same with a man at a Sarozek junction: he fails to get on with his work, to put down roots in the steppe, to adjust to his surroundings; and then he finds he can't settle down. Passengers look out from passing trains, shake their heads and ask: 'God, how can people live here? Nothing but steppe and camels!' But people who have enough patience *can* live here. For three years, or four, with an effort . . . But then they pack up and get as far away as possible. Only two people really put down roots at Boranly–Burannyi – Kazangap and he, Burannyi Yedigei. And how many others came and went! Yedigei, however, was the kind of man who never gave up, and Kazangap, too, worked here for forty-four years – and not because he was thicker than anyone else. No – Yedigei would have swapped any number of other men for one Kazangap. And now he was gone . . .

The trains separated – one to the East, the other to the West. For a time the junction of Boranly–Burannyi was deserted. And all at once everything around was clearer: the stars seemed to shine more brightly from the dark sky and the wind whined more intensely along the embankment and over the gravel ballast between the weakly ringing, clinking rails.

Yedigei did not leave the hut door; he was deep in thought, leaning against the pillar. Far ahead, beyond the railway, he could make out the dim silhouettes of the camels, grazing in the fields. They stood there under the moon, not moving, whiling away the night. And among them Yedigei made out his Bactrian, the large-headed, two-humped male – the strongest in the Sarozek, and fast, too. He was called, like his master, Burannyi-Karanar. Yedigei was proud of him, this animal of rare strength, although he was not easy to cope with. Karanar had remained a full-blooded male; Yedigei had not castrated him when young, and later on had left him untouched.

Among the chores for the coming day, Yedigei remembered that first thing in the morning, he would have to drive Karanar home and saddle him. He was needed for the funeral journey. Then he remembered other things which would have to be done.

At the junction, people were still sleeping peacefully. On one side of the track were the small service buildings belonging to the station; the six prefabricated houses with their standard twin-sloped, slated roofs built by the railway administration; and then Yedigei's house, which he had built himself, and the dead Kazangap's mud-walled house. There were also various stores, outhouses, reed-thatched stables for cattle and other purposes, and in the centre the windmill-driven universal electric pump which had arrived a few years back, and the hand-pump for emergencies. This was the sum total of the settlement of Boranly-Burannyi.

As is usual on a great railway, everything here by the Sary-Ozeki steppe formed part of a great network like a maze of bloodvessels, consisting of other junctions, stations, and towns. And all was laid bare to the winds of heaven, especially in winter, when the Sarozek blizzards whirled, covering the houses up to their windows in snowdrifts and the rails with firm, frozen piles of snow. Hence the name of this junction in the middle of the steppe: Boranly-Burannyi, or 'snow storm', with 'Boranly' written in Kazakh and 'Burannyi' in Russian.

Yedigei remembered that before the snow-clearing machine arrived – the kind that poured out the snow in bullet-like streams and moved it to either side with great blades and other devices – he and Kazangap had had to struggle against the snow on the rails – not so much for life, but to the death, as it were. And it had not been so long ago, either. In 1951 and 1952 they had had very hard winters. Was it only as a soldier that one had, when life demanded it, to do something just the once – one attack, one throw of a grenade under a tank? No, it was the same here. The only difference was that instead of other people killing you, you could kill yourself in the process. How many snowfalls had they fought bare-handed, scraping it up and even shovelling the snow into sacks? That had been at the Seventh Kilometre, where the track ran downhill through a cutting. Each time it had seemed the last time this battle would ever be fought, and for that reason he had never seriously considered chucking up the job. All that he had wanted was to stop hearing the blaring of the engines' whistles out on the steppe and to let them get through!

But the snows melted, the trains went through, the years passed . . .

No one would give a thought to those times now. Perhaps it had happened, perhaps it hadn't. Nowadays when it snowed, the track engineers from the control and repair brigades came out for a short while – noisy types who could not believe or understand or even imagine how it had once been: the Sarozek snowdrifts – and to clear them, just a handful of men with shovels! Wonderful! Some of them just laughed openly. Why was it necessary, they asked, to torture yourself? *We* wouldn't have worn ourselves out like that, not on your life! 'If we'd been told to do that, we'd have chucked it. Told them to go to the devil, and found other work – at the worst, on a building site, or somewhere else where conditions were properly organized. Work so much, pay us so much and if an emergency made it necessary, hold a meeting and pay out the overtime. They took you for fools, you old men, and fools you'll die.'

When they met such arrogance, Kazangap simply took no notice; he would act unconcerned and just laugh, as if he knew something more, something these younger men just could not understand. But Yedigei could not contain himself; he would explode and argue, and the sole result of that was that he got upset and in a bad mood.

Kazangap and he used to talk about those early days – days when all those wise young track engineers had been running around in short trousers. In those days they had discussed life as much as their cautious wisdom would allow and, later on, all the time; those days of 1945 were long past. They discussed things a lot, particularly after Kazangap took his pension. Things did not work out for him. He went to live in the town with his son, but three months later he came back. Then there was even more to discuss.

Kazangap was a wise but simple man. There was much to remember about him . . .

Then suddenly Yedigei realized with awful clarity and grief that he had only his memories now . . .

Hearing the noise as the microphone of the communication set came on, Yedigei hurried into the hut. The radio always gave out a sound of rushing air and whistling, as in a blizzard, before a voice was heard on the stupid set.

'Yedike, hullo, Yedike,' whistled the voice of Shaimerden, the duty man at the junction, 'do you hear me? Answer!'

'I hear you, I'm listening.'

'Can you hear me?'

'I can hear you, yes, I hear you.'

'How do you hear me?'

'As if from another world.'

'What do you mean, from another world?'

'Just that.'

'Ah . . . must be like old Kazangap himself.'

'What do you mean?'

'Well, he's dead, isn't he?' Shaimerden was trying to find something appropriate to say. 'Well, what shall I say? He's sort of, I mean, he's completed his life's journey.'

'Yes,' Yedigei answered laconically. But he thought to himself, *What a brainless ox. He can't even talk about death like any real person would.*

Shaimerden was quiet for a moment. The instrument began to make more wheezing noises, rustling and squeaking. There were sounds of heavy breathing. Then Shaimerden croaked out, 'Yedigei, my dear fellow, don't take me for a fool in this way. If he's dead, what can we do about it? I've no spare people. Why do you have to go and sit beside him? His corpse won't rise again.'

Yedigei was infuriated. 'You've no understanding! What do you mean about taking you for a fool? You've been here less than two years, but he and I worked together for thirty. Think that over! One of us has died; it's not right to leave a dead man alone in an empty house.'

'How can he tell if he's alone or not?'

'*We* know.'

'All right. There's no need to shout so, old man.'

'Let me explain –'

'There's nothing to explain. I've no spare people. What can you do – it's night.'

'I'll pray. I will lay out the dead man. I'll say prayers.'

'Say prayers? You, Burannyi Yedigei?'

'Yes, me. I know all the prayers.'

'And this after, what, sixty years of Soviet rule?'

'What's Soviet rule got to do with it? People have been praying over the dead for centuries. It's a man who's died, not some beast.'

'Well, you go ahead and pray if you must, but do stop making such a fuss. I'll send for Edil'bai – if he agrees, then he'll come and, er, take over from you. But now let's get on with the job – 117 is approaching, be ready to put it on to the second reserve siding line . . .'

And with that Shaimerden rang off, the switch clicked over.

Yedigei hurried back to the signal control and, as he got on

21

with his work, wondered if Edil'bai would agree to come. He began to hope that people really had a conscience when he saw that there were now lights burning brightly in the windows of some of the houses. The dogs were barking too, so evidently his wife was busy spreading the news and getting the people of Boranly out of their beds.

Meanwhile 117 had gone on to the reserve line, and from the other end of the junction an oil train was approaching – all tanker waggons. The two trains passed and separated, one to the East, the other to the West.

It was already two in the morning, and the stars were shining brightly, each one standing out in the sky by itself. The moon was shining over the Sarozek with a brighter, increasing strength, and under its glow the Sarozek sands stretched far away into the distance. Only the shapes of the camels, and among them the twin humps of the giant, Burannyi-Karanar, and the indistinct outlines of the nearest station buildings of the halt stood out; all the rest on either side of the railway stretched away into the endless night. The wind did not sleep, whistling away constantly and rustling among the litter.

Yedigei kept going in and out of the hut; he was waiting to see if Edil'bai would appear, coming along the track. Then he noticed an animal on one side of the track. It was the vixen, her eyes lit up with a greenish, winking glow. She stood dully beneath a telegraph pole – intending neither to approach or run away.

'What are you doing here?' Yedigei muttered, jokingly wagging his finger at her. She was not frightened. 'Look out, I'll get you!' He scraped the ground with his foot. The vixen jumped back, ran a short distance and then sat down again. She gazed quietly, almost sadly at him, or at something close beside him. What had attracted her? Why had she come here? Her behaviour seemed odd to Yedigei. Perhaps the lights had lured her, or hunger. Why not try to hit her with a stone? She was an inviting target. Yedigei found a largish stone on the ground, took aim and made as if to throw, but then dropped the stone at his feet. He had begun to sweat. What strange ideas sometimes come into people's heads! As he had prepared to throw the stone at the fox, he had remembered something that someone had once told him – either a visitor, or a photographer with whom he had talked about God, or someone else – no, it had been Sabitzhan; the devil take him, he was always digging up marvels so that either people would take notice of him or be astonished. It had been about the transmigration of souls after death. Yes, Sabitzhan, Kazangap's son. So that was who he had heard it from – that good-for-nothing chatterbox. Sabitzhan seemed all right at first glance. He knows all this, he has heard all that – the only thing was, he had precious little to show for it all. He had been educated at boarding schools, at institutes – and yet there he was, just another little man; nothing special about him. He liked to boast, to drink, he was good at proposing toasts, but otherwise he was quite useless. In a word, he was shallow – nothing compared to Kazangap, even if he does have a diploma. No, he was not a success, that one, not at all like his father. Well, God be with him, there was nothing else to be said; that was just the way he was.

Once Sabitzhan had been holding forth, saying that in India they believed that when a person died, his soul transferred itself into some other animal – any sort, even an ant. They also believed that every person, once upon a time before they were born, was formerly a bird, or some other animal or insect. Therefore they considered it a sin to kill any living creature, even a snake. If they met such a creature, they did not touch it, simply bowed and let it pass.

There is no limit to the things to wonder at upon the earth, thought Yedigei. How true all this is, who knows? The world is vast and Man cannot know everything. This is what had come into his mind as he had been about to throw a stone at the vixen. What if Kazangap's soul had been in the vixen? What if, having entered the vixen's body, Kazangap had come to see his friend, because it had been so empty in his hut, so lonely and dull?

'I've gone clean round the bend,' Yedigei muttered to himself, ashamed. How could such an idea even be considered?

'Damn it all, I've gone quite addled in my old age.' All the same, he approached the vixen cautiously and spoke to her, as if she could understand what he was saying.

'Off you go! You mustn't stay here – off into the steppe! Do you hear me? Go, go! Not that way – there are dogs there. Go with God, go away into the steppe.'

The vixen turned, looked round once or twice and then disappeared into the darkness.

Meanwhile the next train arrived at the junction. At first it rushed along, then gradually slowed down, carrying with it a flickering cloud of movement – the dust flying above the waggons. When it finally stopped, the driver leaned out of the cab, the engine puffing away at idling.

'*Hi, Yedike, Burannyi, assalam-aleikum!*'

'*Aleikum-assalam!*'

Yedigei stuck his head out so as to see who the driver was. On this line they all knew each other. It was a friend. Yedigei gave him the message for the people of Kumbel', the junction station where Aizada lived and told the driver to tell her about the death of her father. The driver readily agreed to do this out of respect to the memory of Kazangap – and also because at Kumbel' the crews of the brigade changed over. He also promised to bring Aizada and her family on the way back, if she was ready for the journey by then.

He was a reliable man, and Yedigei was considerably relieved. At least one thing was now arranged. The train went off a few minutes later, and as he wished the driver goodbye, Yedigei saw that a tall figure was making its way towards him beside the track. It was Edil'bai.

While Yedigei handed over his duty and he and Edil'bai discussed the news, sighing and reminiscing about Kazangap, another pair of trains arrived at Boranly-Burannyi and went on their way. Then, having completed the handover, Yedigei set off home.

On his way he remembered at last what he had wanted to remind his wife about, or rather discuss with her: the question of how to tell their daughters and sons-in-law about the old man's death. Yedigei's two married daughters lived in the

24

opposite direction, towards Kzyl-Orda. The elder of the two worked on a rice-growing state farm, and her husband was a tractor driver there. The younger girl had lived first on a station near Kazalinsk and had then moved with her family in order to be nearer her sister and to work at the same state farm; her husband was a driver there. Although Kazangap was not their blood relation and they were therefore not bound to come to his funeral, Yedigei knew that Kazangap was dearer to them than any relative. The two daughters had been born at Boranly-Burannyi and knew him well. They had grown up there and had later gone to the station boarding school in Kumbel'. Either he or Kazangap always used to bring them home for the holidays. He thought about the girls, recalling those rides on the camel, younger daughter in front and the elder perched behind. It took Karanar three hours to run at his strong trot from Boranly-Burannyi to Kumbel' – a bit longer in winter. When Yedigei could not make the journey, then Kazangap would take the girls; he was like a father to them. Yedigei decided that in the morning he would send them a telegram and leave it to them to decide what to do. At least they should know that the old man was no more . . .

As he walked on, he decided that in the morning his first task should be to drive Karanar home from the pasture – the camel would be much needed. It is not simple to die, but to bury a person with full honour in this world is also no easy task. One always finds that this or that or the other is not available and everything has to be dealt with in a hurry, starting with the shroud and ending with wood for the stoves for the funeral wake.

It was just at this moment that Yedigei was aware of something moving in the air. It reminded him of his days at the front; the distant shock-wave of a powerful blast, shaking the earth beneath his feet. And as he looked up, he saw right in front of him, far out in the steppe in the direction of the Sarozek cosmodrome, something rise up into the air, literally flaming, with a growing, fiery, fountain-like trail behind it. He was struck dumb by the sight. It was a great rocket rising into space. He had never seen anything like it before.

25

He knew, as did all those who lived in Sarozek, of the existence of the launching-site, the cosmodrome Sary-Ozek-1, some forty kilometres or less from here; he knew also that there was a separate rail-spur from the Torek-Tam junction that led there. People said that out in that direction, in the steppe, a whole town had grown up, complete with big shops, and Yedigei was always hearing on the radio, in people's conversations and in the papers about cosmonauts, space flights and suchlike. At the amateur concert in the oblast' town where Sabitzhan lived – and this town was even further away, about a day and a half's train journey – the children's choir sang a song about how they were the happiest children on earth, because the cosmonaut-uncles went up into space from their land. All this, Yedigei knew, took place somewhere close at hand. But since the cosmodrome and its environs had been declared a closed zone, even though he lived close by, he had had to content himself with finding out about it all at second-hand. This was the first time he had seen with his own eyes a space rocket rising up into the dark, star-lit heavens at an ever-increasing speed, in a raging, concentrated flame, lighting up everything around it with a thrilling, alarming light.

Yedigei felt quite faint. Was there really a man sitting there in the midst of that fire? Or perhaps two? And why, seeing that he had been around for so long, had he never seen the moment of launch before? For they had launched rockets into space so often now that you could hardly keep count any more. Perhaps on other occasions the launches had been by day. In the sunlight, at such a distance, you would not see it so clearly. But why had this one gone up at night? Perhaps there was cause for hurry. Or perhaps the rocket went up in darkness, but straight away came out into the daylight? Sabitzhan had once said, as if he had been there himself, that up in space there was a change from day to night every half hour. He must ask Sabitzhan about this; Sabitzhan knew everything. He wanted so much to be an all-knowing, important person.

Somehow Sabitzhan had got work in the oblast' town. He made no secret of this – and why should he? What you are, so must you be. 'I was there with someone, that well-known person,' Sabitzhan would say. 'I said something weighty to so-and-so . . .' But Tall Edil'bai had told him that once he had met up with Sabitzhan at his place of work and found him racing around at other people's beck and call. 'I understand, Al'zhapar Kakharmanovich! Certainly, Al'zhapar Kakharman-ovich! At once, Al'zhapar Kakharmanovich!' he would say, while his superior, according to Edil'bai, sat there chasing everything and everybody around with the aid of a lot of knobs. They did not have a chance to have a proper talk.

So that is what he is, thought Yedigei, our neighbour from Boranly. God be with him, he is what he is . . . But it was a pity for Kazangap. He had done a very great deal and sacrificed much for his son. To his last day he never said a word against him. He had even moved into the town to live with his son and daughter-in-law; they had invited him, they had taken him there, but it hadn't worked out. However, that was another story . . .

It was with such thoughts that Yedigei walked home from his work that deep night, his gaze still fixed on the space rocket. For a long time he watched it, until finally the fiery ship, getting smaller and smaller, at last disappeared into the black depths of the sky, turning into a small, misty spot. Yedigei shook his head and continued on his way, experiencing strange, contradictory feelings. He was delighted that he had seen it, yet at the same time it was something beyond his ken, causing both wonder and fear. Suddenly he remembered the vixen which had come up to the railway. How would she have reacted when this flame in the sky had startled her out in the empty steppe? No doubt, she would not have known which way to run.

Burannyi Yedigei, the witness of that night flight of the rocket into space, did not suspect, and indeed could not have known, that the space vehicle and its crew of one had been given a special emergency launch, without ceremonies, without journalists and without special reports, and that the launch was connected with a series of extraordinary events aboard the *Parity* space station, which had already been in a special orbit, codenamed *Trampoline*, for a year and a half as part of the American-Soviet space programme. Yedigei had no idea that this event would touch him personally – not simply because of the inseparable link between him and the rest of mankind, but in a most concrete and direct fashion. Nor did he realize that some time after the launch from Sary-Ozek, on the other side of the planet, in Nevada, there rose from a launching site an American vessel with the same mission: to go to the same *Parity* station, on the same *Trampoline* orbit – only approaching from the opposite direction.

The two spacecraft had been launched following an urgent command from the scientific research aircraft carrier *Convention*, which was the floating base of the joint Soviet-American control centre of the *Demiurgos* programme. The aircraft carrier *Convention* was on permanent station in the Pacific Ocean, south of the Aleutian Islands, in a square equidistant from Vladivostok and San Francisco. The joint control centre *Obtsenupr* was now following intently the entry of the two vehicles into the *Trampoline* orbit. So far, all was going satisfactorily. The manoeuvres for the docking with the *Parity* complex were about to begin. The task was extremely complicated as the dockings had to take place, not consecutively, with an appropriate interval between, but simultaneously, from two different directions.

Parity had not acknowledged signals from the joint control centre on *Convention* for more than twelve hours now, and was not reacting to the signals from the two vessels approaching it. They had to find out what had happened to the crew of the *Parity* space station.

28

CHAPTER TWO

Trains in these parts went from East to West and from West to East.

On either side of the railway lines there lay the great wide spaces of the desert – Sary-Ozeki, the Middle lands of the yellow steppes.

In these parts any distance was measured in relation to the railway, as if from the Greenwich meridian . . .

And the trains went from East to West, and from West to East.

From the Boranly-Burannyi junction to the Naiman tribe's cemetery of Ana-Beiit was at least thirty kilometres, measured from the railway – and then only if you went in a straight line across the Sarozek. If you did not want to get lost in the steppe, then it was better to follow the track which ran alongside the railway, but then the distance to the cemetery was even further: some thirty verst on one leg and about the same on the other.

Except for Yedigei, none of the present inhabitants of Boranly had any idea how to get there, although they had all heard about ancient Beiit, for many tales were told of it, some true, some legend. None of them had ever been there; there had been no need, for this was the first time for many years in Boranly-Burannyi, that collection of eight homes on the railway, that a man had died and a funeral had been necessary. Some years ago, a young girl had died within an hour from bronchial pneumonia, but then her parents had taken her body back to their original home in the Ural oblast'; and when Kazangap's wife, the old Bukei, had died at the hospital at Kumbel' some years ago, it was decided to bury her in the churchyard there. There had been no point in taking her back

29

to Boranly-Burannyi. Kumbel' was the largest station in the Sary-Ozeki; furthermore, her daughter Aizada lived there with her husband, and even if he was a useless fellow and a heavy drinker, he was one of the family; they would look after the grave. But at that time Kazangap was alive and he had decided what was best. Now they had to think and consider what to do for him.

Yedigei, however, was quite firm.

'Enough of these words so unworthy of a *dzhigit*' (a dashing, young horseman, the embodiment of all noble qualities), he said to the younger men of the settlement, 'we shall bury him at Ana-Beiit, where his ancestors lie, and where he himself asked to be buried. Now, let's have no more talk and get on with the job. It's quite a way to go and so we'll leave as early as possible tomorrow morning . . .'

Everyone understood: Yedigei had the right to decide and on this all were agreed. Sabitzhan, admittedly, had tried to suggest another plan. He had hurried there that day on a passing freight train – passenger trains did not stop at Boranly. But the fact that he had come to his father's funeral, although he had not known for certain if his father was dead when he set off, already moved and even gladdened Yedigei. Yedigei was surprised at his own reaction. Embracing Sabitzhan and weeping, he found he could not control his feelings and said through his tears, 'It's good that you came, dear one; it's good that you came' – almost as if by coming Sabitzhan could have resurrected Kazangap.

Yedigei could not understand why he had wept so; he had never wept like that before. They wept together for a long time in the courtyard before the door of Kazangap's now-deserted earth home. Something had affected Yedigei. He remembered how Sabitzhan had grown up before his eyes, a young boy, his father's favourite, and how he and Kazangap had taken him to the Kumbel' boarding school for railway-men's children. When there was time to spare, they used to go and see the boy, either on a passing train or on a camel, to find out how he was behaving in the hostel and make sure that he was not teasing the other children or breaking the rules, but was studying determinedly, and to find out what the teachers thought of him. And at holiday time, often wrapping him up in a coat, they had ridden on camels through the Sarozek, in frost and through blizzards, so that he should not be late back for his new term of study.

Oh, those days that one cannot bring back! All this had gone, swept away like a dream. And now here before him stood a grown man, only faintly recognizable as the child of all those years ago, those distant days when he was goggle-eyed and smiling; now he wore spectacles, a dusty hat and a worn tie and worked in the oblast' town and longed to be thought an important and noted worker But life was a treacherous joke. It was not easy to make it to the top, as Sabitzhan often complained – not without strong support or friends or influential relations. And who was he? – just the son of Kazangap from Boranly-Burannyi. So now he was unhappy. Now his father was gone – an unimportant man, but one who, when he was alive, was a thousand times better than any famous dead man; now he was no more.

Finally there were no more tears to shed. They began to talk and get down to business. And that was when Yedigei realized that this devoted son was just the same know-all as before, and that he had not come for the worthy burial of his father, but only to get the job done, to dig a grave somewhere and leave as soon as possible. Sabitzhan began to express such thoughts: why take his father so far out into the steppe, to Ana-Beiit, with desert all around and nothing but the empty Sary-Ozeki steppe stretching as far as the eye could see? They could dig his grave somewhere here, not far away, on a hillock close to the railway. Then he could lie there and hear the trains go by on the line where he had worked all his life. He even quoted as appropriate the old saw about taking leave of the dead and burying them as soon as possible. Why drag out the agony? Why be clever? Was it not all the same to the dead where they are buried – and surely the quicker the better?

And so he argued on, excusing himself by saying that urgent and important matters awaited him back at the office. Time was precious to him, and what did it matter to those in charge

31

whether the place of burial was near or far? – he just had to be back at the office on such a day and at such a time, and that was that. His superiors were his superiors and orders were orders . . .

Yedigei cursed himself as an old fool. He was ashamed at having given way to tears so readily and being taken in by Sabitzhan, even if he was the son of the dead Kazangap. He got up from his seat – there were five of them sitting on some old sleepers made into a bench beside the wall – and he had to make an enormous effort to restrain himself from saying anything hurtful or insulting before other people on such a day. Out of respect to the memory of Kazangap, he just said: 'Of course there are other places close at hand, as many as you could ask for. It's just that people don't bury their dear ones just anywhere. Not without good reason, of course. No one would begrudge any plot of earth.' He paused, and the men of Boranly listened in silence. 'Decide then, consider well! Meanwhile I will go and see how things are out there.'

Off he went, his face dark and hostile, to get away from temptation, his brows furrowed with anger. He was a stern man and a passionate one – another reason he had been given the extra name 'Burannyi' was that his character matched that of a storm. Now, if he had been alone with Sabitzhan, he would have said directly to those shameless eyes all that the man deserved to hear – and in such terms as he would remember all his days. But at the same time he did not want to get embroiled in the women's chatter. They were whispering together and were very angry: look, they were saying, the little son has come to bury his father, just as if he had come on an ordinary visit, with empty hands – and those, too, in his pockets. And he had not brought so much as a packet of tea with him! And his wife, that girl from the town – some daughter-in-law! She could have shown more respect and come, too, to weep and lament a little, just to observe the custom. No shame, no conscience, that girl. When the old man was alive and prospering – with a pair of milking camels and some fifteen sheep and lambs – then he had been a good son. Then she had come, too, and stayed until she was sure

32

everything had been sold. Then she had taken the old man into her home, it seemed; they had even bought some furniture and a car at the same time. But later on, the old man seemed to get in the way . . . Now she would not even show her face at his funeral.

The women wanted to make a scene, but Yedigei forbade them to open their mouths on such a day; this was none of their business; let them sort it out. Instead he went out to the pen near which stood Burannyi-Karanar, who had now been brought in from the pasture and was occasionally and angrily roaring. Except on the two occasions when Karanar came with the rest of the herd to drink water from the well, almost the whole week, day and night, he was free to wander at will. He was scarcely tame and bad-tempered, and now he was showing his displeasure by baring his teeth and now and again howling. It as the old story: tied up again and having to get used to the loss of freedom.

Yedigei approached the camel; he felt thoroughly upset and vexed after the talk with Sabitzhan, although he had known beforehand that there would be just such a discussion. Sabitzhan seemed to think he had done them an honour by coming to the funeral of his own father. At the same time, however, he looked on his filial duties as a halter from which he hoped to free himself as soon as possible. At least the neighbours did not stand idly by. All who were not on duty on the railway helped in the preparation for tomorrow's funeral and the wake afterwards. The women went around collecting dishes; the samovars were polished; pastry was prepared and some baking had even begun; the men fetched water, cut up their last reserves of old sleepers into pieces for the fires – fuel was always a first requisite, along with water, in the bare steppe. Only Sabitzhan got in the way, distracting people from their work, holding forth about this and that – who had been appointed to what post in the oblast', who had been relieved of his post and who had been promoted. The fact that his own wife had not come to bury her father-in-law did not worry him one whit. She had some conference to attend, some foreigners would be present. Nothing was said about Kazangap's grandchildren – they had been left behind to fight for their advancement and good attendance records, in order to get the best attestation for their entry to the Institute.

'What sort of people *are* they, to act thus?' Yedigei asked aloud; he was deeply upset. 'Everything on earth is important to them, except death.' Yet this thought gave him no peace. 'If death is nothing to them, then it follows that life also has no value for them. What is their purpose in life? For what and how do they live?'

In his anger, Yedigei even shouted at Karanar, 'What are you making all that din for, crocodile? Why are you bellowing at the sky as if God himself can hear you?'

Yedigei only called his camel 'crocodile' in the worst situations, when he had already lost control of himself. People who had come and seen the camel had given Burannyi Karanar this nickname because of his tooth-filled mouth and bad temper.

'You bellow at me, crocodile, and I'll break every one of your teeth!'

Now it was time to get on with the saddling of the camel, so he got down to work. Standing back, calmer now, he looked at the animal with delight, for Burannyi Karanar was beautiful and strong. He was also tall – so much so that Yedigei, who was fairly tall himself, could not reach his head. So he had to be cunning; he pressed on the camel's neck and struck the knobbly knees with his whip handle, the while making stern noises to get him down. The camel protested loudly, but all the same obeyed his master and finally folded his legs under him and lay down with his chest on the ground. He, too, seemed calmer now. Yedigei began the main part of his task.

To saddle a camel properly is no small task; it is rather like building a house. The saddle has to be set up and adjusted each time; it requires skill as well as strength, especially when the camel is as huge as Karanar.

Karanar means 'Black Bull', and it was easy to see why the camel had been so named. His head was black and long-haired, with a great powerful black beard growing from it right back to the withers; below, his neck was wreathed in black locks,

34

hanging down to the knees in a thick, unruly mass of hair. On his back were the pride and joy of the male camel – the pair of strong humps rising like black towers on the spine. And to complete everything there was the black end of the docked tail. All the rest of the hair, above the neck, chest, sides and belly were, in contrast, a light chestnut-brown colour. With all his contrasting coat and his height, Burannyi Karanar was a fine sight to behold, and he was now in his prime.

Camels live a long time. Perhaps because of this, no doubt, the females do not give birth until their fifth year and then not every year, but every two years, the young taking longer to gestate than any other animal – twelve months. For the first twelve to eighteen months the little camel must be protected from catching cold, from the piercing wind of the steppe; after that time the little animal grows fast, day by day, and nothing after that time troubles him – neither cold, or heat, nor drought.

Yedigei knew all about camels, and always kept Burannyi Karanar in tiptop condition. The prime sign of health and strength is found in the black humps, and Karanar's looked as if they were made of cast iron. Long ago, in those early days when Yedigei had come back from the war and was settling in at Boranly-Burannyi junction, Kazangap had given him the camel as a suckling, a tiny downy thing like a duckling. Yedigei himself was still young. He was not to know that he would remain here until he became an old man. Sometimes when he looked at old photographs of those days, he found it hard to believe how he had changed. He had become grey-haired; even his eyebrows were now white. His face had changed too, but he had not put on weight as so often happens. Over all this time he had first grown whiskers, then a beard, but now he had shaved it off; it made him seem naked. A whole page of history had passed, one might say, since those old days.

Now he concentrated on saddling Karanar on the ground, soothing him with soft words by waving his hand when the camel showed his teeth or growled like a lion, twisting his untidy head on his long neck. As he did so, Yedigei every now

35

and again cast his thoughts back to those years long ago; it calmed his soul to do so.

He worked for a long while, fixing and then readjusting the harness. This time, before putting the saddle in its final position, he covered Karanar with the best travelling cloth, a piece of old-fashioned work with multi-coloured long tassels and carpet patterning. He could not remember when he had last put this rare piece of harness, carefully preserved by Ukubala, on the camel. But this was just the occasion for it to be used.

When Karanar was saddled, Yedigei made him stand up, and was very satisfied with what he saw. He was really proud of his work. Karanar looked imposing and majestic, decorated with the cloth with its tassels and the fine craftsmanship of the saddle between his humps. Let the younger men admire this – especially Sabitzhan; let them understand that the funeral of a man who has lived a worthy life is not just a chore, not a nuisance, but a great, even if sad, occasion; and that on this occasion there must be special, appropriate honours paid. In some other countries they played music, carried flags; in others they fired their guns into the air; in yet other countries they threw flowers and carried wreaths . . .

But he, Burannyi Yedigei, tomorrow morning would head the procession, mounted on Karanar, decorated with his cloth with its tassels; he would lead the way to Ana-Beiit, accompanying Kazangap to his final resting place. And all the way, Yedigei would think about him as they crossed the great Sarozek desert. And with these thoughts about his friend, he would return him to the earth in the cemetery of his ancestors, as had been agreed. Be it near or far, no one would persuade him, not even the dead man's son, to do otherwise than carry out Kazangap's own expressed wish . . .

Now he would let everyone know that it was to be thus – that was why Karanar was ready saddled and in his best harness. Let them all see.

Yedigei led Karanar on his halter from the pen and around all the houses before tethering him beside Kazangap's home.

Let them all see. He, Burannyi Yedigei, could not do otherwise than keep his word.

As it happened, however, Yedigei's efforts were not needed, for while Yedigei was busy saddling and fitting the harness on the camel, Tall Edil'bai, at an appropriate moment, had taken Sabitzhan to one side for a quiet chat.

They had a short discussion. Edil'bai did not persuade, he just spoke directly and to the point.

'You, Sabitzhan, should thank God that there is one such as Burannyi Yedigei on this earth, your father's friend. Don't prevent us from burying this man as he should be buried. If you're in a hurry to get back, we won't detain you. I'll throw an extra handful of earth into the grave for you.'

'He's my father, and I know myself –'

'– Yes, he's your father. You're inclined to forget that.'

'What do you mean?' Sabitzhan tried to counter. 'All right, let's not argue. Let it be Ana-Beiit. What's the difference? I just thought it was a long way to go.'

On that note their talk finished, and when Yedigei returned, having decked out Karanar for all to see, he said to the men of Boranly, 'Let's have no more words unworthy of a *dzhigit*. We'll bury him at Ana-Beiit!'

No one challenged this proposal and all agreed in silence.

Everyone whiled away the evening and night together in the courtyard in front of the dead man's house. Fortunately, the weather was kind. After the heat of the day, the sharp, early autumn cool of the desert descended. A great twilight calm and silence fell all around. Already the dressing of the lamb killed for the wake had been completed in the darkness, and while they drank their tea beside the smoking samovars, talk revolved around all sorts of subjects. Almost all the preparations for the funeral had been made and now all that was left was to await the morning and the time to leave for Ana-Beiit. The evening hours passed quietly and peacefully, as they should when a very old person has died and when it is painful to grieve.

37

And at Boranly-Burannyi junction, as always, the trains came in and went out, meeting from East and West and separating to East and West . . .

This, then, was the scene that evening on the eve of the departure to Ana-Beiit; and all would have been well had it not been for an unfortunate incident. For just then, Aizada and her husband arrived on a passing train to attend her father's funeral. She announced her arrival with a loud wailing, and at once the women surrounded her and a chorus of weeping started up. Ukubala was especially affected, grieving together with Aizada; she was sorry for her. They wept bitterly and lamented. Yedigei tried to comfort Aizada by saying, 'What can you do now? You cannot die and follow him who has died; you must resign yourself to fate.' But Aizada would not be comforted.

As so often happens, the death of her father opened the floodgates, giving her a reason to bare her soul before everyone – to say all the things which had long been bottled up inside her, unexpressed in words. Weeping loudly, all dishevelled and with tear-swollen eyes, she deplored her fate, as women will, complaining to her dead father that no one understood or appreciated her, that her life had been unhappy from her youth; that her husband was a drunkard, and that her children wandered the streets around the station from morning to evening, uncared for and free to do what they liked; they would turn into hooligans; tomorrow, perhaps, they would be bandits, robbing the trains. The eldest boy had already started to drink, and the police had called to warn her that the case would soon come up before the procurator. What could she do on her own with six of them? If only their father would do something, but . . .

Indeed, her husband did not lift a finger, just sat there, shut up with his own thoughts, confused and looking sad. At least he had come to his father-in-law's funeral, though, even if all he did was sit quietly smoking his stinking, cheap cigarettes. This was not the first time he had seen this performance. He knew how it would go – his old woman would yell and shout until finally she wore herself out.

38

But unfortunately now Sabitzhan decided to intervene. Sabitzhan began to chide his sister: what sort of behaviour was this? Had she come to bury her father or to disgrace herself? Was this the way a Kazakh's daughter should mourn her honoured father? Had not the great grief of Kazakh women been the inspiration of legend and song for their descendants for hundreds of years? they could not raise the dead, but they could at least show respect. By mourning, praise was given to the dead person and all his qualities and achievements offered up to the heavens – that was what the tears of the women of old had meant. And she? She had just wailed out an orphan's tale of woe, saying how bad things were for her, how dreadful was her life on earth.

Aizada had expected this reaction, or something like it. She began to yell with renewed strength and rage, 'You clever and educated one, you've taken full advantage. But you could try teaching your own wife a thing or two first! You should aim these fine words in *her* direction! Why hasn't she come and shown us this supreme grief? And wouldn't it have been fitter if she had honoured our father as she should? Instead that sly piece – with you the worthless worm under her heel – took everything from him and stole every thread from the old man! My husband may be an alcoholic, but at least he's here, but where is your clever little woman?'

Sabitzhan then began to shout at Aizada's husband, telling him to stop Aizada's tirade, but the other suddenly went mad with rage and leapt to his feet, intent on strangling Sabitzhan . . .

With difficulty the people of Boranly tried to calm down the quarrel between the relatives. Everyone felt uncomfortable and ashamed. Yedigei was most upset. He knew these people's worth, but even so he had not expected such a disgraceful scene. Angrily, sternly he warned them, 'You may not respect each other, but at least don't sully the memory of your father. Otherwise I won't let you stay here; I won't stand for this, and you can take all the blame . . .'

Such was the unfortunate incident on the eve of the funeral.

Yedigei was very glum. Once more his brows furrowed

anxiously and the same questions began to nag at him: where had they originated from, they and their children, and why had they become like this? Was this what Kazangap and he had dreamed about, when they had braved the weather to take them to the Kumbel' boarding school in order that they should learn and grow up and not to be stuck on a remote junction in the Sarozek, complaining that their parents never cared about them? And now everything had turned out just the opposite to what they had wished. Why? What had prevented them from growing into people one could be proud of?

Once more Tall Edil'bai came to the rescue, showing understanding and thereby easing Yedigei's difficulty. He understood what all this meant to Yedigei. The dead person's children were always the chief people at a funeral – this was normal. And there was nothing that you could do about them and there was nowhere to go to escape them, however shameless and useless they may be. In order to quell the scene between brother and sister which was depressing everyone present, Edil'bai invited all the men to his house. 'We won't sit here counting the stars – come and drink tea and sit with us . . .'

In Tall Edil'bai's home, Yedigei seemed to be in a different world. He had visited them before as a neighbour, and each time he had felt contentment and his soul had been filled with delight at Edil'bai's family. Today he wanted to stay there as long as possible, the need was so great – it was as if in this home, he could regain the strength which he had lost.

Tall Edil'bai was also a track worker like the others, receiving the same pay and living like everyone else in one half of a prefabricated wooden-board house consisting of two rooms and a kitchen. But the life lived in here was quite different – it was clean, comfortable and light. Although Edil'bai served the same tea as everyone else, here it seemed to Yedigei to be like clear honey straight from the comb. Edil'bai's wife was a handsome woman and an excellent wife, and their children were lively. They would live here in the Sarozek desert as long as they could, thought Yedigei, but no doubt eventually they would go off to some other place. It would be a sad day when they went, though.

Casting off his shoes on the porch, Yedigei went and sat down in the inner room, folding his feet under him. For the first time that day he felt both tired and hungry. He rested his back against the wallboards and was quiet. At once the rest of the guests sat down around the low, round table and talked quietly about this and that.

The main conversation started later – it was a strange discussion. Yedigei had already forgotten about the space vehicle which he had seen the night before. Now people who knew were talking about it, and he began to recall the episode. Yedigei could draw no conclusions of his own about it, but he was amazed at their knowledge about such matters and the fact that he knew nothing. However, he felt no pang of conscience at his ignorance; for him all these space flights which so much interested others were very remote, almost magical and quite outside his experience. His whole attitude to them was careful and respectful, as it would be to some faceless, powerful will, which he for one hardly took into consideration. However, the sight of that rocket going up into space had shaken him and seized his imagination. It was around this that conversation revolved in Tall Edil'bai's house.

At first, however, they sat and drank shubat – kumys from camel's milk. The shubat was excellent, cool, foaming and slightly intoxicating. The control and repair men who came to the junction used to drink a lot of it, calling it Sarozek beer. In this house there was vodka to go with the hot *zakuski*. Usually when it was offered, Yedigei did not refuse, although he only drank in order to keep people company. However, this time he did not drink any, for he thought – and tried to persuade the others – that it would be unwise. Tomorrow would be a hard day, and they had a long journey ahead of them. He was worried that the others, especially Sabitzhan, were getting down to it and drinking vodka *and* shubat. They went well together, admittedly, like two good horses in the same cart, and they were good for raising a man's spirits. But was it wise? Yedigei sighed. You could hardly persuade grown men not to

41

drink. They should know their own limits. At least he was relieved to see that so far Aizada's husband was staying off the vodka; he needed a drink, and if he took both, he would go out like a light. But he was only drinking shubat. Clearly he understood that it would be too much to get drunk at his father-in-law's funeral. But only God himself could tell how long he would hold out against temptation.

So there they sat, talking about this, that and the other; Edil'bai was honouring his guests with the shubat. His hands were very busy, his arms bending forward and back across the table like the bucket of an excavator, and then he suddenly remembered as he passed a cup to Yedigei from the other side of the table.

'Yedike, last night when I took over from you on duty, you'd only just left when something seemed to shake the air all around. I jumped out of my skin. I looked out and there was a rocket rising up into the sky from the cosmodrome launching site! It was vast! Just like a great pole! Did you see it?'

'Indeed, I did! My eyes almost popped out of my head. What power! The whole thing was aflame and going up, up, no end to its climb, no limit. It made me feel strange. Although I've lived here so long, I've never seen the like of it before.'

'Yes – and it's the first time I've seen one. What a sight,' said Edil'bai.

'Well, if it's the first time *you've* seen one, then we down here will have to wait even longer before we see one.' Sabitzhan had decided to make a joke about Edil'bai's height.

Tall Edil'bai laughed politely at this feeble attempt at wit.

'Yes, indeed,' he replied, brushing aside the remark, 'I looked and I couldn't believe my eyes – just a great fire roaring up into the sky. Well, I thought, there's someone else going off into space! Good luck to him! And I quickly turned on my transistor – which I always have with me. Now, I thought, they'll announce something on the radio, of course. Usually there's a report from the launch site soon after; the announcer always speaks with joy in his voice, as if at a meeting. It sends a thrill up your spine. I so wanted to know, Yedike, who it was

42

I'd seen with my own eyes going up on his flight. But I heard nothing reported on the radio.'

'But why?' Before anyone else reacted, Sabitzhan showed his amazement, raising his eyebrows with much meaning and importance. He was already getting drunk and was sweating and red in the face.

'I don't know. They said nothing. I kept tuned in to "Mayak" the whole time, but there was no announcement . . .'

'Surely not! You must be mistaken!' Sabitzhan was unsure and argumentative; he quickly poured himself another shot of vodka and shubat. 'Every flight into space is a world-shaking event . . . You understand? Our prestige – scientific and political – is at stake!'

'I just don't know. And I especially listened to all the latest news bulletins and the newspaper extracts as well . . .'

'*Hm.*' Sabitzhan shook his head. 'If I'd been there – at my office, I mean – I would know of course. What a shame. But perhaps there was something wrong?'

'Who knows? But anyway,' said Tall Edil'bai, 'for me he was my very own cosmonaut. He had taken off before my very eyes. I thought perhaps he might be one of our local lads. That would be really something exciting. Suddenly, one day, I'd meet him. That *would* be something!'

Sabitzhan hurried to interrupt him, excited by a new thought.

'Ah, *I* know what it was. They've launched a pilotless vehicle. No doubt it was an experimental one.'

'How can that be?' asked Edil'bai.

'Well, if it was an experimental variant, it'd be on test, you see. It was probably a pilotless vehicle going into orbit to dock with a station or into orbit on its own, and so far it's not known how things have turned out. If all has gone well, then there'll be an announcement both on the radio and in the papers. If it hasn't gone well, then there'll be no news given out. It'll be regarded as just an experiment.'

'But I thought,' Edil'bai rubbed his forehead angrily, 'that a living person had been launched into space . . .'

Everyone was quiet, a bit dismayed by Sabitzhan's theory.

43

Perhaps the subject would have been dropped if Yedigei hadn't set him off on a new track.

'As I understand it then, dzhigits, a rocket went off into space with no man aboard. But who then controls that rocket?'

'Who?' Sabitzhan waved his hands in wonder and looked triumphantly at the ignoramus, Yedigei. 'Up there, Yedike, everything is done by radio; by commands from the earth, from the control centre. They control everything by radio. Do you see? And even if there is a cosmonaut on board, they still control the flight by radio. The cosmonaut has to receive the decisions in order that he can take action on them. My dear little uncle, it's not like riding on Karanar across the Sarozek sands – it's far more complicated up there.'

'So that's it – tell us more about it,' said Yedigei indistinctly.

Burannyi Yedigei just did not understand the basic principle of radio control. In his book, 'radio' meant words and sounds coming out of the sky from a long way off. How on earth could you control a soulless object in that way? If there was a man inside that object, then that was another story – he would carry out the orders, do this, do that, as he was told. Yedigei would have liked to have asked more about this, but decided that it was not worth it. His heart was not in it, and so he kept quiet. Sabitzhan was already showing off his knowledge in a most condescending way. He was really saying: 'You don't know a thing; you think I'm useless. This brother-in-law of mine, this hopeless alcoholic, has even tried to strangle me. But in fact I understand more than the lot of you about these matters.'

'God be with you,' Yedigei was thinking to himself. 'We were the ones who gave you your education. Indeed, you *should* know more than us in our ignorance.' Then he thought a bit more. 'But what if a man like you should gain power – you'd oppress everyone, make your subordinates pretend to be know-alls; you would have no patience at all with anyone else. At present you're just an office boy running errands, but how much you long for everyone to look up to you; even here, out in the Sarozek desert . . .'

Sabitzhan was indeed striving to amaze and overwhelm these people of Boranly and if it were possible, to raise his standing

44

in their eyes after the disgraceful scene with his sister and brother-in-law. He began to tell them about the most improbable wonders, about the achievements of science, and while he talked, he continued to down the vodka by the glass, chasing it down with shubat. As he warmed to his theme, he began to recount such extraordinary tales that the poor Boranly people did not know what to believe and what not to believe.

'You can judge for yourselves,' he said, his spectacles flashing and his bewitching gaze passing from one face to another in his audience. 'If we think about it, we are the most fortunate people in the history of Mankind. You, Yedike, are now the oldest amongst us. You know, Yedike, how things were in the past and how life is today. This is what I'm talking about – in the past, people believed in gods. In Ancient Greece they were said to live on Mount Olympus. But what sort of gods were they? Stupid! What could they do? They couldn't agree among themselves – they were famous for their quarrels! They couldn't change the pattern of peoples' lives either, and didn't even think to do so. They didn't really exist at all, those gods. All this about them was a series of myths, fairy tales. But our gods, they live right beside us, here, at the cosmodrome on our Sarozek land – and we are proud of that fact and proclaim it to the world. No one of us sees or knows them, and we are not permitted . . . indeed, it isn't the custom for every Myrkinbai-Shyinkinbai to extend their hand and greet them with the words, "Hi, there, how are you?" But they are real gods! You, Yedike, are astonished to learn that they control space vehicles by radio, but this is just child's play, a stage which has already been achieved. Now the equipment, the machines, act according to a programme. The time will come when it will be possible to control people directly by radio, like any other automated systems – you understand? To control *people*, all of them, from the lowest to the highest. There already exist the scientific means to achieve this – in the best interests.'

'Hold on, hold on – how suddenly in the best interests?' Tall Edil'bai broke in. 'You've just said something I can't quite make out. Will each of us always have to have with him a small radio receiver – like a transistor – in order to receive orders? They are already available everywhere.'

'No – that's not what I mean. That's simple, child's play again. No one need carry anything. Go around naked, if you like. No, I'm talking about invisible waves, so-called bio-currents, which work on you, on your conscious self. Where can you run away to then?'

'Is that so?'

'It's true! A person will always do everything in accordance with the central programme. It'll seem to him that he acts and lives of his own volition, but in fact he'll be directed from above. And everything will be exact. If you're required to sing, a signal will be sent and sing you will. If you're to dance – signal – and dance you will. If you're to work, you'll get the signal and you'll work – and so on. Stealing, hooliganism and crime – all these will be forgotten; you'll only read about such things in history books. Everything in a man's behaviour will be foreseen – all his acts, all his thoughts, all his desires. For example, at the present time in the world there is the so-called population explosion; people have produced too many children and there's not enough food to go around. What is to be done about that? Reduce the birth rate. You'll only perform that act with your wife when they send you the signal to do so in the interests of society.'

'*Higher* interests,' Edil'bai corrected, not without a trace of irony.

'Naturally. The interests of the state are the highest of all.'

'But suppose that regardless of those interests, I choose to perform this act with my wife – or even maybe with some other woman?'

'Edil'bai, my dear fellow, nothing like that will happen. The idea won't enter your head. You could be shown the most ravishing creature you've ever set eyes on and you'll not even bat an eyelid. This will be because the bio-currents will cut out this feeling. So that side of your life will be completely under control. There will be complete orderliness, you can rest assured. Or take military matters; all will be done by these signals. If you have to advance under fire, you'll do it; if you've

46

got to make a parachute jump – no trouble either; if you've got to put a bomb under a tank and risk being blown up yourself, you'll do it. How will this be, you ask? If the bio-currents for loss of fear are sent out, that's it; a man will fear nothing. That's how it'll be.'

'Oh, you're going too far! Pull the other one! Is that what you've been learning all these years?' Edil'bai was really astonished.

Those sitting around laughed, shifted in their seats, nodded their heads. Here was this lad pouring out all this nonsense, yet they continued to listen to him. Devilish clever stuff, of course, and something they had never heard before, but everyone realized that he was well and truly sloshed. Drinking vodka like that and chasing it down with shubat, it was hardly surprising. Let him rabbit on. He was probably just repeating something he had heard somewhere – nothing really worth worrying about.

That was so; but Yedigei suddenly began to feel more and more alarmed as the chatterbox jabbered on. There must be *something* behind it all. Supposing there really were people, what's more scientists, who really dreamed up such inventions and sought to control us like gods . . .

Sabitzhan talked on unhindered; he was the centre of attention. His pupils were dilated wide under his misted spectacles, like cats' eyes in the dark, and he went on and on sipping his vodka and now his shubat. Now, waving his hands about, he was telling some tale about the Bermuda Triangle in the ocean, where ships and aircraft disappeared mysteriously without trace.

'Someone from our oblast' at last obtained permission to travel abroad. And you can think what you like about that! Well, off he went – and came to a sticky end. He parted from the other people with him and flew off across the ocean to Uruguay or Paraguay, and that was that. Over the Bermuda Triangle his aircraft disappeared and he vanished with it. But we can get along without Bermuda Triangles. Let us live our healthy life in our own land. Let's drink to our health!'

'Here we go,' Yedigei muttered under his breath, 'now

comes his favourite party piece! What a punishment for us to endure. Once he starts on the drink, he loses all control.'

And so it turned out.

'Let's drink to our health!' Sabitzhan repeated, gazing at those around him with a dull, wavering gaze, but at the same time managing to retain on his face an important expression, full of deep meaning.'For our health is a treasure for the State; our health is the greatest wealth of our country. That's what it is! We're not just simpletons, but the people who make up our State! And I wish to add . . .'

Burannyi Yedigei got quickly to his feet, eager to escape before this toast was completed. He went out. Stumbling around in the dark on the porch, he tripped against an empty bucket. He put on his sandals, now cool after being in the open night air, and went home, sad and angry. 'Oh, poor Kazangap!' He groaned, chewing his moustache. 'What is this? Death is not death, grief is not grief for that one. He sits there, drinking away as if he were at a party, and it all means nothing to him. That wretched speech on the "Health of the State" – we get it every time! Well, please God, tomorrow we'll observe all the honour due, all as it should be and we'll have the burial and the first part of the wake. Then he'll go home and we'll be rid of him. Who needs him here and whom does he need?'

Yedigei took a deep breath of the cooling night air of the Sarozek desert. The weather for tomorrow promised to be as usual – clear and dry and fairly hot. It was always like that – hot by day, and cold, quite chilly, at night. Because of this the dry steppe around was a difficult place for plants to survive in. By day they stretched up towards the sun, opened out and longed for moisture; by night the cold struck them. So only those which could adapt survived: various types of thorn, mainly wormwood, and on the edges of the ravines some other plants that clung in wisps and could be cut and used as hay. The geologist, Yelizarov, an old friend of Burannyi Yedigei, used to tell how once upon a time there were rich grassy places here and a different climate, with three times the present rainfall. Evidently life here was quite different then. Herds of horses and flocks of sheep roamed around. This was long ago – perhaps even before those wild people, the Zhuan'zhuan, came here, as the stories relate. All trace of them had long since gone and now only the legends remained. But how else could so many people exist and be supported in the Sarozek? Not without reason Yelizarov had said, 'The Sarozek is a forgotten book of steppe history.' He also considered that the tale of the Ana-Beiit cemetery fitted in with his theory. Of course some people regarded only what is written down on paper as true history. But if no books were being written at the time, then how could the truth ever be established?

Listening to the trains going through the junction, Yedigei was mysteriously reminded of the storms on the Aral' Sea, on whose shores he had been born and where he had lived before the war. Kazangap had also been an Aral' Kazakh by origin. This fact had brought them closer together and while working on the railway, they often felt a pang for the sea. Not long before Kazangap's death, that spring, they had gone together to the Aral'. The old man had wanted to go and take his leave of the sea. It would have been better if they had not gone, as the trip had upset him. The sea had receded. The Aral' was disappearing, drying up. They had had to walk for ten kilometres over what was once sea bed until they reached the water's edge. Here Kazangap had said, 'How much this land cost – it was at the price of the Aral' Sea. Now it is drying up; one can say much the same about a man's life.' It was then, too, that he said, 'Bury me at Ana-Beiit, Yedigei. This is the last time I shall see the sea.'

As he remembered that occasion, Burannyi Yedigei wiped away a tear on his sleeve, coughed to clear the lump in his throat, then went towards Kazangap's house where Aizada, Ukubala and the other women sat mourning. The Boranly women had come here, one after another as their work permitted, in order to be together and to help in any way needed.

As he went past, Yedigei stopped for a moment by the post dug into the ground where Karanar was tethered; there he was, saddled and ready, wearing his cloth with the tassels. In the light of the moon, the camel appeared vast, powerful and as immovable as an elephant. Yedigei could not resist patting his flank.

'You're a fine, healthy one!'

By the door, for some reason which he could not explain, Yedigei once more remembered the night before. How the steppe vixen had run up to the rails; how he had not dared to throw the stone, and how later as he made his way home, the fiery space rocket had risen up from the launching site in the distance into the black abyss of the sky . . .

CHAPTER THREE

At this time, in the northern latitudes of the Pacific Ocean, it was already nearly eight o'clock in the morning. The brilliant sunny weather cast an interminable light over the boundless, glittering calm of the ocean. There was nothing but sea and sky as far as the eye could see. However, aboard the aircraft carrier *Convention* a drama on a world scale was being played out, unbeknown to anyone outside the ship. This drama had been precipitated by an event hitherto unheard-of in the history of space which had taken place on the American-Soviet *Parity* orbital station.

The aircraft carrier *Convention*, the scientific and strategic staff headquarters of the combined control centre (*Obtsenupr*) for the joint planetological programme *Demiurgos* – named after Plato's creator of the universe – had quickly broken off contact with the outside world. But it remained on permanent station south of the Aleutian Islands in the Pacific Ocean, maintaining its position exactly equidistant by air from Vladivostok and San Francisco.

On the research vessel, various changes took place. On the orders of the American and Soviet co-directors of the programme, both duty operators of the space communications, one Soviet, one American, who were receiving the information about the extraordinary happenings on board *Parity*, were for the time being put into strict isolation to avoid any leakage of information about what had occurred.

A state of special readiness was ordered among the crew of the carrier – although the vessel had no naval status; indeed it carried no armaments and had special international immunity

51

granted by the United Nations. It was the only civilian aircraft carrier in the world.

At eleven o'clock two important commissions were expected to arrive on board *Convention*, with a five-minute gap between them; these would have complete freedom to take special decisions and to take such practical measures as they considered fit in the interests of the security of their two countries and of the whole world.

The choice of the aircraft carrier's position was no accident. Clarity, sagacity and foresight had been shown from the very start of the planning and creation of the *Demiurgos* programme. Even the positioning of the vessel, on which the joint programme of planetological investigation was to be carried out, reflected the principle of full equality adopted by this unique scientific and technological cooperative effort.

The aircraft carrier *Convention* with all its equipment, power and resources, belonged equally to both parties and was thus a cooperative vessel owned jointly by the shareholding states. It had direct and simultaneous radio-telephonic and televisual communications with the Nevada and Sarozek launching sites. Aboard the aircraft carrier there were eight jet aircraft – four for each side – ready to fulfil all the transport requirements of the combined control centre for its daily contact with the mainlands. Also on board the *Convention* were two parity-Captains, Soviet and American: parity-captain 1–2, and parity-captain 2–1. Each of them had full charge when on watch. The whole crew was similarly duplicated, with parity-mates, navigators, mechanics, electricians, seamen and stewards. The scientific and technical staff of the centre was set up in the same way; starting with the general directors of the programme, there were chief parity-planetologists and all the scientific workers and specialists were similarly duplicated. Similarly, the space station on the furthest orbit from the earth, *Trampoline*, was called *Parity* or in Russian *Paritet*, repeating the policy of cooperation followed on earth.

The setting up of all this had been preceded by great and varied preliminary work by scientists, diplomats and administrators in both countries. Many years of work had been required until both sides, in meetings and conferences, had reached an agreement on all general and detailed questions involving the *Demiurgos* programme.

The *Demiurgos* programme represented the most colossal task of the century for space exploration – the study of the planet Ex. The intention was to exploit its mineral resources, which contained an unimaginable wealth, by earth's standards, of energy reserves. A hundred tonnes of Ex's material, which lay practically free for the taking on the planet's surface, could after the appropriate processing ensure an amount of energy, which, when converted into electricity and heat, would be sufficient to meet the needs of the whole of Europe for a year.

Such was the energy content of the planet Ex which had formed under particular conditions of the galaxy, over a period of many milliards of years. This had been shown by soil samples brought back on several occasions by space vehicles from the surface of Ex, and it had also been confirmed by a series of short expeditions to this beautiful planet of our solar system.

The key factor in the decision to develop Ex was that it was the only planetary body known to contain water. The certain presence of water on Ex had been confirmed by borings. According to scientists, under the surface of Ex, there could be a layer of water several kilometres deep, kept in an unchanged state by the cold rocks below. It was the presence of such a quantity of water on Ex which made the great *Demiurgos* programme viable, for water in this case was not only the source of moisture, but the starting material for the synthesis of other elements necessary for the support of life and the normal functioning of man's organism under the conditions of another planet – first of all, air to breathe. In addition, from the production point of view, water played an important part in the proposed technology, which involved floating the Ex rock ore before loading it into trans-space containers.

The question was also being studied as to whether to extract the energy from Ex on orbital stations in space in order to transmit it later to earth on geosynchronized orbits, or to send the material directly to earth. A decision had yet to be reached.

Already a large expedition had been planned, involving a long-term stay by a group of drilling experts and hydrologists, whose task was to set up a permanent, automated, controlled flow of water from the bedrock of Ex into a piped system. The *Parity* orbital station was already fitted with the necessary structural features, for *Parity* was, to use a climber's term, to be the main base camp on the way to Ex. These features would allow the docking, unloading and loading of 'barges' which would run between Ex and *Parity*. In time, with the additional building of modules on *Parity*, over one hundred people would be accommodated on the station in very comfortable conditions, including the continuous reception of television from earth.

In this giant space undertaking, the extraction and analysis of Ex water was to be the first production activity ever set up by Man outside his own planet.

At the Sarozek and Nevada launching sites, the final preparations were being made for the hydrotechnical work on Ex. *Parity* in its *Trampoline* orbit was ready to accept and send on to Ex the first working party of people to open up the virgin lands of space. In fact, Mankind was about to lay the foundation stone of the first extra-terrestrial civilization.

And it was at this very moment, on the eve of the fulfilment of the plan to send this first group of hydrologists to Ex, that the two cosmonauts aboard the *Parity* on its *Trampoline* orbit suddenly disappeared without trace.

Without warning, they stopped answering any signals – either at the prescribed watch times, or at any other time. Except for the signals from the sensors which continually gave the coordinates of the station and the channels correcting its movements, all systems of radio and television communications were dead.

Time passed, and still *Parity* made no reply to any transmissions from earth. Concern aboard *Convention* increased. All kinds of guesses and suggested explanations were put forward. What had happened to the *Parity* cosmonauts, and why were they silent? What if they had been taken ill or had succumbed to food poisoning? Were they still alive?

At last a desperate move was made: a command signal was sent to operate the general fire alarm on board the station. This produced no reaction whatsoever. There was now a serious threat to the whole of the *Demiurgos* programme. Thus it was that the *Obtsenupr* aboard *Convention* finally decided that there was only one way of investigating the situation. Two space ships, two cosmonauts, were sent to dock with *Parity* from the Nevada and Sarozek launching sites.

When the required simultaneous docking – in itself no mean feat – had been made, the first news from the cosmonaut controllers who had searched *Parity* was astonishing; for having gone through all sections, all the laboratories, all stages down to the last corner, they announced that they had not found the cosmonauts. They were not there, alive or dead.

That possibility had never entered anyone's head. Nobody could think what had happened to them. Here had been two men who had spent over two months on board the station and who had until now followed all their instructions to the letter. Where had they suddenly gone? They had not evaporated. Surely they had not gone on a space walk?

The search of *Parity* had been made with direct radio and televisual communications with *Convention*, and with the direct participation of both general co-directors – the chief parity-planetologists. On the many screens in the combined control centre, the cosmonaut controllers could be seen drifting weightlessly, discussing their moves, passing around the station, inspecting all modules and sections. They searched it step by step, reporting back the whole time, and their conversation was recorded on tape:

Parity: 'You see? There's no one aboard; we can find no one.'

Convention: 'Are there any signs of broken objects, destruction or damage on the station?'

Parity: 'No, all looks as if it's intact and in order. Everything is in its proper place.'

55

Convention: 'Any traces of blood?'

Parity: 'None whatsoever.'

Convention: 'What state are the personal belongings of the cosmonauts in?'

Parity: 'Everything seems to be in order. It looks as if they were still here not so long ago. Books, watches, a record player and all the rest are here.'

Convention: 'Good. Are there any reports around? Papers pinned up on the wall?'

Parity: 'We didn't notice anything like that. But . . . hold on! The log is open at a long entry. It's weighted down so that it won't float away and there are clips fastening the pages to leave it open at this spot.'

Convention: 'Read what's written there.'

Parity: 'We'll try. There are two texts, side by side, in English and Russian . . .'

Convention: 'Read on. What are you waiting for?'

Parity: ' "Heading – A message to the people of the earth", and in brackets the words, "An Explanation".'

Convention: 'Stop, don't read it; we'll cease the transmission. Wait until we call back shortly, but continue to listen out for us.'

Parity: 'OK. Roger.'

At this point the discussion between the orbital station and the *Obtsenupr* was halted. Having conferred together, the general co-directors of the *Demiurgos* programme asked everyone except the two duty parity-operators to leave the space communications area. Only after this was done did the two-way communication resume. Here is the text left by the two cosmonauts who had been in *Parity* on the *Trampoline* orbit:

DEAR COLLEAGUES,

Since we are leaving the *Parity* orbital station under exceptional circumstances for an indefinite period, possibly for a very long time indeed – all depends on a host of factors connected with our unprecedented action – we consider it our duty to explain our motives.

56

We well realize that our action will be unexpected and also, properly, quite inadmissible from the point of view of simple discipline. However, the exceptional circumstances which we have encountered while aboard this orbital station in space – circumstances never previously encountered in the whole of human history – entitle us to expect at least some understanding.

Some time ago we began to pick up from among the numerous radio signals emanating from outer space and to a large extent from the earth's ionosphere, which is full of noise and interference, one directionally polarized signal in a very narrow frequency band – this made the tuning much easier. The signal always appeared at the same time and always after the same interval. At first we did not pay it any undue attention, but it continued to intrigue us since it plainly emanated from an exact point in space, in the universe. What was more, it seemed to be beamed directly at our station.

Now we know for certain that these artificially directed radio signals had been going out into the ether long before this third expedition of ours, for *Parity* has been on the *Trampoline* orbit out in deep space for more than eighteen months now already. It is hard to explain why exactly we first became interested in this signal from somewhere out in the universe, but the fact remains that we began to observe, to fix, to study the nature of the phenomenon. And gradually we became more and more convinced that the signal was of artificial origin.

But we did not arrive at that conclusion straight away; we were never without doubts all this time. How could we be sure of the existence of another civilization when all we had to go on was the one fact that, as we thought, there was an artificially produced signal coming to us out of the depths of the universe? We were held back by remembering the fact that repeated scientific attempts to find even the slightest, simplest signs of life on the nearest planets had, as is well known, proved fruitless. The existence of intelligent life outside the earth was now generally considered unlikely and unrealistic. To search for it was regarded as pointless, especially since with every new step in the investigation of space, the chances became theoretically less and less, if not virtually nil. We were therefore not bold enough to report our views. We did not intend to overturn the universally accepted view that life on earth was a singular biological phenomenon quite unrepeated elsewhere in the universe. Nor did we consider ourselves bound to share our findings, since such observations did not enter into the laid-down programme of our tasks and activities on the orbital station. To be honest – quite apart from the reasons given – we did not wish to find ourselves in the position of the cosmonaut who once imagined that he could hear a cow lowing in space, and who later became known as the Cowherd Cosmonaut.

Soon yet another event occurred to add even more convincing proof of the existence of intelligent life elsewhere in the universe, but by then it was too late for us. We had already lived through the springboard feeling of realization and experienced a profound change in our understanding about the world; suddenly we found that we had begun to think in a quite different way. Our entirely new understanding of the structure of the universe, our discovery of a new and inhabited place and of the existence of yet another powerful source of thought, led us to the conclusion that, for a time, we had to refrain from telling the people of earth our news. We felt a new-found anxiety about the fate of the earth. We came to this decision in the best interests of modern society.

Now down to facts. How exactly did this happen? Well, just for curiosity's sake, we decided one day to send an answering radio signal on about the same wavelength and to direct it towards the point in space from which the intriguing, regular signal transmissions seemed to be coming. A miracle happened! Our signal was quickly picked up! Intercepted and understood! In reply, on our receiving band we heard another signal and then another – a whole trio was greeting us; three synchronized signals which continued for several hours, like a triumphal march, bringing us the enthralling news that there *were* thinking beings outside our galaxy who had the ability to make contact with like beings at a very long range. This revolutionized our ideas about space biology, our knowledge of the make-up of time, space and distance . . . So we were indeed not alone in life, not the sole representatives of our kind, in the deserted eternity of the universe.

In order to check whether we had really found an extra-terrestrial civilization, we sent by radio the formula for the mass of the earth, that earth on which our present life arose and exists. In answer they sent us approximately the same formula giving the mass of their planet, and from this we concluded that the newly found, inhabited planet was of fairly large size and possessed a sizeable force of gravity.

Thus we exchanged the first knowledge of physical laws, and thus it was that we had for the first time in history entered into contact with extraterrestrial intelligent beings.

The people of this other planet turned out to be active partners, deepening and bringing our contacts closer all the time. By their efforts these quickly developed, enhanced by new information exchanges; soon we found out that they possessed machines capable of flying at the speed of light. All this and other information we found out initially by way of mathematical and chemical formulae. They then made us understand that they could also communicate by speech. It turned out that for many years, ever since earth people had conquered gravity and set out into space and lived there, these people had studied our languages with the aid of powerful audio-astronomical equipment with which they listened deep into the galaxy. Having intercepted the systematic radio communications between space and earth, they were able by comparison and analysis to determine and work out for their own use the meanings of our words and phrases. We were aware of this when they tried to talk to us in English and Russian. For us, this was yet another unbelievable, amazing discovery.

Now to the heart of the matter. Eventually we gained sufficient courage to contemplate visiting this pleasant planet of Lesnaya Grud' (literally 'Forest Breast' – a rough translation of their name for their planet). The people of Lesnaya Grud' have invited us to come to see them; it was their idea. And we, after much deliberation, have decided to go. They have explained that their machine, flying at the speed of light, will take twenty-six or twenty-seven hours to reach our orbital station, and they have promised to bring us back in the same time – but only if we wish to do that. In answer to our questions about docking, they explained to us that this presents no problem, because their Lesnaya Grud' machine has the capability of making a pressurized attachment to any object or structure; this presumably involves some form of electromagnetic attachment mechanism. We decided that it would be best for us if their machine docks at the hatch used for extravehicular excursions, and by going through this, we could join them aboard their station. We will return in the same way, assuming that the journey to Lesnaya Grud' is successfully completed.

In the meantime we are leaving aboard *Parity* this message, or if you prefer, explanatory note, open letter or declaration. We fully understand what we are undertaking and the burden of responsibility which we have taken upon ourselves. We are only aware that it has pleased fate to offer to us the most astonishing opportunity to render such a service to Mankind, and we can see nothing higher than that.

However the hardest part for us was to overcome the feelings of duty, constraint, responsibility and finally, discipline – all that which has been instilled into us by tradition, law and the normal moral outlook of society. We are leaving *Parity* without having told you first – you, the controllers of *Obtsenupr*. Indeed no one has been told – but this is not because of any contempt or disregard for the rules of behaviour on earth. For us this has been the theme of much heart-searching. We have acted in this way because we can all too easily foresee the various feelings, contradictions, passions which will arise as soon as political forces begin to act – those forces which see in every extra goal in a hockey match a political victory and the superiority of one state system over another. Alas, we know only too well how things are on our earth! Who can be sure that the possibility of contact with an extraterrestrial civilization will not become just another reason for internecine conflict?

On earth it is difficult or almost impossible to get away from political struggle. But after spending a long time – many days, weeks – in outer space, where the world's sphere appears no bigger than a car wheel, we could not help thinking with pain and helpless shame of conditions on earth; of how the present energy crisis, which has led people to rage, to despair, to the desire to take up the atomic bomb, is really just a very big technical problem which all countries could solve if they chose to discuss it.

Because of our fears of aggravating, of complicating an already dangerous situation for Mankind, we have dared to take upon ourselves the unprecedented responsibility of acting as spokesmen before the other people, the bearers of extraterrestrial intelligence, in the name of all Mankind, in accordance with our convictions and conscience. We hope and feel an inner belief that we will fulfil our voluntary mission in a worthy fashion.

Finally, one last point. In our considerations, doubts and waverings, we were in no small way worried lest we should harm the *Demiurgos* programme – this great first step in the geospace history of Man, achieved with so much difficulty by our two countries after long years of mutual distrust. Fortunately, in the end, common sense triumphed and we are conscientiously performing our shared duty to the limits of our strength and skills. But after comparing one mission with the other, and not wishing to harm the *Demiurgos* programme, we have chosen our own way: we are leaving *Parity* temporarily in order, on our return, to take up our post again and continue our work.

If we disappear for good, for ever, or if those in charge consider us unworthy to continue our work on *Parity*, then it will not be difficult to replace us; for there are always people around, who, when needed, will work no worse than us.

We are going out into the Unknown. We are drawn there by the thirst for knowledge and by Man's ancient dream of finding other intelligent beings in other worlds with which to join intellects. However, no one knows what experience awaits us in this new-found civilization. Will it bring good or evil to Mankind? We will try to be objective in our judgements. If we feel that our mission has anything threatening or destructive in it for our earth, then we swear to abandon it. We will never act in a way that might bring harm to the earth.

We say farewell. We can see the earth through our observation windows, shining like an effulgent diamond in the black sea of space. The earth is beautiful, with an unbelievable blueness unseen elsewhere and looks as delicate as a child's head. From out here it seems that all people who live on earth, all of them, are our sisters and brothers and we dare not think of ourselves without them . . . although we know that on earth things are far from being like that.

We say farewell to the globe. In a few hours we shall have to leave the *Trampoline* orbit, and the earth will disappear from view. The Lesnaya Grud' people are already on their way from their planet. In a few hours' time they will arrive. Only a short time remains. Meanwhile we are waiting.

61

One thing more. We are leaving letters for our families. We beg you to deliver our letters to the addressees.

P.S. A note for those who take our place on *Parity*. In the log we have written down the receiving and transmitting channels and frequencies on which we communicated with the people of this other planet. If necessary we will make contact with you on this channel and send our reports. As far as we can tell from the communications which we have had with the people of Lesnaya Grud', the most effective method of communication is to use the onboard systems of the orbital station, since radio signals from space will not reach the earth's surface through the powerful ionosphere layer surrounding the earth's atmosphere.

Identical texts of our message are presented in English and Russian.

Parity–Cosmonaut 1–2
Parity–Cosmonaut 2–1
Aboard the *Parity* orbital station;
3rd watch, 94th day.

Exactly at the appointed time, 11.00 hours Far East Time, one after the other, two jet aircraft landed on the deck of the aircraft carrier *Convention*, bringing the specially appointed plenipotentiaries and commissioners from the American and Soviet sides.

The members of the commission were met strictly according to protocol and were told at once that there would be half an hour in which to take lunch. Immediately after the meal, the members of the commission were to meet in the main mess in closed session to consider the extraordinary situation which had arisen aboard the *Parity* orbital station.

But the meeting had hardly started, when it was unexpectedly adjourned. For just then the replacement cosmonaut-controllers now aboard *Parity* transmitted to the *Obtsenupr* on *Convention* the first message received by them from parity-cosmonauts 1–2 and 2–1 on the planet Lesnaya Grud'.

CHAPTER FOUR

Trains in these parts went from East to West, and from West to East . . .

On either side of the railway lines lay the great wide spaces of the desert – Sary-Ozeki, the Middle lands of the yellow steppes.

In these parts any distance was measured in relation to the railway, as if from the Greenwich meridian . . .

And the trains went from East to West, and from West to East . . .

Say what you like, but it was no small distance to the Naiman tribe's cemetery of Ana-Beiit – it was thirty verst and then only if you go direct, cutting the corners over the Sarozek.

That morning, Burannyi Yedigei had got up early. He had not been able to get much sleep and had not dozed off until dawn. But before then he had been busy laying out and preparing the dead Kazangap. Usually all that was done on the day of the burial, not long before the body was brought out, before the general prayers, or *dzhanaza*, in the dead person's house. But on this occasion all this had to be completed during the night before the burial, so that first thing in the morning they could set off without delay.

He had done all that was necessary by himself, apart from when Tall Edil'bai had brought along the warm water for the washing. Edil'bai had been a bit nervous and had avoided approaching the corpse. Of course it was unpleasant for him.

Yedigei said to him in an off-hand way, 'You should watch what I'm doing, Edil'bai. It can be very useful in life to know how such things are done. People are born, it follows that we must also bury them.'

'Yes, I understand that,' Edil'bai spoke with some uncertainty.

'Suppose, to take a concrete example, I were to die tomorrow. There'd be no one to bury me. You'd probably just shovel me into any old hole.'

'Really!' Edil'bai was shocked as he stood there with the lamp; he was still trying to get used to the idea of being near a corpse. 'Without you around, life would be uninteresting. It'd be better if you went on living . . . the hole can wait awhile.'

Yedigei had spent an hour and a half doing the laying out, but in the end he was content. He had washed the body properly; he had straightened out the arms and legs and arranged them in the right way; he had prepared the white winding sheet and had put it around Kazangap. All was as it should be, and he had done it without skimping on the material. As he did this, he had shown Edil'bai how to sew up the shroud. Then he had got himself ready. He had had a good close shave and trimmed his whiskers, which were like his eyebrows, thick and strong, but with a few grey hairs among them. He then polished his war medals and his shock worker badges, which he fastened on his jacket in readiness for the next day.

So the night had passed. Burannyi Yedigei was surprised at the way he was taking things. He would never have believed that he would have to fulfil such a sad task. It now seemed that he had been predestined to be the man to bury Kazangap. It was strange to think that this had been in his stars ever since he and Kazangap had first met at Kumbel' station. Yedigei had been discharged from the army in '44, suffering from shellshock. Externally all seemed to be in order: he had his arms, legs, his head on his shoulders. But it was this head of his which was not entirely under control. He had a perpetual noise in his ears, a sound like a whistling wind. He would take a few steps and stagger; his head would spin and he would feel sick. Then he would feel cold all over and the next moment he would break out in a hot sweat. His tongue was difficult to control – it seemed an effort to say just one word. He had been

64

severely shaken by the blast wave from that exploding German shell. He had not been killed, but there was no reason why he should have survived. Yedigei was really down in the depths at that time. He looked young and healthy, but what on earth would he be good for when he returned home to the shores of the Aral' Sea? Fortunately he had a good doctor looking after him. He did not give him much special treatment, but examined him, sounded him, checked everything thoroughly. As he now remembered, the doctor had been a red-headed man in a white coat and cap, bright-eyed with a prominent nose. He had slapped him on the shoulder and laughed.

'You see, brother,' he had said, 'the war will soon be over. I could send you back to the front after a short while and you'd fight again. But it'd be better if we let them get on with the war without you until victory is won. In a year or so, perhaps less, all will be well again and you'll be as healthy as a bull. Later, you'll remember what I've just said. Meanwhile get your things together and go home. Don't feel sorry for yourself. People like you live for a hundred years . . .'

Things progressed, just as that red-haired doctor had said they would. True, it was easy to say a year – but a year was a long time. When he left the hospital in his creased tunic, a pack on his back and a stick in case of need, Yedigei felt as if he were walking around in a deep forest. There were those noises in his head, his legs were unsteady, he could not see clearly. But who cared? At the stations and in the train there were crowds of people, the strong ones pushing the others aside. But somehow he dragged himself aboard. After a month of wandering, the train stopped one night at Aral'sk. Train 57, 'The Happy 57th', as it was called; please God, may he never travel on such a train again . . .

But at the time he had been glad to do so. He clambered down from the waggon in the dark, as if from a mountain face; then he stopped in dismay. All around was pitch darkness, save for a few distant station lights. It was windy. But this wind had come to welcome him. It was his own beloved Aral' wind! The sea, too – he could feel the sea. There it was, still down there, splashing right under the railway track. Nowadays

65

you could hardly see it from the station with a pair of binoculars.

He paused for breath. From the steppe came the first faint smell of wormwood, the spirit of awakening spring on the wide open spaces beyond the Aral'. He was home again!

Yedigei knew this place well, the village by the station with its winding streets leading down to the sea shore. The mud was sticking to his boots. He was making his way to the home of friends in order to spend the rest of the night there and in the morning to make his way along to his own fishing village of Zhangel'di, quite a distance away. He did not notice how the street had led him out of the village and down to the sea shore. He could not wait; he went down to the sea. He stopped on the sand by the squelching water's edge. Covered in darkness, the sea could be made out by the dim flashes of white where the waves broke noisily and then disappeared as they drew back from the shore. The moon was fading at the approach of dawn – it was just a faint white spot above the high cloud. So they had met again.

'Good morning, Aral'!' Yedigei whispered. Then he sat down on a stone and lit a cigarette. The doctor had advised him strongly against smoking with his shellshock, and later he gave it up; but at that time he felt free to do as he liked – what did tobacco smoke matter?

It was not yet clear how things would work out for him. To go back to the sea he would need strong hands, a strong body and, most of all, a strong head, so as not to be affected by the pitching of the boat. Before the war, he had worked as a fisherman. But what use was he now? He was a kind of invalid now, not really disabled, but useless all the same. He had no head for fishing, that was clear.

Yedigei was about to get up when a white dog appeared on the shore, trotting along the water's edge. Sometimes it stopped and sniffed at the sand in a business-like way. Yedigei called to it, and trustingly, the dog came up to him and stopped nearby, wagging its tail. Yedigei stroked the furry neck.

'Where are you from? Where are you running away from?

What's your name? Arstan? Zholbars? Boribasar?* Oh, I understand, you're looking for fish washed up on the shore. Good, good. Only the sea doesn't always throw a fish directly in your direction. Sometimes you have to search along the shore. That's why you're so thin. Me? I'm on my way home from near Koenigsberg. I hadn't quite got there when a shell burst beside me and I was left scarcely alive. Now I'm trying to make up my mind what to do next. What are you looking at me for? I've nothing for you. Only orders and medals. It's wartime, my friend, hunger reigns all around . . . It's bad, isn't it? But, wait . . . I've a sweet or two here for my son; no doubt by now he's already running around . . .'

Yedigei did not waste any time, he undid his half-empty haversack, in which there was a handful of sweets twisted up in a bit of newspaper, also a scarf bought for his wife at a wayside railway station, and two bars of soap, also bought from speculators. He was also carrying a spare set of army underwear, his belt, a cap, spare shirt, trousers. That was the sum total of his personal effects.

The dog licked the sweet from his hand, crunched it up, tail wagging the whole time, meanwhile watching him attentively and devotedly with its bright, hopeful eyes.

'That's all, now. Goodbye!'

Yedigei got up and walked further along the shore. He had already decided not to disturb his friends living near the station; dawn was not far off and he should press on to his native village of Zhangel'di.

But it was not until midday that he reached Zhangel'di, walking all the way along the shore. Before he had been shellshocked, he would have taken only two hours to cover this distance. On his arrival he was greeted by dreadful news: his little son was long dead. When Yedigei had been called up, the little boy had been only six months old. But he was unlucky – he died at the age of eleven months. He caught both sorts of measles and could not overcome the fever and died. They never wrote to tell him the news while he was away at the

*Arstan = Lion; Zholbars = tiger; Boribasar = wolfhound

67

front. If he came back alive, he would learn about it on his return home. He would grieve and suffer, but he would get over it. This was the advice friends had given to Ukubala. 'You're young, the war will finish and with God's help you'll have other children. The branch is broken, but it's no tragedy, the main tree is whole.' There were other thoughts also, unspoken but understood. If – for war is war – *if* a bullet has his name on it, at least he will die with hope in that last moment of life; at least he will think the child is alive at home and the line is not broken...

But Ukubala blamed herself for what had happened. She came out in tears, hugging her returned husband. She had awaited this day with hope, but also with an unassuageable pain, tortured by the long weeks of waiting. Through her tears she told everything, just as it had been; how the old women had warned her: *the child has measles, it's a treacherous thing, you must wrap him in camel-hair blankets and keep him in complete darkness; give him cold water; if God is willing, he may live.* But she had not listened to the old women of the village. She had asked her neighbours for a cart and taken the child to the station, to the doctor. But when she had arrived in Aral'sk on that shaking old cart, the boy was already dead. He had reached the crisis of his fever, it had burned him up and he had died. The doctor swore at her and said, *'You should have listened to the older women . . .'*

So that was the news which greeted Yedigei when he arrived home, just as he walked into the house. He turned rigid and black with grief. He had never before thought that he could miss a little child so much, his first-born, whom he had hardly ever held in his arms. That made the loss even harder to bear. He could not forget that little child's toothless smile, trusting, bright, and as he remembered it, so his heart ached.

All the changes began from that moment. Suddenly the *aul* (settlement) became hateful to him. Once, here upon the high shore, there had been fifty houses, and the people had fished the Aral'. Now there were just ten or so earth shacks under the cliff. No men were left – the war had swept them all away, leaving only old people and children, and not many of them.

Many people had gone away to live in the auls of the collective farm, to go as cattle herdsmen so as not to die from starvation. Now there was no one left to go to sea, and the community was dying.

Ukubala also could have returned to her own people – she had come from out on the steppe. Her relations came for her and wanted to take her back with them straight away. You can live with us, things are good for us and when Yedigei returns from the war, you will be free to return at once to your fishing village of Zhangel'di. But Ukubala refused pointblank.

'I'll wait for my husband here. I've lost my little son. If my man returns home, at least he will find his wife at home. I'm not on my own here, there are the old and the young ones. I'll help them and together we'll hold out.'

She had made the right decision. Yedigei from the first day back said that he could not stay by the sea and not work. He was right too. Ukubala's relatives came to see Yedigei and proposed that they should all go back together to their place. 'You can live with us, work with the sheep on the steppe. There you'll recover your health, and find something to do – you know how to look after animals . . .'

Yedigei thanked them, but declined their offer. He knew that it would be difficult. It would be possible to stay as a guest for a day or two with his wife's relations, but afterwards . . . If you can't work, who wants you around?

So Ukubala and he decided to take a chance. They would go to work on the railway. Yedigei was sure to find some suitable work there – as a guard or as a watchman, maybe; or he could open and shut the crossing gates. Surely the railway authorities would help a wounded soldier? This decided, they set out that spring. They were young and they had no ties. At first they spent nights at various stations, but they had no luck in finding suitable work. Living conditions were bad. They lived where they had to, taking up various sorts of casual work on the railways. Ukubala helped – she was healthy and young and did most of the work. Yedigei looked fit and was taken on to do loading and unloading work of various kinds, but it was Ukubala who did most of the physical work.

Thus it was that they turned up, already in mid-spring, at the big junction station of Kumbel'. Here, waggons loaded with coal were put on to the siding right by the back doors of the depot stores and Yedigei and his wife first unloaded the coal on to the ground, so as to free the trucks as quickly as possible, and then, using barrows, took it up the ramps and tipped it out on to the dumps, which were now as high as houses. A whole year's stock was held there and the work was exceedingly heavy, dusty and dirty, but they had to live. Yedigei loaded the coal on to the barrows; Ukubala then pushed it up on the planks, tipped it out and came down again. Once more Yedigei loaded up the barrow, once more Ukubala, working like a horse, shoved the heavy load up to the top of the planks with her last ounce of strength. The days got warmer; they got hotter, until Yedigei felt sick with the heat and the flying coal dust. He felt as if all his strength was leaving him. He felt like lying down there and then on the pile of coal and never getting up again. But most shattering of all was the knowledge that his wife had to do all the hard work which *he* should be doing. He found it hard to even just look at her. She was covered from head to foot in the black coal dust, and only the whites of her eyes and her teeth stood out. She was soaked in sweat, which, blackened by the coal, flowed down in dirty black streams on to her neck, breast and back. If only he could get his former strength back, he would change things! He would have moved tens of trucks-full of this damned coal, only so as not to see the sufferings of his wife.

When they had left the deserted fishing village of Zhangel'di in the hope that Yedigei, as a wounded soldier, would find some suitable work, they had overlooked one thing – that everywhere there were crowds of demobilized soldiers, each and every one of them trying to adapt to normal life once more. At least Yedigei still had his arms and legs. How many crippled men there were – without legs, without arms, on crutches, with artificial limbs – all hanging around the railways! During the long nights, when they would settle down somewhere in a corner in a crowded, stinking station and wait for the night to pass, Ukubala asked first for forgiveness and then thanked

70

God in silence that her husband was beside her; that he had not been struck down by the war, and that their future still held some small shred of hope. For the sights she saw on the station brought her horror and pain: the legless, the armless, people shattered and broken, in worn-out uniforms and rags, sitting on their little trollies, on crutches, the blind being led, homeless and unashamed, wandering about the trains and stations, breaking into restaurants and buffets, with their drunken shouts and groans . . . What did the future hold for them? How could they ever be compensated for what they had gone through and what they now suffered?

It was only because that cruel fate had passed her by – because her husband had returned shellshocked, and not crippled – that Ukubala was ready to perform such gruelling toil. She did not grumble, did not give up, and did not show any signs of her sufferings, even when she could hardly drag her legs along and when it seemed that all her strength had gone.

But this did not make it any easier for Yedigei. Something had to be done; somehow they had to find a more positive place in life. They could not wander around like this for ever. More and more often the thought came to him, 'Supposing I said *"Taubakel"* ' ("Here goes!") and we moved into a town – how would things work out there?' If only his health was restored, if only he could get rid of the effects of this damned shellshock! Then he could fight and stand on his own two feet . . .

Things could change in all kinds of ways in a town. Perhaps they could settle down and become town dwellers like so many others. But fate decreed otherwise. Yes, fate – or whatever you cared to call it – stepped in.

It was the time when they were living so wretched a life at Kumbel', stacking the waggon-loads of coal. Suddenly there appeared in the coal compound a Kazakh riding on a camel, no doubt come in from the steppe on business. That was how it looked at first sight. The new arrival hobbled his camel and put it to graze nearby, looked around with a worried expression

71

and then walked up to Yedigei. He was carrying an empty sack under his arm.

'Hi, brother,' he said to Yedigei, as he walked past, 'be a friend and see that the children behave themselves. They have a very nasty habit of teasing and striking animals here. Sometimes they'll let an animal loose for a joke. I won't be away long.'

'I'll keep an eye on things; don't worry, go about your business,' promised Yedigei, wiping himself with a bit of blackened rag, soaked heavy with sweat.

The sweat poured ceaselessly from his face. Yedigei was most of the time busy near the pile of coal, loading his barrow, so it was a relief to take a look now and again to check that the local tearaways did not tease the camel. Once he had seen them so annoy an animal that it had begun to shriek in rage, spit and try to chase after them. This gave them the very pleasure they sought and, like prehistoric hunters, they surrounded the beast, shouting and throwing sticks and stones at it. The unfortunate animal had had to suffer a great deal before its owner returned.

This time, as if on cue, a noisy horde of tearaways appeared, kicking a football. They began to kick the ball as hard as they could at the hobbled camel. The camel tried to get away, but the boys continued, kicking the ball harder and harder and more and more accurately. Whenever one of them actually hit the camel, there were cheers as if he had scored a goal.

'Go away, be off with you, leave him alone!' Yedigei waved the shovel at the boys. 'Or I'll take you apart!'

The young boys gave up. No doubt they thought he was the camel's owner or perhaps they were impressed by his terrifying coal-blackened appearance. They probably thought he was drunk as well and could have turned unpleasant, so they ran off, kicking the ball in front of them. It never occurred to them that they could have tormented the camel to their hearts' content. Yedigei might have threatened them with his shovel, but in fact he was in such a bad way that he would never have been able to run after them, even if he had wanted to. Every shovelful of coal thrown on to the barrow cost him an enormous effort. He never thought it could be so horrible, so humiliating to be without strength; he felt sick and useless. His head was spinning all the time. The work was exhausting him. He was drained. It was an effort to breathe because of the black coal dust and hard black phlegm which stifled and blocked his chest. Now and again Ukubala broke through to take over the heavier part of the work, so that he could rest a little, sitting on one side while she loaded a barrow herself and then took it to the top of the pile. But Yedigei could not watch idly as she wore herself out; soon he would get up again, stumble to his feet and set to work once more.

The man who had asked him to keep an eye on his camel soon returned, with his load on his back. Having strapped it to the beast and made ready to go, he came up to Yedigei. They started to chat amicably. This man was Kazangap from Boranly-Burannyi junction. It turned out that they both came from the same part of the country. Kazangap said that he also had come from one of the auls by the shore of the Aral' Sea. This quickly gave them a common interest.

At that time neither Yedigei nor Ukubala could have known that this meeting was to determine the course of the rest of their lives. Simply, Kazangap persuaded them both to go back with him to Boranly-Burannyi junction, to live and to work there. There is a certain type of person who attracts at first acquaintance. There was nothing special about Kazangap, but on the other hand his simple appearance showed him to be a man whose wisdom had been learned the hard way. In appearance he was a very ordinary Kazakh, in faded, worn-out clothes which had become moulded to a shape which suited him. His trousers of tanned goatskin were not just worn for appearance, but were comfortable for riding on a camel. But he also knew the value of things: a fairly new railway uniform cap, reserved for special occasions, decorated his large head, and his box calf boots, which he had already worn for many years, were carefully patched and sewn up in many places with thick thread. He was clearly a man of the steppe, a hard worker, as one could tell by his brown face, tanned by the burning sun and continual wind, as well as by his strong,

73

sinewy hands. He stooped prematurely because of his work and his strong shoulders hung down; because of this, his neck seemed long and stretched like that of a gander, although he was of medium height. But he had wonderful eyes, grey, understanding, attentive, smiling, with furrows around them from blinking in the sunshine.

Kazangap was still the right side of forty. Perhaps it was his whiskers, which were cut short into bristles, and his short beard that gave him the appearance of being well-experienced in life. But most of all, he inspired confidence by the serious way he talked. Ukubala at once felt respect for him. All that he said was to the point and he spoke wisely. He said to Yedigei, 'You've had shellshock, and it is still affecting your body. Why punish yourself further? I noticed at once, Yedigei, that this work you're doing was too much for you. You've not recovered sufficient strength, you can hardly move your legs. Now, it'd be far better for you to be out in the fresh air, to drink as much creamy milk as possible. At the junction we're crying out for people for the railway. Our new manager is continually telling me: "You've been here a long time, get hold of some people suitable for the work here." But where are they, these people? All are at the war. Those who are demobilized can find work and enough elsewhere. Of course, it's no bed of roses where we live. We live in a grim place – all around stretches the Sarozek, quite uninhabited, waterless and arid. Water for a week at a time is brought to us in a tanker waggon. Sometimes that arrangement fails. Then we have to ride out to the wells, far out in the desert and bring water back in skins; you set off in the morning and don't get back until evening. But all the same,' added Kazangap, 'it's better to be in your own place in the Sarozek than to wander around, stopping at odd places like you do now. You'll have a roof over your head and permanent work. We'll teach you the job and you can set up your own home. It all depends on how you buckle down. Together the two of you could easily earn enough to live. Time will tell, your health will return. If you don't like it out there, you can always go and look elsewhere . . .'

That was what he said. Yedigei thought over this proposition for a while and then agreed. That very same day they went off together with Kazangap into the Sarozek, to the junction of Boranly-Burannyi. Fortunately at that time it took Yedigei and Ukubala no time at all to pack up their belongings; they collected them together and they were off. What did they have to lose?

Yedigei remembered that journey through the Sarozek from Kumbel' to Boranly-Burannyi for the rest of his life. At first they followed the railway, but gradually they moved away from it, leaving it to one side. Kazangap explained that they were cutting off some ten kilometres, as here the railway made a big loop in order to skirt a great takyr, a place where there had once been a salt lake which had later dried out. Nevertheless every spring, the salty depression came to life and became marshy, soft and difficult to cross. By summer it was covered with a hard layer of salt and turned as hard as iron, remaining so until the following spring. Kazangap explained that he knew all about the vast salt lake there from a geologist who had studied the Sarozek. This was Yelizarov, who later became a very close friend of Yedigei. He was a wise man, was Yelizarov.

Yedigei, as yet not Burannyi Yedigei but simply an Aral' Kazakh, a wounded soldier with his life still in pieces, trusted Kazangap and, together with his wife, went to seek work and a roof over his head in that unknown junction of Boranly-Burannyi. He had no idea that he would stay there for the rest of his days.

The vast boundless wastes of the Sarozek – green only for a short time in spring – made a deep impression on Yedigei. Around the Aral' Sea there were also many steppes and flat plains – the Ustyurt plateau, for example – but this was the first time he had seen such a desert. Later Yedigei understood that only a man who could stand face to face with the silent Sarozek could truly measure the strength of his soul against the vastness of the desert. Yes, the Sarozek was vast, but the living thoughts of a man could contain even this. Yelizarov was wise, he could explain such things and clear away the mists of conjecture.

75

Yedigei and Ukubala would probably have felt very different as they went deeper into the Sarozek, had Kazangap not been there with them, confidently marching on and leading his camel on the rein. Yedigei was perched high on its back, surrounded by all their worldly goods. Of course, Ukubala should have been riding and not he. But Kazangap, and especially Ukubala, begged – in fact practically forced – Yedigei to mount the camel. 'We are healthy people and you must conserve your strength for a while yet. So don't argue, don't hold us up, we've a long journey ahead of us.'

The camel was young, still not quite strong enough for large loads, and so two people had to walk alongside and only one could ride. On Yedigei's Karanar of today, three could easily be carried and they would travel much quicker, trotting along for three and a half to four hours too; but on that day they did not reach Boranly-Burannyi until late at night.

However the journey passed pleasantly enough as they talked and gazed at the new scenery. As they went along, Kazangap told them about living conditions and explained how he had come here to the Sarozek, to the railway. He had been an Aral' Kazakh. His aul of Beshagach was thirty kilometres along the shore from Yedigei's Zhangel'di, but although Kazangap had left there many years ago, he had never been back. There were reasons for this. It seemed that his father had been 'sent away' as part of the liquidation of the kulaks as a class, and had died on his way back from exile after it had been discovered that he had not in fact been a kulak (a small private landowner) at all; someone had exaggerated and the authorities had needlessly, or more exactly mistakenly, treated him as a middle-class owner of property. They announced an amnesty, but by then it was too late. The family had meanwhile gone away in all directions, as far away as they could go, and vanished off the face of the earth. The militant activists were constantly trying to force Kazangap, then a young boy, to speak at meetings, to denounce his father in front of everyone and to say that he held firmly to the view that his father had been rightly condemned as an alien element in society; that he renounced such a father, and that class enemies such as his father had no place on earth and that everywhere they should perish.

Kazangap had to go away to avoid having to do such a shameful thing. For a whole six years he worked in Betpak-Dala in the Hungry Steppe near Samarkand, where they were starting to turn the land, untilled for centuries, into cotton plantations and people were greatly needed. They lived in barracks and dug irrigation ditches. Kazangap worked at the digging, drove a tractor, then was put in charge of a brigade; he even received a certificate of merit for his hard work. Then he got married. People came from all around to the Hungry Steppe in search of work. A Karakalpak girl, Bukei, had come from near Khiva with her brother's family to Betpak-Dala. Fate brought her and Kazangap together. They were married in Betpak-Dala and decided to return to Kazangap's home on the Aral' Sea, to his own people and land. But they overlooked certain things. They travelled for a long time on special, large passenger trains nicknamed 'maxims', with many changes. On one of the stations where they changed trains, Kazangap by chance ran into some people from the Aral' whom he knew. From talking to them he realized that he should not return to Beshagach. It seemed that those same people who had blackened the name of his father were still in charge there. Kazangap decided not to go back to his native aul – not because he feared them, for now he had his certificate from the authorities in Uzbekistan, but because he did not want to see these people still triumphant and jeering at him. How could he still meet them after what had happened? Kazangap did not like to remember all this and did not understand that, apart from him, everyone had long since forgotten the events of those days. In the long, long years after his arrival in the Sarozek, only twice were those memories rekindled. Once it was his son who especially annoyed him and the second time was when Yedigei unwittingly made a joke which turned sour.

On one of Sabitzhan's visits they were sitting together drinking tea, talking and hearing the news from the town. Among other things Sabitzhan was telling – and laughing the while – how those Kazakhs and Kirgiz who had left the country in the years of collectivization and gone to Sin'tsyan (Sinkiang) in China, were now coming back. There the Chinese had forced them into communes where they were forbidden to eat at home, only out of a common pot, three times a day, old and young standing in line holding their bowls. The Chinese had treated them so badly that they had run away, leaving all their possessions behind them. Now they were begging on bended knee to be allowed to come back.

'What sort of news is this?' Kazangap's face was clouded and his lips quivered with rage. Such a thing happened very rarely with him; and equally rarely, one could say almost never, did he speak in such a tone to his son, whom he adored, had taught, to whom he had denied nothing, believing that the boy would make something of himself in the world. 'Why are you laughing about it? It's a human tragedy.'

'What can I say?' said Sabitzhan, 'I'm just describing things as they are.'

His father did not answer, but just pushed away his piala of tea. His silence was unbearable.

'Whom can you blame?' Sabitzhan spoke again, shrugging his shoulders, 'I don't understand. I repeat – whom do you blame? Time? Surely not. And you've no right to blame the government.'

'You know, Sabitzhan, my affairs – those which are in my power to control – are my concern. I don't meddle in other things. But son, I thought you had more sense. One cannot resent God – if he sends death, that's because life has run its course; that's why one was born. But for everything else that happens on earth, there is and must be a reason.'

Kazangap got up and looking at no one, went angrily out of the house without a word.

The second occasion was many years after their departure from Kumbel', when they had settled down and were living in Boranly-Burannyi. The children had now grown up. One spring evening when they were driving in the animals, Yedigei said jokingly as he looked at the sheep with their new lambs, 'We're rich, Kazake. It's time for us to be treated like kulaks!'

78

Kazangap gave him a sharp look and his whiskers gathered together, 'You've said that, but don't say any more!'

'What's up? Can't you take a joke?'

'It's no joking matter.'

'Don't go on, Kazake. A hundred years have passed.'

'What does that mean? You're robbed, but all is not lost – you get over it. But when your soul has been trampled upon, you can never smooth that out again.'

But on that first day, Yedigei, Kazangap and Ukubala made their way across the Sarozek from Kumbel' to Boranly-Burannyi, the days of those exchanges were far off in the future. As yet no one knew how their coming to Boranly-Burannyi junction would work out. Would they be there for a short or a long time? Would they settle down? Or would they go off wandering further about the world? They just talked simply about life, but in the course of the talk, Yedigei was interested to know why it was that Kazangap had not gone to the front; perhaps he had had some illness?

'No, thank God, I'm healthy and well,' answered Kazangap, 'I've never had any illnesses and I would have fought as well as the next man. But everything turned out differently.'

After Kazangap had decided not to go back to Beshagach, he got stuck at Kumbel' and could go no further. To return again to the Hungry Steppe would mean far too long a journey, and why do so in any case when there was no need to leave? They had decided against the Aral'. The station master saw that they were honest people and being a good-hearted man, asked them where they had come from and where they intended to go; he then put them on to a passing freight train to Boranly-Burannyi junction. There, he said, people were badly needed and they would be very welcome. He even wrote a letter about them to the man in charge at the junction.

Life on the Hungry Steppe had been hard, but there had been many people and plenty of work there. After that, the arid Sarozek seemed strange, but they gradually got used to it, settled down and started their new life. It was a poor and strange life, but they were on their own. Both were taken on as track workers on the open line, although they also had to be able to perform all duties within the junction itself.

Thus began life together for Kazangap and his young wife, Bukei, at the lonely Sarozek junction of Boranly-Burannyi. It is true that once or twice during those years, having saved up some money, they would have been glad to move off somewhere else, nearer to the station or even to a town. But while they were thinking about it, the war broke out.

Now the trains went westward from Boranly-Burannyi carrying soldiers and eastwards with refugees; to the west with corn, to the east with wounded. Even at a hole like Boranly-Burannyi, you could at once feel how sharply life had changed.

One after the other the engines blew their whistles at the junction, demanding a change of signals, and from the opposite direction came the same number of whistles. The rails could not take the loads, they became distorted and were wearing out earlier, distorted by the heavy, overloaded trucks. Hardly did they finish repairing one stretch of line than another fell in need of repair.

There was no end to it. Numberless hordes of people, trainful after trainful, went off to the front, by day and night, for weeks on end, months and then years. And all were going westwards where two worlds were fighting, not for life but death . . .

A little later, Kazangap's turn came. A notice was sent to him from Kumbel' ordering him to report to the assembly point. The junction station master clasped his head between his hands and groaned at the news: they were taking away his best track man, and there were only one and a half such men at Boranly-Burannyi in any case! What could he do, who would listen to him now when he complained that the junction could not cope? They would just laugh if he said he needed an extra siding line. What could they do about it? The enemy was at the gates of Moscow.

Already the first winter of the war was at hand, dusk was closing in, and hazy winter was driving in the cold. On the eve of that day, snow began to fall. It fell all night. First powdery snow, then a thick, relentless fall. And among the great silence of the Sarozek, continually spreading, drifting along the valleys, slopes and ravines, down fell a thick covering of pure white from heaven. And straight away, sweeping playfully over the as yet unhardened crust, moved in the Sarozek winds. At first they were light and gusty, then they began to eddy and swirl, to whine; and then the really large snow flurries started. What would happen now to the thin thread of the railway which crossed from one side to the other of the great yellow steppes of the Middle lands, like a vein standing out on a man's temple? Yet still the vein throbbed and the trains kept moving.

So it was on the morning when Kazangap went off to war. He went alone; no one saw him off. When they came out of the house, Bukei stopped and said that the snow was making her head swim. Kazangap took the tightly wrapped bundle of their child from her hands – Aizada had been born by that time. And they walked together, perhaps for the last time, leaving their footprints together in the snow. But his wife would not see Kazangap off – he brought her only as far as the signal box before he got aboard a passing freight train for Kumbel'. For Bukei had to operate the signals in her husband's absence. They said goodbye. All that had to be said had been said, and all the weeping had been done the night before. The engine was waiting, with steam up. The driver was in a hurry, and called to Kazangap to join him on the footplate. Kazangap had only barely clambered up when the engine gave a long blast and slowly gathered speed, clattering over the points, over the crossing where Bukei stood with her scarf tied tight about her head, with her belt, her man's boots, the flag in one hand and her child in her other arm. They waved to each other for the last time. Her face flashed by, a look, a waving hand, and then the signal . . .

By now the train was already moving at speed, while all around the snow covered the Sarozek like a thick blanket, moving in silently from all directions. The wind blew against the engine, adding to the smell of hot burnt ash in the firebox that of fresh, virgin, steppe snow. Kazangap tried to keep this winter fragrance of the Sarozek in his nostrils as long as possible; he realized then that this land meant something to him.

At Kumbel' the mobilized men were being sent on their way. They were lined up in ranks, a roll call was taken and they were allotted to waggons. It was then that something strange happened. As Kazangap was marching with his party to a waggon, one of the Military Commandant's staff caught up with him.

'Asanbaiev, Kazangap! Which one of you is Asanbaiev? Fall out and follow me!'

Kazangap did as he was told.

'Your papers! That's right – you're he. Now follow me.'

They went back to the station, to the office, and the man said, 'Asanbaiev, you're to go home. Go home! You understand?'

'I understand,' Kazangap answered, although he did not really understand at all.

'Get on your way, don't hang around. You're free to go.'

As Kazangap stood there among the noisy crowd of those departing and those seeing them off, he felt completely confused. At first he was delighted at this turn of events, but then he suddenly went hot all over from an idea which had erupted in the depths of his mind. So that's what it was! He began to shove his way through the milling crowd towards the doors, heading for the officer in charge.

'What are you doing, pushing in like that?' shouted others who also wanted to see the officer.

'It's urgent – my train's about to go; it's urgent!'

He pushed past. In the room, filled with a blue haze of cigarette smoke, sitting beside the telephone, surrounded by papers and people, was a greying man with a croaking voice, who lifted up his distorted face when Kazangap reached him.

'What do you want? What's the matter?'

'I protest!'

'What about?'

'My father was pardoned. He was no kulak! Check your papers. He was reinstated as a middle peasant.'

'Hold on! What's all this?'

82

'If you're not taking me because of him, then you're wrong!'

'Listen to me, enough of this nonsense. Kulak, middle peasant – who cares now? Where have you come from? Who are you, anyway?'

'Asanbaiev from Boranly-Burannyi junction.'

The officer looked through his papers.

'You should have said that first. Getting everything confused! Middle, poor, kulak, indeed! You've got a special exemption. You were called up in error. There's an order from Comrade Stalin himself – don't touch the railway workers, all are to remain at their posts. Stop getting in our way, get back to your junction and let us get on with our work . . .'

Sunset found Kazangap, Yedigei and his wife still on their way, but not far from Boranly-Burannyi. Now they were once more approaching the railway line and they could already hear the whistles of the trains going to and fro in both directions and make out the outlines of the waggons. From that far out in the Sarozek, they looked like toys. The sun was already dying behind, lighting up and at the same time darkening the ravines and hills around. Dusk was drawing in now and it was gradually getting dark, making the air a blue colour, with the cool smell of the spring land still holding some of the damp of winter.

'There's our Boranly!' Kazangap pointed, then turned back to look at Yedigei on the camel and Ukubala hurrying along beside. 'There's only a little way to go now; we'll soon be there, and then you can rest.'

Ahead on the empty plateau, where the railway curved slightly, stood several houses and on the reserve line a passing train was waiting for the signal to proceed. Further away on every side there stretched open land, gentle slopes – the voiceless, unending expanse, steppe and steppe beyond . . .

Yedigei's heart sank – he was a man of the steppes by the sea, used to the Aral' desert, but he had not expected this. From the blue, continually changing sea, by whose shore he had grown up, to this dead area without a drop of water in sight! How could he live here?

Ukubala, walking beside him, stretched out her hand to

touch his leg and walked several steps with it resting there. He understood. 'Don't worry,' she was saying. 'The main thing is to get your health back. Then we'll have to wait and see.'

So they came to the place where they were destined, as it turned out later, to spend long years – all the rest of their lives.

Soon the sun set and then it was dark with a multitude of clear, bright stars in the sky over Sarozek; they had reached Boranly-Burannyi.

For several days they lived with Kazangap. Then they moved out, for they were given a room in the barrack reserved for track workers. With that they began their life in their new surroundings.

Amid all the difficulties and trials, especially at first, the empty Sarozek desert gave two gifts of great importance to Yedigei – its air, and camels' milk. The air was virgin clean – another such place would be hard to find; and the milk supply which Kazangap arranged was from one of two young camels which he gave them for milking.

'My wife and I have decided what to do,' he said. 'We have enough milk, and so you take our White Head for your own use. She's a young milking camel with her second young one. Look after her; but be careful not to strain the little suckling camel. He is yours – my wife and I have decided that; he is for you, Yedigei, a gift from me, for breeding. Take good care of him and you'll soon have a herd around him. If you decide to leave this place, then you can sell him. He'll fetch a lot of money.'

White Head's little camel was a tiny, black-headed animal with minute humps, who had been born ten days before. He was lovely, with great, large, damp eyes, bright with a childlike gentleness and inquisitiveness. At times he ran in a comical way, jumping and gambolling around his mother and calling to her when he got left behind in the paddock in an almost human, complaining little voice. Who could have imagined that this was the future Burannyi Karanar, that tireless, powerful animal which in time would become the most famous camel of the district? Karanar was to become closely involved in Burannyi Yedigei's life. But at that time the suckling needed continual care. Yedigei became strongly attached to him and spent all his spare time with the animal. Before, when he had been on the Aral', he had had experience in looking after animals; now he found that experience of great value. By winter, the little Karanar had grown noticeably, and when the cold came, they sewed him a warm cloth which was tied under his belly. In this cloth he looked very funny, with just a head, neck, legs and two humplets showing. In this cloth he went through the whole winter and the beginning of spring, spending whole nights and days in the steppe under the open sky.

By the winter of that year, Yedigei felt that his strength was gradually returning. He did not even notice when his head stopped swimming; also unnoticed, the continual noise in his ears went away; he stopped sweating as he worked and in the middle of winter, when there were big drifts of snow on the tracks, he found he could cope as well as the others with the emergency clearance work. Later on he was to regain his strength to such a degree – he was, of course, young still and energetic by nature – that he even forgot how hard things had been only a short while ago, when he could hardly put one foot in front of the other. The words of the red-bearded doctor had come true.

In moments of good humour, Yedigei would joke with the little camel, stroking and hugging him.

'We're like two brothers, fed with the same milk. You've grown up on White Head's milk and I've got over my shellshock with it. Please God, that's gone for ever. The difference between us is that you sucked at the teat, but I milked out the milk and made it into shubat . . .'

Many years later when Burannyi Karanar had achieved fame in the Sarozek, some people came to photograph him; this was when the war was forgotten and the children were busy at their lessons in school. There was now a water pump in the village, too, and the problem of the water supply had finally been solved. Yedigei by then had a house with a corrugated iron roof. In short, life, after many difficulties, had got into its normal, proper stream. It was then that there took place a conversation which Yedigei remembered for a long time afterwards.

The arrival of the three press photographers was, as they themselves said, an unusual event, if not the only such happening in the whole history of Boranly-Burannyi. The quickly-moving, talkative trio made plenty of promises, claiming that they would splash pictures of Burannyi Karanar and his owners over all the newspapers and magazines. However, the noise and bustle of excitement around him were not much to Karanar's liking and he shrieked with annoyance, grinding his teeth and lifting his head high up out of reach, pleading to be left in peace. The visitors continually asked Yedigei to calm the camel down, turn him this way and that, and Yedigei in his turn called in the children, women and Kazangap in order that not just he, but everyone else should be in the pictures – he thought this would be better. The photographers put up with this willingly and clicked away with their various cameras. The high point came when all the children were sat on Burannyi Karanar's back – two on his neck, five on his back and Yedigei in the middle, so as to demonstrate what power the camel possessed. There was plenty of noise and fun, but in the end the photographers revealed that it was most important for them to photograph the camel by himself, without people around. Well, well!

They now proceeded to take more pictures of Burannyi Karanar, from the side, from in front, from close up and from farther away, as best they could. Then, with the help of Yedigei and Kazangap, they measured the camel – height at withers, chest, wrist, length – and all of them made notes.

'A magnificent Bactrian! Here's a case of the genes performing to the very best effect! The classical Bactrian! What a powerful chest, what a conformation!'

It was, of course, flattering for Yedigei to hear these exclamations, but he had to ask about the meaning of those words which were not familiar to him – such as 'Bactrian'. It turned out that this was the name used by scientists for the ancient race of twin-humped camels.

'So he's a Bactrian?'

'Of rare purity, a diamond of the first water.'

'Why do you need the measurements?'

'For scientific data.'

In claiming to represent newspapers and magazines, the visitors were, of course, deceiving the people of Boranly – it was just to impress them. But six months afterwards, they did send a packet containing a textbook on camel breeding, intended for the use of zoological faculty students; on its cover was the picture of a classical Bactrian – Burannyi Karanar himself. They also sent a whole stack of prints, including some in colour. From these pictures one could see clearly that this had been a happy, joyous time for the people. The trials of the post-war years were behind, the children were not yet grown up, the adults were active and healthy, and old age was still hiding behind the hills.

That day, in honour of the guests, Yedigei killed a lamb and arranged a fine feast for all the people of Boranly. There was plenty of shubat, vodka and other luxuries. At that time a mobile ship from the workers' supply organization used to call at the junction, bringing everything they could desire: crab, black and red caviare, various fish preserves, cognacs, sausages, sweets, and so on. Now, it seemed, everything was available, but all the same they did not usually buy very much. Why should they buy such things? Now this mobile shop has long since vanished.

They had an excellent time, even drinking Burannyi Karanar's health. In conversation it came out that the three visitors had heard about Karanar from Yelizarov. Yelizarov had told them that out in the Sarozek lived his friend Burannyi Yedigei and that he owned one of the most handsome camels on earth! Yelizarov, Yelizarov! A fine man, with a vast store of knowledge of the Sarozek, a scientist . . . When Yelizarov came to Boranly-Burannyi, all three used to meet at Kazangap's house and they would talk all night.

At the party for the photographers, first Kazangap, then Yedigei, each continuing or embellishing what the other had said, told the visitors the Sarozek legend of the original mother of the local race of camels, the famous white-headed camel,

87

Akmaya, and her no less famous owner Naiman-Ana, who was buried in the ancient cemetery of Ana-Beiit. This was the line from which Burannyi Karanar had sprung. The people of Boranly hoped that perhaps they would print this old tale in the newspaper. The visitors listened with interest, but no doubt considered that this was just another local legend handed down from generation to generation. Yelizarov thought differently. He considered that the legend about Akmaya reflected correctly the facts of history; indeed, as he said, it was historical fact. He loved to hear such tales, and himself knew no small number of steppe legends . . .

The visitors left towards evening. Yedigei was satisfied and proud. Afterwards, however, he went on to say something without thinking first. But then, he had been drinking with the guests.

'Well, Kazake, tell me,' he said to Kazangap, 'are you not sorry you gave me the suckling Karanar?'

Kazangap looked at him and smiled. He had not expected that. After a moment's silence, he answered, 'We're all human. But do you know there is a law laid down by our forefathers which says "An animal's master is sent by God." This is God's work. It is determined in this way. Karanar was destined to be yours, you had to be his owner. If he'd fallen into other hands, who knows how he would have fared? Perhaps he wouldn't have grown up, died – anything might have happened. He might have fallen down a ravine. He *had* to belong to you. I've had camels before – not bad ones, either. And also from White Head, who gave birth to Karanar. But he was born to be yours, a gift . . . Please God, he will serve you for a hundred years. Don't ever think that I regret giving him to you.'

'I'm sorry. I apologize, Kazake,' Yedigei was ashamed, sorry that he had blurted out that inane question.

In the course of their talk, Kazangap had enlarged on his views. According to the legend, the golden mother, Akmaya, had had seven young ones – four females and three males. From that time on, all the females had had bright white heads and all the males of the line had black fur on their heads and chestnut coats. Thus Karanar was from this line, a black-headed male camel from a white-headed mother. Who knows how many years have passed since then? Two, three, five hundred or more. But in the Sarozek the line from Akmaya still continued, and now and again a wonder-camel, a *verblyud-syrttan*, such as Burannyi Karanar would appear. Yedigei was fortunate indeed. It was a joy to him that Karanar had been born, and a piece of great good fortune that he had come into his hands.

Eventually the time came for something to be done about Karanar – either to castrate him or to hobble him; he was now beginning to get very wild, not letting people approach him, running away and disappearing for several days on end.

When Yedigei had asked for advice, Kazangap had said, 'It's up to you; if you want a quiet life, go ahead and castrate him. If you want real glory, then don't touch him. But if you do that, then you take on a big responsibility. You'll need strength and patience. He'll be wild for three years, but then he'll walk obediently behind you.'

Yedigei did not touch Burannyi Karanar. He could not raise his hand against him. He left him as a full-blooded male. But then afterwards there were moments when he wept tears of blood . . .

CHAPTER FIVE

Trains in these parts went from East to West, and from West to East.

On either side of the railway lines in these parts lay the great wide spaces of the desert – Sary-Ozeki, the Middle lands of the yellow steppes.

In these parts any distance was measured in relation to the railway, as if from the Greenwich meridian.

And the trains went from East to West, and from West to East.

Early in the morning, all was ready. The body of Kazangap, tightly bound up in a stout rug, tied outside with wool braid and with wrapping around his head, was put into a tractor trailer whose floor had first been strewn with sawdust, shavings and clean hay. There was no time to waste if they were to be back from the cemetery by five or six o'clock. There were thirty kilometres to cover each way, and then there was the digging and the burial to be performed. They had to be back by six, to leave time for the wake and funeral feast.

Now all was ready. Holding on to the leading rein of the harnessed and decorated Karanar, who had been ready since the evening before, Burannyi Yedigei instructed his party to hurry up and stop fussing around. Although he had not slept all night, he looked fresh and alert, but his face was worn. Smartly shaven, the grey-whiskered and grey-eyebrowed Yedigei was in his best clothes, his box-calf boots, his velvet breeches, a black jacket over a white shirt and on his head his best railway uniform cap. On his breast shone all his army decorations and even the shock-worker badges of the various Five Year Plans. All this suited him and gave him an imposing appearance. This, of course, was just how Burannyi Yedigei should look at Kazangap's funeral.

Boranly people, from little ones to the old, had turned out to see them off, crowding around the trailer, waiting for the departure. The women were weeping unceasingly. Burannyi Yedigei decided to make a short speech to them.

'We are now leaving for Ana-Beiit, the most revered and ancient cemetery in the Sarozek. The late Kazangap-ata deserved this; he asked to be buried there.' Yedigei paused as he considered what to say next, and then continued. 'The water and salt given to him at birth have run out. This man worked at our junction for forty-four years, all his life. When he started here, there wasn't even a water pump. Water was brought in in tankers every week. At that time, too, there was no snow-clearing and other machinery, such as we have now. There wasn't even a tractor such as this one which we are using to take him to his burial. But all the same the trains went through and the line was always ready for them. All his life he worked honourably at Boranly-Burannyi. As you all know, he was a good man. Now we are going. We haven't the means for everyone to travel with us, and even if we had, we couldn't leave the railway unattended. The six of us will go and we will do all that is necessary. The rest of you must wait for us here and get ready, for on our return you are all bidden to come to the funeral feast; I invite and summon you in the name of his children – here they are, his son and his daughter . . .'

Although Yedigei had not thought about it in this way, this had really been a small mourning meeting. Then they left. The people of Boranly followed the trailer a little of the way and then stopped in a group just beyond the houses. For some time a great wailing could be heard – this was from Aizada and Ukubala. Then the cries became silent and the six of them moved off from the line of the railway and headed deep into the desert. Burannyi Yedigei sighed with relief. Now they were all on their own, and he knew what had to be done.

The sun had already risen above the horizon and was filling the Sarozek with generous and comforting light. As yet, it was still cool on the steppe and there was little to hinder their progress or make the going difficult. Alone high above them, two kites soared, and occasionally larks rose up from the ground at their feet, twittering anxiously and fluttering their wings as they flew off.

'Soon they'll be leaving,' thought Yedigei. 'With the first snow, they'll gather into flocks and fly away.' He imagined for a moment the falling snow and the little birds flying off among the snowflakes. Once again, he recalled the vixen he had seen two nights before, running towards the railway. He even looked to one side in case she was following them. Once more, too, he thought about that fiery rocket which had ascended into space that night over the Sarozek desert. Surprised by these thoughts he tried to put them at the back of his mind; this was not the time for them, even if the journey was long and tedious.

Mounted on Karanar, Burannyi Yedigei rode in front, leading the way to Ana-Beiit. Karanar was going at a nice bold trot, getting more and more into a rhythm. To a person who appreciated such points, Karanar's movement and gait were especially beautiful. The camel's head on its proud, bent neck, seemed to be swimming over waves yet remaining practically motionless, while his very long legs cut through the air as they tirelessly measured out the steps over the ground. Yedigei was seated between the humps, secure, comfortable and confident. He was pleased to find that Karanar needed no urging; he was moving easily and exactly following his master's instructions. Yedigei's orders and medals tinkled together on his chest and flashed in the sun as he moved along. This did not disturb him.

Behind him was the *Belarus'* tractor with its trailer. In the cabin, beside the young tractor driver, Kalibek, sat Sabitzhan. Yesterday he had had his full share of drink, entertaining the people of Boranly with all sorts of tales about radio-controlled people and all sorts of other gossip, but now he was subdued and silent. Sabitzhan's head rocked from side to side, and Yedigei was concerned that he might break his glasses. In the trailer beside Kazangap, sat Aizada's husband, looking sad. He was blinking his eyes at the sun and occasionally looked round. Today this useless alcoholic was on his best behaviour. He had not taken a drop, and had tried in all sorts of ways to be helpful. When they were carrying the body, he had been particularly active, getting his shoulder right underneath. When Yedigei suggested that he should sit behind him on the camel, he had refused. 'No,' he said, 'I will sit together with my father-in-law and be with him from beginning to end of the journey.'

Yedigei approved of this, as did the people of Boranly. And while they were leaving, he had wept louder than anyone else, as he sat there in the trailer, holding on to the felt bundle of the dead man's body. 'What if, suddenly, he comes to his senses and gives up the drink?' thought Yedigei. 'What a joy that'd be for Aizada and the children!' He even began to have some hope of this happening.

The wheeled *Belarus'* excavator brought up the rear of this small, strange procession through the desert steppe. In the cabin of the digging machine were Edil'bai and Zhumagali. The thick-set Zhumagali, black as coal, was driving; usually he used this machine on various railway tasks. He had arrived at Boranly-Burannyi not so long before and had not decided how long he would stay there. Edil'bai, beside him, was a good head taller; they were engaged in a lively conversation all the way.

The station master at the junction, Ospan, had turned up trumps. He had allotted for the funeral all the special equipment which was available at the junction. And the young manager had made a good decision – if they were to go such a long way and then dig a grave by hand, they would be hard put to it to get back by evening, for they would have to dig a very deep hole, with the side recess of the Moslem tradition.

At first Burannyi Yedigei had been a bit taken aback by the proposal. It would never have occurred to him to think of digging a grave other than by hand, least of all with a mechanical excavator! As he sat opposite Ospan and talked, his forehead puckered up, full of doubts. But Ospan had found a way to persuade the old man,

'Yedike, I'm talking sense. To avoid upsetting your sensibilities, start off digging by hand – well, the first few spade cuts. Then the digger will do the main work in two ticks. The ground in the Sarozek has dried right out – it's as hard as stone, as you well know. You can dig as deep as is necessary with the machine and then at the end you can finish the work by hand to complete the job properly. You'll save time and still keep to the traditional rules . . .'

Now that he was far out in the remote Sarozek, Yedigei found Ospan's advice entirely reasonable and acceptable. He was even surprised that he had had any doubts about it. Yes, they would do that when, God willing, they reached Ana-Beiit. They would select a suitable place at the cemetery in order to lay the dead man with his head facing the direction of the eternal Kaaba at Mecca; they would begin with spade and shovel, which they had brought with them in the trailer; then, after they had made a start, the digger could dig the hole to the bottom and also begin the niche, the *kazanak*, to one side. Finally they would complete the resting place for the body by hand. This would be quicker and surer.

With this plan, they were making their way across the Sarozek. Now they appeared at the top of a ridge; then they disappeared into a deep hollow, then once more they found themselves on a flat area. Still Yedigei rode in front; after him came the wheeled tractor and trailer and behind that, looking like some beetle, the angular *Belarus'* excavator, with the bulldozer scraper in front and the excavator shovel at the rear, pointing backwards.

It was only as he took a last look back towards the junction that Yedigei noticed, to his great amazement, the rusty-coloured dog, Zholbars (Tiger), who was trotting beside them in a most businesslike manner. When had he joined them? Well, now! There had been no sign of him around when they had left Boranly-Burannyi. He might have known the dog would have done something like this. He should have left him tied up. The cunning animal! The moment he noticed that Yedigei was going off somewhere on Karanar, he always tagged along behind. This time he had appeared as if by magic. God be with him, decided Yedigei. It was too late to drive him

94

away or send him home. There was no point in wasting time over the dog – let him come along with them.

As if reading his master's mind, Zholbars ran past the tractor and took up station a bit ahead of and to one side of Karanar. Yedigei pretended to threaten him with the whip, but the dog did not bat an eyelid. He knew it was too late for Yedigei to be threatening him! And anyway, why shouldn't he have joined them? Broad-chested, with his strong, shaggy neck, his tattered ears and wise, quiet expression, the rusty-coloured Zholbars was in his way handsome and worthy of admiration.

Meanwhile various thoughts came to Yedigei's mind on the way to Ana-Beiit. He noticed how the sun had risen above the horizon, measuring the passage of time, and once more his thoughts turned to life in the past. He recalled those days when Kazangap and he had been young and in their prime. Then, they had formed the chief permanent staff at the junction, for the others did not stay long at Boranly-Burannyi; they came and went. Kazangap and he had no time to rest properly because, want to or not, they could not count on anything and had to do all the jobs which needed to be done. Now it was embarrassing to recall that time. The young men had laughed at them; 'Old fools, you've ruined your own life, and for what?' But it *had* been for something.

Once during the blizzards, they had fought for two days without stopping to clear the snow from the tracks. During the night an engine fitted with headlights was brought up to illuminate the area where they were working. The snow kept on falling and the wind blowing. As soon as they cleared away the snow on one side, a new drift formed on the other. It was cold – but not just cold in the ordinary sense: your face and hands swelled up with it. You got up on to the engine footplate to warm up a bit, and then out again after five minutes, back to the deadly task. The engine was already up to its wheels in a drift. That day, towards evening, three new arrivals walked out in disgust, roundly cursing life on the Sarozek with the vilest curses they could muster, using the full extent of their vocabulary. We are not animals, they said; even in jail they allow you time to sleep. And with this, they up and left; next

95

morning as soon as the trains were running, they were whistling farewell and shouting, 'You idiots! You can keep your job!'

Kazangap and he had come to blows during that same blizzard. It happened thus. That night, work became impossible. The snow was still falling, although less heavily, but the wind continued to blow from all points of the compass, biting like a dog and going right through you. There was no way that you could avoid it. The engine was giving off steam, yet this merely produced a fog, and the headlights hardly gave any light. After the three 'helpers' had left, Kazangap and he remained, removing the snow with a small cart drawn by a pair of camels. But the beasts refused to move, they were cold through and through and were fed up with the whirling snow and wind. On one side, the snow came up to their chests. Kazangap dragged the camels along by seizing hold of their lips, forcing them to follow him; meanwhile, Yedigei on the cart, belted them with a whip. They carried on like this until midnight, then the camels just lay down in the snow, as if to say: beat us or beat us not, we can do no more. They were exhausted. What was to be done? Surely they would have to pack up until the weather improved? They stood near the railway engine, sheltering from the wind.

'That's enough, Kazake. Let's get up on the engine and then we can see what the weather's going to do,' said Yedigei, beating his frozen gloves together.

'The weather's as it was, and as it will be. Our job is to clear the line. Let's do it with shovels; we've no right to stand around like this.'

'Aren't we people?'

'Not people, but fools. Even the wolves have hidden away in their lairs.'

'You swine!' Yedigei was furious. 'May you die out here, as you surely will!' And he struck Kazangap in the face.

They grappled, and each suffered cut lips. It was as well that the fireman jumped down from the engine and parted them. Yedigei smiled as he remembered. But that showed what Kazangap was like. They don't make them like that any more; there are no Kazangaps around today. We are carrying the last of his line to his grave. It only remains to hide him under the earth, say a few words of farewell, and that will be 'Amen' to that.

Thinking about this, Burannyi Yedigei repeated to himself the half-forgotten prayers, in order to remind himself of the proper order of words, to organize in his mind the correct sequence of thoughts, the appeals to God – for only He, unknown and unseen, could reconcile the unreconcilable in a man's consciousness of the beginning and end of life and of death. It was to this end that the prayers had been composed. You did not simply shout at God, 'Why have you arranged things so that people are born and die?' Man has lived with this since the world began – although he cannot accept it, at least he can become reconciled to it. These prayers have been unchanged since then and everything in them has stayed the same; one did not grumble in vain, but in order that a man might be calmed. These words, polished over thousands of years like bars of gold, were the last a living man had to say over a dead man. That was the custom.

Quite apart from the question of whether there *is* a God or not, a man remembered Him mostly when he took it into his head to do so – although that was hardly the right way to go about it. Because of this, no doubt, arose the saying that the unbeliever does not remember about God until his head aches. However, whether or not that was so, one should know the prayers.

Looking at his young companions on the tractor, Burannyi Yedigei was genuinely distressed and sorry to think that none of them knew a single prayer. How then could they bury one another? With what words, covering the beginning and end of life, would they sum up the departure of a man into the unknown, into non-existence? 'Farewell, comrade, we will remember you'. Or with some other sort of nonsense?

Once he had to attend a funeral at the regional centre town. Burannyi Yedigei had been amazed. At the cemetery it was just like being at some sort of meeting. The speakers read out from scraps of paper and each said exactly the same thing about the dead man lying there in his coffin – what his job had been, at what and how he had worked, whom he had served under, and how. The band had then struck up and they had covered the grave with flowers. No one had found the time to say anything about death, as the prayers did, uniting, from time past, the sequence of life and non-life. It was as if before this time no one had died and afterwards no one would die. Unhappy people – they were without death! They had pronounced, in spite of all the evidence to the contrary: 'Man has become immortal'.

Yedigei knew well the place through which they were now passing. What was more, perched on Burannyi Karanar, he could see for a long way all around. He tried to keep to as straight a track as possible across the Sarozek to Ana-Beiit, only making a detour in order that it would be easier for the tractors to go around the more uneven spots.

All was going as he had planned. Neither quickly, nor slowly, but steadily they had already gone a third of the way. On went Burannyi Karanar at his tireless trot, following his master's wishes exactly. Behind him, rattling along, went the tractor with the trailer, and behind the trailer, the *Belarus'* excavator.

However, ahead unforeseen happenings awaited them; and remarkable as it might seem, these had some connection with the events now taking place at the Sary-Ozeki launching site.

The aircraft carrier *Convention* was at this time on station in the Pacific Ocean, south of the Aleutians, at a strictly equal distance by air from Vladivostok and San Francisco.

The weather on the ocean was unchanged. For the first half of the day the same blinding sun shone over the continually glittering surface of the water. Nothing on the horizon boded any atmospheric change.

Aboard the carrier, all services were on standby. This included the wing of aircraft and the internal security group, although there was no visible reason for their state of alert. The reasons were out beyond the limits of the galaxy.

The messages coming to *Convention* from the planet Lesnaya

Grud' and relayed by the *Parity* cosmonauts had thrown those in charge of the *Obtsenupr* and the members of the special plenipotentiary commissions into complete confusion. The embarrassment was such that both sides decided that, first of all, they must hold separate meetings in order to consider the situation from the point of view of their own interests, and only after those to meet for joint deliberations about the affair.

The world as yet knew nothing about the unprecedented discovery of the existence of an extraterrestrial civilization on the planet Lesnaya Grud'. Even the two governments involved, who had been informed under conditions of the strictest secrecy about the events, did not have any further information and were now awaiting the verdict of the competent commissions. Aboard the aircraft carrier a strict regime was in force: no one, including the aircraft wing personnel, was allowed to leave the vessel and no other vessel was permitted to approach nearer than fifty kilometres. Aircraft flying over the area had to change course in order not to come within three hundred kilometres of the carrier's position.

Now the general meeting had been adjourned and each commission, together with its respective co-director, was considering the reports of *Parity* cosmonauts 1-2 and 2-1, sent by them from the planet Lesnaya Grud'.

Their words came from an unimaginable distance out into space:

Listen, listen! We are sending a trans-galaxy transmission back to earth! It is impossible to explain everything, since there are many things on Lesnaya Grud' for which there are no names on earth. However, there is much in common. The inhabitants are man-like creatures, people very like us! Here evolution has produced a model of a hominoid on a universal principle! These are beautiful hominoid types from another planet! They are dark-skinned, with light blue hair, lilac and green eyes, with thick white eyelashes.

We first saw them in their transparent pressure suits when they docked with our orbital station. They smiled from the stern of their space vehicle and invited us aboard.

And so we stepped from one civilization into another.

They undocked their screw-shaped craft and at the speed of light – which can in no way be felt inside the vehicle – we moved off, overcoming the passage of time, out into space. The first thing that we noticed and which was an unexpected relief, was an absence of the sensation of weightlessness. How they have achieved that we cannot yet explain.

In a mixture of Russian and English, they said their first phrase to us: *'Well come our galaxy!'* And then we realized that with a little practice, we could exchange thoughts. These people are tall, about two metres high, and there were four, no – five in all, including one woman. The woman was distinguishable not by height, but by her womanly figure and light-coloured skin. All the light-blue-haired people of Lesnaya Grud' are dark-skinned, resembling our northern Arab peoples. From the first, we felt an instinctive trust in them.

Three of them were the pilots of the vehicle and, with the one other man and the woman, they knew earth languages. They had gained their knowledge and systematized it by way of radio message interception in space of English and Russian words, and had thus formed a vocabulary. When we met them, this amounted to over two thousand five hundred words and terms. With the help of this linguistic fund, our intercommunication started. They themselves speak a language which we cannot understand, but in sound it resembles Spanish.

Eleven hours after leaving *Parity* we crossed the boundary of our solar system. This change from one galaxy to another was accomplished without any special sensation. The material of the universe is the same everywhere. But ahead of us (evidently, such was the position and state of the other system's bodies) a bright glow gradually appeared. This glow grew and moved in the distance in limitless space. Meanwhile, on our way we passed several planets, at that time dark on one side and illuminated on the other, and a multitude of suns and moons.

It was as if we were travelling from night into day. For then, suddenly, we moved into a blindingly clear and boundless light coming from a vast and powerful sun in that until now unknown sky.

'We're in our galaxy! That's the light of our Derzhatel' (*Upholder*); soon Lesnaya Grud' will be visible!' announced our woman linguist.

We found that in intensity of radiation and size, Derzhatel' was greater than our sun. Incidentally, because of this and because a day on Lesnaya Grud' lasts twenty-eight hours, there are a whole range of geobiological differences between our world and theirs.

But we will try to say more about this next time, or on our return to *Parity*. For now we will just give a few important details. The planet, Lesnaya Grud', seen from above, resembles our earth, being surrounded by similar atmospheric clouds. But closer in, from a height of about five or six kilometres – the Lesnaya Grud' people gave us a special flight over the surface – it is a spectacle of unprecedented beauty, with bright green mountain ranges and hills, and between them, rivers, seas, and lakes. However in some parts of the planet – chiefly in the remote polar areas – there are vast stretches of lifeless desert, where there are dust storms. The greatest impression made on us was by the towns and inhabited areas. These islands of buildings among the Lesnaya Grud' landscape demonstrate the exceptionally high degree of urbanization. Even Manhattan cannot be compared with the cities built by the inhabitants of this planet.

The people of Lesnaya Grud', we consider, are a unique race of rational beings. Their gestation period is eleven Lesnaya Grud' months. They have a great lifespan, although they themselves consider that the main problem of society is this prolongation of life. They live for an average of a hundred and thirty to a hundred and fifty years, and some individuals live to two hundred. The population of the planet is ten thousand million people.

At this stage we are not in a position to report systematically about the lifestyle of these light-blue-haired people and the achievements of their civilization. Therefore we will give a fragmentary report about those things that have impressed us most.

They know how to obtain energy from the sun, or rather Derzhatel', turning it into heat and electrical energy with a high level of efficiency – far more efficient than our own hydroelectrical methods. They also are able – and it is an exceptionally useful achievement – to synthesize energy from the difference between day and night temperatures.

They have also learned to control their climate. When we were making our observation flight over the planet, the vehicle in which we were travelling dispersed clouds and fog concentrations by means of radiation. We know, too, that these people can influence the movement of air masses and water currents in the seas and oceans. By these means they control the humidity and the temperature on the surface of their planet.

However, they have one colossal problem which, as far as we know, has not been encountered on earth. Because they can control the climate, they do not suffer from droughts and so far they have no shortages in food production – and this with a population twice that of the earth. But a large area of their planet is gradually becoming uninhabitable. In these regions everything dies. This phenomenon they call 'internal withering'. On our flight we saw the dust storms in the south-eastern area of Lesnaya Grud'. As a result of some reaction deep down inside the planet, perhaps something akin to a volcanic process but more likely some form of slow dispersal of radiation, the upper surface is being broken down and is losing its strength, and in the process all humus-producing organisms are being burnt up. Every year in this area of Lesnaya Grud', a desert the size of the Sahara encroaches on the space inhabited by the light-blue-haired people of the planet. This is their greatest concern. They have not yet been able to find a way to control the process going on deep inside their planet. Nevertheless, against this threat of internal withering, they have deployed vast scientific and material resources. They have no moon in their galaxy, but they know about our moon and have, indeed, visited it. They consider that our moon went through a similar process. Having heard about their visits, we thought: 'it is not far from the moon to the earth; are we prepared for a meeting with these people? What could be the results? Is it not time we abandoned conflict and lack of cooperation and set about learning from our neighbours in the universe?'

At the present time on Lesnaya Grud', there is an all-planet discussion in progress as to whether they should expend efforts in attempting to discover the cause of the internal withering and a means of stopping this catastrophe – or whether they should find a new planet in the universe which meets their living requirements and then begin a mass transfer of the population to this new planet with the purpose of exporting their civilization and setting it up there. So far it is not yet clear which new planet they are considering. At present they still have several million years yet to live on their parent planet, and we found it remarkable that they have already been thinking about a time so far ahead in the future and are filled with the same fire and energy about it as if the problem affected the present generation. Surely the thought has arisen in many minds, 'Will the grass not grow when we are gone?' We were ashamed that we on earth had not considered anything like that when we heard that a considerable part of the planet's gross product goes on a programme of preventing internal withering from within the depths of the planet. This involves the setting up of a barrier stretching over many thousand kilometres, along the whole line of advance of the desert, by drilling ultra-deep borings and introducing into the bedrock long-term neutralizing substances which, they consider, will halt the internal poison-producing reactions within the planet.

Of course, inevitably there are social problems on the planet such as always cause concern and are a heavy burden – problems of behaviour, morals and intellectual matters. It is quite clear that ten thousand million people living together are bound to have conflicts, whatever level of civilization they may have achieved. But the remarkable thing is that they do not know of states as such; they know nothing of weapons; they do not even know what war is. We do not know; perhaps in the distant past they had wars and separate states and money and all the social factors of a similar character; but at the present time they have no conception of such institutions of force as the state and such forms of struggle as war. If we have to explain the fact of our continuous wars on earth, will it not seem inconceivable to them? Will it not also seem a barbaric way of solving problems?

Their life is organized on quite a different basis, not completely comprehensible to us, and quite unachieved by us in our stereotyped earth-bound way of thinking.

They have achieved a level of collective planetary consciousness that categorically excludes war as a means of struggle, and in all probability theirs is the most advanced form of civilization among rational beings in the universe. It is possible that they have achieved a level of scientific development which will one day allow the humanization of time and space to become the main purpose of rational human beings, and so allow the world to evolve to a new, higher, eternal phase.

103

We do not intend to compare things which cannot be compared. In due course no doubt people on earth will also achieve great progress, and even we have much to be proud of. But, all the same, a troublesome thought gnaws at us: Is Man on earth to continue in his present tragic state of error? Must all history be a history of wars? Is this not a dead end for Mankind? Where are we going and to what will all this lead us? Will Mankind find the courage to avoid total cataclysm? Since we have been fated to be the first to see an extraterrestrial civilization, we are experiencing complicated reactions – fear for the future of the people of the earth, and at the same time hope, since at last we have found an example of a vast communal life, an advancing movement, which lies outside those forms of contradiction which are decided by wars . . .

The people of Lesnaya Grud' know of the existence of the earth at the extreme limits of the universe. They are filled with a wish to make contact with the people of earth, not only from natural curiosity but, as they think, above all for the sake of the triumph of human intelligence; for the opportunity to exchange experiences and compare civilizations; for the sake of a new era in the development of thought and of the spirit of universal intellect-possessing people.

In all this they foresee more possibilities than might be thought. Their interest in the people of the earth is dictated by the fact that in the union of the power of these two worlds of intelligent behaviour, they see a basic way of ensuring the limitless continuation of life in nature. At the same time they are aware that all life inevitably decays and that any planet is doomed to destruction eventually . . . They are concerned *now* with the problem of 'the end of the world', which may be some thousands of millions of years away, and are even now working on cosmological projects for the organization of a new basis for contacts between all living beings in the universe.

With their vehicles which fly at the speed of light, they could have already visited our earth. But they do not wish to do so without the consent and invitation of the people of the earth. They do not wish to come to earth as uninvited guests. In making this point, they told us that they have long sought a means of getting to know us. Ever since our space stations started spending some time in orbit, it became clear to them that the time of a possible meeting was approaching and that they should take some initiative. They prepared in detail, awaiting a suitable opportunity. Thus we became involved as we were in an intermediate situation, aboard an orbiting station . . .

Entirely understandably, our arrival on their planet caused a sensation. A system of global telecontact reserved for special occasions was used. In the bright air around us, we could see people and objects which were in fact thousands of kilometres away – yet we could communicate, looking one another in the face, smile, shake hands with them, speak joyfully and exclaim loudly, as if they were right in front of us. They are very beautiful, these people of Lesnaya Grud' – their hair colour varies from dark-blue through to ultramarine. The old people go grey, just as our old people do. The anthropological types are also varied, and several different ethnic groups exist.

We will tell of this and of much else no less remarkable when we return to *Parity* or to earth. Now for the most important part. The people here ask us to convey a message via the *Parity* relay system about their wish to visit our planet when this would be convenient to the people of earth. Before this, they propose the building of an inter-galactical station which would serve as a place for initial meetings and then, in the future, would act as a permanent base on the way for mutual research work. We have promised to bring this proposal to the attention of our fellow earth-dwellers. However, we are now worried about something else in this connection. Are we, the people of earth, ready for such intergalactical meetings? Are we sufficiently developed, as thinking beings, for this? Could we, in our varied society and with our existing contradictions, speak with one voice, as plenipotentiaries of the whole human race, in the name of the whole earth? We beg of you to avoid a new outburst of rivalry and struggle for supremacy, and to give the final decision on this matter over to the United Nations. We beg that in this matter the right of veto should not be misused; indeed, perhaps on this occasion that right could be suspended. It is bitter and hard to think about such things when we are beyond the confines of our galaxy, but we are people of earth and we know how things are on our planet.

Finally, about ourselves, about what we have done. We realize what confusion and extraordinary measures our disappearance from the orbital station will have set in train. We deeply regret that we have caused such trouble. However, this was an event unique in the world's experience. We could not, had not the right to refuse to do this, the most important act in our life. Being people accustomed to direct control, we were bound for the sake of such a purpose to act 'contrary to regulations'.

Let this be on our conscience and let us bear whatever punishment is necessary. But for the moment forget about that. We have sent you a signal from outer space. We are giving you a sign from the previously unknown galaxy of Derzhatel', the Upholder. The light-blue-haired people of Lesnaya Grud' are the creators of the highest form of modern civilization. A meeting with them might make a profound change in our lives, in the lives of all Mankind. Are we bold enough to do this, taking account, of course, first of all, of the interests of earth?

These people do not threaten us. At least, that is how it seems to us. But we could gain immensely from their experience; we could change our way of life, learning how to obtain energy from the material of the world around us, and how to live without weapons, without force and without wars. This last will no doubt appear to you as a wild flight of fancy, but we solemnly declare that it is just in this way that the life of these rational beings on Lesnaya Grud' is organized; they have achieved just such a precious state, inhabiting as they do an environment equal in mass to that of the earth. Being the possessors of a universal and highly civilized thought process, they are ready for open contacts with their fellow intelligent beings, the people of earth, in such forms as will benefit both sides.

Although we are fascinated and amazed by the discovery of an extraterrestrial civilization, we nevertheless long to return as soon as possible in order to tell people about all that we have seen while in this distant galaxy.

We intend in twenty-eight hours time, that is in a day's time after this session, to return to *Parity*. On arrival, we will put ourselves at the full disposal of *Obtsenupr*. Meanwhile, farewell. Before we set off for the solar system, we will send our ETA at *Parity*. With this we conclude our first report from the planet Lesnaya Grud'. Until our next meeting. We beg you to tell our families not to worry about us.

Parity-Cosmonaut 1-2
Parity-Cosmonaut 2-1

The adjourned and then separate sessions of the plenipotentiary commissions on board the aircraft carrier *Convention*, which had been investigating the extraordinary happenings on the *Parity* orbital station, concluded with both commissions flying off to consult their superiors in each country. One aircraft took off from the carrier's deck and set course for San Francisco; a few minutes later another aircraft set off for Vladivostok.

The aircraft carrier *Convention* remained on permanent station in the Pacific Ocean, south of the Aleutians. On board strict discipline reigned. Each man was busy at his own work. And all kept silent.

The trains in these parts went from East to West, and from West to East.

On either side of the railway lines in these parts lay the great wide spaces of the desert – Sary-Ozek, the Middle lands of the yellow steppes.

Already one third of the way to Ana-Beitt had been covered. The sun, which had at first risen quickly above the earth, now seemed to have frozen in place over the Sarozek. Dawn had become day. The usual burning heat prevailed.

Looking first at his watch, then up at the sun and then at the open steppe ahead, Burannyi Yedigei decided that the journey was going as it should. He was in front on his camel, behind him was the tractor with its trailer and behind that was the wheeled *Belarus'* digger, while on one side the rusty-coloured Zholbars ran along.

'It seems a person can't stop thinking for one second. Whether you like it or not, one thought follows another, and so on without end. No doubt it'll go on like that until you die!' Yedigei came to this conclusion when he realized that all through the journey he was thinking about something. Thought followed thought, just as one wave follows another wave at sea. As a child he had watched for hours on end how on the Aral' Sea during windy weather the white running seas had appeared far out in the distance and how they had approached, forming boiling white horses, each wave giving birth to another wave. At one and the same moment there occurred the birth, the destruction and again the birth and the stilling of the living flesh of the sea. At that time, as a boy, he had longed to turn into a seagull and fly above the waves, above the glittering splashes, in order to study from above the life of the vast deep.

The emptiness of the landscape and the even sound of the trotting camel soon set Burannyi Yedigei's thoughts wandering, and he let them roam freely. Fortunately the way ahead was long and nothing impeded their progress. Karanar, as always on long journeys, had warmed up as he went along and now began to produce a strong musk-like smell from his mane and neck. 'Well, well,' Yedigei chuckled to himself with satisfaction, 'you're already in a lather! You beast, you young stallion! You're bad, bad!'

Yedigei thought about the past, when Kazangap had still been young and healthy; and, from a chain of things remembered, an unwanted, long felt and bitter sadness fell upon him. The prayers did not help, although he murmured them aloud over and over again, repeating them in order to drive away the constant returning pain. But his soul was not to be stilled. Burannyi Yedigei was sad; needlessly he struck out from time to time at the flanks of the conscientiously trotting camel; he pulled the peak of his cap down over his eyes and did not even look at the tractor following behind. Let them follow, keep up with him. What did they care, those green young men?

The event he recalled took place long ago. He and his wife never spoke about it any more, but at the time Kazangap had pronounced his judgement on it, as always, wisely and honestly. Only he could pass such judgement on Yedigei. Had anyone else spoken to him so, Yedigei would long ago have quitted his work at the Boranly-Burannyi junction.

At the end of the year 1951, a family came to the junction: a husband, wife and their two children, both boys. The elder, Daul, was five, the younger, Ermek, was three. Abutalip was the same age as Yedigei. Before the war, as a young man, he had been a teacher in a village school – just a small aul. In the summer of 1941, he had been called up and gone to the front.

At the end of the war, or soon after, he had married Zaripa. Before they came to the junction she, too, had been a teacher, working with the youngest children. Now fate had forced them out into the Sarozek, to Boranly-Burannyi.

It was clear at once that they had not led an easy life, otherwise they would not have come to this Sarozek backwater. Abutalip and Zaripa could have easily got work somewhere else. But, as it turned out, circumstances had allowed them no choice. At first, the people of Boranly thought that they would not stay long and would soon go as far away as they could. But these were not the sort of people who would come to and then leave Boranly-Burannyi. This was also the view of Yedigei and Kazangap. Their relations with Abutalip's family were nonetheless founded on immediate respect. They were well-mannered and cultured people, and they had been in trouble. Like everyone else, both husband and wife worked. They heaved around sleepers and they froze in the snowstorms. In effect they did the job of track workers. However, this good, pleasant, friendly family were unhappy and this was because Abutalip had been a prisoner of war with the Germans. At that time the passions of the war years had subsided. People no longer regarded former prisoners of war as traitors and enemies of the people. As for the people of Boranly, they could not have cared less. All they knew was that the war had ended in their victory, and that everybody had suffered in that terrifying world upheaval. Others to this day wandered restlessly about the world. The spectre of war was still ever-present. Thus, the people of Boranly did not ask too many questions about these people who had arrived. Why make their life more miserable, when they had clearly drunk their cup to the bitter dregs?

As time passed, Yedigei and Abutalip became friends. He was a wise man and Yedigei was attracted to him because he was not sorry for himself in his unfortunate plight. He behaved honourably and did not complain about his fate. He had reconciled himself to the way things were on earth. He understood that this was the fate he had been assigned, and both he and his wife, Zaripa, were filled with a sense of duty. Being at inner peace about the inevitable price which they were paying, they found the meaning of life in an unusual sensitivity and closeness one to the other. Yedigei understood later that this was the way they lived, defending themselves together and thus protecting themselves and their family from the fierce winds of those days.

Abutalip refused to live one day away from his wife and children. His sons meant everything to him and all his spare minutes were spent with them. He taught them grammar, told them stories, riddles and devised games for them. When he and his wife went off to work, at first they left the children on their own in the barrack room. But Ukubala could not calmly stand by and watch this happen; she began to take the boys into her home. It was warm in their house and life was more congenial than in the barrack room house of the new arrivals. This brought their two families together. Yedigei's two daughters were growing up, too, and were the same age as Abutalip's boys.

Once when Yedigei was calling in to collect the boys after work, Abutalip suggested, 'What do you say, Yedigei? Shall I teach your girls as well? I have to work with my boys. Now they've all four become friends and play together, let them be together in your house during the days and in the evenings the girls can come over to our place. Life out here is a bit empty, so there is even more reason to spend time with the children. Nowadays knowledge is needed from an early age. A child today needs to know as much as a youth in the past. Otherwise he'll not get a full education.'

Burannyi Yedigei was to realize the full meaning of these efforts of Abutalip when, later on, disaster struck. Then he realized that this had been all that Abutalip had been able to do for his children, given the conditions at Boranly. It was as if he was anxious to give his children as much as he possibly could of himself; as if he wished, in this way, to be stamped in their memory and so that he could live again through them.

In the evenings, therefore, when he had returned from work, Abutalip and Zaripa set up something very like a kindergarten school for their own and Yedigei's children. They learned the alphabet, played, drew, competed to see who could do the best and listened while the parents read to them, and together they even learned various songs. All this was so fascinating that even Yedigei began to take an interest and came to see how well everything was going. Ukubala would also drop in frequently as if there was something for her to do, but really only to look at her children at work. Burannyi Yedigei was touched by all this; touched to the depths of his soul. So this is what educated people, teachers, were like! It was a delight to see how they knew how to work with children, how they could enter into the children's world and stop being grown-ups. On such evenings Yedigei tried not to get in the way, but sat quietly on one side. But when he arrived, he would doff his hat at the door and say, 'Good evening! Here's your fifth pupil!'

The children got used to him being there. His daughters were happy, and with their father there they tried harder. Yedigei and Ukubala stoked the stove in turn, so that it was warm and comfortable in the barrack room for the children.

So this was the family that settled down that year at Boranly-Burannyi. But strange as it may seem, such people are not usually lucky. Abutalip Kuttybaev's trouble was not just that he had been a prisoner of war under the Germans, but that, luckily or unluckily, having escaped with a group of other prisoners from a camp in South Germany, he had found himself in 1943 in the ranks of the Yugoslav partisans and had fought in the Yugoslav Liberation Army until the end of the war. He was wounded and recovered there. He was awarded Yugoslav military decorations. They wrote about him in the partisan newspapers and printed his photograph. All this was very helpful when his case was considered by the Control and Filtering Commission on his return to the Motherland in 1945. Of the twelve who had escaped from the camp, only four survived and all four were lucky, because the Soviet Control Commission worked directly with units of the Yugoslav army and the Yugoslav commanders wrote reports on the military and moral characteristics of these four Soviet ex-prisoners of war and praised the part they had played in the partisans' battle with the fascists.

So it was that two months after many enquiries, interrogations, face-to-face confrontations, waiting, hope and despair, Abutalip Kuttybaev returned to his native Kazakhstan without any loss of rights, but without the extra privileges which demobilized servicemen normally received. Abutalip Kuttybaev did not mind. Having been a geography teacher before the war, he returned to the same job. Here, in one of the regional central schools, he met the young elementary class teacher, Zaripa. There are such cases of such shared happiness – not very often, but there certainly are. Without them there would not be much in life.

Meanwhile, the first years after victory passed. After the triumph and the rejoicings, the Cold War was beginning to cast its shadows over the world. In various troubled parts of the world, events began to take a dangerous course.

For Abutalip, the crisis came in one of his geography lessons. Sooner or later, it had to happen. If not with him, then with someone else like him. While telling the eighth-year pupils about Europe, Abutalip Kuttybaev recounted how on one occasion he and his friends were taken from the camp in the South Bavarian Alps to a quarry; and he told how, having disarmed their guards, they succeeded in escaping and joined up with the Yugoslav partisans. He told how he had traversed half of Europe during the war, had been on the shores of the Adriatic and Mediterranean Seas; how he knew the scenery well there, and also told about the life of the local people and said that all this could not be written into a school book. The teacher considered that in this way he was enriching the subject with his eyewitness account.

His pointer moved over the blue, green and brown map of Europe hanging on the board; his pointer followed the heights, the plains; went along the rivers, every now and again touching those places he still dreamed of – where he had fought day in, day out, many summers and winters. And perhaps the pointer even touched that minute spot where his blood had been shed when a burst of enemy automatic fire from the flank had ripped into him and he had fallen slowly down the slope, reddening the grass and stones with his blood. That patch of bright red blood could have covered the whole map, and for a moment he was reliving that moment, seeing that blood once more, this time flowing on to the map. And he remembered how he had become giddy and things had become dark; his eyes were swimming and, as he fell, so the mountains seemed also to be falling. He had called out for help to his Polish friend with whom he had run away the year before from that Bavarian stone quarry: '*Kazimir! Kazimir!*' But Kazimir had not heard him, for although he thought he was shouting at the top of his voice, in fact he made no sound and only came round in the partisan hospital after he had been given a blood transfusion.

As he told his pupils about Europe, Abutalip Kuttybaev was surprised to find that after all he had lived through, he could talk about that part which concerned elementary school geography in so matter-of-fact, in so detached a fashion.

And then suddenly a hand was raised in the front row.

'Agai, teacher, so you were a prisoner of war?'

The child's pitiless eyes were looking at him with a cold brightness. The boy's head was thrown back slightly; he stood at attention, and for some reason Abutalip always remembered his teeth – the lower ones stuck out, covering the upper ones.

'Yes, I was . . .'

'Why didn't you shoot yourself?'

'Why should I kill myself? I was wounded.'

'Because one mustn't surrender when captured – that was the order.'

'Whose order?'

'One from higher authority.'

'How do you know?'

'I know all about it. We have people to stay from Alma-Ata, from Moscow even. So you didn't obey the order from higher authority?'

'Was your father at the front?'

'No, he was concerned with mobilization arrangements.'

'Then he probably wouldn't understand. I can only say that I had no other way out.'

'All the same, you should have obeyed that order.'

'What are you going on about?' Another pupil had stood up. 'Our teacher fought alongside the Yugoslav partisans. What more do you want?'

'All the same, he should have obeyed that order!' The first boy was adamant.

The class began to buzz and the normal quiet was broken. 'He should have done!' 'He shouldn't!' 'That's right!' 'I don't agree!'

The teacher struck his desk with his fist.

'Stop this noise! This is a geography lesson! How I fought and what happened is known to those who need to know. Now we'll get back to the map.'

Again, no one in the class could have seen that minute, almost invisible point on the map whence had come that burst of automatic fire; nor could they have seen how their teacher, now standing with his pointer by the map-board, had slowly fallen down the slope, covering the blue, green and brown map of Europe with his blood . . .

A few days later he was summoned to the regional peoples' education section. There it was put to him in a few words that he should be taken off teaching 'at his own request'. As a former prisoner of war, he had no moral right to be teaching the rising generation.

Abutalip Kuttybaev and Zaripa, together with their first-born, had to move away to a different region, further away from the oblast' town. He found a place in an aul school. Somehow they settled down in that village and found somewhere to live. Zaripa, a young and able teacher, took charge. But then there occurred the events in 1948 connected with Yugoslavia. Now Abutalip Kuttybaev was not merely a former prisoner of war, but a suspicious character who had had a long association with Yugoslavia. And although he could prove that all he had done was to serve with the Yugoslav partisan comrades, no one took any notice of that. All understood; they even sympathized; but no one dared take upon themselves any responsibility in this matter. Once again he was summoned to the regional peoples' education centre; again he was taken off teaching, 'at his own request'.

Having been forced to move many times from place to place, the family of Abutalip Kuttybaev at the end of 1951, in the middle of winter, finally turned up in the Sarozek, at the Boranly-Burrannyi junction.

In 1952 the summer was even hotter than usual. The ground dried out and became so hot that even the Sarozek lizards did not know what to do; they lost their fear of people and were to be found sitting on the doorstep, their throats quivering, with mouths wide open, trying somehow to find shelter from the sun. Meanwhile, the kites were trying to get cool by soaring to such heights that you could no longer see them with the naked eye. Just now and again they gave themselves away with a single cry and then once more they became silent in the hot, quivering, mirage-laden air.

But there was still duty to be done. The trains kept on going from East to West and from West to East, and many of them passed through Boranly-Burannyi. It would take more than the heat to prevent the movement of trains on the great state main line.

Work had to go on as usual. They had to wear gloves as it was too hot to touch stones, still less any metal objects. The sun was up there overhead, burning down with oven-like heat. Water was, as usual, brought to them in tankers, and while it was there in the open, it heated up almost to boiling point. Clothes on the shoulders were bleached colourless in a couple of days. It was easier for a man to work in the Sarozek in winter, even with the hardest frost, than in such summer heat.

Burannyi Yedigei tried to cheer Abutalip up.

'We don't always have such a summer. You've picked a bad year.' He was making excuses, almost as if he himself was to blame. 'Fifteen more days, twenty at the most, and the heat will become less, it'll decrease. Damn it, it's a torture for everyone. But here in the Sarozek at the end of summer, there's usually a break; there's a sudden change. Then for the whole of the autumn until winter comes, the weather's fine – it's cool, and the animals put on weight. I reckon the signs are there – this year there'll be a change. So be patient, there'll be a good autumn.'

'You can guarantee that?' Abutalip smiled understandingly.

'Let's say I almost can!'

'Well, thanks for that. Just now I feel as if I was in a Turkish bath. But my soul is very heavy. Zaripa and I can stand it. We've learned to be patient, but I'm sorry for the children . . . I can hardly bear to look at them.'

The children at Boranly were miserable and tired, their faces drawn, and there was nowhere for them to escape from the oppressive, exhausting heat. There was not one tree around, nor a stream – things so essential for a child's world. In the spring when the Sarozek became alive and for a while it was green around the valley and the halt, then the children enjoyed themselves. They played ball, hide-and-seek, ran out into the steppe and chased the marmots. It was a delight to hear their voices ringing out in the distance.

Summer destroyed all that. And that year the unusual heat wore down even their restless spirits. They hid from the heat in the shade by the houses and only looked out when the trains were passing through. This was their amusement – to count how many trains went one way and how many the other; how many passenger carriages and how many freight trucks. And sometimes when the trains with passengers merely slowed down to pass through the junction, it seemed to the children that they would stop, so they ran after them, panting and sheltering themselves from the sun with their arms raised, perhaps in a vain hope of getting protection from the heat. It was hard to see the envy and unchildlike sorrow of the small boys of Boranly when they watched the waggons rumble on their way without stopping. The passengers in these carriages, with wide-open windows and doors, were also out of their minds with the oppressive heat, the smells and the flies, but at least they knew that within a couple of days they could recover later amid cool rivers and green forests.

Everyone was worried about the children that summer, all the adults, the mothers and fathers; but what Abutalip suffered, only Yedigei and Zaripa could understand. At this time Zaripa and he had their first talk about this subject. In that talk something more about the fate of these two was revealed. That day they were working on the track, renewing the ballast, scattering the metal and raking it into the spaces under the sleepers and rails so as to reinforce the embankment against the strain of the vibration. They had to work in bursts, between the passing of the trains. It was long, wearisome work in that heat. Nearer to midday, Abutalip took the empty can and went, as he put it, for some more hot water, to the tanker in the siding. At the same time he wanted to check to see how the children were getting on.

He walked quickly along the track, in spite of the heat. He was hurrying to see the children and was not thinking about himself. Over his bony shoulders he wore a vest of indeterminate colour; on his head was a scruffy straw hat; his trousers were hanging loosely on his thin body, while on his feet were his laceless working shoes. He walked with the soles of his shoes pattering on the sleepers, paying no attention to anything. When a train came up behind him, he did not even look round.

'Hi, Abutalip, get off the line! Are you deaf?' Yedigei yelled.

But he didn't hear. Only when the engine whistled did he climb down the embankment and even then, he did not so much as look at the train and never saw the driver shake his fist at him.

During the war, in captivity, he had not turned grey – he was, of course, younger then; he had gone to the front as a junior lieutenant of nineteen. But that summer he did go grey – Sarozek grey. The greyness showed up almost white here and there in his matted, thick, mane-like hair. Then it spread to his temples. In good times, he would have been a handsome, a presentable man, broad-browed, with a hooked nose, protruding Adam's apple, strong mouth and wide, oblong eyes. Zaripa joked bitterly, 'You're unlucky, Abu. You should have played Othello on the stage!' Abutalip had laughed back, 'Then I would have had to strangle you, and you wouldn't have liked that!'

Abutalip's slow reaction to the train coming up behind him had really worried Yedigei.

'You should say something to him, ask him what on earth he

was thinking about!' he said to Zaripa, half in reproach. 'The driver couldn't be held responsible – it's forbidden to walk along the line. Why did he take such a risk?'

Zaripa sighed deeply and wiped the sweat with her sleeve from her black, sunburnt face. 'I'm afraid for him.'

'What?'

'I'm afraid, Yedike. Oh, what have we to hide from you! He is being punished instead of the children and me. When I was to be married, I didn't listen to my relations. My elder brother was furious about it. He said, "You'll regret this for a hundred years, you fool! You're not getting married, you're seeking your own unhappiness and that of your children and their children, not yet born; they're already condemned to sorrow. If your beloved has a head on his shoulders, he wouldn't raise a family, he'd hang himself! That'd be the best thing for him!" But we went our own way. We hoped that since the war was over, there would be no more reckonings between the living and the dead. We kept away from everyone and from his and my relations. Imagine it – recently my brother wrote a statement that he'd warned me against our marriage; he added that he had nothing to do with me, and even less with a person who had spent a long time in Yugoslavia, as Abutalip Kutty-baev had! Well, after that, naturally everthing started up again. Wherever we go, we're turned away. And now we're here, we can go no further.'

She was silent, furiously raking the packed gravel under the sleeper. Ahead the next train was approaching. They walked back, away from the line, taking their shovels and barrows with them.

Yedigei felt that he had to help in some way when people were in such a situation. But he could change nothing; the cause of the trouble lay far beyond the bounds of his Sarozek world.

'We have now lived here for many years,' he replied. 'You'll get used to it, settle down. You must live.'

As he looked directly into her face, he thought: yes, bread in the Sarozek is earned the hard way. When they arrived in the winter, her face was still pale, but now it looked like the earth itself. He was sad to see this – sad to see her beauty fading before his eyes. But her hair was still fine, although bleached; even her eyelashes had been burnt by the sun. Her lips were cracked and bleeding. She was going through a really difficult time; she was not used to this sort of life. However, she would stick it, she would not run away. Where could she run to? She had her two children. In all, she was a fine, brave person.

Meanwhile, that next train, stirring up the hot, motionless air, rattled past along the line, sounding like a burst of automatic fire. Once again they picked up their tools, went back and continued their work on the track.

'Listen, Zaripa,' said Yedigei in an attempt to strengthen her will, to make her get to grips with reality, 'of course, it's very hard for the children here, I won't deny that. My heart aches too, when I look at my own – but this heat won't last for ever. It'll give way. And again, just think: you're not alone here in the Sarozek; there are other people around. At the worst, there's us! Don't let it get you down, because of all that's happened in your life.'

'That's just what I say to him, Yedike. I try not to say anything unnecessary. I can understand how things are for him.'

'Then you act quite rightly in what you do. I've wanted to say this to you, Zaripa – I've just been waiting for the opportunity. Now you know. Forgive me.'

'Of course, there are times when I despair. Then I'm sorry for myself, for him and even more so for the children. Although he's not to blame, he feels that it's his fault – he brought us here. But he can't change anything. Of course, where we come from, among the Ala-tau mountains and rivers, it was quite a different life, altogether another climate. If only we could send the children there for the summer – but to whom? We know no old people, they died early on. Brothers, sisters, relations – it's hard to criticize them, they're not to blame. Formerly they avoided us; now they've given us up completely. Why should they worry about our children? So we are tortured, fearing that we are stuck here for our whole life, although we never mention it openly. But I see how things are for him. What lies ahead for us, God only knows.'

There was a heavy silence. They did not return to the subject, but worked on, pausing to let the trains pass and then restarting work. What else could they do? How could he console them? How could he help them? They were not beggars, thought Yedigei. They could live on what they both earned. No one has imprisoned them. Yet they could not escape from here – not tomorrow, nor the day after.

Yedigei was surprised at himself, how he felt, at his anger and bitterness on behalf of this family; it was as if their troubles were his. Who were they to him? But could he say to himself, 'This isn't my problem. What business is it of mine?' Was he the sort of person to judge or take a stand on something which did not concern him? A hard worker, a man of the steppe – there were countless others like him on the earth. Why should he be upset? Why should he worry or trouble his conscience with questions about what is fair or unfair in life? No doubt those responsible for Abutalip's plight knew a thousand times more then he, Burannyi Yedigei. They could see things more clearly than him, out here in the Sarozek. Was it his business? But all the same, he could not rest. And for some reason he felt the most concern for Zaripa. Her loyalty, her reserve, her brave fight with adversity amazed and overwhelmed him. She was like a bird trying to protect her nest from the storm with her wings. Any other person would have cried, given up, and heeded her relations. Now she was paying, equally with her husband, for the past, for those war years. And what worried Yedigei above all else was the fact that there was no way in which he could defend her, or her children, or her husband . . .

Later on there were moments when he regretted bitterly that Fate had brought this family to settle at Boranly-Burannyi. Yet why was he so worried? He could have shut himself off from such things and lived quietly, as before.

CHAPTER SIX

Towards the second half of the day, the waves began to get up on the Pacific Ocean, south of the Aleutians. The south-easterly wind coming up from the lower latitudes of the American continent had gradually increased in strength and settled down in direction. The vast, open spaces of water now began to surge gently, to break, and then the waves took up a continuous pattern in rows, one after the other. This confirmed, if not the beginning of a storm, then at any rate a long period of unsettled weather.

Such waves in the open ocean did not present any danger to the aircraft carrier *Convention*. Any other time its position would have stayed unchanged. But since any minute now the aircraft was expected to return with the special plenipotentiary commissions after their consultations with their superiors, the carrier was headed into the wind to reduce the roll. All went normally: first the aircraft from San Francisco and then the one from Vladivostok landed safely.

The commissions had come back in full strength but they were very quiet and preoccupied. Fifteen minutes after landing they were already in closed session around the table, and five minutes after they had started work, a coded message was sent off into space to the *Parity* orbital station for retransmission to the parity-cosmonauts 1–2 and 2–1 out in the Derzhatel' galaxy. It read:

To cosmonaut-controllers 1–2 and 2–1 of the *Parity* orbital station. This message is to warn the parity-cosmonauts 1–2 and 2–1, now outside the limits of the solar system, not to take any action. You are to remain where you are, pending further special instructions from *Obtsenupr*.

After this message had been sent and without wasting any time, the special plenipotentiary commissions prepared to present their positions and the proposals of the two sides for the resolution of the crisis.

The aircraft carrier *Convention* stood bow to wind among the Pacific waves, endlessly bearing down. No one in the world knew that aboard the ship at that time the fate of the planet was being decided.

Trains in these parts went from East to West, and from West to East.

And on either side of the railway line in these parts lay the great wide spaces of the desert – Sary-Ozeki, the Middle lands of the yellow steppes.

In these parts any distance was measured in relation to the railway, as if from the Greenwich meridian.

And the trains went from East to West, and from West to East.

There were only two hours more to go before they reached the Ana-Beiit cemetery. The funeral procession was continuing its journey over the Sarozek as before. Burannyi Yedigei, on his camel, was leading the way, his Karanar still making his bold, untiring pace, while behind was the tractor with its trailer in which the son-in-law, the husband of Aizada, was sitting patiently and alone with the dead Kazangap. Behind came the *Belarus'* excavator, and at the side, now ahead, now dropping behind, having stopped for some important reason, ran the businesslike and confident, big-chested, rusty-coloured dog, Zholbars.

The sun was burning hot as it reached its zenith. The greater part of the journey was behind them now and the great Sarozek opened out with every rise crossed, with further new desert lands stretching away to the horizon. The expanse of the desert was vast. Long ago in these places had lived the Zhuan'zhuan of evil memory, who had come and seized almost all the

Sarozek region and had held it for a long time. Other nomadic peoples lived here, waging continual wars for pastures and for wells. Now one tribe took the upper land, now another. But conquerors and conquered remained in their territories, some losing, some gaining their hold on the area where they lived. Yelizarov used to say that the living space of the Sarozek was the prize of this struggle.

In those times there were heavy rains in both spring and autumn, and the resultant grasslands supported many herds of large and small livestock. Then, too, traders passed through the region and conducted their business. But suddenly there seemed to have been a change in the climate; the rains ceased, the wells dried up and the supply of fodder withered away. The peoples and the tribes departed in various directions and the Zhuan'zhuan disappeared completely. They moved off towards the Edil', as the Volga was then called, and it was somewhere around there that they disappeared into oblivion. No one found out where they had come from and no one knew where they had disappeared to. It was said that a curse had fallen on them and that when they were crossing the frozen Edil', the ice on the river moved, broke, and all of them, together with their herds, and flocks, disappeared under the ice . . .

The native inhabitants of the Sarozek, the Kazakh nomads, at that time, did not leave their country but remained in those places where they had struck water in newly dug wells. But the busiest time in the Sarozek deserts came with the recent post-war years, when water carriers arrived. One water carrier – if the driver knew the country well – could supply three or four remote points. The lessors of the Sarozek pastures, the Collective and State Farms of the adjacent oblast's, were considering the setting up of permanent bases in the Sarozek for pasturing remote flocks, and were currently engaged in estimating and assessing the costs of such a project. Fortunately, however, they took their time and did not hurry. Almost unnoticed, near Ana-Beiit, a town with no name other than 'Letter Box' came into existence. People would say, 'I've been to Letter Box . . . I was at Letter Box . . . We bought this in Letter Box... I saw this in Letter Box . . .' Letter Box grew and spread, was built up – and then was closed to outsiders. A tarmac road connected it in one direction with the rocket launching site, or cosmodrome, and in the other direction with the railway station. Thus grew up a new, industrialized population in the Sarozek.

As a reminder of the past, there remained only the Ana-Beiit cemetery on two hills which touched like the twin humps of a camel – Egiz and Tyube. This was the most revered spot for burial in the whole area of the Sarozek. In olden times people sometimes brought their dead there from far away – so far away that they had to spend a night in the desert steppe on their way there. For that reason the descendants of those buried at Ana-Beiit were rightly proud that they had given such a special honour to the memory of their forebears. Here were buried the most respected and best known people of the tribes – those who lived many years, and knew much and who had earned honour by word and deed. Yelizarov, who knew all about this, called the place the Sarozek Pantheon.

So it was that that day the strange funeral procession of camel, tractors and dog approached the cemetery from the direction of Boranly-Burannyi junction.

The Ana-Beiit cemetery had its own history, dating back to the time when the Zhuan'zhuan were in the process of conquering the Sarozek and treated captive warriors with exceptional cruelty. Those who were sold into slavery in neighbouring lands were considered fortunate, because sooner or later they could escape and return to their homeland. But a monstrous fate awaited those whom the Zhuan'zhuan kept as slaves for themselves. They destroyed their slaves' memory by a terrible torture – the putting of the *shiri* on to the head of the victim. This fate was reserved for young men captured in battle. First of all their heads were completely shaved and every single hair was taken out by the root. When this was completed, expert Zhuan'zhuan butchers killed a nearby nursing mother camel and skinned it. First they removed the heavy udder with its matted hair. Then they divided it into several pieces and, in its still warm state, stretched it over the shaven heads of the prisoners. At once it stuck in place like a sticking plaster, looking rather like a present-day swimming cap. The man who was subjected to the ensuing torture either died because he could not stand it, or he lost his memory of the past for ever. He had become a *mankurt*, or slave, who could not remember his past life.

Each udder skin made five or six *shiri*. After the *shiri* had been put on, each condemned man was shackled and fitted with a wooden collar, so that he could not touch the ground with his head. In this state the men were taken far away from inhabited places so that their unavailing, soul-searing cries could not reach other people's ears. Then they were thrown down on to the open ground, with hands and feet bound, under the searing sun, without water or food. The torture lasted several days. Increased patrols were mounted to cut off access to the victims, in case any fellow tribesmen tried to help them while they were still alive. But such attempts at rescue were not often made, because any movement in the open steppe could be seen at once. If afterwards it was heard that someone had been made into a *mankurt* by the Zhuan'zhuan, then not even his nearest and dearest tried to save him or pay a ransom, because all they ever recovered was a living carcase of the former man.

There was only one Naiman mother, named in the legend as Naiman-Ana, who was not prepared to accept such a fate for her son. The Sarozek legend tells of this, and from the story comes the name of the Ana-Beiit cemetery – the Mother's Resting Place.

The men left out there on the ground for the appalling torture mostly perished under the Sarozek sun. Only one or two survived as *mankurts* out of five or six so treated. They had died, not from hunger, nor even from thirst, but from the pressure exerted on their heads by the drying-out of the raw camel skin. Mercilessly contracting under the burning rays of the sun, the *shiri* constricted and pressed on to the shaven head of the slave-to-be, just as if an iron ring was being tightened. By the second day the shaven hairs of the victims were beginning to grow. The hard, unyielding Asiatic hair grew into the raw camel skin and being unable in most cases to break through, bent back and once more penetrated the skin of the man's head, causing even greater agony. This final trial drove the victim to the brink of insanity and beyond.

Only on the fifth day did the Zhuan'zhuan come out to see who had survived out of their prisoners. If even one of those tortured was found to be alive, it was considered that a satisfactory result had been achieved. They gave him water, released him from his bonds and, in due time, restored to him his physical strength. The result was the *mankurt* slave, forcibly deprived of his memory and therefore very valuable, being worth ten healthy, untreated prisoners. There was even a law which ordained that if a *mankurt* slave was accidentally killed in a fight, the damages for loss were set at three times those of a free, untreated man.

The *mankurt* did not know who he had been, whence and from what tribe he had come, did not know his name, could not remember his childhood, father or mother – in short, he could not recognize himself as a human being. Deprived of any understanding of his own ego, the *mankurt* was, from his master's point of view, possessed of a whole range of advantages. He was the equivalent of a dumb animal and therefore absolutely obedient and safe. He never thought of trying to escape. For any slave owner, the most frightening thing was the possibility of a revolt of these slaves, since each slave was a potential rebel. The *mankurt* was the exception: he was absolutely impervious to any incitement to revolt, quite innocent. He knew of no such passions. As a result, there was no need to keep him confined, to guard him and even less to suspect him of having any sinister intentions. The *mankurt*, like a dog, only recognized his masters. He would have nothing to do with other people. All his thoughts were concerned with satisfying his belly's needs. He had no other worries. He performed the work given to him blindly, willingly and single-mindedly.

Mankurts were given the dirtiest and hardest work or the dullest, hardest tasks which demanded dumb patience. Only a *mankurt* could endure the endless silence and emptiness of the Sarozek, completely cut off with nothing to keep him company but a herd of camels. On his own he could replace a large number of workers. All that was required was to provide him with his food and then he could stay out there without relief, winter and summer. He was unworried by the isolation and had no complaint about what he might have lacked. His master's command and order was the highest thing of all for the *mankurt*. He wanted nothing for himself, save food and such clothing as would prevent him from freezing to death out in the steppe.

It would have been much easier simply to cut off the prisoner's head, or cause him some other harm to terrify him into subjection; instead, the Zhuan'zhuan chose to annihilate his memory, destroy his reason, to draw out by the roots that which otherwise stays with a man to his last breath, remaining uniquely his, and which dies with him and which cannot be reached by other people. This most cruel form of barbarism, resurrected from the dark past of the nomadic Zhuan'zhuan, encroached on the sacred being of a man. For they had discovered the means of removing from slaves their living memory, in this way causing to a human being the most dreadful of all imaginable or unimaginable evils. Lamenting over her son, turned into a *mankurt*, Naiman-Ana said in her frenzy of grief and despair:

'When they tore your memory from you, crushing your head like a nut in tongs, tightening the pressure on your skull with the slow twisting of the drying camel skin; when they fastened that unseen ring on your head so that your eyes stood out of their sockets, filled with the fluid of fear; when the raging thirst of the Sarozek tormented you, and there was not even one drop to fall from the sky to your lips – did not the sun, which gives everyone life, become for you a hateful, blinding body, the blackest of all the heavenly bodies in creation?

'When, tortured with pain, your screaming filled the desert, when you shouted and writhed, calling to God day and night; when you awaited help from heaven in vain; when choking in phlegm thrown out by your tortured flesh, you writhed in the vile excrement flowing from your body as it twisted in its convulsions; when you sank into that stinking mass, losing your reason, plagued and eaten by clouds of flies – did you not with your last breath curse God who has created us all in that world which he has deserted?

'When the dusk of darkness covered for ever your mind, racked by torture; when your memory, forcibly destroyed, lost for ever its links with the past; when in your wild struggles you forgot how your mother looked, the noise of the stream by the mountains where you played as a child; when you lost your own name and that of your father in your desolated consciousness; when the faces of people among whom you had grown up faded away, as did also the name of the girl who had smiled modestly at you – did you not then curse with the most terrible curses, as you fell into the bottomless pit of forgetfulness, your own mother, because she had dared to conceive you in her womb and given you birth into God's light just to live to this day . . . ?'

This story comes from those times when the Zhuan'zhuan had been driven out of the southern parts of nomadic Asia and were spreading out to the north. Having gained possession of the Sarozek and held it for a long time, they waged endless war with the purpose of increasing the area under their control and of getting more slaves. At first, taking advantage of surprise, they took many prisoners in the lands adjoining the Sarozek, including women and children. However, resistance to the alien invaders grew and fierce battles began to rage. The Zhuan'zhuan had no intention of giving up their Sarozek gains, but on the other hand they were intent on consolidating their hold on these wide open steppes. For their part, the local tribes were not prepared to put up with the loss of their lands and were determined, sooner or later, to exert their right and duty to drive out the invaders.

In small and large battles there were gains and losses on both sides, but even in these exhausting wars there were periods of calm. In one of these periods of peace some traders, who had come with a caravan of goods into the Naiman lands, told as they sat drinking tea, how they had passed through the Sarozek steppes without encountering any undue interference from the Zhuan'zhuan at the wells. They told, also, that out in the Sarozek, they had met a young herdsman tending a large herd of camels. The traders had engaged him in conversation, and discovered that he was a *mankurt*. He had a strong and healthy appearance and the traders were surprised to learn that he had suffered such a fate. No doubt once upon a time he had been as bright and talkative as anyone else; he was still young, his beard was only just sprouting and his general mien was good. But when you spoke to him it was just as if he had been born yesterday; the poor fellow could not remember his own name, or that of his father or mother. Nor did he know what the Zhuan'zhuan had done to him or from whence he had come. You would ask him a question and he had nothing to say but 'yes' and 'no' and all the while he clutched at his cap, which was firmly pressed down on his head. Although it was a sin, people sometimes laughed at such a misfortune; they laughed also at the fact that there were *mankurts* on whose head in places the camel skin had grown into the skin of the man. For such a *mankurt* the worst punishment of all was to frighten them by saying that you would steam their head. They would fight like a wild horse rather than let you touch their head. They did not remove their cap by day or night and even slept in it.

This *mankurt*, the traders continued, might have lost his reason, but he was nonetheless intent on his work the whole time. His watchful eyes followed them until the caravan had gone right away from the place where the herd of camels was grazing. One outrider decided to play a joke on the *mankurt* before he rode off.

'We've a long ride before us. To whom shall we give your greetings? To some girl perhaps? But where? Tell us! Perhaps we could give her a scarf from you.'

The *mankurt* was silent for a long time as he looked at the outrider, and then he said, 'Every night I look up at the moon and she looks at me. But we don't hear one another. There's someone up there . . .'

While the traders were telling their tale, a woman in the yurta served them with tea. It was Naiman-Ana. It is with this

129

name that she is preserved in the Sarozek legend. While the guests were there, Naiman-Ana did not react. Indeed, nobody noticed how greatly the tale had affected her, nor how her expression had changed. She had longed to ask the traders some questions about this young *mankurt*, but she was afraid to do so, to find out more than had already been said. She knew how to keep quiet and held in check her growing alarm, as she might a shrieking, wounded bird . . .

By now the conversation had passed on to some other subject; no one was any longer concerned about the fate of the *mankurt* – such unfortunate happenings were common in life. But Naiman-Ana was still trying to get over the fear which was filling her and control the shaking of her hands. It was as if she was indeed cradling that wounded bird against her body. But all that she did was to draw down lower over her face the black mourning scarf which she had long ago taken to wearing on her grey-haired head.

The traders and their caravan went on their way. During the sleepless night which followed, Naiman-Ana realized that she would find no peace until she had searched out in the Sarozek that *mankurt* herdsman and had confirmed for herself that he was not her son. The nagging, terrible thought revived again in her heart – that doubt which had long been kept hidden as a dim premonition; that her son had not died on the field of battle, as she had been told. And, of course, it would be better to bury him twice than to be tormented by continual fear, continual pain, continual doubt.

Her son had been killed in one of the battles against the Zhuan'zhuan, out in the Sarozek. Her husband had been killed a year earlier. He had been a famous man among the Naiman. His son had then gone out with the first expedition to avenge the loss of his father. The dead were not expected to be left on the battlefield; it was the duty of their fellow tribesmen to bring home the bodies. But it seemed that this had been impossible. Many veterans of that great battle had reported that when they had engaged with the enemy, her son had fallen over the mane of his horse, and the animal, excited and then terrified by the noise of battle, had bolted. He had then fallen from the saddle, but one foot was trapped in the stirrup and he had hung motionless on one side of the animal. This had frightened the animal yet further, and it had dragged the breathless body at full gallop over the steppe. To make matters worse, the horse had bolted towards enemy-held territory. In spite of the fierce and bloody battle, in which everyone was needed in the fight, two fellow tribesmen had raced off in pursuit in order to catch the runaway horse and recover the body. However, a party of shouting, mounted Zhuan'zhuan lying in ambush in a valley, had cut them off; one Naiman was killed by an arrow and the other was badly wounded and unable to rejoin his companions before he slumped to the ground. This incident helped the Naiman to locate the position of the Zhuan'zhuan ambush before they were able to launch an outflanking move at the most decisive moment. So the Naiman hurriedly retreated to regroup and to advance again into battle. Of course, by now no one was able to concern themselves with the fate of their young comrade, the son of Naiman-Ana . . .

The wounded Naiman, who at last succeeded in riding back, told later that he had tried to pursue the son's horse, but that eventually the animal had disappeared.

Several days running the Naiman warriors went out to search for the body, but they could find no trace of him, his horse, weapons or any other clues. Even if he had only been wounded, at this time of year he would have died out in the steppe from thirst or lack of blood. They mourned him; they grieved that their young comrade lay unburied out there in the uninhabited Sarozek steppe. It was a shameful thing for everyone. The women wailed in Naiman-Ana's yurta and reproached their husbands and brothers thus:

'The vultures have picked the flesh from his bones and the jackals have scattered his bones. How dare you walk around in your men's hats after this!'

And so the empty days on the empty earth dragged by for Naiman-Ana. She was accustomed to the idea that people were killed in war, but the thought that her son was lying abandoned on the battlefield, that his body had not been committed to the earth, gave her no peace. The mother was tormented by unceasing, bitter thoughts. She had no one with whom to share them and so make her grief easier to bear, and there was no one to turn to, except to God himself.

In order to stop thinking about all this, she had to be convinced with her own eyes that her son was dead. Who then would dispute the will of Fate? Most of all, she was puzzled that her son's horse had disappeared leaving no trace. The horse itself had not been hurt, it had merely bolted in fright. Like any other horse from the herd, it would be bound, sooner or later, to return to its familiar haunts, dragging behind it the body of its rider, his foot tangled in the stirrup. No doubt it would be a terrible sight, but at least she could weep and wail over her son's body, tearing her face with her nails and lamenting until God in his heaven finally wearied of her cries. At least then she would no longer be bottling up these doubts in the depths of her soul and would be prepared for death with cold reasoning, awaiting it at any time, not holding on, continuing to live in hope. But her son's body had not been found, and his horse had not returned.

Doubts still tortured the mother, although the other people of the tribe began gradually to forget about the war. All losses, after a while, become less sharp and are gradually forgotten. Yet she, the man's mother, could not become resigned and forget. Her thoughts went round and round in the same circle: what had happened to his horse? Where was the harness, his weapons? You would only have to look at them, just glance, and it would be possible to determine what had happened to her son. Of course, it could have been that the Zhuan'zhuan had caught up with the horse somewhere out in the Sarozek, when it was exhausted and could be caught. A horse, with good harness, was worthwhile booty. But what would they have done with her son, dragged along by the stirrup? Buried him or thrown him out to be torn apart by the wild animals? And what if he were still alive, still living by some miracle? Would they have finished him off with a *coup de grâce* or thrown him out to expire on the ground? Supposing . . .

There was no end to her doubts. And when the traders had

spoken about the young *mankurt* who had met them out in the Sarozek, they had had no idea that their words had kindled a flame in the aching soul of Naiman-Ana. Now her heart beat with an alarming premonition. The thought that this might be her lost son more and more certainly and strongly possessed her heart and mind. She knew now that she would not rest until she had found and seen this *mankurt* and had been convinced that he was not her lost son.

Among the hills on the edge of the steppe where the Naiman lived in summer, there flowed small streams with stony bottoms. All night long Naiman-Ana lay there, listening to the gurgle of the flowing water, before she set out into the silence of the Sarozek. She knew how dangerous it was to go out alone into the desert, but she did not wish to confide her plans to anyone. No one would understand. Not even her nearest and dearest would approve of her plan. How could she go out in search of her long-dead son? And if by some chance he was still alive and had been made into a *mankurt*, it was even more unthinkable to search him out, to break her heart in vain; for a *mankurt* was merely the outer covering, the skin of the former man . . .

That night, before she left, she stepped outside her yurta several times and looked around, listening, trying to concentrate and collect her thoughts. The midnight moon was high above her head in a cloudless sky, filling the earth around with an even, milky-pale light. The many white yurtas scattered around at the foot of the hills resembled a flock of large birds, roosting here by the banks of the noisy streams. Beside the aul, where the sheep were kept and further on from the ravines where the herds of horses were grazing, the barking of the dogs and the indistinct voices of people could be heard. But above all, came the sound of girls' voices, cheerfully singing by the sheepfold on the nearest side of the village. The sound touched Naiman-Ana. She had once sung those night songs herself. They had stopped here every summer for as long as she could remember, ever since she had first come here as a bride. All her life had been spent in these places. While the family had been growing up, there had been their four yurtas here – one for cooking in, one for receiving guests and two to live in. Now, after the attack by the Zhuan'zhuan, there was only hers left.

And now she was leaving her single yurta. The evening before, she had prepared for her journey. She had collected together food and taken extra water, filling two skins, in case she could not find wells straight away out in the Sarozek. Tethered close to the yurta was her camel, Akmaya, her hope and her companion. She would never have been bold enough to venture out alone into the silent Sarozek if she had not possessed Akmaya, with her strength and speed! That year Akmaya was barren and she was resting after two calvings. She was in excellent condition for riding: lean, with strong legs, and strong soles to her feet, she had not yet been spoilt by heavy loads and age and she had a strong pair of humps and a fine head that sat beautifully on her strong, muscular neck. She had ever-moving, light nostrils that fluttered like the wings of a butterfly, catching the air as she went along. The white she-camel Akmaya was worth more than a whole herd of ordinary beasts. For such a fast-moving beast in her prime, people would have given several tens of head of fattening young animals in order that she might breed. She was the last treasure Naiman-Ana possessed – the last memory of her former wealth. The rest had vanished, like dust washed from the hands. All she had left were her duties – the forty-day and annual memorial prayers for the departed, for her son, whom she was now setting out to find. Naiman-Ana still felt enormous weariness and grief, for not long ago the final memorial service had been held in the presence of many people, all the Naiman from far around.

At dawn she came out of her yurta, prepared to leave without delay. She stopped as she crossed the threshold and leant against the door post, thinking, casting a glance around the sleeping aul, before she left it. Still possessed of a handsome figure and all her former beauty, Naiman-Ana had tied on her belt, as was the custom before going on a long journey. She had on her boots, wide trousers, a little sleeveless coat or kamzol over her dress, and a shawl hanging free from her

134

legend time

shoulders. She had tied a white scarf around her head, tucking in the ends at the back of her neck. She had decided on this during the night – after all, if she was hoping to see her son alive, why go off in mourning? And if her hope was not fulfilled, then there was time enough to cover her head with a black scarf.

At that time of day, the dawn light concealed the greyness of her hair and the marks of deep grief on her face – the lines deeply furrowed her sad, mother's countenance. Her eyes were wet at that moment and she sighed deeply. Had she ever thought or guessed that she might have to live through such a trial? But now she summoned up all her strength of character. *'Ashvadan lya illa khil' alla,'* she said, whispering the first line of the prayer. 'There is no god, but Allah.' And with this in her mind she went purposefully out to the camel and bade her go down on to her knees.

Complaining quietly, Akmaya unhurriedly lowered her chest to the ground. Quickly throwing the various bags across the saddle, Naiman-Ana climbed up to the riding position, urging the camel with her heels. Up got Akmaya, straightening out her legs and lifting her mistress high above the ground. Now Akmaya realized there was a journey ahead of her.

No one in the aul knew about Naiman-Ana's departure and except for her drowsy sister-in-law servant, who every now and again yawned widely, no one saw her off. The servant had been told the evening before that Naiman-Ana was going to visit relations and that afterwards, if there were pilgrims about, she would be joining up with them to go to the Kipchak lands to pray at the shrine of the saint, Yassavi. She was leaving as early as possible to avoid questions.

When she had gone some way off from the aul, Naiman-Ana turned in the direction of the Sarozek, which in its emptiness gave no hint of what lay ahead . . .

The trains in these parts went from East to West, and from West to East.

On either side of the railway line in these parts there lay the great

135

wide spaces of the desert – Sary-Ozeki, the Middle lands of the
yellow steppes.

In these parts any distance was measured in relation to the
railway, as if from the Greenwich meridian.

And the trains went from East to West, and from West to
East . . .

On board the aircraft carrier *Convention* another coded radio
message was sent to the cosmonaut-controllers on the *Parity*
orbital station. In this signal, orders were given in the same
admonitory tone that they should not get into radio contact
with the parity-cosmonauts 1–2 and 2–1, who were outside the
solar system, nor should they discuss with them arrangements
for their return to the orbital station. They were to await the
orders of *Obtsenupr*.

Out on the ocean a full gale was blowing and the aircraft
carrier was pitching and rolling as the Pacific waters broke
around the stern of the vast vessel. All the same, the sun was
shining over the wide spaces of the sea, which was continually
boiling with white foam capping the waves. The wind was
blowing steadily, like a man's even breathing. All the services
aboard *Convention*, including the aircraft and security personnel were on watch, at full readiness.

It was now some time since that the white camel, Akmaya, had
begun trotting over the level Sarozek and along the ravines.
She was now complaining monotonously as she went, her feet
scraping almost noiselessly, while her mistress drove her on,
urging her on across the hot desert. They only stopped when
night fell and they reached some remote well. Next morning
they were off once more in search of the large herd of camels
to be found somewhere in the Sarozek. Here in this region,
not far from the precipitous, reddy-sandy Malakumdychap
area, which stretched for many kilometres, the traders had
met up with the *mankurt* herdsman for whom Naiman-Ana
was now searching. Already she had been searching around
and near Malakumdychap for some two days. She was terrified
of meeting up with the Zhuan'zhuan, but wherever she looked,

wherever she wandered, she saw only the empty steppe, and deceptive mirages. Once she was taken in by such a mirage and made a great detour towards a town swimming in the air, with minarets and fortress walls. Perhaps she would find her son there in the slave market . . . Then she could set him on Akmaya, to sit there behind her, and *then* let them try to catch her . . . It was distressing out there in the desert; perhaps that was why the sight appeared to be so real . . .

Of course it was difficult to find just one person in the Sarozek. Out here a man was like a grain of sand. But if he was with a big flock or herd grazing over a wide area, then sooner or later you would see an animal from far off, then you would find others; and with the herd, there would be the herdsman. That was what Naiman-Ana hoped, at any rate.

But so far she had found nothing anywhere. She was already starting to fear that the herd had been driven elsewhere, or that the Zhuan'zhuan had sent all the camels to be sold in Khiva or Bukhara. Would the herdsman then return from such faraway places? When she had set off from the aul, worn out with worry and doubt, she had had but one dream – just to see her son alive, even if he were a *mankurt*. Perhaps he would remember nothing, understand nothing, but let it be her son, living, just alive . . .

It was a lot to ask. But as she went deep into the Sarozek and approached the place where she hoped to find the herdsman whom the traders with their caravan had met as they passed through not long ago, she became more and more disturbed at the thought of finding that her son's mind had been crippled. This fear now bore down on her oppressively and she began to pray to God that it would not be him, her son, but some other unfortunate. She was even ready to accept unconditionally that her son was no more and could no longer be alive. But on she went in order just to look at this *mankurt* and be convinced that her doubts were in vain; perhaps having been convinced, she could return home and stop being tormented and would live out her years as Fate decreed.

But then once more she began to be oppressed by a longing

to find in the Sarozek, not just anyone, but her son. Whatever the cost.

She was just crossing a sloping ridge, wrestling with these contrary feelings, when she suddenly caught sight of a large herd of camels, grazing freely all over a wide valley. The brown fattening camels wandered between the small bushes and thorn plants, chewing at their tops. Naiman-Ana spurred on her Akmaya to full speed. At first she was breathless with joy because she had at last found the herd; then she became frightened, and a shiver passed through her, because the thought that she would now be seeing her son who had been turned into a *mankurt* was so very terrifying. Then she became glad again and gave up trying to understand what was going on inside her mind.

There was the grazing herd, but where was the herdsman? He must be somewhere nearby. Then she saw a man on the other side of the valley. From a distance she could not make out who he was. The herdsman stood there with a long staff in one hand, while in the other hand he held the halter of his riding camel, which stood just behind him with its loaded panniers. He was watching her approach, calmly, from under the peak of his cap, which was pulled down hard over his eyes. When she came closer and recognized her son, Naiman-Ana could not remember afterwards how she had managed to get down from her camel. She must have just fallen off, but it did not worry her at all.

'My son, my own one! And I've been searching for you all around!' She dashed up to him. 'I'm your mother!'

At once she understood everything and wept, stamping at the ground, bitterly, terribly, her lips moving feverishly as she tried to stop, but she could not control herself. In order to stand still, she seized the shoulder of her indifferent son and wept and wept, overcome with the grief which had been so long pent up and now was pouring out. As she wept, she gazed through her tears, through the strands of wet, grey hair, through her shaking fingers with which she was spreading the dust of the journey all over her face; gazed at the familiar features of her son, all the while trying to catch his glance,

138

hoping against all hope that he would recognize her. Surely it was so simple to do – to recognize his own mother?

But her appearance had not the slightest effect on him; it was just as if she came here often, visiting him out here in the steppe every day. He did not even ask who she was, or why she was crying. Then suddenly the herdsman took her hand from his shoulder and walked away, pulling the inseparable riding camel with its load behind him, and made his way towards the other side of the herd in order to make sure the young animals had not run too far away in their play. Naiman-Ana remained where she was and squatted down, sobbing, pressing her face with her hands and not raising her head. Then she gathered her strength and walked over to her son, trying to keep calm.

Her *mankurt*-son seemed devoid of thoughts or emotion and looked at her from under the peak of his cap. Then a weak sort of smile passed quickly over his thin, roughened face, blackened by the wind. But his eyes, reflecting a complete absence of interest in anything, remained, as before, quite aloof.

'Sit down, let's talk,' said Naiman-Ana with a deep sigh.

They sat down on the ground.

'Do you recognize me?' asked the mother.

The *mankurt* shook his head.

'What do they call you?'

'*Mankurt*,' he answered.

'That's what you're called now. But do you remember your old name? Try to remember your real name.'

The *mankurt* was silent. His mother could see that he was making a great effort to remember, for beads of sweat were coming out on the bridge of his nose and his eyes were filled with a misty look. But between them there had arisen an invisible barrier which he could not cross.

'What was your father's name? And who are you? Where did you come from? Where were you born – do you know?'

No, there was nothing that he could remember; he knew nothing.

'What have they done to you?' His mother whispered, and once again her lips began to tremble against her will, but also

139

partly from anger, hate and grief. Again she began to sob, at the same time trying to calm herself. The sorrow of his mother in no way touched the *mankurt*.

'They can take your land, your wealth, even your life,' she said aloud, 'but who ever thought, who ever *dared* to attack a man's memory? Oh God, if You do exist, how did You give such power to people? Isn't there evil enough on earth without this?'

And then, as she looked upon her *mankurt*-son, she uttered her famous words of sorrow about the sun, about God, about herself; those words which people recite to this day when Sarozek history is being recalled.

Then she began her lament:

'*Men botasy olgen boz maya, tulybyn kelep iskegen . . .*'

'I am a she-camel who has lost her young one, come to sniff the smell of a young camel's skin stuffed with straw . . .'

Then there burst from her soul an endless succession of heartbroken cries that echoed long and loud among the silent, endless Sarozek.

But nothing of this meant a thing to her son, the *mankurt*.

Then Naiman-Ana decided to abandon questions, but to use suggestions to try and remind her son know who he had been and was.

'Your name is Zholaman. Can you hear? You are Zholaman. And your father's name was Donenbai. Surely you remember your father? In your childhood, he taught you to shoot with the bow. I'm your mother and you are my son. You are from the Naiman tribe, do you understand? You are a Naiman . . .'

As she said this, he listened with a complete lack of interest, just as if she were saying nothing at all – as if he were listening to the chirping of a cricket in the grass.

And then Naiman-Ana asked her son, the *mankurt*, 'What happened before you came here?'

'Nothing,' he said.

'Was it night or day?'

'Nothing,' he said.

'With whom do you like to talk?'

'With the moon. But we don't hear each other. Someone is sitting up there.'

'What more do you want from life?'

'A pigtail on my head, like the one my master has.'

'Let me see what they've done to your head.' Naiman-Ana stretched out her hand towards him.

The *mankurt* quickly jumped back, took hold of his hat and looked away from his mother, who immediately realized her mistake.

It was at that moment that a man appeared in the distance, riding towards them on a camel.

'Who's that?' asked Naiman-Ana.

'He brings me my food,' answered her son.

Naiman-Ana was worried. She had to hide quickly before the Zhuan'zhuan man saw her. She brought her camel down and got into the saddle.

'Say nothing. I'll be back soon,' she promised.

Her son did not answer; he remained as indifferent as ever.

Naiman-Ana soon realized that she had made a mistake in riding away through the grazing herd. But it was already too late. The Zhuan'zhuan approaching the herd would be sure to see her riding away on the white she-camel. She should have walked away on foot, hiding among the grazing animals.

After going some way from the grazing herd, Naiman-Ana entered a deep ravine overgrown with wormwood. Here she dismounted, leaving Akmaya on the floor of the ravine, while she climbed up and observed what was happening. Yes – the man had noticed her. He soon appeared, his camel coming at a trot. The Zhuan'zhuan was armed with a lance and a bow and arrows and was clearly concerned, looking around and obviously wondering where the rider on the white camel – and he had seen her clearly – could have disappeared to. He could not make up his mind which was the best direction to follow. First he rode one way, then another. The final time he came very close to the ravine. It was just as well that Naiman-Ana had tied up Akmaya's muzzle with a scarf. If her camel had uttered a sound, it would have been the end.

Hidden behind the wormwood on the precipice edge,

Naiman-Ana could see the Zhuan'zhuan quite clearly. He was mounted on a shaggy camel and was looking from side to side as he went along. His face was puffy and intent, and on his head was a boat-shaped hat with the ends turned up; behind, shining black and dry, was a double-plaited pigtail. The Zhuan'zhuan was standing up in his stirrups, his lance at the ready, turning his head as he searched, eyes shining. Here was one of the enemy who had seized the Sarozek and driven no small a number of people into slavery and caused untold misery to her family. But what could she, an unarmed woman, do against a fierce Zhuan'zhuan warrior? She began to wonder what could have brought these people to such a state of cruelty and savagery as to destroy a slave's memory.

Having trotted to and fro, the Zhuan'zhuan soon went back to the herd. It was now evening and the sun had set, but its glow still hung over the steppe for a long while; then, suddenly, darkness fell and the silence of night descended. Naiman-Ana spent that night entirely alone out in the steppe, not far away from her wretched *mankurt*-son. Yet she was afraid to go back to him, for that Zhuan'zhuan man might have stayed to spend the night with the herd.

She had made a decision not to leave her son in slavery, but to try and take him away from there with her. Even if he was now a *mankurt*, even if he could understand nothing at all, he would be better off at home, among his own people, rather than serving the Zhuan'zhuan as a herdsman out in the empty Sarozek. This is what her soul, a mother's soul, prompted her to do. She could not leave one of her own blood in slavery. In familiar surroundings his mind might return to him and he would remember his childhood.

Next morning, Naiman-Ana again mounted Akmaya. After long diversions and circlings, she finally reached the herd, which during the night had moved some way off. Having found it, she looked around for some time to make certain there was no Zhuan'zhuan around. When she was sure that there was no one, she called to her son by his name.

'Zholaman! Zholaman! Good morning!'

Her son looked around and the mother cried out in joy, but

at once realized that he was merely reacting to the sound of a voice.

Again, Naiman-Ana tried to rekindle her son's lost memory.

'Remember your name – please remember your name!' she begged. 'Your father's name was Donenbai, don't you know that? Your name is not *Mankurt*, but Zholaman – it means "God's help on a journey". We called you that because you were born on a journey during a migration of the Naiman tribe. When you were born, everyone stopped for three days of rejoicing and celebration.'

All this made no impression on her *mankurt*-son, but his mother continued, hoping vainly that suddenly there would be some flash of recognition in his subconscious mind. But she was beating against a firmly closed door.

Again and again she repeated, 'Do you know your name? Your father was Donenbai.' Then she fed him and gave him water from her own supplies and began to sing him cradle songs. He liked those songs. He enjoyed hearing them and something living, a fleeting expression of warmth appeared on his tanned face. Then his mother began to attempt to persuade him to leave this place, to leave the Zhuan'zhuan and to go away with her back to his own home. The *mankurt* could not understand how it was possible just to get up and go. What would happen to the herd? No – his master had told him to stay with the herd always – that was what he had said. He could not go away and leave the herd . . .

Again and again Naiman-Ana tried to break down the door to her son's ruined memory.

'Remember whose son you are? What's your name? Your father was Donenbai!'

Naiman-Ana did not notice how much time had passed in these vain attempts; she only remembered when she suddenly noticed the Zhuan'zhuan appear again on the edge of the herd, mounted on his camel. This time he was much closer and travelling fast, clearly intent on catching her. Naiman-Ana wasted no time and got up on Akmaya. But then from the other direction appeared a second Zhuan'zhuan, also on a camel.

143

Naiman-Ana, spurring on Akmaya, passed between them, the fleet-footed white Akmaya carrying her forward and ahead with the Zhuan'zhuan in hot pursuit, shouting and waving their lances. They stood no chance of catching up with Akmaya and dropped further and further behind on their shaggy camels, while Akmaya, getting her second wind, sped over the Sarozek, carrying Naiman-Ana away from her pursuers at a remarkable speed.

Naiman-Ana was not to know, however, that when the angered Zhuan'zhuan returned, they beat the *mankurt* cruelly. But all that the *mankurt* said was:

'She said that she's my mother.'

'She's not your mother! You've no mother! You know why she came? Do you know? She wants to tear off your cap and steam your head!'

So they frightened the unhappy *mankurt*.

On hearing their words, the *mankurt* paled and his black face became ashen grey. He hunched his neck down between his shoulders and, taking a firm hold of his cap, began to gaze around like a frightened animal.

'Don't be scared! Come on, take this!' The elder Zhuan'zhuan put a bow and arrows into his hand.

'Now take aim.' And the younger Zhuan'zhuan threw his hat high into the air.

The arrow pierced the hat.

'Look at that!' The owner of the hat was amazed. 'Your hand hasn't lost its memory!'

Like a bird disturbed from her nest, Naiman-Ana circled around that area of the Sarozek, not knowing what to do, or what to expect. Would the Zhuan'zhuan now drive off the whole herd and her son with it? Would they send the *mankurt*, her son, to some place she could not reach, nearer to their own herd? Or would they try to track and capture her? Lost in guesses, she moved about, hiding from view, until finally she was delighted to see that the Zhuan'zhuan had left the herd. Indeed, one rode close by, but not searching. For a long time Naiman-Ana kept them under observation and when they at last disappeared into the distance, she decided to return to her son. Now, whatever happened, she was determined to take him away with her. Whatever he had now become and was to be, it was not his fault that Fate had turned against him, that his enemies mocked and despised him; his mother would not leave him in slavery. Let the Naiman people see how the invaders crippled captured *dzhigits*, how they humiliated them and deprived them of their reason; let the sight enrage them and make them take up arms. It was not just a matter of land – there was enough land for everyone; the Zhuan'zhuan evil was unbearable, even for neighbours who had had no contact with them.

Thinking these thoughts Naiman-Ana returned to her son, all the way thinking how she might persuade him to run away with her that very night.

It was already getting dark over the great Sarozek, and another night in the procession of countless past and future nights was coming down, stealing in invisibly over ravines and hills and bringing the reddish tones of dusk.

The white she-camel Akmaya carried her mistress lightly and easily towards the great herd. The rays of the dying sun picked out her figure, clearly, seated between the humps. Ever watchful and worried beyond all measure, Naiman-Ana looked pale and stern. Her grey hairs, the lines on her face, her passive expression matched the look in her eyes, which were like Sarozek twilights, witnesses to her unending pain.

Now that she had reached the herd, she rode between the grazing animals and began to look around, but there was no sign of her son. His camel, with its load, was for some reason grazing free, dragging its halter over the ground behind it. But he was not there.

What had happened to him?

'Zholaman! My son Zholaman, where are you?' Naiman-Ana began to call. No one appeared. No one answered her call.

As she looked around anxiously, she did not notice that her son, the *mankurt*, was hiding in the shadow cast by the camel, was already on his knee, taking aim with an arrow stretched on the bowstring. The light of the setting sun was hindering his aim and he was waiting for a suitable moment to shoot.

'Zholaman! My son!' Naiman-Ana called, fearing that something had happened to him. Then she turned round in her saddle and saw him. 'Don't shoot!' She had only to spur on her camel and turn her face away; but before she could do so, the arrow whistled and struck her on the left side, under her arm.

That was the fatal shot. Naiman-Ana fell forward and continued to fall, clutching at the camel's neck. But just before her white headscarf fell from her head, it turned into a white bird, which flew away, crying, 'Do you remember whose child you are? What's your name? Your father was Donenbai! Donenbai! Donenbai!'

Ever since that time, so they say, there flew over the Sarozek at night a bird called Donenbai. Whenever it meets a traveller, the Donenbai bird flies close to him, calling, 'Do you remember whose child you are? Who are you? What is your name? Your father was Donenbai, Donenbai, Donenbai, Donenbai, Donenbai . . .'

The place where Naiman-Ana was buried became known in the Sarozek as the cemetery of Ana-Beiit, or the Mother's Resting Place.

There were many descendants of the white she-camel, Akmaya. She-camels from her direct line were white-headed young ones, well known all around, but the young males, by contrast, were black and powerful, like the Burannyi Karanar of today.

The dead Kazangap, whom they were now taking to his burial at Ana-Beiit, always said that Burannyi Karanar was not just any camel, but came from that line of Akmaya, the famous, white she-camel herself, who remained out in the Sarozek after Naiman-Ana's death.

Yedigei was quite prepared to believe Kazangap. Why not? Burannyi Karanar was worthy of it. How many trials they had gone through in good times and in bad, yet always Karanar had brought them through. Recently, however, he had become very troublesome when the urge came upon him – this always happened at the coldest times of the year, and he raged terribly – as terribly as the winter itself. This had now happened two winters in succession, and during such days there was no joy in life. Once he let Yedigei down, let him down thoroughly, and if Yedigei had not been, shall we say, human, but a logical being, he would never have forgiven Burannyi Karanar. But what can you expect from a camel during the rut? How could Burannyi Karanar be blamed? Kazangap knew this story well, and he pronounced his judgement on it. Who could have known how things would turn out?

Chapter Seven

Burannyi Yedigei remembered the end of that summer and the start of the autumn of 1952 with a special feeling of happiness past. It was almost magical how his prophecy about the weather came true. After that dreadful heat, in which even the Sarozek lizards ran on to the very thresholds of the houses to escape the sun, the weather in the middle of August suddenly changed very markedly. The unbearable heat went away suddenly and gradually the cooler weather came along; at any rate, one could sleep peacefully at night. Such a boon did not come every year in the Sarozek, but it usually did. The winters were constant; they were always severe. But in the summers, there sometimes was a blessed break. This happened, said Yelizarov, when strong shifts occur in the upper layers of the airflow, and the direction changes. Yelizarov loved to talk about such things. He said that up there in the sky flowed great invisible rivers with banks and floods. These rivers, being in continuous movement, washed around the earth's sphere; thus wrapped around with winds, the earth continued on its orbit – and time passed. It was fascinating to listen to Yelizarov. It was hard to find such people; he was a man of rare character. Burannyi Yedigei respected him and he respected Yedigei. So there it was; that heavenly river which was bringing cooling air down to the Sarozek had somehow come down from its place on high and, as it came down, had met the Himalayas. These Himalayas were God only knew how far away, but in the scale of global distance they were quite close. The river of air struck the Himalayas and reflected back from them, not going on into India or Pakistan; there the heat remained as it was and the air flowed back over the

148

Sarozek, because the Sarozek, like the sea, is an open space without any obstacles. So this river brought in the cool air from the Himalayas . . .

Whatever the cause, the end of that summer and the beginning of autumn of that year was a wonderful time. Rain in the Sarozek was very uncommon, and was long remembered when it did fall. But that particular rain Burannyi Yedigei was to remember for the rest of his life. At first the clouds piled up – it was unusual to see the normally empty depths of the hot, stifling Sarozek sky covered over. Then it began to get hot and sticky, with an unbearable heaviness in the air. That day Yedigei was working, coupling up trucks. On the junction siding there were three flat cars after the gravel, and a load of pine sleepers on them had been unloaded the day before. As always they had been told to do that as a rush job, but then it turned out that the haste had been quite unnecessary. Twelve hours after being unloaded the flats were still there in the siding. Everyone had been put on the 'urgent' work: Kazangap, Abutalip, Zaripa, Ukubala, and Bukei. In those days everything had to be done manually. Oh, what heat! Why on earth did those flat cars have to come along during such a boiling heat? But if it had to be done, then it had to be done. They had set to work. Ukubala had soon felt faint and began to be sick. She could not stand the hot, resinous smell of the sleepers; they had to send her home. Then all the women had gone home to join their children who were worn out too from the oppressive heat. The men had remained, strained away and finished the job.

Next day, when it was raining, the empty flat cars had to be coupled up and taken back to Kumbel'. While they were shunting and coupling up the waggons, Yedigei became worn out with the heat and the damp; he felt just as if he were in a soldiers' bath house. What a driver they had to work with, too – he dragged every bit of the work out, just a teaspoonful at a time. As far as he was concerned, they could go to hell under the flat cars. Yedigei swore his best at the man, as he deserved, and the driver gave as good as he got. He too was having a rough time, beside the engine firebox. People went mad in that sort of heat. At last, thank God, the goods train went away, taking the flats with it.

Now the rain poured down in buckets – a downpour, to pay them back for all the days of drought. The ground shook, and at once was covered with puddles. The rain went on and on, raging down madly, having collected huge reserves of cool moisture, if Yelizarov was to be believed, up on the snowy ranges of the Himalayas.

What power there was up in those mountains!

Yedigei ran home. Why he ran, he did not know; he just did. A man caught in the rain always runs home, or to the nearest shelter. It was a habit. But *why* shelter from such rain? He stopped as soon as he saw how the whole Kuttybaev family – Abutalip, Zaripa and their two sons, Daul and Ermek – had joined hands and were dancing and jumping out in the rain near their hut. This amazed Yedigei. Not because they were playing and were delighted with the rain, but because, before it had begun, Abutalip and Zaripa had hurried away from work, marching directly over the tracks. Now he understood. They had wanted to be with their children when the rain came. Yedigei had never thought of such a thing before. And there they were, bathing in it, dancing and shouting like migrating geese on the Aral' Sea! It was a real celebration for them, this shower bath from heaven. They had been worn out by the Sarozek heat, waiting, longing for this rain to come. And Yedigei felt delighted, sad and amazed all at the same time – and also sorry that it should take a shower of rain to brighten up their life at Boranly-Burannyi junction.

'Yedigei! Come and join us!' Abutalip shouted through the pouring rain, waving his hand as if he were swimming.

'Uncle Yedigei!' The boys in their turn rushed towards him.

The youngest, Ermek, who was only just over two, was Yedigei's favourite and he ran up to him, his arms wide to embrace Yedigei, his mouth wide open, swallowing down the rain. His eyes were filled with indescribable delight, heroism and excitement. Yedigei picked him up and whirled him around in his arms. He did not know what to do next. He had not intended to join in this family game. But then, from around the corner, with loud squeals of excitement, appeared his daughters, Saule and Sharapat. They had run out, hearing the noise made by the Kuttybaevs. They were also happy. 'Papa, let's run!' they demanded. And this call removed Yedigei's doubts. Now they were all together, united, and they went wild under the unending downpour.

Yedigei held on tight to little Ermek, fearing he would fall over into a puddle. Abutalip sat the smaller girl, Sharapat, on his shoulder. And then away they ran, giving the children a treat. Ermek wriggled in Yedigei's arms, shouting, and when he choked a bit, quickly and firmly pressed his little wet face against Yedigei's neck. It was touching, and Yedigei several times caught the happy, grateful looks of Abutalip and Zaripa, pleased that their little boy was enjoying himself so much with his Uncle Yedigei. But Yedigei and his girls were also very happy in this rainy commotion started by the Kuttybaev family. And, unwittingly, Yedigei noticed how beautiful Zaripa was. The rain had plastered her black hair down over her face, neck and shoulders, while the water flowed over her strong young body, showing up her neck, arms, thighs and the calves of her bare legs. Her eyes were shining with joy and excitement and her white teeth were flashing happily.

For the Sarozek rain is not like fodder stored for a horse. The melting snows are gradually absorbed into the soil. But rain in the Sarozek is like mercury on one's hand – it runs over the surface of the ground into the ravines and gorges, gurgles noisily – and vanishes.

Even after a few minutes of this downpour, streams and currents formed, strong, fast-flowing and foaming, and the people of Boranly began to run out and jump around, launching basins and troughs on to the water. The older children, Daul and Saule, even sailed down a stream sitting in basins. They had to put the smaller ones together in a trough, and they, too, floated away.

Still the rain went on. Excited by their voyages in the basins, the children got as far as the rails below the embankment, at the beginning of the junction. At that moment a passenger train was passing through Boranly-Burannyi junction, and the passengers leaned out of the wide open windows and doors of the train to look at the children of these strange unhappy desert people. They shouted at them, 'Don't drown!', laughing helplessly, whistling and then laughing some more. No doubt, the children down below the train did look funny. Then off went the train, well washed by the rain, taking the passengers away. Perhaps in a day or two they would tell what they had seen to amuse their listeners.

Yedigei would have thought nothing about all this, if he had not had the impression that Zaripa was crying. When rainwater is streaming down a person's face, it is hard to tell if they are crying or not. But Zaripa *was* crying. Although she was pretending that she was laughing, that she was wildly happy, she was indeed crying, holding back the sobs, shedding tears mingled with laughter and exclamations. Abutalip took her hand.

'What's wrong? Don't you feel well? Shall we go home?'

'No, I've just got the hiccups,' said Zaripa, and they began again to amuse their children, trying to enjoy to the utmost this gift of the sudden rain.

Yedigei felt uneasy. He thought how hard it must be for them to know that there was another sort of life which had been torn away from them – a life where rain was not a special event, an occasion, where people bathe and swim in clean, clear water, where there are other conditions, other things to amuse the children . . .

But in order not to embarrass Abutalip and Zaripa, who, of course, had only started these games for their children's sake, Yedigei went on joining in the fun.

They went on until they played themselves to a standstill, yet still the rain came down. They ran home. And as he watched them with sympathy, Yedigei noticed how the Kuttybaevs, father, mother and children, ran together. All were wet through, yet it was a day of happiness in the Sarozek.

Carrying his youngest and holding his eldest daughter's hand, Yedigei arrived on his own doorstep. Ukubala seeing them, threw up her hands in alarm.

152

'Oh, what have you been doing? You look like nothing on earth!'

'Don't be frightened, Mother,' Yedigei calmed his wife and laughed. 'When the old camel gets drunk, he plays with his young ones!'

'Oh, I see – you're just the same as an old camel.' Ukubala laughed, but there was a mild reproach in her voice. 'Now get your soaked clothes off and stop standing there like wet hens.'

The rain soon stopped, but it was still pouring down elsewhere in the depths of the Sarozek until dawn, judging by the heavy growling of distant thunder which they heard during the night. Yedigei woke up several times because of this. This surprised him. By the Aral' Sea a storm might rage overhead and he would sleep right through it. Of course, it was different there – storms were a frequent occurrence. Half-awake, Yedigei tried to guess through his half-open eyelids how far away it was, as the distant watery sheet lightning, breaking out over various places in the steppe, was reflected in the glass of the window.

That night Burannyi Yedigei dreamed once again that he was at the front, lying pinned down under an artillery barrage. But the shells fell without noise. The explosions were noiseless black clouds falling slowly and heavily through the air. One such explosion threw him up into the air, and he fell for a long time, falling with a slowing heartbeat into a dreadful emptiness . . . Then he was running into the attack. There were many soldiers in grey uniforms also attacking, but he could not make out their faces; it was as if the uniforms were running on their own, their weapons firing automatically. Suddenly the uniforms ahead of Yedigei shouted 'Hurrah!', and Zaripa appeared, wet from the rain and laughing. This was extraordinary. There she was in her cotton dress, with her hair soaking wet and lying across her face and she was laughing without stopping. Yedigei could not halt as he was taking part in the attack. 'Why are you laughing so, Zaripa? This can bring us no good!' he shouted. 'But I'm not laughing, I'm crying,' she answered, and went on laughing under the teeming rain . . .

Next day he wanted to tell Abutalip and his wife about the dream, but he had second thoughts. It had been a bad dream. Why worry people unnecessarily?

After this great rain, the hot spell in the Sarozek was at an end for that year, and as Kazangap put it, the summer's tricks were over. There were still some more hot days, but they were bearable. Then gradually autumn set in, the grace and delight of the Sarozek. The Boranly chidren were freed from the dreadful heat and came to life again and their voices rang out. Then a message came from Kumbel': that Kzyl-Orda water melons and other melons had come in; let the people of Boranly decide – they could either have their share sent, or they could come and choose. Yedigei took the second course. He persuaded the junction station master that they should go, since otherwise they would be sent God knows what, stuff that would be no good to them at all. The station master agreed: 'Good, you go with Kuttybaev and select the best.' This was just what Yedigei wanted; he wanted to take Abutalip, Zaripa and their children away from Boranly-Burannyi for at least one day. It would do them good to get a change of air. So off they went, all in their best clothes, the two families and their children, early in the morning on a passing train to Kumbel'.

It was a fine day. The children thought that they were off to some magic land. The whole way there they were excited and asking question after question.

'Do trees grow there?'

'They do.'

'Is there green grass there?'

'There is – and flowers also.'

'And are there big houses and cars driving along the streets?'

'And are there melons and water melons there? And is there ice cream there? And is the sea there?'

The wind beat against their goods waggon and flowed through the open doors, giving an even, pleasant current. The opening between the doors was protected by a wooden barrier, so that the children could not fall out; in any case, Yedigei and Abutalip were sitting there by the edge on empty boxes, chatting away and answering the children's questions. Burannyi

Yedigei was happy that here they were travelling together. The weather was good and the children were enjoying themselves. But most of all he was pleased, not for the little ones, but for Abutalip and Zaripa. Their faces were lit up. They were free for once, unfettered at least for a time from their continual cares and inner worries. The thought came to Yedigei, as he mused, that perhaps Abutalip would be allowed to live in the Sarozek as long as he liked. Please God, grant this!

It was nice to see Zaripa and Ukubala chatting away together closely about household matters. They, too, were happy. That was how it should be – people do not need so much . . . Yedigei wished dearly that the Kuttybaevs could forget all their troubles, get strong and get used to this life at Boranly, if no other choice lay open to them. He was flattered, too, that Abutalip was sitting beside him, their shoulders touching; that Abutalip knew he could trust Yedigei and that they understood each other without any unnecessary words and did not touch needlessly on delicate matters about which it was better to say nothing. Yedigei valued Abutalip's wisdom, his self-control, but most of all his concern for his family; he lived for them, refusing to give up and drawing his strength from them. As he listened to what Abutalip was saying, Yedigei came to the conclusion that the very best thing a man could do for others was to bring up his children as worthy people. Not just with someone else's help, but by his own efforts, day by day, step by step, putting one's whole effort into it – to be with the children as much as possible and for as long as possible.

Look at Sabitzhan. It seemed that wherever Sabitzhan had been educated, from his earliest years, in boarding school, at the Institute, and on various courses of study, he had always made progress. Poor Kazangap had given everything, all he earned or obtained, in order that his Sabitzhan should not be worse off than anyone else. But what use had it all been? He was just a know-all and useless, and would remain that way.

This is what Yedigei was thinking about, then, on the way to Kumbel' to fetch the melons – that there was no better outcome than that Abutalip Kuttybaev should settle down in

Boranly-Burannyi. He should get his home fixed up, get some livestock and bring up his sons in the Sarozek as best as he could. It is true that he did not want to tell Abutalip what to do, but he had the feeling from their talk that Abutalip was in favour of doing something like this and intended to do so. He was asking how to get together a stock of potatoes, where was the best place to buy felt boots – *valenki* – for the winter for his wife and the boys. He, himself, would be wearing leather boots. He also wanted to know if there was a library in Kumbel' and if they lent out books to people living outside the town.

Towards the evening of that day, they went back on yet another goods train, coming home with the melons and water melons which had been set aside by the local trade association for the people of Boranly.

By evening, of course, the children were worn out, but very contented. They had seen the world in Kumbel'; had bought toys, eaten ice cream and done all kinds of other things. But there had been one small incident in the local hairdressers. They had decided to get the chilren's hair cut. And when it had come to Ermek's turn, he set up such a great display of shouting and tears, that there was nothing they could do with the boy. Everyone got worn out, but he was afraid, struggled to escape and called for his father. Abutalip was at that time absent in a nearby shop. Zaripa did not know what to do, alternately blushing and turning pale with shame. She apologized by saying she had not had the boy's hair cut from birth and that it was a pity, because he had such very curly hair. Indeed, Ermek's hair was exceptionally thick and wavy, just like his mother's. In general he took after Zaripa: just wash their hair and comb their curls and they would both look beautiful.

So Ukubala decided to have Saule's hair cut. 'Look, the little girl is not afraid!' This might have had some effect, but no sooner did the hairdresser take up the clippers in his hand than once again the shouting and wailing started. Ermek struggled free just as Abutalip came through the shop door and rushed up to his father, who picked him up and pressed

156

him tightly in a hug – he soon saw that the boy should not be tormented any more.

'Forgive us,' he said to the hairdresser, 'it'll have to be some other time. We'll be prepared then. In the meantime he'll have to walk around looking like this. There's no hurry. Another time will do . . .'

In the course of the extraordinary session of the special plenipotentiaries commission aboard the aircraft carrier *Convention*, it was agreed by both sides that yet another coded radio signal should be sent to the *Parity* orbital station for relaying to the parity-cosmonauts 1-2 and 2-1 now on the planet Lesnaya Grud'. In it they were told categorically not to take any action and to stay where they were until a special order came from the *Obtsenupr*.

As before, the session took place behind closed doors. As before, the aircraft carrier *Convention* was on its station in the Pacific Ocean, south of the Aleutians, at a strictly equal distance by air from San Francisco and Vladivostok. No one else in the world knew of the extraordinary intergalactical event that had taken place: the discovery of an extraterrestrial civilization of rational beings, who hoped to make contact with the inhabitants of the earth.

At the extraordinary session, the two sides had fully discussed this unusual and unexpected problem. On the table before each commission member, besides the various other papers, was a dossier containing a full transcript of the text of the message sent by parity-cosmonauts 1-2 and 2-1. Every thought was studied, every word of the documents pondered. Each detail of life on the planet Lesnaya Grud' was looked at from the point of view of its possible consequences, its compatibility or otherwise with civilization on earth and with the interests of the leading countries on the planet earth. None of those present had ever had to deal with problems of this nature, and it was necessary to decide urgently on what was to be done.

On the Pacific, as before, the storm continued unabated.

*

After the Kuttybaev family had gone through the very worst of the summer heat in the Sarozek and had not collected their things together and moved away from Boranly-Burannyi in despair, the people of Boranly realized that there was a family that would stick it here and hold on longer still. Abutalip Kuttybaev was noticeably more confident now and entered more fully into the Boranly daily toil. He was now accustomed to the way of life at the junction. Like everyone else, he complained that Boranly was the worst place on earth; that even the water had to be brought there in a tank waggon by rail and that a man who wanted to drink his fill of really fresh water had to saddle a camel and set off with skins to one of the wells, 'thirty-nine lands away', to a place that no one except Yedigei and Kazangap had the courage to visit. Yes – that was how things were in the Fifties and right up to the Sixties. Eventually, of course, they installed a deep electric pump for water, powered by a windmill generator, but at that time no one ever dreamed of such a thing. However, in spite of all these privations, Abutalip never really cursed the Boranly-Burannyi junction, nor the Sarozek. He took the bad as it came, and the good in its turn. After all, the land was not to blame. It was up to the individual to decide whether to live here or not . . .

In this land, people tried to settle down to live as comfortably as possible. When the Kuttybaevs were finally convinced that their home was here at Boranly-Burannyi, that they did not have to move on further and that it was essential to settle down permanently, then they found there was little spare time in which to get their home in order. Every day and every shift had to be worked, and in their free time there were always endless jobs to be done. Abutalip was busy the whole time and sweated away, preparing their home for the winter: he refitted the stove, insulated the door, adjusted the frames and made good. He had no particular skills at such work, but Yedigei helped with tools and materials and made sure he was not left to cope all on his own. When they began to dig an underground store near the barn, Kazangap also joined in, and the three of them made a small cellar with a cover consisting of old sleepers topped with straw and mud. They made the top as strong as possible so that nobody's cattle would fall through the hole. Whatever they were doing, Abutalip's little boys were always there, close at hand. Even if they did get in the way sometimes, it was more fun and pleasant to have them around. Yedigei and Kazangap thought that they could help Abutalip to set up his 'farm' and had given him some things. They decided that in spring they would give him a milking camel. The main requirement was to teach him how to milk; it was not the same as with a cow – you had to milk a camel standing up. You also had to follow her out into the steppe, chiefly to keep an eye on the suckling calf, put him to the udder in time and also remove him at the right time. There was plenty to think about, and it all had to be done properly . . .

But what delighted Burannyi Yedigei most was that not only was Abutalip busy the whole time with the house and with the children of both families – for he and Zaripa taught them to read and draw; but he also made even more effort to get to grips with the hard life of Boranly. Yet still he had time to be busy on his own account – for Abutalip Kuttybaev was an educated man. He read, wrote down his notes – this was his world. Secretly, Yedigei was proud he had such a friend and was greatly drawn to him. As with Yelizarov, the Sarozek geologist who was often in these parts, this friendship was no accident. Yedigei respected educated people, scientists, people with knowledge. And Abutalip, like Yelizarov, knew a great deal, although he rarely displayed his wisdom.

Once, however, they did have a particularly serious conversation. One evening they were coming home from work on the railway track. That day they had been putting up snow fences at the Seventh Kilometre point, where there was always much drifting snow. Although autumn had only just arrived, these preparations had to be put in hand in good time. So there they were coming home from work. It was a fine bright evening, just right for a talk. On such evenings the Sarozek all around could just be made out in the mist of the sunset, like the bed of the Aral' Sea, which was visible from a boat in calm weather.

'Well, Abu, in the evening when I walk past, there's always

your head there bent over the window sill. Are you writing or mending something? There's always a lamp beside you.' This was Yedigei's question.

'It's quite simple,' Abutalip answered willingly, shifting his spade from one shoulder to the other, 'I have no writing table. As soon as my brood settle down to sleep, Zaripa reads, and I write down things while I can still remember what happened – about the war, and especially my years in Yugoslavia. Time passes and the past goes further away into the distance.' He was silent and then added, 'All the time I'm thinking about what I can do for my children. Obviously I feed them, give them to drink and educate them. I do all that I can. But I've been through so much – things that other people, please God, will not experience in a hundred years. I'm still alive and healthy, so no doubt Fate gave me those experiences for a purpose. Perhaps so that I can tell others about them, first and foremost my children. Of course there is a general truth for everyone, but everyone has his own understanding about things, and this understanding dies with him. When a man hovers between life and death in the midst of a world conflict; when he is nearly killed a hundred times over and yet still survives, then he has learnt a great deal about good and evil, truth and falsehood . . .'

'One moment, there's something I don't understand,' Yedigei interrupted in amazement. 'Perhaps you are telling the truth, but your sons are still little lads with running noses, and are afraid of the hairdresser's clippers – what can they understand of this?'

'That's why I'm writing all this down. I want to keep it for them. No one can tell whether I'll be alive or dead. I've been thinking for three days now how, like a fool, I nearly fell under a train. Kazangap was there and able to push me out of its way. But he really laid into me afterwards. He said: "Let your children thank the Lord God on their knees!" '

'He was right. I warned you about that long ago. And I spoke to Zaripa.' Yedigei was angry in his turn and took the opportunity to express his concern once more. 'Why do you walk along the track like that? It's as if you expected the train to leave the rails to let you pass. There are the safety regulations. You're an educated man – how many more times do we have to tell you? Even now you're walking on the railway, just as you would in the bazaar. You'll buy it one day – it's no joke.'

'Well, if something happens, it'll have been my fault,' he agreed gloomily. 'But listen to me first, then you can say your piece.'

'I've said all that had to be said, now go on!'

'In the past, people left their children things when they died – for better or for worse, there was always a legacy. How many books have been written, how many plays performed in theatres about those times – how they divided up the spoils and what happened to those who received things. And why? Because these legacies usually consisted of things obtained as a result of other people's sufferings, other people's work, deception and so they brought evil, sin and injustice. But I console myself with the thought that we, thank God, are free of that. My legacy will bring no harm to anyone. My legacy is my soul, my writings, and in them is all that I understood and learnt from the war. I have no greater riches to leave to my children. Here in the Sarozek desert, I have come to the conclusion that life has been directing me here, so that I might be lost, disappear and then write down for them everything that I have thought and worked out. Thus I will live on in my children. Perhaps they will succeed in achieving that which I did not succeed in doing . . . They will find it harder to live than we do. So let them amass knowledge while they're young.'

They walked on for some time in silence, each with his own thoughts. Yedigei found it strange to listen to such words. He was surprised that it was possible to give meaning to one's existence on earth in this way. All the same he decided to get clearer in his mind exactly what it was that surprised him so.

'They say on the radio that our children will live better, easier lives in the future, but clearly you think that things will be more difficult for them than it has been for us. There'll be an atomic war, perhaps?'

'Well, yes and no; but it's not only to do with the bomb.

161

Perhaps there won't be a war at all – even if there is, it'll not be soon. Nor am I talking about food problems. Simply, the wheel of time is gathering speed. They'll have to approach everything on their own, using their own mind, and partly they'll have to answer for what we did in the past. It's always hard to have to think things out. Therefore, I say, life will be harder for them than it has been for us.'

Yedigei did not take the trouble to find out just why he thought it was always hard to think things out. It was unfortunate that he did not ask, and later on, remembering this talk, he was to regret not doing so. He should have asked more questions and found out what was in Abutalip's mind . . .

'I'll say this,' Abutalip went on, as if in answer to Yedigei's doubts, 'to little children, grown-up people always seem wise and to speak with authority. Then they grow up and see that the teachers – our generation – didn't know so very much and were not as clever as they seemed. It's possible to laugh at them, too; their ideas seem completely out of date. The wheel of time is turning ever faster and faster. But we, ourselves, need to say the last word about ourselves. Our ancestors tried to do this in their legends. They wanted to prove to their descendants that they had once been great. And we judge them now by their spirit, as they show it. This is what I am doing for my sons as they grow. My legends are in my war years. I am writing about them in my "Partisan" books. All as it was, all that I saw and all that I went through. That should be useful to them when they grow up. But there are other things as well, other thoughts. They've had to grow up in the Sarozek. Again, when they grow up, I don't want them to think that they lived in an empty, desert place. So I'm writing down our old songs from here. Otherwise these also will be forgotten. A song, as I understand it, is a statement from the past. Your Ukubala seems to know many of them, and she's promised to remember others for me.'

'Well, yes, of course she is from the Aral',' Yedigei said proudly. 'Aral' Kazakhs live by the sea; and it's good to sing when you're at sea. The sea understands everything. Say what you will, everything from the heart is harmonious at sea.'

'You're right, exactly so. Not long ago I read aloud something I'd written down, and Zaripa and I were nearly in tears. How beautifully they sang long ago. Every song is a whole page of history. You can imagine those people, see them, you want to be at one with them. To suffer and to love like them. That's the sort of memorial they've left for themselves. I've also been on at Kazangap's Bukei. "Remember," I told her, "your Karakalpak songs. I'll write them down in a separate notebook; a Karakalpak notebook." '

And so they walked unhurriedly along the railway line. It was a rare occasion. The end of that day came peacefully, easily, like a long sigh, in that pre-autumn time. Although there were no woods, rivers or fields in the Sarozek, the setting sun gave the impression of a complete landscape, thanks to the subtle movement of light and shade over the face of the steppe. The dim flowing blue of the wide-open space seized hold of your soul, lifted up your thoughts, making you want to live long and think deeply . . .

'Listen, Yedigei,' Abutalip began to speak again, having remembered something he had put on one side until there was a suitable moment to ask, 'I've been meaning to ask you for some time. The bird Donenbai – what do you think? Is there really a bird called Donenbai in nature? Have you ever seen such a bird?'

'Oh, it's just part of the legend.'

'I know. But it often happens that a legend overlaps with fact. For example, we have the oriole which all day long in the Semirech'ye sings in the gardens on the hillsides, "Who is my love?" It's just a freak of nature, the sounds are similar. But there's a legend about this bird, explaining why it sings this song. So perhaps there's a similar basis in this story also. Perhaps there exists in the steppe a bird whose call is similar to the name "Donenbai" and because of this it was brought into the legend.'

'I don't know. I haven't thought about that.' Yedigei was doubtful. 'However, I've travelled a lot over this area and I've never come across a bird with that call. I don't think there is one.'

'Maybe . . .' Abutalip answered thoughtfully.

'But if there *isn't* such a bird, surely that doesn't necessarily cast doubt on the legend?' Yedigei was now worried.

'No, why should that be so? The legend explains why the Ana-Beiit cemetery is there and evidently something did happen there. For my part, I still think that there is such a bird and that sometime, someone will see it. That's why I'm writing it all down for the children.'

'Well, if it's for the chidren,' Yedigei blurted out, 'then that's all right . . .'

As far as Burannyi Yedigei could remember, only two people ever wrote down the Sarozek legend about Naiman-Ana. First, Abutalip Kuttybaev wrote it down for his children, for when they grew up – this was at the end of 1952. However, this manuscript was lost. How much sorrow had to be endured after that. How much, indeed! Then, some years later in 1957, Afanasii Ivanovich Yelizarov wrote it down. Now, he, Yelizarov, was dead. His manuscript was probably among his papers at Alma-Ata, but who could say for certain? Both men wrote it down directly from Kazangap's lips. Yedigei had been there also, taking part, but more in the role of a prompter and commentator.

'So the years pass, my God! This was all long ago,' thought Burannyi Yedigei as he rocked between the twin humps of Karanar, covered with his cloth. Now he was taking Kazangap to the Ana-Beiit cemetery. It was as if the circle had closed. The man who used to tell the legend was now to have his final resting place at the cemetery; he who had preserved the tale and had passed it on to others.

'Only we remain – I and Ana-Beiit. And soon it'll be my turn to be brought here. Life leads only to that.' Thus thought Yedigei as he went on his way on his camel, leading the strange funeral procession across the steppe – the tractor and trailer and the *Belarus'* excavator following close behind. The rusty-coloured Zholbars, who had joined up with the procession, was sometimes in front, sometimes at the back, sometimes on either side and sometimes was off somewhere else – for a short while. He carried his tail proudly, as if he were in charge of the whole proceedings, and kept a close watch, busily, on both sides.

The sun was now overhead: it was midday. There was not much farther to go to Ana-Beiit.

CHAPTER EIGHT

The end of 1952, or rather the whole of the autumn and the start of the winter (which was late and without blizzards) – these were the best days that the handful of inhabitants of Boranly-Burannyi junction were to know. Later, Yedigei often thought back to them nostalgically.

At that time, Kazangap, as the patriarch of the people of Boranly, was always very tactful, never interfering in other people's business, and was still strong and in excellent health. Sabitzhan was still at the Kumbel' boarding school, and by then the Kuttybaev family was firmly settled down in the Sarozek. By winter they had made their barrack hut warm, laid in a store of potatoes, had obtained the *valenki* for Zaripa and the boys, and had had a whole sack of flour brought in from Kumbel'. Yedigei had brought a load himself from the supply section on the young Karanar, who was at that time approaching his full strength. Abutalip was working well and, as before, spent all his spare time with the children and at night working diligently away at his writing, sitting there under the lamp.

There were two or three other families of workers at the station, but it seemed that they were only temporarily at the junction. The man then in charge was Abilov – not a bad chap. No one was ill at Boranly. The work went on, the children were growing up. All the pre-winter work programme to protect the tracks and all necessary repairs had been carried out on schedule.

It was excellent weather for the Sarozek, and the autumn colour was like breadcrust brown. Then the winter hurried in. Pure white snow lay all around – and that, too, was beautiful.

Among the great white silence, the railway stretched away like a black thread and along it, the trains went back and forth as usual. On one side of the tracks, among the snowy hillocks, huddled the little village – the Boranly-Burannyi junction siding. Passing train passengers either threw a disinterested glance from the carriages, and occasionally, for a moment, there arose in their hearts a fleeting pity for the lonely inhabitants of the junction.

But this pity was unnecessary. The people of Boranly-Burannyi had had a good year – apart from the stifling summer heat, which was long in the past. In general, everywhere life was getting a little better – with some small setbacks – after the war years. In the New Year they could expect a reduction in prices of food and manufactured goods and although, in the shops, the shelves were far from groaning, things were improving year by year.

Usually the people of Boranly did not bother to wait up for midnight and see the New Year in. Work at the junction went on as usual, and the trains went through, not for one moment considering when or where they would greet the New Year on their journey. In winter, there was more to be done at home, too. There were the stoves to be attended to; the animals needed more attention, both out on the pastures and in the pens. A man got worn out during the day, and after work was over, it seemed better to rest and go to bed early.

So the years had passed, one after the other.

However, the eve of 1953 saw a real celebration at Boranly-Burannyi. Of course, it was arranged by the Kuttybaev family. Yedigei joined in, helping with the last-minute New Year preparations. It had all started when the Kuttybaevs had decided to give their children a New Year tree. And how did you get one of those in the Sarozek? It was easier to find the fossilized eggs of a dinosaur! Yelizarov had in fact found some dinosaur eggs, millions of years old, in the Sarozek, in the course of his geological wanderings. Those eggs, each about the size of a large water melon, had turned to stone. The find had been taken to the Alma-Ata Museum. The newspapers had reported the event.

In the end, Abutalip Kuttybaev had to go to Kumbel' in the freezing cold and there ask at the local committee office for one of the five trees sent to the big station to be given to Boranly-Burannyi instead. This was agreed, and all went ahead.

Yedigei was standing by the stores, having just drawn on his new working gloves, when a long goods train braked to a noisy halt on No. 1 track, all rusty from the steppe wind and made up of four-axle sealed waggons. Abutalip, moving with difficulty for his legs were stiff from the cold even in his leather boots, clambered down from the open platform of the last truck, and the guard, clad in a vast sheepskin coat, his fur hat tied tightly down, moved clumsily down the platform and then handed down a bulky object to Abutalip.

'It must be the tree!' guessed Yedigei in amazement.

'Hi, Yedigei! You, Burannyi! Come and help!' the guard shouted to him, leaning out from the steps of the waggon.

Yedigei hurried up and when he got there he was alarmed, for Abutalip, white to his eyebrows, was all covered with powdery snow and was so frozen that he could hardly move his lips. Nor could he move his hands much. Beside him was the New Year tree – a prickly fir, for which Abutalip had nearly gone to the next world.

'What sort of people *are* you here, to travel dressed like that?' The guard croaked this out in irritation. 'His soul could have flown away on the wind behind us. I wanted to take off my coat to put on him, but then I'd have been cold.'

Still hardly able to move his lips, Abutalip apologized. 'I'm sorry about that. I'll soon warm up now – my home's just over there.'

'I told him,' the guard grumbled on to Yedigei, 'I'm wearing my sheepskin coat, and under that the quilted things; *valenki* on my feet; fur hat – but each time I step outside to give the signal to leave, my eyes nearly pop out from the cold. How can he manage like that?'

Yedigei was embarrassed. 'All right, we'll make sure he wraps up next time, Trofim! Thank you, off you go and a good journey to you.'

He picked up the tree. It was cold. It was not a very big one, just about the height of a man, and it smelt of winter pine forest. Yedigei's heart began to beat strongly; he was recalling those pine forests at the front. There had been masses of pine trees there, crushed by tanks and torn apart by shells. Certainly no one had thought it would cost dear to enjoy the smell of a pine forest.

'Come on,' said Yedigei, and looking at Abutalip, threw the tree up on to his shoulder. Lively, joyful and triumphant eyes shone out from under the white eyebrows of Abutalip's drawn, grey face, with tears formed by the cold glistening on his cheeks. Yedigei was suddenly afraid: would the children appreciate what their father's care had cost? So often in life things are quite the opposite from what one expects – in place of gratitude, there is indifference, even hate. 'God preserve him from that. He has enough other troubles,' thought Yedigei.

The first to see the tree was the elder of the little Kuttybaev boys, Daul. He shouted out with joy and slipped out through the door of the hut, followed out by Zaripa and Ermek, without any coats on.

'The tree! The tree! Look what a fine tree!' Daul was overjoyed and leapt around. Zaripa was no less excited.

'So you got it, after all! That's splendid!'

But Ermek, it turned out, had never seen a New Year's tree before. He gazed at what Uncle Yedigei was carrying, not taking his eyes off it.

'Mama, that's the tree, isn't it? It's good, isn't it? Will it live with us inside the house?'

'Zaripa,' said Yedigei, 'because of this *yölka-palka* (fir-stick) as the Russians call it, you nearly got a frost-bitten husband! Get him indoors quickly and warm him up. First of all, we must get his boots off.'

The boots were frozen on his feet. Abutalip frowned, gritting his teeth and groaning when everyone tried to take them off. The children were especially assiduous. They seized hold of the heavy boots with their little hands, but it was no good – they were stuck to his feet like stone by the frost.

'Boys, don't get in the way, let me do it!' Their mother pushed them aside.

Yedigei felt it necessary to whisper to her, 'Don't stop them, Zaripa. Let them try. Let them help.' For inside he felt that this fervour was the highest and best gift Abutalip could receive – the love, the excitement of his two children. It meant that they were already individuals, they already had their own thoughts. It was especially touching, as well as amusing, to watch the little fellows. For some reason, Ermek called his father 'Papika'. No one corrected him, since this was his own modification of one of the eternal and most basic words in human language.

'Papika! Papika!' He was quite red in the face from his exertions. His hair was thick, his eyes bursting with the will to do what was needed, but he was so serious about it that you had to laugh. Of course, something had to be done to help the boys achieve their aim. Yedigei found a way. By this time the boots had begun to thaw out and they could be twisted without causing pain to Abutalip.

'Come on, lads, sit behind me. We'll be like a train, one will draw along the other. Daul, you take hold of me. Ermek you take hold of Daul!'

Abutalip understood Yedigei's idea and nodded in agreement, smiling through his tears which were welling up as he felt the change from cold to warmth. Yedigei sat opposite Abutalip, the boys formed the 'train' behind him, and when everyone was ready, Yedigei began to pull at the boots.

'Now lads, pull harder, pull as a team! I can't do it alone. I'm not strong enough. Come on, Daul, Ermek! Pull harder!'

The boys were puffing away behind him, doing their best to help, and Zaripa was cheering them on, like a supporter. Yedigei was pretending that it was a great effort, and when the first boot came off, the little fellows shouted in triumph. Zaripa hurried in to massage her husband's limb with some knitting, but Yedigei stopped everyone.

'Come on lads, come on, Mama! What's this? Who's going to pull off the other boot? Or shall we leave your father with one bare foot and the other still in a cold boot? Is that right?'

170

Everyone burst out laughing. They laughed for a long time, all rolling on the floor – especially the boys and Abutalip himself.

Burannyi Yedigei often remembered that moment later, when he tried to solve the terrible riddle. For who knows? Perhaps at that very second, somewhere far away from Boranly-Burannyi, the name of Abutalip Kuttybaev had once more surfaced on some anonymous official-looking form, and even then the Kuttybaev family's fate was being decided.

The tragedy overtook them by stealth – although perhaps Yedigei, being more experienced in these matters, more cunning, might have had some dim premonition or inkling in his heart of the danger to come.

What was there for them to be worried about? Always, towards the end of the year, an inspector came to the junction. According to a time-table of visits he went from one junction, one siding, to the next, from station to station. He would arrive, stay two or three days, check how the staff were being paid; check the amounts of materials being used and other such points. Then he would sign his name, together with the man in charge of the place, on his report; some other individual from among the workers would also countersign, and finally he would move on by the next train to his next destination. What a lot there was to be checked, even at a small junction! Yedigei was the usual person to sign the inspector's report, as the workers' representative.

On this occasion the inspector spent three days at Boranly-Burannyi and slept the night in the duty hut by the main building, where there was also the communications centre and the small room for the man in charge, usually proudly called his 'office'. Abilov fussed around the whole time and brought the inspector tea in a tea pot. Yedigei called in to see the inspector. There he sat, smoking and looking at some papers. Yedigei had thought perhaps the inspector might be someone who had been there before, someone whom he knew; but, no, he had never seen this one before. Ruddy cheeks, a few teeth left, glasses, hair going grey. A strange, sticky sort of smile flashed in his eyes.

They met again later that evening. Yedigei was returning from his shift, looked up, and there was the inspector walking under the lamp by the duty hut. He had turned up his lambskin collar, he was wearing his lambskin hat, spectacles, and he was puffing thoughtfully at a cigarette and stamping on the sand beneath his boots.

'Good evening. Come out to have a smoke? Had a good day's work?' Yedigei asked him in a friendly tone.

'Yes, of course,' answered the other with a trace of a smile, 'though it's not easy.' Again that half-smile.

'Of course, of course.' Yedigei agreed politely.

'I'm off tomorrow,' announced the inspector,' when No. 17 train comes in, it'll stop and I'll board it.' Again he gave his half-smile. He had a quiet voice, a bit forced. His eyes were penetrating and intense. 'You must be Yedigei Zhangel'din?' asked the inspector.

'Yes, that's me.'

'I thought so.' The inspector confidently puffed out the smoke between his remaining teeth. 'An old soldier. You've been here since 1944. The men working on the track nick-named you "Burannyi".'

'Yes, indeed.' Yedigei answered simply; he was pleased that this man knew so much about him, but at the same time surprised as to why and how the inspector had found out all this – and, what was more, remembered it.

'I've a good memory,' the inspector went on, as if he had been reading Yedigei's thoughts. 'I write, too – like your Kuttybaev here.' He nodded, directing a puff of smoke in the direction of the lighted window where, as always, Abutalip's head was bent over his papers. 'This is the third day I've seen this. He writes and writes the whole time, I understand. I write myself, only I write poetry. They print my verses almost every month in the depot magazine. We have a literary circle which I run. Some of my verses have been published in the oblast' newspaper, once on International Women's Day and this year on 1st May.'

They were silent. Yedigei was preparing to say goodbye and be on his way home, but the inspector began to speak again.

'He's writing about Yugoslavia, isn't he?'

'I honestly don't know,' answered Yedigei, 'it may be so. He fought there as a partisan for many years. He's writing for his children.'

'So I've heard. I asked Abilov here. It seems that he was a prisoner of war; then he was a teacher for a number of years. Now he intends to develop his skill with the pen.' He laughed hoarsely, 'It's not as simple as it might seem, I can tell you. I'm also considering some larger work – about the front, the rear areas and my work. But I've no time at all. I'm always travelling around on this job . . .'

'He only writes at night. He works all day,' Yedigei replied.

Again they were silent; but again Yedigei did not succeed in getting away. 'So he writes and writes and doesn't raise his head, eh?' The inspector gave his half-smile again and looked in the direction of the silhouette of Abutalip in the window.

'Well, you have to do something,' Yedigei said. 'He's an educated man, after all. No one or nothing around, so he writes.'

'Aha, that's a thought. No one and nothing around.' The inspector frowned as if imagining something, and murmured, 'And you're free; on your own – no one and nothing . . .'

With this they said goodbye.

Over the following days Yedigei meant to tell Abutalip about this incidental conversation with the inspector, but somehow he did not get round to doing so. Finally he forgot all about it.

There was much to be done before winter. Karanar had started off on a major campaign. What a trial, what a punishing time for his master! As a young male, Karanar had become mature two years ago; but in those two years his passions had not yet fully awoken; you could still calm him down, frighten him and call him to order with a sharp shout. Also, the old male in the Boranly herd, for a long time one of Kazangap's camels, kept him under control. He kicked him, bit him and chased him away from the females. But the steppe was vast. Chase him away from one place and he would succeed elsewhere. Thus the old male chased him for a whole day, but eventually was exhausted, whereupon the young, hot-blooded *atansha* (young male) Karanar achieved his aim, not so much in the struggle of the rut, but by his powers of running. In this latest season, as the winter cold approached, when the blood of camels again awoke to the ancient natural call, Karanar had become chief of the Boranly herd. He had become powerful and had developed extra strength. He had chased Kazangap's old male into a ravine out there in the empty steppe, and had kicked him, trampled him and bitten him until he was half dead; fortunately someone arrived on the scene and they were separated. Nature was pitiless; it would take its course, come what may. And now it was Karanar's turn to raise progeny.

It was through this incident that Kazangap and Yedigei first quarrelled. Kazangap could not control his anger when he saw the pitiful sight of the old male trampled in the ravine. He came back from the pasture very angry and upset and shouted at Yedigei, 'How did you let such a thing happen? They're animals, but we are human beings. Your Karanar has started on a murderous course, yet you let him go out into the steppe without any qualms.'

'I didn't let him go out, Kazake. He just went of his own accord. How can you expect me to keep him penned up? With chains? He'd break them. You know the old saying, "*Kyush atasyn tanimaidy*" ("Strength doesn't recognize its father"). His time has now come.'

'So you're glad, are you? But, you see, there'll be more trouble. You're sorry for him, you don't want to pierce his nostrils and put a *shish* (a piece of wood) in his upper lip. But you'll shed tears when you have to chase after him. A beast like him won't be satisfied with the herd here. He'll go and fight over the whole Sarozek. And there'll be no holding him. You'll remember my words then . . .'

Yedigei did not argue with Kazangap; he respected him and he knew that he was right in what he had said. So he just said placidly, 'You gave him to me as a suckling and now you're swearing. All right, I understand. I'll do something about keeping him in check.'

But to spoil such a handsome beast as Karanar – to pierce his nostrils and put in a *shish*? Yedigei could not bring himself to do that. Later on he often remembered those words of Kazangap, and many times, angered to the point of madness, he swore he would do something, but in fact he never touched the camel. Once he considered castrating him, but he did not do that either; he could not overcome his feelings. The years passed and every time, with the start of the winter and the rutting season, the endless searches for the lust-inflamed Karanar resumed.

Everything began with that winter. While Yedigei tried to keep Karanar under control and strengthened the pen so as to keep him shut in more securely, the New Year came along. And then the Kuttybaevs started their plans for the party with the New Year's tree. It was a great event for all the Boranly children. Ukubala and her daughters moved in to the Kutty-baev's barrack hut and they spent the whole day preparing and decorating the tree. Before he left for work and as soon as he got back, Yedigei's first act was to go in and see how the tree was getting on at the Kuttybaevs. It became more and more beautiful as the decoration progressed, and was covered with ribbons and various home-made toys. One had to give credit to the two women, Zaripa and Ukubala; they had done marvels for the children and really put all their skill into the work. For them, it was not merely a tree, it was a symbol of their hopes for the New Year, of everyone's expectation of happiness around the corner.

Abutalip was not content with this – he led the children outside and there began to make a big snowman. At first Yedigei thought they would simply play, but he was delighted at the result. A huge snowman, about the height of a real person, with black eyes and eyebrows of coal, a red nose and smiling mouth, with one of Kazangap's worn-out malakhai hats on its head, had taken up position at the front of the junction, waiting for the trains. In one hand the snowman held a green flag and in the other a board with the greeting, 'Happy New Year – 1953'. It was a fine effort. This snowman still stood there after 1st January.

Until the evening of 31st December of the dying year, the Boranly children played around the tree and outside. Those grown-ups not on duty were also there. Abutalip told Yedigei that early that morning, his children had crept into his bed, sniffing, fussing around while he pretended to be still sound asleep.

'Get up, Papika, get up!' Ermek had told him. 'Soon Grandfather Frost will be here. Let's go and meet him!'

'Good,' said Abutalip. 'Now we'll get out of bed, wash, dress and go along to see. He did promise to come.'

'On what train?' Daul asked.

'He might be on any train,' replied Abutalip. 'Grandfather Frost can arrange for any train to be stopped, even at our junction.'

'Then we must get up as quickly as possible!'

'Yes, we must meet him properly, with due ceremony!'

'What about Mama?' Daul asked. 'She'll want to meet Grandfather Frost too, won't she?'

'Of course she will. Go and call her.'

Together they had left the house, the boys running ahead to the duty hut. There they had searched everywhere, but found no sign of Grandfather Frost.

'Papika, where is he?' Ermek had asked.

'Just one moment,' said Abutalip. 'Don't be in such a hurry. I'll go and have a word with whoever's on duty.'

So saying, Abutalip had disappeared into the duty hut where he had hidden a letter from Grandfather Frost the previous evening, together with a sack of presents. The moment he came out, the boys asked, 'Well, Papika?'

'This is what's happened,' he said. 'Grandfather Frost has left you a letter – here it is. It reads: "Dear Boys, Daul and Ermek! I arrived here at your famous Boranly-Burannyi junction early this morning at five o'clock. You were still asleep and it was very cold. I was cold, too – my beard was like a frozen sheepskin! The train only stopped for two minutes, but I managed to write this letter and to leave your presents. In the bag there's an apple and two nuts each for every child at the junction. Don't be angry with me for not waiting, I've much to do. I've other children to see – they're also expecting

176

me. I'll try and come next New Year, so that we can meet. Until then, your Ayaz-Ata, Grandfather Frost." '

'Wait,' said Abutalip, 'there's a PS. It's written in a hurry – no doubt the train was waiting to go. It says, "Daul, don't beat your little dog. Someone told me that once it squealed when you hit it with a galosh. But I've not heard any more, so perhaps you're treating it better now. That's all! Once again, your Ayaz-Ata!" Wait – there's something else scribbled here . . . "Your snowman is very fine. Congratulations! I shook his hand!" '

Well, of course they had been delighted, for Grandfather Frost's letter had convinced them straight away, and they did not think to complain about not seeing him. Only then they had begun to argue over who should carry the sack with the presents. Their mother had had to intervene.

'First, Daul will carry it for ten paces, as he's the eldest; then you, Ermek, as the youngest, can carry it for ten, and so on.'

Yedigei laughed with all his heart when he heard about all this. 'If I'd been in their place, I'd have been convinced too!'

That afternoon, Uncle Yedigei achieved the summit of popularity with the children. He arranged a ride for them on Kazangap's old sleigh. One of Kazangap's camels, a quiet animal which pulled gently when fitted with a breast harness, was chosen (Karanar, of course, would have been quite unsuitable for the task). The camel was harnessed up, and off they went with much noise. Yedigei was driving, and the children were all sitting close together, all eager to sit beside him, and begging, 'Faster, let's go faster!' Abutalip and Zaripa walked or ran alongside, and when they were going downhill, they sat on the edge of the sleigh. They went about two kilometres away from the junction, turned round on a hilltop and then went downhill again all the way home. The camel got quite tired, and every now and then they had to stop to let it rest.

It was a lovely day. Over the endless snow-covered Sarozek, as far as the eye could see and the sound could carry, there was a white, unbroken, virgin silence. All around stretched the steppe – slopes, hills, valleys and sky. The Sarozek had a soft light, giving a brief midday warmth, and you could feel the breeze as it caressed your ears. Ahead of them on the railway line there was a long red and yellow train pulled by two engines in tandem, both puffing out smoke and steam. The smoke hung in the air, dispersing slowly in the form of rings. As the train approached the first signal, the front engine gave a long, powerful blast on its whistle. It repeated this twice to make sure everyone knew, for it was a through train and rumbled noisily through the junction without slowing down, past the signals and the half dozen little houses huddled beside the line. Then all went quiet and peaceful again. Not a thing moved, only the black smoke from the stoves turning and twisting above the roofs of the Boranly houses. All was quiet; even the children, over-excited by their ride, were silent. Then Zaripa whispered, so that only her husband could hear, 'Oh, how beautiful it is, but yet so frightening.'

'You're right,' answered Abutalip, also quietly.

Yedigei glanced at them out of the corner of his eye, not turning his head. They were very much alike, standing there. Zaripa's quietly spoken words worried Yedigei, although they had not been intended for his ears. He understood suddenly with what melancholy and fear she was gazing at those little houses with the smoke rising above them. But there was no way in which Yedigei could help them, for that place beside the railway was the only place for them to be living.

Yedigei urged on the camel, gave it a touch of the whip, and the sleigh headed back towards the junction.

That evening of New Year's night, all the people of Boranly gathered at Yedigei and Ukubala's home, as had been arranged some days before.

'Since the Kuttybaevs, the new arrivals, have arranged the party and the New Year tree for the children, it's up to us not to spare any effort!'

This is what Ukubala had said, and Yedigei was delighted at it. Of course, not everyone could come at the same time – some would be on duty, others would have to go on duty during the course of the evening. The trains kept on running;

178

to them holidays and ordinary working days were all the same. Kazangap could only be there at the start of the party. At nine o'clock he went off to duty on the points, and Yedigei was on the shift roster to start at six a.m. on 1st January. That was the price you had to pay. But in spite of this, it was a most enjoyable evening. Everyone was in good spirits and, although they met at least ten times each day, they had changed into their best clothes for the occasion, just as if they were guests who had come from far away. Ukubala was at the peak of her cooking form and had prepared all kinds of delicacies. There was vodka and champagne – as much as you wanted to drink – and for those who preferred it, there was the winter shubat from the milking camels. In the winter, Bukei, Kazangap's tireless wife, took on the job of milking them.

But the party really got under way after the first dishes had been sampled, the first glasses drunk, and they started to sing. Now the initial worries of the hosts were over; the guests were relaxed and everyone could forget their troubles and enjoy a rare moment of pleasure, a good drink and a talk. Of course, the guests saw each other every day and knew each other well, but a party has the power to change people, to reveal new sides to them. Of course, sometimes the change can be for the worse, but not here among the people of Boranly. To live in the Sarozek, and have the reputation of being difficult to get on with or the type who makes scenes . . . not likely!

Yedigei became slightly intoxicated. However, this suited him. Ukubala, without any special alarm, merely reminded her husband, 'Don't forget – you're to be at work at 6 o'clock in the morning.'

'All right, Uku. Message received and understood!' he answered.

Sitting beside Ukubala, his arm around her neck, he began to sing – not always in tune, admittedly, but with feeling. He was in that excellent state of spirit when a clear brain and excitement mix harmlessly together. As he sang, he looked kindly on the faces of his guests, giving everyone a happy, heartfelt smile, sure that everyone was enjoying the party as much as himself. And he was handsome – still the black-browed, black-moustached Burannyi Yedigei, with flashing grey eyes and a complete row of strong white teeth. Not even the most lively imagination could have foretold then how he would look when he was old. He was attentive to everyone. He patted the shoulder of the plump and kindly Bukei, calling her the Boranly Mama, and drank a toast to her, saying that in toasting her, he was toasting the whole Karakalpak people, who once upon a time had lived on the banks of the Amu-Dar'ya. He also persuaded her not to be upset that her Kazangap had had to leave the party.

'I'd got tired of him!' Bukei answered boldly.

That evening Yedigei called Ukubala only by her full name, Uku balasy – child of the owl, or owlet. For everyone he had a kind, heartfelt word; everyone in that circle was to him a beloved brother or sister, including the man in charge of the junction, Abilov, who found it hard to endure the work of a small track worker out in the Sarozek, and his wife, Saken, pale of face and pregnant, who would shortly have to go to the Station Maternity Home at Kumbel'. Yedigei honestly believed that he was surrounded by inseparably close friends. Why should he have believed otherwise?

For a moment, in the middle of a song, he felt he had to close his eyes. He saw in his mind's eye the vast, snow-covered Sarozek and the people in his house, all come together like one family. But most of all he was glad for Abutalip and Zaripa. This couple deserved the best. Zaripa sang and played on the mandolin, quickly taking up the tunes of the songs, one after the other. Her voice was ringing and pure. Abutalip led with a deep-chested, muffled, drawn out voice. They sang together with spirit, especially the Tartar songs. These they sang in the *almak-calmak* style, one singer answering the other. As they sang, the other people joined in. They had already sung many old and new songs, yet they were quite unwearied. On the contrary, they sang with even greater enthusiasm. So their guests were happy. Sitting opposite Zaripa and Abutalip, Yedigei looked at them the whole time and was moved. They would always have been like this, were it not for that bitter fate which gave them no peace of mind . . .

In that dreadful summer heat, Zaripa's face had been grey like a tree scorched in a fire, her brown hair bleached to the roots, and her lips caked with dried black blood. Now she was a different person. Black-eyed, those eyes shining, and with her open, smooth-skinned Asiatic face beaming – today she was beautiful. Her lively, well-marked eyebrows showed most clearly her state of mind, for they were joining in the song, now rising, now knitted, now running free in the full flight of the ancient songs. With especial feeling, she stressed each word, Abutalip repeating after her, rocking from side to side:

> "*. . . like the trace of the girth on the pacer's side,*
> *The days of a departed love are not erased from the*
> *memory . . .*'

As Zaripa played upon the strings of the mandolin, her hands made the music ring out and groan with suffering in that close circle of friends that New Year's night. She floated along on her song, and it seemed to Yedigei that she was somewhere far away, running, breathing lightly, roaming freely over the snows of the Sarozek, in her lilac-coloured knitted blouse with its separate white collar, with the mandolin sounding faintly in the darkness. As she went further away, she disappeared into the mist and only the mandolin could be heard. Then, as she remembered that at Boranly junction there were people who would miss her, she returned once more and was with them again, singing at the table . . .

Then Abutalip demonstrated how the partisans had danced, putting their hands on each others' shoulders and beating time with their feet. While Zaripa leapt up and down, Abutalip sang a provocative Serbian song and then everyone danced in a circle, hands on each others' shoulders and shouting, '*Oplya! Oplya!*'

Then they sang and drank some more, clinking glasses, and wished each other a Happy New Year. Someone left and someone came in to join the party. Abilov and his pregnant wife had left before the dancing started. Time passed.

Zaripa went out for a breath of fresh air, followed by Abutalip. Ukubala made everyone put on a coat before they went out, so as not to feel the cold too much after getting so warm. For a long time Zaripa and Abutalip did not return. In the end, Yedigei decided to go out and look for them, for without them the party would lose its momentum.

As he left, Ukubala called to him, 'Put your coat on, Yedigei! Where're you off to like that? You'll catch cold!'

'I'll be back soon. 'And Yedigei stepped out on to the porch in the cold, clear midnight air. 'Abutalip! Zaripa!' he called, as he looked around.

There was no answer. Behind the house he heard voices. He stopped, undecided, not knowing what to do. Should he go away and leave them, or should he go to them and bring them back? Something was happening between them.

'. . . I didn't want you to notice,' Zaripa was sobbing. 'Forgive me. I suddenly felt so sad. Forgive me, please!'

'I understand,' Abutalip was consoling her, 'I understand completely. But I can't help the way I am. If only this was just my problem, but what affects me affects you too. Perhaps if we weren't so close to one another . . .' They were silent, and then he said, 'Our children will be free. In that lies my hope, all of it.'

Not understanding what all this was about, Yedigei walked away on tiptoe, shrugging his shoulders from the cold, and returned without a sound. When he entered the house, all the brightness had faded and the party was over.

On 5th January 1953, at ten in the morning, a passenger train stopped at Boranly-Burannyi junction – although the track ahead was clear and it could have gone through without stopping, as it usually did. It stopped for only a minute and a half, but it was long enough. Three figures – all in standard pattern black chrome leather boots – stepped down from the train and went straight into the duty hut. They walked with an air of determination, not saying a word and did not look around, but they stopped for a second by the snowman and looked in silence at the greeting on the piece of plywood, and at the ridiculous *malakhai*, Kazangap's old worn-out hat, stretched on the snowman's head. Then they went into the office.

A moment later, Abilov, in charge of the junction, hurried out of the door. He nearly ran full tilt into the snowman, swore, and hurried on, almost at a run, something he never did normally. Ten minutes later, puffing and blowing, he was on his way back. With him was Abutalip Kuttybaev whom he had searched out at work. Abutalip was pale and holding his cap in his hand. They went into the hut together. However, very soon, out he came again with two of the men, in their chrome leather boots, and all three men went into the Kuttybaevs' hut. They soon came out again, the two men closely escorting Abutalip and carrying some papers which they had taken from the house.

Then all was quiet. No one entered or left the duty hut.

Yedigei heard about this from Ukubala. On Abilov's instructions, she ran out to the Fourth Kilometre point, where they were working on the line that day, and immediately took Yedigei on one side.

'They're interrogating Abutalip.'

'Who are?'

'I don't know – some people who came here on the train. Abilov told me to tell you that, if they don't ask, then don't say anything about our celebration on New Year's Eve with Abutalip and Zaripa.'

'And what does that mean?'

'I don't know. He just asked me to say that to you. Also, that you're to report there at two. They want to ask you some questions about Abutalip.'

'What do they want to know?'

'How do I know? Abilov was properly scared when he came, and all he said is what I've already told you. Then I came straight out here.'

Yedigei had to come home for lunch at two in any case. All the way back he tried to make out what was happening, but could not find the answer. Surely it could not be about the past again, his time as a prisoner of war? They had checked on all that long ago. What else could it be? He felt worried and alarmed. He swallowed two spoonfuls of *lapsha* and then pushed the rest of the plate of noodles to one side. He looked at the time: five to two. Since they had said two, then two it had to be. He went out of his house. Near the hut, Abilov was walking to and fro. He looked a sorry sight, downcast and shattered.

'What's happened?'

'It's bad, it's bad, Yedike,' said Abilov, looking fearfully at the door. His lips trembled. 'They've got Kuttybaev.'

'What for?'

'They've found some forbidden writing he's been doing in his hut. Of course, he was busy writing away every evening – everyone knows that. Now he's written too much.'

'He was doing all that for his children's benefit.'

'I don't know about that. I don't know who he wrote it for. I know nothing. Go on in, they're waiting for you.'

In the little so-called 'office' of the junction chief sat a man of about Yedigei's age or a little younger, waiting for him. He was thick-set, with a large head covered with close-cropped hair. His large nose with its wide nostrils was sweating from the effort of concentration, and he was reading some papers. He wiped at his nose with his handkerchief; there was a frown on his high, heavy brow. Later, all through their talk, he continually wiped his sweating nose. He pulled a long cigarette from a packet of *Kazbek* on the table, twisted the tube and lit up. He turned his clear, hawk-like eyes on to Yedigei, who was standing in the doorway, and said sharply:

'Sit down!'

Yedigei sat down on a stool in front of the table.

'So that there'll be no doubt . . .' said Hawkeye, and took from the breast pocket of his civilian jacket a piece of brown cardboard, opened it out and at once took it back, blurting out something like 'Tansykbaev' or 'Tysykbaev', so that Yedigei did not really have a chance to catch his name.

'Well, then, let's get down to business. They say you're Kuttybaev's best friend and comrade?'

'Perhaps, yes. Why?'

'*Perhaps, yes.*' Hawkeye drew on his *Kazbek* as if making

184

clear what he'd heard, 'Perhaps, yes . . . All right, that's clear.'
And then he said sharply, with an unexpected trace of a smile,
a joyful prepared look of pleasure in his glassy, clear eyes,
'Well, my friend, what are we going to write down?'

'Write down . . . ? I don't understand what you're talking
about.'

'Don't you? Well, think about it.'

'I don't know what you're talking about.'

'What was Kuttybaev writing about?'

'I don't know.'

'How is it you don't know. Everyone else knows except you,
but you don't know.'

'I know that he's been writing something. But how should
I know exactly what it was? Is it my business? A person wants
to write, let him write. Whose affair is it?'

'So whose business is it?' Hawkeye jumped in surprise,
frowning, focusing his penetrating gaze on Yedigei. 'So if
someone wants to write, you say let him write? He convinced
you about that?'

'He didn't convince me about anything like that.'

But Hawkeye took no notice of this answer. He was very
upset.

'So that's it! Hostile agitation – and you say: what does it
matter if all and sundry begin to write? You say: *what does it
matter?* So every person has the right to express whatever
comes into his head. That's it, is it? Where have you got such
alien ideas from? No, my friend, we don't allow that. Such
counter-revolutionary tendencies must not pass unchecked.'

Yedigei was silent, crushed and confused by the words flung
at him. He was amazed to see that all around him nothing had
changed, everything was the same as ever. Through the
window he could see the Tashkent train passing through, and
imagined for a second the people sitting there in the carriages,
going about their business and needs as usual; drinking tea or
vodka, talking to each other . . . Not one of them had a clue
that at that moment in that same Boranly-Burannyi junction
he, Yedigei, was sitting there opposite Hawkeye, who had
dropped down on his head from heaven knows where . . . He

felt an infuriating pain in his chest that made him long to rush out of the hut, catch up with the train and travel on it to the ends of the earth – anything rather than remain here now.

'Well, has the point of the question now got home to you?' Hawkeye continued.

'It has, it has.' Yedigei answered. 'Only I want to know one thing. All he wanted was to write his memoirs for his children. How things were at the front, then as a prisoner of war and with the partisans. What's wrong with that?'

'For his children!' The other exclaimed. 'And you believed that? Who writes for two children hardly a year old? Fairy tales! That's how an experienced enemy works. He hides himself away in the depths of the country where there's no one around, where no one keeps an eye on him, and he gets down to writing his memoirs!'

'But that was all he wanted to do,' said Yedigei. 'He wanted, no doubt, to express in his own words something from himself, some of his thoughts, so that his children, so that they could read it when they grew up.'

'Now it's his "own words"! What on earth does that mean?' Reproachfully shaking his head, Hawkeye sighed. '*Some of his thoughts* – is that what you mean? His own point of view? His own special opinion? That cannot be allowed. Once a thought is down on paper, it's no longer personal. That which is written with a pen cannot be cut out with an axe. Everyone will wish to express his own thoughts. That would be *rich*! Here they are, his so-called "Partisan note books"; he's subtitled them, "Days and Nights in Yugoslavia". Disgraceful! And here you are, trying to shield your friend. But we've unmasked him!' He threw down three thick bound notebooks on to the table.

'How have you unmasked him? In what way?'

Hawkeye jumped up in his chair and once again radiated pleasure and delight, although his eyes remained bright, clear and penetrating.

'I do not propose to reveal in what way we have unmasked him,' he said, revelling in the effect produced by his words. 'That is *our* business. I do not have to answer or report to everyone.'

186

'Well, if it's like that . . .' said Yedigei in confusion.

'His memories are hostile to the State and must be suppressed,' said Hawkeye, and began to scribble something down. 'And I thought you were cleverer – that you were one of us. A leading worker. A former soldier at the front. I thought that you'd help us unmask the enemy.'

Yedigei drew himself up and said quietly, but clearly, in a tone which left no room for doubt, 'I won't sign anything. I'm telling you that straight away.'

Hawkeye threw him a devastating look. 'We've no need of your signature. Do you really think that if you don't sign, the matter will be shelved? Then you're wrong. We have enough material to bring him to account without your signature.'

Yedigei was quiet. He felt humiliated, devastated. And with this his anger rose up within him like a wave on the Aral' Sea, an utter fury at what was going on. All of a sudden he wanted to throttle this Hawkeye like a mad dog – and he knew that he could do it. That fascist whom he had strangled with his bare hands had had a similar, sinewy, strong neck. There had been no other way out then. The two of them had come unexpectedly face-to-face in a trench when the Soviet forces had driven the enemy from a defensive position. They had come in from the flank, hurling grenades into the trench and spraying all around with automatic fire. The line seemed to have been cleared and they were hurrying on further, when suddenly there he was. He must have been a machine gunner who had been firing his last remaining rounds from near the dug-out. It would be best to take him alive – that thought had flashed through Yedigei's mind; but just then the other man had raised a knife above his head. Yedigei had butted him in the face with his helmet and they had both gone down. There was nothing for it but to go for his throat. The other man twisted, choked and groped with his fingers for the knife, which had been knocked from his hand. Every moment Yedigei expected to feel that knife in his back, and so with an unyielding, inhuman, animal effort, he pressed, grunting as he tightened his grip on the cartilage of his enemy's neck. The man's teeth bared and his face gradually turned black. Then suddenly he stopped breathing and there

187

was a pungent smell of piss. Yedigei loosened his fingers from their feverish hold. He threw up at once and, covered with his own vomit, crawled away with a groan and with his vision blurred. He had never told anyone about it then or afterwards. Sometimes he would relive the whole scene in a nightmare, and the next day he would find that he was unable to settle down to anything and did not want to live . . .

Now Yedigei remembered this with a cold shiver. However, he realized that Hawkeye would triumph through cunning and mental superiority. This fact maddened him. While the other was writing away, Yedigei searched for the flaws in Hawkeye's argument. From what Hawkeye had said, one thought struck Yedigei with its lack of logic, its devilish inconsequence. How was it possible to accuse anyone of having hostile memories? For memories were things that happened at some time in the past; they no longer existed. In other words, a man could only remember something which had already happened.

'I want to ask you something,' said Yedigei, feeling his throat go dry from emotion, but forcing himself to enunciate his words clearly, even calmly. 'You say' – he was deliberately addressing the other in the familiar form so that he would understand that Yedigei was in no mood to cringe and cower; after all, he could not be exiled any further out in the wild than the Sarozek – 'you say,' he repeated, 'his memories were hostile. Now, what am I to understand by that? How can memories be hostile or not hostile? As I see it, a man remembers something that happened and how it happened, long ago – it's something long past. Or are we to say: if a thing is good, remember it; if it is something bad or inconvenient, then don't remember it, just forget it? Forget that it has ever been? If, for example, you have a dream, then if it was good, remember it; but if it was frightening and bad, no good to anyone, then . . . ?'

'So that's the sort you are, is it? The devil take you!' Hawkeye was astonished. 'You like to ponder, you want to argue. You're the local philosopher. Oh, well, let me see.' He paused. He seemed to be trying something out in his mind; then he sorted it out and pronounced solemnly, 'In life, anything can be an historical event in a sense. What we are concerned with here is not *what* happened and *how* it happened. What matters is that when we describe the past, when we speak of it – and even more so when we write about it – we should do so in the way that is needed now, as is appropriate now, for us. Things that are of no use to us at the present time must not be mentioned. And if you do mention them, it means that you are acting in a hostile and antisocial fashion.'

'I don't agree,' said Yedigei, 'that cannot be.'

'But no one needs your agreement. That's by the by. You have asked and I, because I'm good-natured, have explained. I do not have to indulge in such discussion with you. Good – then we'll go on from words to the actual matter under consideration. Tell me, did Kuttybaev when talking frankly, or when you were drinking together, give or tell you any English names?'

'Why do you want to know that?' Now it was Yedigei's turn to be amazed.

'This is why.' Hawkeye opened one of Abutalip's 'Partisan Note Books' and read out the following passage, underlined with red pencil marks: ' "On 27th September an English mission arrived at our post – a colonel and two majors. We paraded before them and marched past. They saluted us, and then joined us for a meal in our CO's tent. He had invited us as foreign partisans serving with the Yugoslavs. When I was introduced to the colonel, he shook me politely by the hand and asked, through the interpreter, where I'd come from and how I'd got there. I told him in a few words. I was handed a glass of wine and we drank together. Then we talked for a long time. I was pleased to find that the English were simple, direct people. The colonel said that it was a great good fortune – his actual words were, 'an act of Providence' – that all of us in Europe had united against fascism. And that without this, the battle against Hitler would have been even harder. Possibly, if nations had remained isolated and standing alone, the war could have ended in tragedy." And so on in that sort of vein.'

Hawkeye put the book on one side, lit another *Kazbek* and sat in silence, puffing away. Then he continued.

189

'So it appears, Kuttybaev did not say to that English colonel that without the genius of Stalin, victory would have been impossible, no matter how long they danced round and round in Europe with the partisans – or anyone else, for that matter. So he was not keeping Comrade Stalin in the forefront of his thoughts! Do you see my point?'

'Perhaps he did say something,' Yedigei made an attempt to defend Abutalip, 'but he forgot to write it down.'

'Where is this stated? You can't show! In addition, we have had another look at the evidence Kuttybaev gave in 1945, when he was screened by the Control Commission on his return from the Yugoslav partisans. There is no mention of this meeting with the English mission. That means that there's something very wrong. Who can be sure that he was not caught up by British Intelligence?'

Once again Yedigei felt sick at heart. He could not understand what Hawkeye was getting at.

'Now think carefully. Kuttybaev didn't say anything to you about the English? Or mention any English names? It's important to us to know who were these people he met in the English Mission.'

'What sort of names would they have had?'

'Well, for instance, John, Clark, Smith, Jack . . .'

'I've never heard anything like those.'

Hawkeye was thinking; he was looking downcast. Not everything had gone as he had wanted in this interrogation of Yedigei. Then he said insinuatingly, 'He started a sort of school here, I believe. Taught the children . . . ?'

'What do you mean by a school?' Yedigei couldn't help laughing. 'He has his own two little boys and I have my two girls – that's the sum total of the school. The eldest are five and the youngest both three. At this age our children have nowhere to go – there's desert all around. He and his wife worked with the children, educated them. They are former teachers, after all. All the children do is learn to read, draw, write and count. That's all that goes on in the school.'

'What sort of songs did they sing?'

'Oh, children's songs. I can't remember.'

'What did he teach them? What did they write?'

'They learn their letters. And then some ordinary words.'

'For example?'

'I don't remember.'

'Well, there,' Hawkeye took out from among some papers some sheets from exercise books covered with childish writing and scribbling. 'Here are these first words. On this sheet a child has written, "Our home." But why not, "Our victory"? Think. What surely should be the first words on a child's lips today? They should be "Our victory", isn't that so? But for some reason that didn't enter his head. Victory and Stalin are indivisible.'

Yedigei felt confused, humiliated by all of this, and above all, sorry for Abutalip and Zaripa, who had put so much effort and time into working with the children – children who could not yet understand such things. He dared to say, 'If that's so, then first they should write "Our Lenin". After all, it's Lenin who should take first place.'

Hawkeye gaped at this unexpected reply and choked on his cigarette. Then he got up, clearly needing to stretch his legs, but there was no room in the tiny office.

'When we say "Stalin", that *includes* Lenin,' he said sharply and in a ringing tone. Then he breathed more easily, and added, in a more conciliatory tone, 'Good, then we'll consider that this discussion did not take place between us.'

He sat down and, once more on his inscrutable face, his unworried bright eyes gleamed like those of a gyrfalcon.

'We have information that Kuttybaev spoke out against teaching children in boarding schools. What have you to say about that – were you present on that occasion?'

'Where did you get that information? Who told you?' Yedigei was astonished, but he guessed at once that it had been Abilov, the chief of the junction, who was to blame for all of this; he had repeated this because such a conversation had taken place when he had been there. But Yedigei's question really riled Hawkeye.

'Listen, I've already told you – where we get our information, what sort of information, that's our affair. We don't have to account for it to any Tom, Dick or Harry. Make an effort to remember. Tell me, what did he say?'

'What did he say? I'll try to remember. Well, the son of our oldest worker at the junction here – Kazangap, that is – is being educated at the boarding school at Kumbel'. That lad, it's clear, misbehaves there and even tells lies. On 1st September his father was taking him back to school on the camel. His mother – that's Kazangap's wife Bukei – began to cry and complain, "It's a shame – since he's been to boarding school, he's become kind of estranged. He's no longer tied heart and soul to his home, his father and mother, as he was before." Well, that's an uneducated woman talking. Of course, their son has to get his education, but he's always away from home . . .'

'So far, so good,' broke in Hawkeye. 'But what did Kuttybaev have to say about that?'

'He was also there with us all. He said that the boy's mother felt in her heart that something was wrong. He had to be at the boarding school on account of the difficulties of our life here. The boarding school sort of took away, well, separated the child from his family, father and mother. He went on to say that it was a very difficult question, but what could you do in the absence of other arrangements? I understood what he was getting at. Our children are also growing up. Our souls are pained – how will things work out, what will come from this parting? Of course it's bad.'

'We can come back to that later,' Hawkeye interrupted him. 'So he said that the Soviet boarding school was a bad thing?'

'He didn't say "Soviet". He simply said "boarding school". Ours is in Kumbel'. It was I who said the word "bad".'

'That's not important. Kumbel' is in the Soviet Union.'

'What do you mean, it's "not important"?' Yedigei was furious; he felt that the other man was trying to trick him. 'Why write down something that this man didn't say? I think the same as he does. If I lived elsewhere and not at this junction, I wouldn't send my children to any boarding school at any price. There it is – that's how I feel. What do you say to that?'

'Think, think!' Hawkeye started to speak again, trying to stop the discussion. Then, after a short silence, he said, 'Well, it seems we can reach some conclusions. So he's against collective education – that's so, isn't it?'

'He's against no such thing!' Yedigei could not stand this. 'How can you say that? It just doesn't follow?'

'Don't worry – forget it!' Hawkeye waved his hand as if to brush the matter aside, judging it unnecessary to explain. 'Now, tell me, what is this book called "The Donenbai Bird"? Kuttybaev said that he'd written it down from the words of Kazangap and also partly from what you had told him. Is that so?'

'Yes.' Yedigei revived. 'There's a story, a legend here in the Sarozek. Not far away from here there's a Naiman cemetery. Once it was for the Naiman tribe only, but now it's used by everyone. We call it Ana-Beiit. Naiman-Ana was buried there – she was killed by her own *mankurt* son.'

'That's enough about that; let's read this and see what's hidden here behind this bird,' said Hawkeye, and began to flip over the pages, once more thinking aloud and expanding on his views. 'The bird Donenbai, hmm. Can't you think of anything better? A bird with a man's name. So I've unearthed a new writer. A new Mukhtav Auzov has appeared on the scene – think of it, a writer of ancient legends. The Donenbai bird, hmm . . . He thinks that we won't bother to look into this. And he does this writing silently, secretively, for his children. And this? Do you think this is also for the children?'

Hawkeye held up to Yedigei's face yet another book, bound in oil cloth.

'What's this?' Yedigei was puzzled.

'What is it? You should know. It's called "The Words Of Raimaly-Aga To His Brother Abdil'khan.'

'Oh, yes, indeed; that's another legend,' Yedigei began. 'It's an old story. The old people know it well.'

'Don't worry, I know also,' interrupted Hawkeye, 'I've heard it, too. An old man, out of his mind, falls in love with a young girl of nineteen. What's good about that? This Kutty-baev is not only a hostile type; it appears he's also morally depraved. See how he worked away, writing down all this muck in lurid detail.'

Yedigei blushed, not from shame or embarrassment, but because his soul was filled with rage. Such an injustice to Abutalip could not be tolerated. So he said, scarcely controlling himself, 'You . . . I don't know what post you hold, what you're in charge of, but let's get one thing straight and understood. The Kuttybaevs are lucky to have such a father, such a husband, and here anyone will tell you the sort of man he is. You can count all of us here on your fingers, and we all know each other through and through.'

'All right, all right, calm yourself!' said Hawkeye. 'I can see he's addled all your brains here properly. The enemy always pretends to be something else. But we will expose him. That's all. You're free to go.'

Yedigei stood up. As he put on his hat he felt confused. 'What will happen to him? What now? Will he be sent to prison because of this writing – just for that?'

Hawkeye got up quickly from his chair. 'Listen, I'll repeat – it's none of your business! We know how to deal with this sort of thing – how to sniff out an enemy, how to treat him, how to punish him. Don't give yourself a headache over this! Keep to your own affairs! Off you go!'

That same day, late in the evening, a passenger train stopped once more at Boranly-Burannyi junction. Only this time the train was going in the opposite direction. It did not stop for long. Three minutes. Once more the three men in chrome leather boots were standing there by No. 1 track; they were taking Abutalip Kuttybaev away with them.

There also, standing on one side and separated from Abutalip by the backs of the three officials, stood the people of Boranly – Zaripa with the little boys, Yedigei and Ukubala, and the chief at the junction, Abilov, who was walking up and down, fussing about stupid little things, because the train was half an hour behind time. What good was he doing there? thought Yedigei. He could have been standing quietly by himself. Besides, Kazangap, who had also been put through an interrogation about the unlucky legends found in Abutalip's home, was at the points lever. This meant that he, with his own hands, would have to despatch the train on which they were taking Abutalip away, far away from the Sarozek. Bukei had stayed at home with Yedigei's little girls.

The three men in their boots, with their collars raised against the wind, keeping Abutalip apart from his own people with their backs, were stolidly silent. The people of Boranly, who had gathered to say goodbye to him, were equally silent. The wind swept through the place. It chased the snowy air across the ground with a rustling sound and a scarcely audible whistle. It looked as if a blizzard was on its way. The cold mist swelled and strained up in the impenetrable Sarozek sky, wildly, dully and emptily. The moon hardly shone through it, it was just a single, faded spot of light. The frost stung the people's cheeks.

Zaripa was weeping quietly; she held in her hands a bag with food and clothes which she intended to give to her husband. The heavy sighs of Ukubala were revealed in the clouds of mist which came from her mouth. Under her coat she was shielding Daul. Daul seemed to have an idea that something was wrong; he was quiet but worried as he clung to his Auntie Ukubala. But most of the trouble was with Ermek, whom Yedigei was holding in his arms, protecting him from the wind with his body. Ermek did not suspect a thing.

'Papika! Papika!' he called to his father, 'Come over here with us. We're going with you.'

Abutalip started at the sound of the voice; he could not help it. He turned to say something, but they did not even let him look around. One of the three shouted, 'Don't stand here! Do you hear? Go away now; later on, you can come up here.'

Now, in the distance, the lights of the engine came into view. Everyone moved a bit and started to walk. Zaripa could not stand it and sobbed more loudly than ever. Ukubala wept with her, for the train was bringing closer the moment of parting. With its headlight piercing through the thick, frosty, swirling mist, it came on, a dark, threatening, clattering mass. As it approached, the blazing headlight and the other lights seemed to rise higher above the ground; the snowy air above the rails became more visible in the beams, and the heavy noise of the cranks and pistons grew louder. Now the outline of the engine was visible.

'Papika! Papika! Look, the train's coming!' Ermek was shouting – then he too became silent, surprised that his father did not answer. Once more he tried again to attract his attention. 'Papika! Papika!'

The chief of the junction, Abilov, fussing around nearby, came up to the three men. 'The Post Office van will be at the front. Please come along, I beg you. There it is!'

Everyone followed in the direction he indicated, moving at a brisk pace, for the engine had already gone past. In front of the party, not looking round, walked Hawkeye with his briefcase, and a little behind him, went his two broad-shouldered assistants, escorting Abutalip. A little way behind them hurried Zaripa, then Ukubala holding Daul by the hand. To the side and a little further back was Yedigei, with Ermek in his arms. While they walked, he fought back his tears, for he could not break down in front of the women and children. Desperately he tried to swallow the lump rising in his throat.

'You're a good boy, Ermek. You're clever, aren't you? Then don't cry – all right?' He blurted out the words, hugging the boy close.

The train meanwhile was slowing to a halt. The boy in Yedigei's arms had shivered with fright when it had come level with them, and had jumped as the train gave out steam with a sudden hiss. Now there was a piercing whistle from the guard.

'Don't be frightened, don't be scared!' Yedigei said. 'There's no need to be scared while I'm with you. I'll always be with you!'

The train stopped with a long, heavy screeching, the waggons rusty from the frost and snow, windows blind with their covering of ice. At last it was at a standstill, and all was quiet. Then suddenly the engine let out a great hiss of steam as it prepared for departure. The postal waggon was behind the engine, after the luggage van, its windows covered with mesh. The double doors in the middle opened from the inside and a man and a woman peered out, wearing post office caps, thick padded trousers and warm jackets. The woman, who carried a torch, was clearly in charge. She was heavily built and full breasted.

'It's you, then,' she said, holding the torch high above her head so that she lit up everyone around. 'We're expecting you. The place is ready.'

Hawkeye with his large briefcase was the first to get aboard. 'Come on, come on, don't waste time!' The other two men hurried after him.

'I'll soon be back. There's been a misunderstanding,' said Abutalip rapidly. 'I'll be back, you wait and see!'

Ukubala could not stand it. She wept loudly as Abutalip began to say goodbye to the children. He hugged them with all his strength and kissed them, saying something to them; they were frightened, not understanding at all. The engine already had steam up. All this took place by the light of the torch. Once more there ran along the train the penetrating, terrifying sound of the whistle.

'Come on, come on! Get aboard and sit down!' The two men dragged Abutalip to the steps of the waggon.

Yedigei and Abutalip managed to have a final embrace, holding each other for a second, understanding with mind, heart and whole being as they pressed their wet, bristled cheeks together.

'Tell them about the sea!' Abutalip whispered.

Those were his last words. Yedigei knew what he meant. Their father was begging him to tell his sons about the Aral' Sea.

'That's enough! Come on! Come on now, get on board!'

They were pushed apart.

Shoving at him from behind with their shoulders, the two officials forced Abutalip into the waggon. Then and only then did the terrible reality of parting come to the understanding of the boys. At once they burst into tears, shouting together:

'Papika! Papa! Papika! Papa!'

Yedigei, with Ermek in his arms, leapt towards the waggon. 'Where're you going? Where are you going? God be with you!' Then the woman pushed him back, thrusting her torch into his chest and covering the entrance with her massive shoulders.

No one understood that, at that moment, Yedigei was ready, if that were possible, to go himself, in Abutalip's place. He was ready to strangle Hawkeye with his bare hands, so unbearably painful was it to hear the cries of Abutalip's two boys.

'Don't stand there! Go away! Stand back!' yelled the woman with the torch, and her breath, smoke-laden yet mingled with a smell of onions, struck Yedigei full in the face.

Then Zaripa remembered that she still had the bag in her hand.

'Here, give this to him, it's his food!' And she threw the bag into the waggon.

And then the doors of the waggon slammed shut and all went quiet. The engine sounded its whistle and moved off. Away it went, its wheels shrieking as they turned, slipping, and then the train slowly gathered speed in the frosty air.

The people of Boranly could not help following after the departing train, walking along beside the sealed waggon. Ukubala was first to come to her senses. She grasped hold of Zaripa and pressed her to her breast, holding her tight.

'Daul, stay here! Stay here and hold your Mama's hand!' She commanded this in a loud voice that sounded above the noise of the wheels accelerating and rushing past.

But Yedigei, with Ermek in his arms, still ran on beside the train, and only when the last waggon went past him did he stop. The train went on its way, the noise of its wheels fading and its lights slowly growing dim. The last, drawn out whistle of the departing engine sounded, and only then did Yedigei turn back. For a long time he could bring no comfort to the weeping boy.

They were back at home, sitting dumbly by the stove in the middle of the night when Yedigei remembered about Abilov. Quietly he got up and began to put on his coat. Ukubala guessed at once.

'Where are you off to?' She seized hold of her husband.

'Don't touch him, don't even lay a finger on him! His wife is expecting. In any case you haven't the right. How could you prove it?'

'Don't worry,' Yedigei answered calmly, 'I won't touch him. But he should realize that he'd best go away to some other place. I promise you, not a hair of his head will be harmed. Believe me!' He took his hand from hers and went out of the house.

The windows of the Abilovs' house were still lit up. So they, too, had not yet gone to bed. Crushing the snow down on the path, Yedigei came up to the cold door and knocked loudly. Abilov opened the door.

'Ah, Yedike, come in, come in,' he said, looking fearful and pale, and stepped aside to let the visitor in. Yedigei entered without a word, bringing with him clouds of frosty breath. He stopped and shut the door behind him.

'Why did you do it – making orphans of those unhappy children?' As he spoke the words, he had to make an effort to control himself.

Suddenly Abilov fell on his knees and literally crawled, clutching the hem of Yedigei's coat. 'Oh God, it wasn't me, Yedike! Otherwise may my wife not give birth to her child!' As he protested his innocence, he turned towards his alarmed pregnant wife. Then he spoke again, hurriedly, stammering. 'In God's name, it wasn't me, Yedike. How could I? It was that inspector! You remember he spent his time asking questions and then asking again about what he was writing and why? It was him – that inspector! How could *I* have done such a thing? Then may my wife not give birth to this child! And all that time by that train, I just didn't know where to go; I was ready to vanish, rather than see that! Then I remembered the inspector, with his discussions and questions about everything . . . How was I to know? If only I had known . . .'

'That's enough,' Yedigei interrupted. 'Get up and let's talk like human beings before your wife. May all be well with her! No doubt it's all the same to you where you are; but we will probably be here until we die. So you just think. You might be well advised to change to some other work. That's my advice.

199

That's all that I have to say. We won't speak of this again.'

And with that Yedigei went out of the house, shutting the door behind him.

CHAPTER NINE

On the Pacific Ocean, south of the Aleutians, it was long past midday. The storm still continued with no let-up, and everywhere the waves were sweeping on in foaming lines, one after the other, forming a boundless watery confusion as far as the eye could see. The aircraft carrier *Convention* was rolling lightly on the waves. It was still on its former station, at a point strictly equidistant from San Francisco and Vladivostok. All the services of the international scientific programme were on full alert.

At this time aboard the aircraft carrier, the extraordinary session of the special plenipotentiary commissions was in progress, investigating the situation which had arisen as a result of the discovery of the extraterrestrial civilization in the Derzhatel' system. The parity-cosmonauts 1-2 and 2-1, who had of their own volition abandoned their orbital station, were still on Lesnaya Grud', but had been warned three times by *Obtsenupr* not to take any action until they received further special instructions.

These categorical orders of *Obtsenupr* reflected in reality, not only the confusion of minds, but also the exceptionally complicated and strained situation on board *Convention*. The deepening disagreement between the two sides now threatened to bring about a complete breakdown of cooperation and, even worse, a full and direct confrontation. That which not long ago had brought the two leading powers together – the *Demiurgos* programme – had now receded into insignificance compared with the problems posed by the discovery of the extraterrestrial civilization. The members of the commissions clearly understood one thing – that this was a remarkable and incomparable discovery which represented a supreme challenge for world cooperation, for all that had been taught, all the culture that had been handed down, and for all that had been developed in the conscience of generations over the centuries.

Yet dare they take the risky step of establishing contact with an alien planet, and in so doing, perhaps endangering the security of the earth?

Here, once again, as always in critical moments of history, the root contradictions of the two social and political systems on earth were laid bare.

The consideration of the situation had led to heated debate. The differences in approach more and more took on the character of irreconcilable positions. Things were rapidly headed for a collision, towards a conflict, which, if it was allowed to escalate, might turn into a world war. Each side was therefore trying to hold back from the brink, to bear in mind the appalling danger of such a development. But an even greater restraining factor was the unimaginable consequences if the news of the discovery of an extraterrestrial civilization became a matter of public knowledge. No one could be sure what the result of such a development might be . . .

Common sense won. The two sides came to a compromise agreement – a necessary one, and on a strictly balanced basis. In connection with this compromise, an *Obtsenupr* coded message was sent to the *Parity* orbital station in the following terms:

To cosmonaut-controllers 1-2 and 2-1:
    You are required, without delay, to make radio contact with the aid of the *Parity* communications system with parity-cosmonauts 1-2 and 2-1, now in the so-called Derzhatel' system, on the planet Lesnaya Grud'. You must inform them immediately that, on the basis of an agreement between the two commissions who have been studying the information about the extraterrestrial civilization discovered by them, the *Obtsenupr* has come to the following irrevocable decisions:

    (*a*) Not to allow the return of former parity-cosmonauts 1-2 and 2-1 to the *Parity* orbital station, and still less to earth, as people not desirable for the world civilization.

(*b*) To inform the inhabitants of the planet Lesnaya Grud' of our refusal to enter into any form of contact with them, as being in conflict with the historical experience, the present interests and the particular stage of development of human society on earth.

(*c*) To warn the former parity-cosmonauts 1-2 and 2-1 and also those people of the other planet now in contact with them, that they should make no attempt to get into communication with the people of earth or, even less, enter the areas around the earth, as took place recently in the visit made by extraterrestrials to the *Parity* orbital station in its *Trampoline* orbit.

(*d*) To inform them that in order to isolate the space around the earth from possible incursions by vehicles originating from the other planet, *Obtsenupr* announces the setting up, as a matter of urgency, of an Extraordinary Transcosmic System, codenamed *Operation Hoop*, in which is programmed a series of standing patrols of automated military rockets assigned to certain orbits and intended to destroy by nuclear and laser radiation means any object approaching the earth from space.

(*e*) To bring to the attention of the former parity-cosmonauts, who of their own volition made contact with creatures from another planet, that no communication can be entered into with them. This is in the interests of security and in order to maintain the present stability of the geopolitical structure of the peoples of the earth. Later, all security measures will be taken to preserve the information about these events and about the measures taken to prevent any further contact. To this end, the orbit of the *Parity* station will very shortly be changed and the radio channels of the station will be recoded and reprogrammed.

(*f*) To warn the inhabitants of Lesnaya Grud' once again of the danger of approaching the *Operation Hoop* zones around the earth.

> *Obtsenupr*, aboard the aircraft carrier
> *Convention*

In taking these defensive measure, the *Obtsenupr* had to postpone indefinitely the whole *Demiurgos* programme of developing the planet Ex. The *Parity* orbital station parameters were changed and the station was employed instead on routine space observations. It was decided to hand over the cooperatively operated aircraft carrier *Convention* to the custody of neutral Finland. After the launch into distant space of the *Hoop* system, all parity-personnel were to be released after signing a most solemn undertaking to remain silent until their death about the reasons behind the change in activity of *Obtsenupr*.

For the benefit of the general public everywhere, it was proposed to announce that work on the *Demiurgos* project was to be suspended for an indefinite period, while radical investigations and adjustments of the programme on the planet Ex were carried out.

Everything was carefully worked out in detail; all of this would be done immediately after the extraordinary *Operation Hoop* had been set in train. Before this, and directly after the final session of the commissions, all documents, ciphers, and information concerning the former parity-cosmonauts, all reports, films and papers having any connection with this sad story, were destroyed.

On the Pacific Ocean, south of the Aleutians, the end of the day was approaching. The weather was still tolerable, but all the same the sea was getting rougher and the ship was pitching heavily in the swell.

The flight personnel on board the carrier were waiting for the moment when the members of the special commission came out of their conference and made their way up to the aircraft. Now they were leaving the conference room and taking their leave of each other. Some went to the first aircraft, others to the second one. In spite of the rolling motion of the ship, the take-offs passed without a hitch. One aircraft set course for San Francisco, the other for Vladivostok.

Washed by the upper winds, the earth continued along its appointed orbit. It was like a grain of sand in the immense eternity of the universe. There were very many such grains of sand in the whole of creation, but only upon the planet earth did people exist. They lived as best they could, as best as they knew how, and sometimes, when their curiosity was greatly aroused, they tried to find out if, somewhere, on other planets, there were beings like them. They argued, formed hypotheses, went to the moon and sent automated stations to other heavenly bodies. But each time they were bitterly disappointed to find that nowhere else in the solar system was there anyone or anything resembling them; indeed, there were no signs of other life. In the end they forgot about this quest; they had no time for it, and besides, it was by no means easy for them to succceed in living and agreeing among themselves; food also cost great effort to obtain. Many considered that the matter was none of their concern. The earth spun on along its appointed orbit.

The whole of that January was very frosty and misty. From where had so much cold come to the Sarozek? The trains went back and forth with frozen axle boxes, heated inside but all white and icy outside. It was strange to see the normally black tank cars which stopped on the siding white and completely covered in hoarfrost. It was so cold that the engines could barely get the trucks to move. Coupled in pairs, they tugged, jerked, literally tearing the wheels from the rails, to which the trucks had become frozen. These efforts of the engines could be heard in the thin air far around as a great noise of grating steel, which woke the Boranly children up at night.

It was now that the drifts began to form on the tracks. One merged into the other. In the Sarozek there was endless space for the winds to play in, and you could never tell which direction the next blizzard would come from. It seemed to the people of Boranly that the wind had the ability to drive snowdrifts on to the railway anywhere it chose. It just looked for a place through which it could blow in order to come down as a blizzard and cover the tracks with a heavy pile of snow.

All Yedigei, Kazangap and three other track workers knew was that as soon as they had cleared the snow from one end of the line it was time for them to go back and start all over again at the other. The camel-drawn rakes helped. The whole heavy upper layer of snow was dragged off the track and into the ditch by the rakes, but the rest had to be dealt with by hand. Yedigei put Karanar to work on this and he was glad of the chance to wear him out and to calm his tempestuous strength. He would harness him up with another camel to give the pull required and, urged on with the whip, they would take away the top of the drift with a transverse board, with a counter-weight behind. He stood on this board, pressing down on it with his own weight. There were no other devices or aids available at that time. People said that the factories were now turning out special snow-clearing machinery such as snow-ploughs on locomotives, which pushed the drifts to the side of the line. They were promised that these would be arriving soon, but for the present these promises remained unfulfilled.

That summer they had been subjected to two months of heat sufficient to drive them out of their minds; but now the frosty air was so cold it seemed as if their lungs would burst each time they breathed it. Yet still the trains were coming and going as usual and the job had to be done. Yedigei let his beard become bristly and that winter for the first time grey hairs appeared here and there. His eyes became swollen from lack of sleep, and in the mirror his face was an awful sight; it looked as if it were made of cast iron. He spent all his time in his short sheepskin coat, and on top of it he always wore a canvas cape with a hood, while on his feet were felt *valenki*.

Whatever Yedigei was doing, however hard he worked, he could not forget what had happened to Abutalip Kuttybaev. The thought was continually, painfully nagging away inside him. Often he and Kazangap would sit and wonder what had happened, and how it would end. Kazangap spent more and more time saying nothing, simply frowning and keeping his thoughts to himself.

Once he said, 'It's always the same. They're probably still considering the case. In the old days, they used to say with good reason, "The Khan's not a god. He doesn't always know what those around him are doing, and those around him don't know about those who are engaged in extortion in the bazaar." It's the same now.'

'Just listen to you! What a wise man you are!' Yedigei

scoffed, not at all pleased. 'They threw out the Khans long ago – it can't still be like that!'

'Then why did they take him? What's the reason?' Kazangap asked.

'The reason? The reason?' Yedigei said this with irritation, but had no answer to give. He continued walking around with this problem still in his head and still no sign of an answer.

It is well known that troubles never come singly. Daul, the elder of the two Kuttybaev boys, caught a severe chill. He ran a high temperature and became delirious. His cough was bad and he had a sore throat. Zaripa said that he had tonsilitis and treated him with various tablets, but she could not be with her children the whole time; she had her work on the points, and she had to live. She was on duty, sometimes at night, sometimes on the day shift. So Ukubala took over the job of looking after the boys, as well as her own two girls; she coped with this, for she knew what a desperate position the family were in. Yedigei also helped as best as he could. Early in the morning he brought in coal for them from the barn, and if there was time, lit the stove. There is a knack to starting a coal stove. He would put in a whole bucket and a half once it was going, and then the children would be warm for the whole day. He also brought them water from the tanker waggon on the siding, and chopped their kindling wood. It cost him little to do this. The real burden was emotional. It was impossible, an unbearable torture to look into the eyes of Abutalip's boys, to answer their questions. At this time the elder boy was lying there ill, and in any event he was also the more reserved of the two; but the younger, Ermek, was like his mother – lively, loving, very sensitive – and he had been deeply hurt by what had happened. When Yedigei brought in the coal in the morning and dealt with the stove, he tried hard not to wake up the boys. However, it was not often that he got away unnoticed. The curly, black-haired Ermek usually woke up at once, and his first question as soon as he opened his eyes was:

'Uncle Yedigei, will Papika come back today?'

The little boy ran up to him, still in his nightclothes, barefoot and with unconquerable hope in his eyes. What would

Yedigei have given to see Abutalip back home with them again! He cuddled the thin, warm, little body and put the boy back into his bed, then talked with him as if he were grown-up.

'I don't know, Ermek, if your Papika will come today or not; but they will have to let us know the time and the train number from the station. You know yourself that passenger trains do not stop here. They can only do so on the instructions of the Chief Traffic Superintendent of the line. I think that they should radio any day now. Then we'll go, together with Daul, if he's better, and meet the train and your father.'

'We'll say, "Papika, here we are!" – just like that, won't we?' said Ermek, embellishing the grown-up's imagined scene.

'Of course! We'll say that!' Yedigei agreed cheerfully.

But it was not easy to persuade the little lad for long. 'Uncle Yedigei, let's do as we did last time. We'll get aboard a goods train and go together to see this Chief Traffic Superintendent of the line. And we'll tell him to stop Papika's train right here!'

Yedigei had a hard time getting out of that one.

'But it was summer then and it was warm. How could you travel on a goods train now? It's very cold and very draughty. You can see how the windows are covered with hoarfrost. We wouldn't get there, we'd freeze like pieces of ice. No, that'd be very dangerous.'

The boy was downcast and had nothing to say.

'You lie there and I'll go over and take a look at Daul.'

With a sigh of relief, Yedigei went over to the sick boy's bed and laid his heavy, gnarled hand on the boy's forehead. The boy opened his eyes with difficulty, smiling weakly, his lips caked from the fever, which was still raging.

'Don't throw off your bedclothes – you're sweating. Do you hear me, Daul? You could get even more of a chill. You, Ermek, bring him the pot when he wants to pee, then he won't have to get out of bed to do it. You've heard what I've said? Soon your Mama will be home from her duty, and Auntie Ukubala will come soon to give you something to eat. When Daul's better, you'll come to our house to play with Saule and Sharapat. Now I must be off to work. There's so much snow,

208

it might stop the trains!' Yedigei said this as he was about to leave. But Ermek was not to be appeased.

'Uncle Yedigei,' he said, as Yedigei reached the door. 'If there's a lot of snow when Papika's train is coming, I'll come and help to clear the snow too. I've got a little spade.'

Yedigei left them with a heavy, aching heart. He was burning with resentment, a feeling of helplessness and pity. Furious with everything, he took it out on the snow, the wind, the drifts and the camels, which he drove pitilessly. He himself worked like an animal, as if he, on his own, could halt the Sarozek blizzards.

The days went past like raindrops falling relentlessly, one after the other. January was over now, and the cold was beginning to give way a little. Still there was no news of Abutalip Kuttybaev. Yedigei and Kazangap were now at a loss to know what had become of him, but imagined all kinds of things as they went over the case again and again. Both thought that the authorities would soon let him go – after all, what was so terrible about writing for oneself, for one's own children? They had such firm hopes and they did their best to pass on their confidence to Zaripa, so that she would find strength and not give way. She had to keep firm for the sake of the children. She had in fact become very hard by now; she kept quiet and her lips were closed, and only her bright eyes showed her worry. Who knew how much self-control she had? It was at this time that Burannyi Yedigei decided to go out into the steppe to see how the camel herd was grazing and, chiefly, to find out how Karanar was behaving. Had he injured any of the other camels? Had he started the rut yet? It was due.

He went on skis, for it was not far to go, and came back in good time. First he meant to go and tell Kazangap that all was in order and that the animals had been grazing in the Fox's Tail Hollow; there was almost no snow there, for the wind blew through it, carrying it on and away, and so the grass was uncovered; they had no need to worry. Yedigei decided to go home first to leave his skis.

His elder daughter, Saule, looked out of the door as he

approached and she was clearly alarmed. 'Papa, Mama is crying!'

Yedigei threw down the skis and, worried, went straight into the house and found Ukubala wailing loudly.

'What's up? What's happened?'

'May everything be damned in this damned world!' Ukubala lamented, swallowing as she wept.

Yedigei had never seen his wife in such a state before. Ukubala was normally a strong, level-headed woman.

'You're to blame for this, it's your fault, everything!'

'For what? For what am I to blame?' Yedigei was astounded.

'For what you said to those unhappy children. Not long ago a passenger train stopped here – the one coming the other way had priority, so the passenger train stopped to let it go through. God knows why they had to meet at our junction. Anyway, both of Abutalip's boys saw that the passenger train was standing there, so off they rushed, shouting, "Papa! Papika! Papika has come home!" And there they were, running towards the train with me chasing after them. They were running from carriage to carriage and shouting all the time, "Papa, Papika! Where's our Papika?" I thought they'd fall under the train. They ran right from one end to the other, calling for their father. Not one door opened. On they ran. The whole length of the train. How they ran! And before I caught up with them and got hold of the younger one, before I'd taken hold of the elder one's hand, the train started to pull out. They broke away from me. "Our Papika is in there, he didn't manage to get off the train!" And what a wailing they set up then! My heart went numb. I thought I'd go mad, they were shouting and crying so much. Ermek's in a dreadful state. Go and calm the child down. *Go!* It's you who told them that their father would return when a passenger train stopped here. If you'd only seen what happened to them when the train left and their father hadn't appeared! If only you'd seen! Why are things so ordered in this life? *Why* must a father be so terribly attached to his children and the children to their father? Why is there so much suffering?'

Yedigei went off to see them, as if he was going to his own

execution. He prayed that God would grant one thing – that He would be merciful and forgive him before punishing him for this unwitting deception of those trusting little souls. Naturally the last thing he had wanted was to harm them. But what would he say? What answer would he give to their questions?

As he appeared, Ermek and Daul, their faces all tear-stained and so swollen that they could hardly be recognized, ran up to him with cries, choking with their tears; sobbing, crying, they tried to tell him, one out-shouting the other, how a train had stopped at the junction, how their father had not managed to get out, and how he, Uncle Yedigei, must arrange for the train to be stopped . . .

'We miss him so, we've been so worried about Papika!' Ermek was yelling, begging him for help with all the trust, hope and grief he could muster.

'I'll find out everything. Quieten down, quiet, don't cry . . .'

Yedigei tried to bring some reason back, somehow to calm the boys, so overwhelmed with their crying. But it required all his strength not to give way or to reveal his own despair. He was determined not to let the children see his own weakness and helplessness.

'Now, we'll go . . . we'll go . . .' (*Where shall we go? Where? To whom? What shall we do?*' he was thinking.) 'We'll go outside and talk it over.' Yedigei promised nothing definite; he was merely saying something for the sake of it.

First, however, he went in to see Zaripa, who was lying on her bed with her face buried in her pillow.

'Zaripa, Zaripa!' Yedigei touched her shoulder. But she did not even lift her head. 'We're going out for a walk, wander around for a bit and then we'll go back to our house.' Then he added, 'I'm taking the boys.'

It was all he could think of to calm them, to distract them, and give himself time to think things over. He lifted Ermek up on to his back and took Daul's hand, and they walked off aimlessly along the railway track.

Never before had Burannyi Yedigei experienced such a heavy burden of suffering and misfortune. Ermek was sitting up on his back, still sobbing and breathing heavily and damply on to the back of Yedigei's head. Pained and grief-stricken beyond measure, he clung so trustingly to him that Yedigei was ready to shout to high heaven with pain and pity for him.

So they walked along the railway line, amid the Sarozek desert, while the trains thundered past in both directions. Once more Yedigei had to tell the boys an untruth. He told them that they had been mistaken. That the train which had stopped was going in the wrong direction and had only stopped by chance. Their Papika would come from the other direction. But he would not be coming back soon. It seemed that he had been sent as a sailor on some voyage and would not return until his ship came home. Meanwhile they would have to wait. In his view this should help them to hold on until the untruth was overtaken by the truth. For Yedigei did not doubt for one moment that Abutalip Kuttybaev would come back. Time would pass, the affair would be reviewed and he would return the moment he was freed. A father who loved his children as much as Abutalip did would not delay for one second. So Yedigei told this untruth.

Knowing Abutalip as well as he did, Yedigei could imagine what the break from his family meant to him. Another man might not suffer so much or so deeply from the temporary parting; his own strength of character, and the hope that he would soon be back, would see him through. But for Abutalip, Yedigei had no doubt that this break was much the worst punishment he could suffer. Yedigei was frightened for him. Would he hold out? Would he be able to wait while the matter was being reviewed?

Meanwhile Zaripa had by that time written several letters to the 'appropriate authorities', asking about her husband and if she could visit him. So far, no reply had been received. Kazangap and Yedigei racked their brains for an explanation. They were inclined to believe that the delay had been caused by the fact that Boranly-Burannyi did not have a direct postal service. Letters had to be sent either by giving them to someone to take, or by going to Kumbel' yourself. Similarly, letters coming to the junction had to be brought by hand from

Kumbel'. It was obvious that it was not the quickest method of communication. Maybe that was what had been happening in this case.

In the last days of February Kazangap went to Kumbel' to visit his son, Sabitzhan, at the boarding school. He rode there on his camel, as in winter it was too cold to go there on a passing goods train. You were not allowed to go inside the waggon, and out on the open platform the cold was unbearable. But on a camel, if you were well and warmly wrapped up, and went at a fair pace, you could be there and back in the day and still have time for any business in the town.

Kazangap returned that same evening, and as he dismounted, Yedigei noticed that he looked worried. He thought that perhaps his son had been misbehaving at the school and in any case he would be tired after his ride to the town and back.

'What sort of a ride did you have?' he asked.

'All right,' answered Kazangap matter-of-factly as he busied himself with his load. Then he turned round and after a pause for thought, said, 'Are you going to be at home tonight?'

'I will be.'

'I've something to talk to you about. I'll drop in in a few minutes.'

'Come along as soon as you're ready.'

Kazangap wasted little time. He came together with Bukei. He walked in front, his wife behind. He looked tired, his neck seemed longer, his shoulders were drooping, and so was his moustache. The plump Bukei was breathing heavily.

'You two look as though you've been quarrelling – you haven't, have you?' Ukubala was joking. 'Have you come to make it up? Please sit down.'

'If only we had just been quarrelling,' Bukei blurted out, in between puffs.

Kazangap looked around and asked, 'Where are your little girls?'

'They're over at Zaripa's, playing with the boys,' answered Yedigei. 'Why do you ask?'

'I have some very bad news for you,' said Kazangap, looking

213

at Yedigei and Ukubala. 'The children should not be told yet. There's been a real tragedy. Our Abutalip is dead!'

'What are you saying?' Yedigei had jumped to his feet. Ukubala gave a sharp cry, and then, putting her hand over her mouth, went white as a limed wall.

'He's dead? *Dead!* Those unhappy children, unhappy orphans!' Bukei lamented, half-croaking, half-whispering.

'How did he die?' Yedigei went fearfully up to Kazangap, still unable to believe what he had heard.

'A paper has come to the station.'

Everyone went quiet, not looking at each other.

'How terrible! How awful!' Ukubala clasped her head and groaned, rocking from side to side.

'Where is this paper?' Yedigei asked at last.

'It's still there at the station.' Then Kazangap began to tell what had happened.

'I'd been at the school, and suddenly I thought I'd drop in to the shop in the station waiting-room to get some soap Bukei had asked me to buy. I'd just reached the door when the station master, Chernov, came out to meet me. We greeted each other – we've known one another for years – and then he said to me, "It's lucky that I ran into you. Come to my office. There's a letter for you to take back to the junction with you." He opened his office door and we went inside. He picked up an envelope from the table, with the address typed on it. He said, "Abutalip Kuttybaev used to work at the junction with you, didn't he?" "Yes," I answered. "What's all this about?" "We've had this paper here for three days and there's been no one to take it on to Boranly-Burannyi. Here it is – give it to his wife. It gives the answer to her questions . . . He's dead . . . It's written down here" – and he said a word I didn't understand: "From an infarct." "What's an infarct?" I asked. He answered, "It's a sort of heart failure. His heart just gave way." I just sat there. I was so overwhelmed, I didn't believe it at first. I picked up the piece of paper, and on it was written, *"To the Station Master, Kumbel'. Please forward to Boranly-Burannyi – in answer to Citizeness So-and-so . . ."* And it went on to say that Abutalip Kuttybaev, under investigation, had

214

died of a heart attack. That's what it said. I read it through to the end, looked at him and didn't know what to say or do. "So there it is," said Chernov, and waved his hands in the air, "take it and give it to her." I said, "No, we don't do things that way. I've no wish to be the bearer of bad news. His children are little, how can I crush them with this? No!" I said. "We at Boranly-Burannyi will first of all discuss the matter and then we'll decide. One of us will come especially to fetch this paper, as is suitable for such terrible news. It's not a sparrow that's perished, but a human being. Most likely his wife, Zaripa Kuttybaeva, will wish to come herself and receive it from your hands. You can then explain and tell her what has happened." He said to me, "It's your affair how you arrange it. But what can I explain? I don't know any more details than you do. My duty is to hand over this paper to someone, and that's all."

' "Well then," I said, "excuse me, but let the paper stay here and I'll tell the others and we'll decide what to do." "You know best." So I left and all the way back, I've been urging on the camel, and my heart aches. What can we do? Which of us has the heart to tell them this?'

Kazangap was silent. Yedigei was bent double, as if he were carrying a mountain on his shoulders.

'What will happen now?' Kazangap put the question, but no one answered him.

'I knew this would happen.' Yedigei slowly shook his head. 'He couldn't stand the parting from his children. It was exactly what I feared most of all. He just couldn't stand being parted from them. Longing is a terrible thing. Look how his children long for their father – you can hardly bear to look at them. If he'd been different . . . Supposing, let's say, he'd been tried for something – I don't know what – but he'd been tried. Well, he'd have sat there in jail for a year or two, or however long it had to be, and returned home. Abutalip had been a prisoner of war in Germany; he'd been in concentration camps. And it can't have been a picnic fighting with the partisans in a strange country, either. He hadn't given way then, he'd stood it out, because then he'd been on his own, he'd had no family. But this time they divided him from his own flesh and blood, from the most precious of his possessions, his children. That's why this tragedy happened.'

'I agree,' Kazangap exclaimed. 'Although I would never have believed that a man could die from being parted from his family – and certainly not he; he was young, clever and well-read. He could have waited, so I thought, while they investigated, and then they'd have released him. He wasn't in any way guilty. He understood, of course, but his heart couldn't stand it. He loved his children so very much that it cost him his life.'

Then they all sat for a long while, considering the situation, trying to think how to prepare Zaripa for the news, but however much they thought or tried to foresee, it all came back to the one fact: the family had lost their father, and now the children were orphans and Zaripa was a widow. You could neither add nor take away anything from that.

Ukubala made the most reasonable suggestion. 'Let Zaripa receive the paper herself, at the station. Let her receive the blow there, and not in front of her children. Let her decide – either there at the station or on the way back, while there's time to consider everything – whether she wants to tell the children then or perhaps wait until later. Perhaps she'll decide to wait a bit, let them grow a little older, forget their father a little. It's hard to say what's for the best.'

'You're right,' Yedigei supported her view, 'she's their mother, let her decide whether she'll tell the boys about Abutalip's death now or later. Myself, I could not . . .' Yedigei could say no more, for just then he seemed to lose control of his tongue and had to cough so as to clear the lump from his throat.

When they had agreed generally on this, Ukubala added some more advice.

'Kazake, you should tell Zaripa that there's a letter awaiting her at the station, in the office there. Tell her that some answers have come to her enquiries, but they've asked her to go there herself, that it's essential. Another thing: Zaripa shouldn't go there on her own on such a day. They have no

216

close friends or relations here. And the worst thing in grief is to be alone. You, Yedigei, go with her, be at her side at this time. Anything might happen at such a tragic time. Say you've got to go to the station too, suggest you travel together. The children can stay here with us in the house.'

'That's a good idea,' agreed Yedigei. 'Tomorrow I'll tell Abilov that we have to take Zaripa to the station hospital. Let him stop a passing train for a minute.'

So they decided, but it was not until two days later that it was possible to stop a train on the junction chief's order. It was the 5th March, a day that Burannyi Yedigei would always remember.

They travelled in an uncompartmented coach. There were many people on board, families with children, loaded down with all the things needed for a journey. People passed to and fro continually, and there was a constant buzz of conversation as women talked in half-whispers to each other about the difficulties of life; drunken husbands, divorce, marriages and funerals . . . These people were travelling a long way and seemed to have brought all their possessions along with them. They had their own troubles and grief, to which were added, for a short time, those of Zaripa and Yedigei.

Zaripa, of course, was not at all well. She was quiet, worried, saying not a word the whole way, no doubt wondering about the sort of answers that were awaiting her at the station master's office. Yedigei, too, was silent most of the time.

There are in this world compassionate, sensitive people who can notice at once when something is wrong with a person. When Zaripa got up and walked through the carriage to stand by the window at the end, an old Russian woman sitting opposite Yedigei, her once-blue eyes now dimmed by age, addressed him.

'What's wrong, my son? Is your wife ill?'

Yedigei jumped. 'She's not my wife, she's my sister, Mamasha. I'm taking her to the hospital.'

'I can see that something is worrying her, poor soul. And she is very thin, her eyes are dull through grief. No doubt she has some fear in her heart; perhaps she is afraid they'll diagnose some dreadful disease. Oh, what a life it is! You're hardly born, you've hardly seen the light of day before you have to start fending off the trials of this world! That's how it is. But God is merciful. She's still young, perhaps she'll pull through.' In some way she seemed to sense that there were stresses and sadness which were filling Zaripa more and more as they approached the station.

It was an hour and a half's journey to Kumbel'. The other people in the train were uninterested in the places through which they were passing that day. They just asked dully what the next stop was. And all around was the vast Sarozek, still covered in snow, a silent, endless kingdom of uninhabited space. But there were some first signs of the end of winter appearing. On the slopes, thawed outcrops appeared in places as bold patches; the ragged edges of ravines were showing through; there were other patches on the lower slopes, and everywhere the snow was beginning to disappear under the influence of the moist, warm wind coming in to the steppes with the arrival of March. However, there was still some snow hiding among the thick, low clouds, grey and watery-looking. Winter was still alive: the wet snow on the ground might be melting, but another blizzard could still come in again.

Yedigei stayed in his seat opposite the compassionate old woman, sometimes talking to her, sometimes looking through the window. But he left Zaripa alone. He thought that she should be on her own for a while; let her stay by the carriage window and think things over. Perhaps some inner premonition might tell her something. Perhaps she was remembering that journey at the start of autumn last year, when they had all set out together, both families, on a passing goods train to Kumbel' to fetch the melons. They had been very happy, and it had been an unforgettable day for the children. It hardly seemed any time ago. Then, Yedigei and Abutalip had sat by the open doors of the waggon in the breeze, and talked about all kinds of things; the children had been playing round them, watching the country going by, and the two wives, Zaripa and Ukubala, had been enjoying a heart-to-heart talk about domestic things. Then they had walked around the shops and the little square; they had been to the cinema and to the hairdresser. They had eaten ice cream. But the main tragi-comedy had been when even their combined efforts had failed to persuade Ermek to have his hair cut. For some reason he was afraid of the touch of the clippers upon his head. And Yedigei remembered how, at that moment, Abutalip had appeared in the doorway of the hairdresser's shop, and how his little son had rushed to him; how his father had picked him up and hugged him, as if instinctively protecting him from the hairdresser. Abutalip had said that they would have to pluck up courage and do the job the next time they came. They would wait. Ermechik with his curly black hair would grow up. Yet there he was now, with his hair still uncut since birth – and now he had no father . . .

Once more Burannyi Yedigei tried to understand why Abutalip Kuttybaev had died, and why he had not waited for his case to be fully investigated. Again he came to the same conclusion: that his pining for his children had torn his heart apart. The parting, the unimaginable strain of it, the sad realization that his sons, his purpose and meaning in life, were cut off from him, abandoned by Fate at a lonely junction in the uninhabited drought of the Sarozek – that was what had killed him.

Yedigei was still thinking about this as he sat on a seat in the little square opposite the station, awaiting Zaripa's return. They had arranged that he would be waiting for her on this seat while she went to see the letter and papers at the station master's office.

It was now midday and the weather was still bad. The low, cloudy sky had still not cleared. Now and again something would fall, sometimes snowflakes, sometimes raindrops. The wind blowing in from the steppe was damp, carrying with it the smell of the melting, stale snow. Yedigei felt chilled and uncomfortable. Usually he loved to be among the people in the bustle of the station – when he was not going far, and had nothing to worry about and could watch the trains, see how the passengers got out and walked quickly along the platform. But this time all this was of no interest to him. He was

219

amazed what bored, drab faces people had, how featureless, how unconcerned they looked, how tired and cut off from one another. Added to which, the radio music on the public address sounded as if it were suffering from a throaty cold, filling the whole station square with its monotonously flowing dull noise and adding to the general misery. What sort of music was this? What a programme! There weren't even the grand, pompous voices of the announcers! They were just serving up this music.

Already twenty minutes or more had passed since Zaripa had disappeared into the station building, and Yedigei was beginning to be worried. Although they had firmly agreed that he would be waiting for her on this seat, the very one where they had sat with Abutalip and the children, eating their ice cream, he decided to go and look for her, to see what was going on in there. At that moment he saw her at the door, and shivered involuntarily. She stood out among the crowd going in and out. She looked so detached from all around her. Her face was deathly pale and she was walking without looking where she was going, as if she were in a dream. She did not stumble against anyone or anything; it was as if nothing existed around her and she was walking out in the desert, holding her head straight and sorrowfully, her lips pressed tightly together. As she approached, Yedigei got up. She seemed to be walking towards him for a long time, again as if in a dream – it was very strange how aloof she looked as she slowly approached, eyes lowered. A whole eternity of long-drawn-out and unendurable waiting seemed to pass until she came up to him, holding in her hand that very piece of paper in the compact envelope with the typed address that Kazangap had described. And as she came close, she opened her lips and asked, 'You knew?'

He slowly bowed his head.

Zaripa sat down on the seat and covering her face with her hands, pressed them tightly to her head, as if it might cave in or fly to pieces. She wept bitterly, completely retreating into herself, into her pain and her loss. And as she cried, she formed herself into a tortured, shaking huddle, falling deeper and deeper into herself, into her immeasurable suffering.

Meanwhile Yedigei sat there beside her. He would have been more than ready, as he had been when they had taken Abutalip away, to take Abutalip's place and accept his sufferings – anything, if only he could free this woman from the pain which she now suffered. And yet he knew that there was no way in which he could console or comfort her until the first over-whelming wave of the tragedy had receded.

So they sat there on the seat in the square in front of the station. Zaripa was sobbing feverishly now, and at one point, without looking, pushed away the crumpled envelope with its wretched bit of paper inside. Who needed that paper now that he was no longer living? But Yedigei picked up the envelope and put it into his pocket. Then he got out his handerchief and, forcibly opening her fingers, made the weeping Zaripa take the handkerchief and wipe away the tears. But this did not really help. The radio music played on all over the station, as if aware of Zaripa's bereavement, for it was mournful and exceedingly painful. The March sky, grey and deep, hung over their heads; the gusty wind wore out one's very soul. Yedigei was conscious of passers-by staring at them and probably thinking that they had had a violent quarrel. He had insulted her, no doubt. But it turned out that not everyone was thinking about them.

'Weep, good people, weep!' From nearby came the sound of a voice full of sorrow. 'We've lost our dearest father! What will happen now?'

Yedigei lifted his head and saw a woman walking by on crutches, dressed in an old uniform jacket. One of her legs had been amputated at the hip. He knew her by sight. She had served at the front and now worked as a clerk in the booking office. She had been weeping bitterly and, still weeping, walked on, repeating, 'Weep! Weep! What will happen now?' As she went on her way, to every two sounds of the crutches was added the scraping sound of the sole of her remaining foot, on which she wore an old soldier's boot.

The reason for her words at last got through to Yedigei when he noticed that people were gathering in front of the station entrance. Lifting their heads, they were watching some men

221

put up a ladder and set about hanging a large portrait of Stalin in military uniform, with a black mourning border around it, high above the door.

Now he understood why the radio music had been so mournful. At any other time, he would have got up too and joined the crowd of people, eager to find out what had happened to this great man, without whom no one could imagine the earth revolving on its axis. But for now he had grief enough of his own. He did not utter a word. Moreover Zaripa was not interested in anyone or anything else.

The trains, however, were running as usual, as they had to, whatever else might be happening on earth. In half an hour the long-distance train, No. 17, was due to arrive. Like all passenger trains, it did not normally stop at junctions such as Boranly-Burannyi. Its time-table did not permit it. This time, however, train No. 17 would indeed have to stop at Boranly-Burannyi. Yedigei had decided on this quite firmly and calmly.

He said to Zaripa, 'Zaripa, we must soon return home. There's only half an hour to wait before our train goes. You must now consider very carefully and thoroughly what you are to do. Will you tell the boys about their father's death now, or will you wait a while? I will not calm you or try to whisper advice. You are your own mistress. Now you'll have to be both father and mother to them. But you must think very hard about this while we're on the journey. If you decide not to tell the boys, then take yourself firmly in hand; you mustn't shed tears in front of them. Can you do that? Have you strength enough? And we must also know how we're to behave with them. That's the problem – do you understand?'

'It's all right, I understand everything,' answered Zaripa through her tears. 'While we're travelling, I'll collect my thoughts and tell you what we're going to do. I'll try and pull myself together. Now . . .'

On the return journey the train was the same: crowds of people, clouds of tobacco smoke, everybody still travelling, ploughing their way through the vast country from one end to the other.

Zaripa and Yedigei got into a compartmented carriage. Here

there were less people, and they sat down in the gangway, close to the window, so as not to get in anyone's way and to talk about their affairs. Yedigei was sitting on a tip-up seat in the corridor, while Zaripa stood beside him, looking through the window. He had offered her the seat, but she preferred to stand.

Although she still sobbed now and again as she grappled with the tragedy which had fallen on her shoulders, she tried to concentrate as she looked through the window, to consider her new life as a widow. Before, there had been a hope that one day all would come right again, like waking from a nightmare; that sooner or later Abutalip would return – that they would sort out this misunderstanding, and they would all be together again as a family. All would work out; they would find a way of living, however hard, and they would educate their sons. But now that hope had gone. She had plenty to think about . . .

Burannyi Yedigei was also thinking, for he could not stop worrying over the fate of this family. But he knew that now, more than ever, he had to be self-controlled and calm, and that only in this way could he give Zaripa some degree of confidence. He was not hurrying her. And he was right. Having shed her tears, it was she who began to talk.

'For the present I must keep from the boys the news that their father is dead.' Zaripa was speaking in a hesitating voice, still swallowing and driving back her tears. 'I cannot tell them now. Especially not Ermek . . . Why must these bonds be so close? It's frightening. How can I destroy their dreams? What will happen to them? They live only for the return of their father – they wait and wait from one day to the next, every minute . . . In due course we'll have to go away from here, have a change from this place. But I must let them grow a bit more. I am very fearful about Ermek. He'll certainly have to grow up a bit more . . . Then I'll tell them; perhaps by then they will have guessed a bit . . . But not now, I haven't the strength. Let me do what I can . . . I will write to the brothers and sisters, mine and his . . . Why should they be afraid of us now? They'll rise to the occasion, I hope, and will help us to move somewhere else . . . Then things will be clearer . . . Now, as he is no more, my only task is to bring up Abutalip's children . . .'

This was how she saw the situation. Burannyi Yedigei listened in silence, taking account of the thought behind each of her words, knowing of course that this was but a fraction of all the thoughts and emotions that whirled around within her. You cannot say everything on such an occasion. Trying not to widen the scope of their conversation, he said, 'I think that's the right decision, Zaripa . . . If I didn't know the boys, I might be doubtful. But in your place I would do what you propose. You must wait for a while. But while your relatives are considering, have no doubt about how we stand. As we have always done, so we will continue. You can work as before, the children will be together with ours. You know that Ukubala loves your boys as she does our own girls. The rest will become clear in time . . .'

With a deep sigh Zaripa added some more thoughts. 'That's how life is arranged, it seems. So frightening, so wise and all interdependent. The end, the beginning, the continuation . . . If it wasn't for the children, on my honour, Yedigei, I wouldn't go on living. I'd even go that far! Why should I live? But children give you a responsibility; they must be looked after, it is they who keep me from . . . doing that thing. In this is my salvation, and the continuation of life. It's a bitter fate, it's hard, but I must continue . . . It terrifies me to think not only how it will be when they learn the truth – you can never escape that – but about the sort of future which lies before us. What happened to their father will always be with them, like an open wound. When they go to school, at work, they'll have in some way to justify themselves in the eyes of society; with their name, they'll have no easy life . . . It seems to me that we have an immense barrier to cross. Abutalip and I avoided such talk. I spared him, and he me. I was sure with him that our children would grow up as people of worth. This thought protected us from destruction and difficulties. Now, I don't know . . . I cannot take his place for them, because he was just – himself. He used to do so much for them. He wanted, as it were, to transfer himself to them and become part of them. That is why he died – because they took him away from them.'

Yedigei listened attentively to Zaripa. These words were said to him as the person closest to her, and they roused in him the sincere wish, somehow to answer, to protect, to help; but the realization of his powerlessness depressed him, bringing out a dull, but hidden feeling of exasperation.

They were already approaching Boranly-Burannyi and were passing places which they knew, along the line where Burannyi Yedigei had worked for so many summers and so many winters.

He said to Zaripa, 'We're nearly there. Get ready. So we've decided to say nothing to the children for the present. It's good that we know that. You mustn't give yourself away. Now make yourself tidy and go to the end of the carriage. Stand by the door. As soon as the train stops, get out of the carriage calmly and wait for me. I'll get out and we'll go home together.'

'What do you plan to do?'

'Don't worry. Leave it to me. In any event, you have the right to leave the train.'

As always, passenger train No. 17 was scheduled to go through the junction without stopping; it would just slow down by the signal. But at this moment, just as the train entered Boranly-Burannyi, it suddenly braked with a squealing and a terrible grinding noise from the axle boxes. Everyone got up in alarm. There were shouts and whistles along the whole length of the train.

'What's happened?'

'Has someone pulled the emergency brake?'

'Who's done that?'

'Where?'

'In the compartmented coach!'

By that time Yedigei had opened the door for Zaripa and she had got down. He waited until the guard and conductor came to the end of the coach.

'Stop! Who operated the emergency brake?'

'I did,' said Yedigei.

'Who are you? Why did you pull it?'

'It had to be done.'

'What do you mean, it had to be done? What are you up to? Do you want to be charged?'

'There's nothing to worry about. Write in your report to the court, or wherever, that former soldier, now track worker, Yedigei Zhangel'din – here are my documents – operated the emergency brakes and stopped the train at Boranly-Burannyi junction as an expression of mourning on the day of the death of Comrade Stalin.'

'What's that? Is Stalin dead?'

'Yes, it's been announced on the radio. You should listen to it.'

'Well, that's a different matter.' The two men were taken aback and did not wish to detain Yedigei. 'Be on your way then.'

In a few minutes train No. 17 was on its way, continuing its journey.

And again the trains went from East to West, and from West to East.

And on either side of the railway lines in these parts there lay, the same as ever, the untouched spaces of the desert – the Sary-Ozeki, the Middle lands of the yellow steppes.

Cosmodrome Sary-Ozek-1 did not then exist, and there was no trace of it in the bounds of the desert. It is possible that it existed only in the minds of the future creators of space travel.

And the trains still went from East to West, and from West to East.

The summer and the autumn of 1953 were the hardest Burannyi Yedigei had ever known. Whether it was snowfalls on the line, Sarozek heat, lack of water, or other trials or tribulations, nothing, not even the war – and he had gone as far as Koenigsberg and could have been killed a thousand times over, wounded or crippled – nothing ever caused Yedigei as much suffering as those days of 1953.

Afanasii Ivanovich Yelizarov once explained to Burannyi Yedigei how landslides are caused – those inevitable movements when whole slopes collapse, or sometimes the whole side of a mountain falls away, leaving gaping chasms in the thick crust of the earth, and snatching away the ground from under our feet. The danger of landslides is that the catastrophe develops unnoticed, from day to day; underground waters gradually wash away the base of the subsoil, and then there has only to be a slight shaking of the earth, thunder or heavy rain, before the mountain begins slowly and relentlessly to flow downwards. An ordinary earth fall happens unexpectedly and suddenly. The landslide moves threateningly, and there is no force which can stop it. Something very much like this can happen with a man, when he is left on his own with his irresistible conflicts; he struggles, his soul so shattered that he cannot tell his trouble to anyone, because there is no one on earth in a position to either help or even understand him. He knows this, it frightens him. And this weighs down on him . . .

The first time that Yedigei felt within himself such a movement and clearly realized what this meant was two months after the journey with Zaripa to Kumbel'. He was going there again on business and he had promised Zaripa that he would look in at the post office to see if there were any letters for her; if not, then he was to send off three telegrams to three addresses which she had given him. Up until then she had not received one letter of reply from her relatives. Now she simply wanted to know if they had received her letters or not – she had written so in the text of the telegrams; it was an earnest request simply asking whether the letters had been received, yes or no. So far it appeared that the brothers and sisters did not even wish to be in correspondence with the family of Abutalip.

Yedigei set off on Burannyi Karanar in the morning, so as to be back by evening. Of course, normally when he went on his own without any packages, any driver known to him would gladly pick him up, and in an hour and a half he would be in Kumbel'. However, he had started to be wary of making such journeys on passenger trains, because of Abutalip's boys. Both of them, elder and younger, were still waiting, day after day, for the return of their father. In their games, talks, riddles and

227

in the pictures which they drew, in all aspects of their innocent childish life, the return of their father was the one theme, dominating all they thought and did. And there was no doubt that during this period Uncle Yedigei was the most important figure of authority for them, who, they were convinced, should know everything and be able to help them.

Yedigei himself knew that without him, the boys' life at the junction would be even harder and they would feel more helpless, so he tried to spend almost all his free time with them and thus take their minds off their vain expectations. Remembering the last wish of Abutalip that he should tell the boys about the sea, he spent his time recounting new details of his childhood and youth as a fisherman in all sorts of tales, true and legendary, about the Aral' Sea for the little lads. Each time he was astonished by the ability, brightness, impressionability and memory which they showed. And this pleased him greatly, for it showed the results of their father's teaching. When he was telling a story, Yedigei aimed it mostly at young Ermek. However, the boy was by no means behind his elder brother, and among all four of his listeners – the children from both houses – he was the closest to Yedigei, although Yedigei tried not to favour him. Ermek turned out to be the most interested listener and the best interpreter of his stories. Whatever the subject was, any event, any interesting turn in the story, and he at once related it to his father. His father was to be found in everything. For example, there would be such a conversation as this:

'. . . And by the Aral' Sea there are lakes and shores where the reeds grow very thickly, and in these reeds hide the wildfowlers with their guns. And the ducks come every spring to the Aral' Sea. In the winter they live in other, warmer countries; but as soon as the ice melts on the Aral' Sea, they fly back there as quickly as possible, travelling night and day, because they miss those places so much. They fly in a great flock, and after their long flight they like to swim, to dive into the water, and so they come down lower and lower towards the shoreline. Then suddenly there's a burst of smoke and flame from the reeds – *Bang! Bang!* That's the wildfowlers shooting.

The ducks are hit and fall into the water. Those not hit fly in fright to the middle of the sea and do not know what to do, where to live. They circle over the water, calling. They are used to swimming near the shore, but now they're afraid to approach it—'

'Uncle Yedigei, but didn't one duck fly back to the place she'd come from?'

'Why should she fly back there?'

'Because my Papika's a sailor there, he's there aboard a big ship. You told us that yourself, Uncle Yedigei.'

'Yes, so I did,' said Yedigei, realizing that he had put his foot in it again, 'so what happens next?'

'This duck comes and says to my Papika that the wildfowlers are hiding in the reeds and have shot at them and now they have nowhere to live.'

'Yes, yes. And?'

'And Papika says to that duck that he will be coming soon, that at the junction he has two boys, Daul and Ermek, and also Uncle Yedigei. And when he comes back, we'll all go together to the Aral' Sea and chase those wildfowlers who shot at the ducks out of the reeds. And once more everything will be all right for the ducks on the Aral' Sea. They'll swim and dive and wave their feet in the air . . .'

When they tired of stories, Burannyi Yedigei showed them fortune-telling with pebbles, for he always carried with him his forty-one pebbles, all about the size of a large pea. This most ancient way of telling fortunes has its own complicated symbolism and its ancient terms and language. The children watched attentively as Yedigei laid out the stones, spoke and adjured them to answer honestly and correctly; he asked if the man called Abutalip was alive, where was he and would there soon be a journey before him and what was the expression on his face and what thought was there in his heart. The children listened silently, following how the stones were positioned. Once Yedigei heard some shuffling and quiet talking round the corner. He looked round cautiously and saw that it was Abutalip's sons. Ermek was now consulting the stones himself. Laying them out as best he knew, he brought each pebble up

229

to his lips and said, '. . . And I love you. You're a wise, good pebble. Don't you make any mistake, don't stumble; tell honestly and directly, just like Uncle Yedigei's pebbles do.' Then he began to tell his elder brother the meaning of the cast he had made, exactly repeating what Yedigei had said. 'Look, Daul, the general picture isn't bad, not bad at all. This is a road. But the road's a bit foggy. There's a fog, but it's nothing. Uncle Yedigei says that there's never a journey without some such difficulties. Father is getting ready to come. He wants to sit in the saddle, but the girth is a bit loose. You see, the girth isn't tight enough, it must be tightened up a bit more. That means that something is still holding Father up, Daul. We must wait. Now let's look again. What's on the right rib and what's on the left? They're intact, that's good. And what's that on his forehead? He's worried about us, Daul. Look at this stone on the heart – there's pain and longing in his heart, he's missing our home very much. Will he come soon? Soon. But the shoe on one of the horse's back hooves is loose. That means it must be reshod. We'll have to wait a bit longer. What's in the saddlebags? Oh, in the saddlebags are things he's bought in the bazaar. And now, will the stars be in good positions? Look, this star is the Golden Halter and there are tracks from it, but not clear tracks – not yet. That means he must soon untie his horse and set off on his journey . . .'

Burannyi Yedigei went away unnoticed, touched, angry and surprised at all this, and from that day on he tried to avoid telling the future with his pebbles.

But children will be children. It was possible to console them in other ways, to give them hope and occasionally to lay to one's charge a sin and to deceive them from time to time. But now one more sorrowful thought had settled in Burannyi Yedigei's heart and soul. Perhaps given these events, it had to arise; and now it was like that landslide – it had at some time to start moving. Then he knew he would never be able to stop it.

He was continually worrying about her, about Zaripa. Although there was no conversation between them except about matters of everyday life, although she never gave him

230

any cause to do so, Yedigei was thinking about her all the time. But he did not simply feel sorry for her or sympathize with her as anyone and everyone would; he did not simply suffer with her because of all that he saw and knew about the trials which beset her – for that would have given no cause for concern or alarm. No – he thought about her with love, and with an inner readiness to become the person on whom she could depend in everything which concerned her life. And he would have been happy for her to know that – to know that he, Burannyi Yedigei, was the person most devoted to her and the person who loved her most in all the world.

It was torture to have to behave as if he felt nothing special about her, yet he knew that there could not and must not be anything between them.

All the way to Kumbel' he was preoccupied with these thoughts. He thought about the situation in various ways. He experienced a strange changeable state of mind; it was as though first he was expecting an imminent celebration, then an unavoidable illness. And in this state, he felt as if he was back on the sea again. At sea a man feels different, not like he does back on dry land, even if all is calm around and no storm is threatening. However freely, however delightful it sometimes is to wander over the waves, even if you are busy with necessary tasks on board ship, however beautiful the reflections of sunsets or sunrises on the smooth water, you still have to return to shore eventually – your own or another, but still to shore. You can never be at sea for ever. And ashore quite a different life awaits you. The sea is temporary, the dry land is permanent. If it frightens you to go ashore, then you must find an island, a place of your own, and there you must always remain. Burannyi began to imagine such an island and dream of taking Zaripa and the children to live there. He would get the boys used to the ways of the sea, and he would spend the rest of his life on this island in the middle of the sea, not bemoaning his fate, but being happy. All he wanted was to know that she would be there, and that he would be the only person whom she needed and wanted, the person most dear to her . . .

231

Then he became ashamed of himself for having such desires. He even began to blush, although for hundreds and hundreds of kilometres around there was not a single other soul. Like a small boy, he had let his dream take him over. He longed to go to that island, and he became quite lost in fantasies, he who had been tied hand and foot all his life, by his family, his children and his work, by the railway and finally by the Sarozek, to which he had got so accustomed without even noticing it. But did Zaripa need him, even if she was in such enormous difficulties? Why must he always have to think about himself, why did he have to be dear to her? As far as the boys were concerned, he had no doubts – he doted on them and they were very fond of him. But why should Zaripa want that? And had he the right to think thus, when life had set him down firmly in this one place where he would no doubt stay until the end of his days?

As Burannyi Karanar went along the track so familiar to him and which he had covered so often, he knew exactly how much of the journey was left to go and needed no prompting from his master. He was keeping up a fast pace, calling and breathing heavily as he ran, and covering the distance over the vast Sarozek rapidly, past the spring slopes, the hills, past a long-dried-up salt lake . . . But Yedigei was suffering. He was grieving, shut up within himself, filled with contradictory feelings. He could not settle, and his heart found no comfort in the vast space of the Sary-Ozeki. It was more than he could stand.

It was in this state of mind that he arrived at Kumbel'. Of course, he wanted Zaripa to receive at long last the answers from her relatives, but the thought that those same relatives might come and fetch the orphaned family and take them away to distant parts, or might write to tell them to come and join them there made Yedigei feel ill. Once again in the post office the clerk at the *poste restante* window said in answer to his question that there were no letters for Zaripa Kuttybaeva. Quite unexpectedly, Yedigei found he was glad. A bad, wild thought flashed through his mind, in spite of himself. 'How fine that there aren't any replies!' Then he conscientiously carried out her instructions and sent off the three telegrams. This done, he set off home and arrived towards evening.

Meanwhile spring gave way to summer, and the Sarozek became golden. The grass disappeared like a dream, and the yellow steppe was yellow once more. The air heated up and the hot season was daily coming closer. Still there was no word from the Kuttybaevs' relations. They answered neither letters nor the telegrams. The trains rattled on through Boranly-Burannyi, and life went on as always.

Zaripa no longer expected an answer; there was no point in counting on help from her relations, it was not worth burdening them any more with letters or calls for help. Convinced of this, she fell into a mood of silent despair. Where should she go, what should she do? How would she tell the children about their father? How would she rebuild her shattered life? As yet she had not found the answers to these questions.

Perhaps no less than Zaripa, Yedigei took all this to heart, as did all the people of Boranly. But Yedigei was especially close to her, as this family tragedy affected him personally. He could not stand apart from them. From one day to the next his fate was inextricably bound up with the fate of these boys and Zaripa. He was also in a state of intense apprehension about what would happen to them – and not only about what would happen to them, but also himself. How could he cope with himself, how could he stifle the voice inside him, calling him to her? He found no answer at all. He had never imagined that in the course of his life he would find himself in such a situation . . .

Many times Yedigei was on the verge of making a confession of his love to her; he yearned to tell her directly how he felt and to say that he was ready to take all her troubles on to his shoulders, that he could not imagine himself separated from her and the boys – but how was he to do this? Would she understand him? Surely it would be too much for her in her present state. Here she was, alone and facing all these troubles which had come down upon her head; and now here was he, crawling up to her expressing all these feelings! What help would this be? As he wrestled with the problem, he became gloomy and flustered, and he had to make no small effort to conceal his feelings when other people were around.

However, all the same, he did say something. He was returning from an inspection of the track when he noticed in the distance that Zaripa was taking her buckets to the water tanker. He had to go to her. And he went. Of course, it was a convenient excuse to offer to carry the buckets for her. But it was also more than that. Almost every other day, and often daily, they were working side by side on the tracks and they could talk together as much as they wanted. But at that particular moment Yedigei felt the need to go to her and to say that which was begging to be brought out into the open. In his passion, he thought this was the best way; even if she did not understand, even if she repulsed him, at least he would feel easier and his heart and soul would be calmer . . .

She did not see or hear him approach. She was standing with her back towards him, holding the tap on the tanker. One bucket was already filled and the second was under the tap and overflowing. The tap was turned fully on and the water was bubbling, splashing and flowing around in puddles, yet she seemed unaware of this as she stood there, depressed, leaning with her shoulder against the tanker. She was wearing that same cotton dress in which she had greeted the great downpour of rain last year.

Yedigei looked at the pigtails made from her curly hair, the hair at her temples and behind her ears – Ermek had got his curly hair from her; he saw her face, her thin neck, her drooping shoulders and her arm resting on her thigh. Was the sound of the water bewitching her, reminding her of the mountain streams and the irrigation ditches of the Seven Rivers? Or had she simply turned her thoughts inwards, distracted by those sad reflections? Only God knew.

But Yedigei had a tight feeling in his chest at the sight of her. All of her was eternally dear to him and he felt an urgent desire to caress her, to protect her, to defend her from everything which was oppressing her. But this could not be done. Instead he quietly turned the tap off, stopping the flow of water. She looked at him without surprise, but with a long, penetrating stare, as if he were not standing beside her at all, but somewhere a long way off.

'What's up? What's the matter?' he asked sympathetically.

She said nothing, just smiled at the corners of her mouth and vaguely raised her eyebrows above her bright eyes, as if to say: things aren't good, not good at all . . .

'Things are bad, are they?' Yedigei asked.

'Bad,' she admitted with a deep sigh.

Yedigei shrugged his shoulders in confusion. 'Why do you exhaust yourself like this?' There was pity in his tone, mingled with unintended reproach. 'How much can you bear? It doesn't help. It's hard for us' – he wanted to say 'for me' – 'to look at you, and it's hard for the children too. Do understand. There's no need to go on like this. You must do something.' As he said this, he tried to select the words he so much wanted, which he *had* to say to her; that it was he, more than anyone else in the world, who felt for her and loved her. 'Think about it. What if they don't answer your letters? Well then, God be with them – but we won't vanish. All of us here' – again, he wanted to say 'You and I' – 'are like one family. Only don't lose heart. Work, hold on. And the boys will grow up here amongst us. All will work out. Why should you go away? All of us here are one family. As you know, not a day goes by without my seeing your children.' And then he stopped, for he had said as much as he could.

'I understand all of that, Yedike,' answered Zaripa. 'And I'm grateful, of course. I know that we won't be abandoned in our plight. But we have to go away from here; so that the boys will forget everything that happened here. Then I will tell them the truth. You know, yourself, that this cannot continue . . . That's what I think we must do . . .'

'Yes, I suppose that's so,' Yedigei had to agree, 'only don't be in a hurry. Think a bit more. Where could you go with these little ones? And I'm afraid when I think how I'll manage here without you . . .'

And he really was fearful for them – for her and for the children. Because of this he tried not to look further than one day ahead. But he also understood that the present situation

235

could not go on much longer. A few days after this conversation, there was an occasion when he gave himself away completely, and he regretted it and suffered from it for a long time afterwards and was unable to excuse the way he behaved.

Many months had passed since that memorable day's journey to Kumbel' when Ermek had been scared of the hairdresser and had refused to let his hair be cut. In the meantime the boy had gone around with his hair untrimmed, and although the black curls were very nice, the obstinate little coward was now long overdue for a haircut. When he could, Yedigei would kiss the little lad's thick hair and breathe in the smell of his head. However, Ermek's hair was now nearly down to his shoulders and got in the way when he was playing and running. Yet, the need for the haircut was something the boy found hard to understand. He would give in to no one. In the end Kazangap, seeing the trouble, managed to persuade him. He even frightened the boy a bit by telling him that goats did not like people with long hair and butted them. So then it happened – and it was a tragedy on a global scale!

Later on, Zaripa described how the haircutting operation began and ended. They had not expected such fierce resistance. Ermek had begun to cry and struggle, and Kazangap had to employ strength. He held the boy firmly between his legs and got to work with the hair clippers. The wailing could be heard all over the junction. And when the job was completed, the kindly Bukei, hoping to calm down the boy, handed him a mirror and said, 'Look how nice you are!' The boy took one look, did not recognize himself, and yelled even louder. It was in this state, with Ermek yelling as loud as he could, that Yedigei met them as they returned home from Kazangap's house.

The completely shorn Ermek, quite unlike his former self, with a bare, thin neck, ears sticking out, and tear-stained face, immediately broke away from his mother and rushed over to Yedigei.

'Uncle Yedigei, look what they've done to me!'

If Burannyi Yedigei had been told beforehand what his reaction would be, he would never have believed it. He took hold of the boy in his arms and hugged him close, sharing in the disaster with his whole being, sharing the child's feeling of grief and betrayal just as if the tragedy had happened to him. He began kissing the boy and said, his voice breaking from anger and love, hardly realizing what he was saying, 'Calm down, my dearest one! Don't cry! I won't let anyone hurt you. I'll be like a father to you. I will love you like a father, only don't cry!' But as he looked across to Zaripa, who had already frozen on the spot, distraught, he was aware that he had crossed a forbidden line. Suddenly he became very confused; he hurried away from her, the boy still in his arms, mumbling the same words, but all mixed up now: 'Don't cry! I'll show that Kazangap! I'll show him!'

For several days after this incident, Yedigei avoided Zaripa. And he was aware that she avoided meeting him. He was deeply sorry that he had spoken so unwisely and had embarrassed the blameless young woman. She already had more than enough troubles and worries, and now how much more pain he had added! Yedigei could not forgive himself, or justify his behaviour. But at the same time, for many long years, perhaps to his last breath, he would remember that moment when he had felt with his whole being the hurt of that defenceless child, when his heart had been moved with love and rage. And he would also recall how, overwhelmed by this scene, Zaripa had looked at him with a silent cry on her lips and grief in her eyes.

After this incident, Burannyi Yedigei kept quiet for a time, and all the feelings that he had to hide within himself and stifle, he transferred to the children. He could find no other way. He looked after them whenever he was free and continued to tell them stories; often he had to repeat himself, but he also found that he was constantly remembering new details about the sea, their favourite subject. About gulls, about fishes, migrating birds, about the Aral' Islands on which there still survived rare animals which had disappeared elsewhere. In telling these things to the boys, Yedigei recalled more and more often and clearly his own life on the Aral' Sea – and in particular, one true story from it which he preferred not to tell to anyone else. This certainly was no tale for children. Only two people, he and Ukubala, knew it, and they never spoke about it, for it was concerned with their first-born son, who had died. If he had lived, he would now have been much older than the Boranly children – older even than Kazangap's Sabitzhan by two years. But he had not. Of course, people always await any child with the hope that he will be born safely and live long, very long; it is hard to imagine how otherwise they would bring children into the world.

During Yedigei's time as a fisherman, in their young years not long before the war, Ukubala and he experienced a remarkable incident, the kind of event that only happened once in a lifetime.

Ever since they had got married, all the time Yedigei was at sea, he always wanted to return home as quickly as possible. He knew that she would be waiting for him. He loved Ukubala. At this time there was no woman he desired more. And this desire to return home as quickly as possible filled him and occupied all his thoughts while he was away. It seemed to him sometimes that he existed in order to spend his whole time thinking about her, to collect and to store within himself the power and strength of the sea and the sun, and then to give himself to her, his waiting wife; because from this giving came their mutual happiness, the happiness in the very depths of his heart. Everything else outside merely added to and enriched this happiness, this mutual rapture which had been given to him by the sun and the sea. And when Ukubala had announced that something was happening inside her, that she had conceived and soon would be a mother, then to the constant waiting to meet again after he had been to sea was added the expectation of the arrival of their first-born to be. This was a cloudless time in their life.

Later that autumn, just before the winter set in, on Ukubala's face began to appear freckles, which could be seen if you looked closely. And already her belly was becoming prominent and rounded. Once she asked him what sort of fish was the *altyn mekre* – the golden sturgeon. 'I've heard about it, but never seen one,' she said. He told her that it was a very uncommon fish, a form of sturgeon which lived in deep water.

It was quite large, but its main feature was its beautiful appearance. The fish was speckled blue, but the top of its head, fins and the cartilage plates on its back from head to tail tip, was of pure gold and shone with a wonderful golden sheen. From this came its name: *altyn mekre*, the golden sturgeon.

The next time they talked, Ukubala said that she had had a dream about the golden sturgeon. It was as if the fish had swum around her and she had tried to catch hold of it. All she had wanted was to hold the fish and feel its golden flesh, and then set it free. She had so wanted to press the fish to herself that in her dream she had chased after it. The fish had eluded her, and when she awoke, Ukubala could not calm down for a long while and felt a strange disappointment, as if she had failed to achieve some important aim. It was strange, but even after she had woken she still felt badly that she must catch and hold a golden sturgeon.

Yedigei pondered this as he was dragging his nets from the sea and, as it turned out later, he interpreted correctly what her wish meant, this wish that had started as a dream but had remained on waking. He understood that he must, come what may, catch a golden sturgeon, because the feeling which the pregnant Ukubala had had was one of her longings, a *talgak*. Many women when carrying a child, feel some form of unfulfilled longing; this is often shown in a desire to eat something acid, salty, very sharp or bitter; others desire the roast meat of some wild animal or bird. Yedigei was not surprised at his wife's particular longing. Coming from the wife of a professional fisherman, it was entirely appropriate. God himself had implanted this desire to see with her own eyes and to hold in her hands the golden body of this large fish. Yedigei had heard, too, that if a pregnant woman's longing is not fulfilled, then this can lead to harm to the child in the womb.

Ukubala's longing was so unusual that she could not admit to it aloud; but Yedigei did not try to get her to be more precise and did not question her, because it was by no means certain that he could catch such a very rare fish. He decided to catch the fish first and then find out later if it was indeed the object of her longing.

By that time the main fishing season on the Aral' Sea, from July to November, was coming to an end for that year. The cold breath of winter could already be felt, and the group of fishermen with whom Yedigei worked was getting ready for their winter operation of fishing through the ice. Along the whole shoreline of one and a half thousand kilometres, the sea was covered with thick ice and large holes had to be made, weighted nets let down and dragged from one hole to another with the help of harnessed camels, the irreplaceable tugs of the steppes. The wind blew, and the fish which were caught in the nets could not move on being lifted out of the water, for they were instantly sheathed with ice from the Aral' cold . . .

Although Yedigei had fished a long time with his group, winter and summer, and had caught many valuable and less valuable sorts, he could not ever recall a golden sturgeon falling into the nets. Occasionally this fish would be caught on hook or spinner, but that would be a memorable event for the lucky fisherman. Indeed, they always used to say that a golden sturgeon brought luck to whoever caught it.

So early one morning he set off to sea, telling his wife that he would catch some fish before the ice formed. The evening before, Ukubala had tried to dissuade him when he had told her of his intention.

'The house is full of all sorts of fish. Is it worth going? The weather's already cold.'

But Yedigei was firm in his intention. 'What's in the house is there,' he said, 'but you yourself said that Auntie Sagyn is very ill. What she needs is some soup, hot and made from fresh fish – a barbel or a *zherekh*. It's the best thing for her, but who's going to catch it if not me?'

With this as the reason, Yedigei started off as early as possible that morning to catch a golden sturgeon. He had earlier prepared all his lines and the necessary tackle for the method he had decided to employ. All was put into the bow of the boat. He wrapped himself up well, with his raincoat and hood on the top of everything else, and set off.

240

It was a misty day, half autumn, half winter. Crossing the swell at an angle, Yedigei rowed out into the open sea to a point where he thought the feeding grounds of the golden sturgeon should be. Everything depended on luck, because there was nothing less likely than the catching of a seafish on a single hook. On dry land, however difficult it may be otherwise, the hunter and his quarry are at least in the same element; the hunter can follow the animal, approach, conceal himself, wait and then strike. The fisherman has no such advantage. Having lowered his line, he must wait until the fish turns up, and even if it does, there is no guarantee that it will then take the bait.

In his heart Yedigei was confident of success, because this time he had not gone to sea for the sake of gain, as usual, but to fulfil this longing of his pregnant wife. With this in mind, he rowed on. Yedigei, as a young man, was a strong and powerful oarsman. Tireless, evenly pushing aside the swell and current, he brought the boat out into the open sea athwart the twisting, unsteady waves that the Aral' Sea fishermen called *Iirek tolkun*, or 'lop-sided waves'. *Iirek tolkun* were the early signs of an approaching storm, but in themselves they were not dangerous and there was no reason to be fearful about heading further out to sea.

As he went further from the land, the shore with its steep clay cliff and the stony strip of surf at the edge of the water gradually decreased in size, becoming less clear. Soon they turned into a vague line, at times disappearing. The clouds hung above, scarcely moving, but below them there was a noticeably strong wind, licking at the watery ripples it had formed.

After two hours, Yedigei stopped, shipped the oars and started to set up his tackle. He had two reels and a home-made device to keep the line taut. One of these he fixed up on the stern, letting down the line and weight through a fork piece to about a hundred metres, and leaving some twenty metres remaining. The other line he set up at the bow. Then he took up the oars again in order to keep the boat in the same position in relation to wind and current and, of course, to keep the two lines apart from each other.

That done, he began to wait. In his opinion, the golden sturgeon should be found in this spot. He had no proof of this, just his own intuition. Moreover, he believed that the fish had to appear – absolutely had to appear. He could not return home without it. He needed it, not for amusement, but for a very important reason.

After some time, fish began to bite, but not the right one. First a *zherekh* was hooked. As Yedigei pulled it in, he knew it was not a golden sturgeon. It was impossible that a golden sturgeon should be the first to bite. That would mean that life on earth had become too simple, if not dull. Yedigei was prepared to work and wait. Next he hooked a large barbel, one of the best, if not the best of the fish in the Aral' Sea. That he stunned and threw into the bottom of the boat. At any rate now there was more than enough fish for Auntie Sagyn's soup. Then he caught a *tran* – the Aral' bream. What was it doing down at the depth where he was fishing? Usually the *tran* was found near the surface. God be with it, it had only itself to blame. After this there was a long period of waiting . . . 'No, I'll stay on,' said Yedigei to himself. 'Although I said nothing, she'll know that I've come out to get a golden sturgeon. And I *must* catch one, so that the child in her womb does not suffer. Our child-to-be wants his or her mother to hold in her hands a golden sturgeon. Why the child should want that, no one knows. But the mother wants it too, and as I'm the father, I shall do everything I can to see that the desire is fulfilled.'

The *Iirek tolkun* played around, turning the boat, for they are lop-sided, unsteady waves. Yedigei began to get frozen from sitting still, but all the while he was keeping a sharp watch on the reels. Was there a pull? Was the line moving within the fork? No, neither fore nor aft were there any such signs. However, Yedigei did not lose patience. He knew, he believed, that the golden sturgeon must come to him. Only the sea must be patient, too. Already the lop-sided waves were beginning to play up. What did that mean? Surely the storm could not get up so soon? More likely it would come towards

242

evening or during the night. *Alabashi*, or 'howling' waves would come, and then the terrible Aral' would be boiling from one shore to the other and covered with white foam. No one would dare put to sea then, but meanwhile it was all right; there was still time to stay out there . . .

All ruffled up, frozen and looking around, Yedigei waited for his fish to bite. 'What are you waiting for, why so slow? For God's sake, don't be afraid! I promise I'll put you back. You say that such things don't happen? Well, you're wrong – they do. I won't eat you. We have food and fish a-plenty at home. And there are three other fish on the bottom of the boat already. Would I be waiting just for the chance of eating you, golden sturgeon? No! We're awaiting our first-born, and not long ago my wife had a dream about you; since then she's had no peace – she doesn't say so, but I can see it all. I can't explain why this is so, but it's vital that she sees you and holds you in her hands – and I give you my word that after she's done that, I'll put you back into the sea. The fact is that you're a very special and uncommon fish. You have a golden top to your head, fins and tail, and your back is golden too. Try to see our point of view. She's longing to see you as you are, in reality; she wants to touch you and to feel you in her hands, to know how you feel, golden sturgeon. Don't think that because you're a fish you have no relationship to us. Although you're a fish, she longs for you as if you were a sister or brother, and she wants to see you before she gives birth. And the child within her womb will be pleased. This is what all this is about. Help me, my golden sturgeon. Come to me, I give you my word I won't hurt you. If I meant you harm, you would know. On each hook I have put a large piece of meat; choose either. The meat is a bit smelly so that you will notice it from far away. Come along, and don't think badly of me. If I'd used a spinner, then that would have been unworthy, although you'd go for a spinner more quickly. You'd probably swallow it and then you'd have had that piece of metal in your belly when I put you back into the sea. Then I would have deceived you. I offer you the hook honestly. Your lips will be a bit wounded, but that'll be all. Don't worry, I've brought along a large goatskin and I'll fill it with water and you'll lie in there for a while, and afterwards you'll swim out to freedom again. But I won't leave here without you. Time is getting on. Can't you see that the wind's getting up and the waves are rising? Surely you don't want our first-born to be an orphan, without a father? Think it over, and help me . . .'

It was already getting dark in the grey wastes of the cold pre-winter sea. The boat was one minute rising on the crest of the waves, the next disappearing in the troughs, steadily heading towards the shore. It went with difficulty, fighting with the breakers, and the sea was already noisy, gradually boiling up, rocking, gathering up its strength for the storm. Icy spray flew in his face, and his hands on the oars were cold and wet.

Ukubala was walking along the shore. Some time before, feeling very worried, she had gone down to the seashore to wait there for her husband. When she had agreed to marry a fisherman, her steppe relations, cattle herders all, had said, 'Think well before you give your word. You're unaccustomed to such a hard life. You'll be married to the sea and many times you will be washed with tears because of the sea, as you offer prayers to it.' But she did not refuse Yedigei; she just said, 'As my husband is, so will I be . . .' So it had turned out.

But this time he had gone out, not with the rest of the fishermen, but on his own. Now it was getting dark quickly and the sea was noisy and rough.

Then amid the waves the blades of the oars flashed, and there was his boat rising up on a wave. Her head in a scarf, her belly already protruding, Ukubala came right down to the water's edge and waited there until Yedigei came ashore. With a mighty lift, the waves carried the boat into the shallows. Yedigei jumped at once into the water and dragged the boat ashore, as he might have dragged a bull. When he stood up, all wet and salty, Ukubala came up and hugged his wet neck, under the cold hard mackintosh.

'I've been straining my eyes looking for you. Why have you been so long?'

244

'It didn't appear all day, and then suddenly towards the end it took the bait.'

'So you were after the golden sturgeon?'

'Yes, I begged it to come. You can look at it.'

Yedigei took hold of the heavy skin filled with water, undid it and poured out the water, together with the golden sturgeon, on to the pebbles. It was a large fish, a powerful and beautiful fish. It flapped its golden tail feverishly, twisting, jumping and throwing the wet pebbles around; at the same time, with its rosy mouth open, it turned towards the sea, struggling to get back to its own element, back to the surf. For a second or so it was suddenly still and quiet, looking around with its unblinking, reproachful eyes, round and clear, trying to adjust to the new world in which it had found itself. Even in the dusky evening of the wintry day, the unfamiliar light was like a blow on the head. The fish saw the shining eyes of the two people leaning over it, a bit of the shore and the sky; in the distance far away out over the sea, it could make out on the horizon, behind thin clouds, the unbearably bright light of the setting sun. It began to gasp. It gave a jerk. It beat and twisted with a new effort, trying to get back to the water. Yedigei lifted the golden sturgeon up, holding it below the gills.

'Hold out your hands and take it in them.' He said to Ukubala.

Ukubala took the fish and cradled it as if it were a child in both her hands, pressing it to her breast.

'What a firm fish!' Ukubala cried, feeling the fish's inner strength, like a coiled spring. 'It's as heavy as a log! And what a beautiful smell of the sea! Oh, it's beautiful! There you are, Yedigei, take it from me. I'm so pleased, so happy. My wish has been granted. Now put it back into the water as quickly as you can . . .'

Yedigei carried the golden sturgeon to the sea, wading into the surf up to his knees; then he let the fish slide down. For a fleeting moment as the golden sturgeon fell into the water, the whole golden colour and sheen of the fish from head to tail was reflected in the thick blue air of evening. Then, in a flash, parting the water with its speeding body, the fish swam away once more into the depths . . .

That night a great storm broke out at sea. The sea roared beyond the wall, under the cliff. Once more Yedigei realized that not for nothing were the lop-sided waves regarded as harbingers of a coming storm. It was already late into the night. Half-asleep, he listened to the wild surf, and as he did so, he remembered the cherished sturgeon. Where was his fish now? No doubt down in the deep darkness, the fish was listening to the waves raging overhead, at the surface. Yedigei smiled happily at this thought and as he dropped off to sleep, he put his hand against his wife's side. Suddenly he felt the child stirring in her womb. His first-born was making his presence felt. At this, Yedigei smiled happily once more and fell peacefully asleep.

He little knew that not a year would pass before the war broke out and his whole life changed irrevocably; nor that he would leave the sea for ever and it would remain only in his memory – especially when the difficult times came along . . .

Trains in these parts went from East to West, and from West to East.

On either side of the railway lines in these parts there lay the great wide spaces of the desert – Sary-Ozeki, the Middle lands of the yellow steppes.

In that terrible year for Burannyi Yedigei, 1953, winter came early. Never before had such a thing happened in the Sarozek. By the end of October the snow was lying all about and the cold had begun. It was good that before that happened, he had managed to bring potatoes from Kumbel' for himself, Zaripa and the children. As soon as he realized what was happening, he wasted no time. The final trip he made on the camel, for he was afraid that if he went on a passing goods train, the potatoes would freeze on the open platform during the journey, and frozen potatoes would be no use to anyone. So he went there on Burannyi Karanar. Having placed on him the two sacks making up the load – he had not been able to lift them on his

246

own, but fortunately some men had helped him – he put a felt rug on top to keep the cold out and tucked in the edges to protect against the wind. Then he got up on the very top of the load, between the sacks, and calmly set off home to Boranly-Burannyi.

Sitting up there on Karanar, he looked as if he were riding an elephant. Indeed, this thought occurred to Yedigei. Until then no one there had given any thought to riding elephants or how it was done, but recently the first Indian film to reach there had just been shown at the station. All the people of Kumbel' from small to large had come to see it, curious to find out about this country they had never seen before. As well as endless songs and dances, the film showed how people went out into the jungle to hunt tigers and how they sat on elephants to do so. Yedigei and the chief of the junction had been attending a general trades union meeting as the Boranly delegates, and when the meeting was over, they had showed this Indian film in the depot club. From this it began. The railwaymen had been flabbergasted to see how people rode on elephants in India and as they left the cinema, various discussions started.

Someone remarked loudly, 'What about those elephants, eh? Yedigei's Burannyi Karanar is no less remarkable – load him up and off he goes, looking just like an elephant!' 'It's true!' People laughed. Another voice called out. 'What good's an elephant? It can only live in hot countries. Try one in the Sarozek in winter! Your elephant would be lying on his back with his feet in the air! It couldn't compete with Karanar!'

'Listen, Yedigei! Why don't you fit up a hut on Karanar, like they do in India? Then you'd ride around like one of those rich Maharajahs!'

Yedigei laughed. His friends might have been joking, but all the same it had been flattering to hear such words about his famous male camel. Nevertheless, Yedigei had a heavy share of trouble, worry and grief thanks to Karanar . . .

It had all begun as the cold set in. That day the first snowfall caught him out while he was on his journey. A light snow flurry had fallen several times and had melted straight away.

But then it had really come down! The sky had closed in over the Sarozek in an impenetrable gloom and the wind had got up. The snow fell heavily and in big thick flakes. It was not especially cold, but it was wet and unpleasant. The main thing was that you could not make anything out all around. What should he do? In the Sarozek there were no places where you could stop and wait for the weather to clear. There was only one thing for it, and that was to trust in the strength and sense of direction of Burannyi Karanar. He would bring them safely home.

Yedigei gave the camel his head, put up his collar, pulled down his hat, shut his hood around and sat there, trying patiently to make out any landmarks or familiar objects on either side. But all he could see was an impenetrable curtain of snow. On went Karanar into this whirling snow, not slowing up at all. He seemed to understand that his master was no longer directing him, for Yedigei was sitting there silently on top of the load and not interfering. Karanar needed all his vast strength to be able to carry such a large load over the steppe in a snowstorm. The powerful animal, breathing hotly as he carried his master, called and roared and now and then gave a wail that lengthened into a drawn-out blast, but all the time he continued on, not stopping, through the snow which was flying towards them . . .

No wonder that the journey seemed long to Yedigei. If only we had set out earlier, he thought, and then imagined to himself how worried they would be at home, knowing that he was out in such weather. Ukubala would be anxious about him, but would not say a word. She was not the type to reveal all that she was thinking. Perhaps Zaripa was wondering what had happened? Of course she would be. But she was even less likely to say anything and was trying to avoid him and all conversation with him. But what reason was there, when nothing untoward had passed between them? Not by word or deed had he, Yedigei, given any grounds for anyone to think that there was anything wrong. As things were before, so they remained. All that had happened was that two travellers through life had suddenly looked around as they went along

248

the same road . . . And then they had continued on their way. That was all there was to it. What had happened to him, that was *his* trouble . . . That was his fate from birth; no doubt he had been fated to be torn between two fires. Let no one else worry; it was his problem, working out how to live with himself and his much-suffering heart. Whose business was it, what his life was and what lay ahead of him? He was not a little child; somehow he would untie that tight knot which, at present, by his own fault, was drawing tighter still . . .

These were frightening thoughts, and there seemed to be no escape from them. Winter had already come to the Sarozek, yet still he could not forget Zaripa, nor could he even in thought renounce Ukubala. It was his misfortune that he needed both at the same time. They, surely seeing and being aware of this, were trying not to hurry things, so as to help him to determine his fate quickly. Outwardly, everything was just as before – the easy relations between the two women and the children of both households; it was as if they were one family, growing up together at the junction; their children were always playing together, sometimes in one house, sometimes in the other. So the summer had passed, and now autumn was over . . .

Burannyi Yedigei, alone in the storm, felt like an orphan without shelter. Down came the snow; the emptiness was all around. Every now and then Karanar shook lumps of snow from his mane and, as he ran along, broke the silence with roars and cries.

Yedigei was suffering on that journey, yet he could do nothing about his feelings; he could not calm down, or see anything clearly or free of argument and conditions. He was unable to declare his love unreservedly to Zaripa, and he could not give up Ukubala. He began to curse and to call himself by the harshest names: 'Beast, *khaivan*, you're no better than your camel! Swine! Dog! Madman!' With these and similar names, mingled with the strongest oaths, he castigated himself, scolding himself in an effort to come out of his stupor, to come to his senses, to think, to stop . . . But all to no avail. The landslide was about to start on its way. The sole delight which awaited him was the prospect of seeing the children. They accepted him as he was, without argument, and gave him no problems. To help them, to bring something for them, to repair something in the house for them – this gave him the greatest of pleasure, just as now he was bringing them the potatoes for the winter in the two huge sacks, loaded on Karanar. He had ensured their supply of fuel for the winter.

To think about the boys was a form of escape for Yedigei – then he could be at peace with himself. He imagined how he would arrive back at Boranly-Burannyi, how the boys would run out of the house when they heard him coming, and how it would be impossible to chase them back indoors, even with the snow falling; they would be jumping around with loud shouts: 'Uncle Yedigei has come back! He's on Karanar! He's brought the potatoes!' Then he would show them how strict and powerful he could be by ordering the camel to lie down on the ground; then, all covered in snow, he would climb down from Karanar's back and, after shaking off some of the snow, pat the children on the head. Then he would unload the sacks of potatoes and look around to see if Zaripa was around. He would say nothing special to her, nor she to him; just look into her face and be happy. Then he would begin to feel ill and saddened – because where could he go from there? Meanwhile the boys would play nearby, getting in the way and every now and again would run up to him, scared by the camel's roars; then, their fears overcome, they would try to help him and that would be his reward for all his sufferings . . .

So he prepared for the meeting with Abutalip's boys. He also thought in advance about the story which he would tell them, his ever-hungry listeners. Should he tell them about the Aral' Sea again? Their favourite stories were about things that happened at sea, which they would then inevitably elaborate by bringing in their father; in this way they contrived, albeit unconsciously, to keep in touch with him and to keep their memories of him fresh. But Yedigei had already told them all he knew about the sea several times over; that is, all except the story about the golden sturgeon. Yet how could he tell that story? How could he explain, except to himself, the real tale behind that incident so long ago?

So this was how he made his journey home on that snowy day. All the way he could not get rid of his doubts and thoughts; and all the way the snow went on falling . . .

That snowfall heralded the start of winter in the Sarozek, early and chill from the very first. With the start of the cold weather Burannyi Karanar became restless, angry and irritable, as once again his male instincts rebelled within him. No one and no thing could be permitted to encroach on his freedom. During this time even his master had to retreat on occasions and bow to the inevitable.

On the third day after the snowfall there was a frosty wind blowing over the Sarozek, and suddenly there arose a thick, chilly haze just like steam over the steppe. You could hear footsteps crunching in the snow far away, and any sound, even the faintest rustling, was carried through the air with exceptional clarity. The trains could be heard coming along the lines when they were still many kilometres away. And when at dawn Yedigei heard the waking roar of Burannyi Karanar in the fold and heard him trampling and noisily shaking the fence behind the house, he knew only too well that he was in for trouble. He dressed quickly and stepping out into the darkness, walked over to the fold. There he shouted, his voice hoarse from the astringent air, 'What's all this about? Is it the end of the world again? You want to drink my blood? You lecherous beast!'

But he was wasting his breath. The camel, excited by his awakening passions, took not the slightest notice of his master. He was going to have his way, come what may. He roared, snorted and ground his teeth threateningly and broke down part of the fence.

'So you've sniffed something in the air, then?' His master changed from anger to reproach. 'It's obvious you want to go out to the herd. You reckon some young she-camel is ready for you, do you? Ai! Ai! Why on earth did God create you like this? Why do you have to have it once a year instead of doing it every day without all this noise and fuss? You'd think

251

nothing else matters – and it's the end of the world when you can't get it!'

But Burannyi Yedigei well knew his own helplessness. There was nothing that could be done about it, no point in throwing words aimlessly on the winds, so he just opened the gate. He had hardly succeeded in starting to move the heavy gate made of hurdles and about the height of a man and held in place by a strong chain, when Karanar, nearly throwing him to the ground, burst through and ran out into the steppe with a fierce howl and a roar, his vast legs at full stretch and his firm black humps shaking as he went. In a moment he was out of sight, obscured by the clouds of snow rising up behind him.

'Pox on you!' his master spat after him; then added in heartfelt sympathy. 'Run – hurry up, you fool, or you'll be too late!'

Yedigei had to go to work that morning, so he could not deal with the effects of Karanar's revolt until later on. But if he had known how all this was going to end, he would not have let him go for the world. But who could have coped with the maddened camel without Yedigei there? No – the only thing to do was to let him go as far away as possible. Yedigei hoped that the camel, running free, would get some fresh air and perhaps his hot blood might cool a bit . . .

At midday Kazangap came up to him and said, partly with a laugh, partly sympathetically, 'Well, *bai*, you're in real trouble! I've just been out on the pasture. Your Karanar has set off on what I think will be a long expedition. It seems the young females here aren't good enough for him!'

'He's run right off? Where to? Don't joke, tell me the truth!'

'I'm serious. I tell you he's away after the other herds. The beast feels something in the air. I went to see how things were with him out on the loose. I went into the big gorge, looked around, and what do I see? There was something running over the steppe, making the earth shake – it's old Karanar himself! His eyes were out like organ stops, he was roaring at full power and the saliva was flowing from his muzzle! He looked just like a locomotive as he ran along! There was a whole blizzard rising up behind him. I thought he'd trample me, but he raced past without even seeing me. He was heading in the direction of

Malakumdychap. Over there, under the cliff, there are herds much bigger than ours. He's not interested in what's around here. He needs things on the grand scale. The beast is at the height of his powers.'

Yedigei was really upset. He could just imagine the head-aches and unpleasantness that would result from this.

'Don't worry. There are some good males over there, they'll fight him, and he'll return like a whipped dog,' said Kazangap, attempting to console Yedigei.

Next day news began to come in, like communiqués from the front in wartime, about the activities of Karanar. The picture which emerged gave little comfort. You only had to stop a train at Boranly-Burannyi and the driver, fireman or guard would compete to tell you about the atrocities and havoc being wrought by Karanar among the camel herds around stations and junctions along the line. They said that at Malak-umdychap, Karanar had battered two males to death and then had driven off four females with him into the steppe. With difficulty the owners had eventually managed to get them away from Karanar. Shots had been fired into the air. In another place, Karanar had thrown the owner of a she-camel from his saddle, and then had chased him off before making off with her. He, a blockhead from heaven, had waited for two hours, thinking that when Karanar had had his fun, he would let the she-camel go in peace – although she, incidentally, had not the slightest intention of leaving this impudent camel. The man had started to approach in order to catch her and ride her home, when Karanar had rushed at him like a wild beast and chased him again. He would have trampled him if the man had not succeeded in jumping into a deep hole and had hidden there, quiet as a mouse, neither alive nor dead. Then he had recovered and hurried off home, making his way along a ravine further away from where he had last seen Karanar. He was glad to have escaped with his life.

The Sarozek bush telegraph brought other, similar stories about Karanar's wild behaviour, but the most worrying and indeed threatening item came in from the Ak-Moinak junction. It was in the form of a written complaint. So that was where he had got to, the devil – to Ak-Moinak, beyond Kumbel'! A certain Kospan sent his despatch from that station. This is what was written in that historic note:

Salaam, respected Yedigei-aga! Although you are a notable figure in the Sarozek, you nevertheless must hear some unpleasant news. I had thought you were a man of strong character. Why then have you let loose your giant Karanar? We did not expect this from you. Here he has inflicted great fear upon us. He has crippled our male camels and he has taken away three of the best females. In addition, he arrived here, not on his own, but driving before him a saddled she-camel, whose owner he had evidently thrown from the saddle. For why otherwise would she be going around saddled? Now he has driven these she-camels out into the steppe and allows neither man nor beast to approach him. What good can come of this? One of our young male camels has already died – his ribs were shattered. I wanted to fire into the air to frighten Karanar and to recover our she-camels, but what good would that do? He fears nothing. He is ready to bite, to chew any living person, anything in order that they should not interfere with his business. He doesn't eat, he doesn't drink, he just covers these she-camels in turn, making the earth shake as he does so. It is revolting to see how brutally he does this! And he roars out over the whole steppe when he does it, as if the end of the world was at hand! We have not the strength to listen to this! And it seems to me he could go on for a hundred years without a break! I have never seen such a monster. In our village everyone is scared. The women and children are afraid to go far from the houses. Therefore I demand that you come at once and remove your Karanar. I will set you a time limit. If in two days you are not here and have not freed us from this affliction, then do not be angry, dear aga. I have a heavy calibre gun. Its bullets can fell a bear. I will fire into his head in the presence of witnesses, and that will be the end of the matter. I will send you the skin on a passing goods train. I do not care if it is Burannyi Karanar. I intend to keep my word. Come before it is too late,

Your young brother at Ak-Moinak,
Kospan

254

So this is what was going on. Although the letter was written by a real character with a sense of humour, the warning contained in it was serious. He discussed it with Kazangap and they decided that Yedigei must set off without delay for the Ak-Moinak junction.

This, however, was easier said than done. He had to get to Ak-Moinak, catch Karanar out in the steppe, and return home in extremely cold weather, while a blizzard might blow up at any time. The simplest way would be to dress up as warmly as possible, get on to a passing goods train and on arrival at Ak-Moinak, ride out into the steppe. But who knows how far out into the steppe Karanar had now gone with his harem? Judging by the tone of the letter, the people were so upset that they might not lend him a camel, and in that case, worst of all, he would have to chase Karanar on foot over the snowdrifts.

Yedigei set off in the morning. Ukubala had prepared him food for the journey, and he was well wrapped up. Over his quilted, padded trousers and warm, sleeveless jacket, he wore a sheepskin-lined top coat; on his feet were *valenki* and on his head a foxskin *malakhai* hat with triple-sided flaps, the sort that keeps wind out at back and sides and surrounds the whole of your head and neck with fur. On his hands were warm sheepskin gloves. When he had saddled the she-camel on which he was to ride to Ak-Moinak, up ran Abutalip's two boys. Daul had brought him a hand-knitted wool scarf.

'Uncle Yedigei, Mama said that it was so that your neck didn't get cold,' said the boy as he handed the scarf to him.

Joyfully Yedigei began to squeeze the boy and kiss him; he was so touched that he was momentarily lost for words. His very soul was delighted, he was like a boy, for this was the first sign of attention from her.

'Tell your Mama,' he said to the children as he left, 'that I'll soon be back – if God wills, perhaps tomorrow. I won't stay a minute longer than is necessary. Then we'll all drink tea together.'

How Burannyi Yedigei longed to get back from that dreaded Ak-Moinak and see Zaripa again! To look into her eyes, and be sure that this scarf was not just a chance gift . . . He folded

255

it carefully and hid it in the inner pocket of his jacket. Even after he had left, and was some way from home, he was scarcely able to prevent himself from turning back. That mad Karanar! Let this Kospan shoot him if he wants to and send back his skin; after all, how long was he to act as a nanny to this camel with his wild desires? Let Fate punish him! It would serve him right! Such were his thoughts as he set out. But then he was ashamed. He realized he would be a real fool to turn back, that he would be shamed in the eyes of other people, and most of all, in the eyes of Ukubala and Zaripa. He cooled off, persuading himself that there was only one way of dealing with his impatience to get back, and that was to go there and return as soon as possible.

With this thought he pushed on. It was fairly frosty and an even but strong wind was blowing. The frost on the wind covered his face, and especially the fur of the foxskin *malakhai* hat, with a fluffy hoarfrost. The white hoarfrost from the breath of the brown camel covered her from neck to withers. Winter had indeed arrived in full force. In the far distance it was misty, and when he looked, he could see that at the limit of visibility there was a foggy line which seemed all the time to be moving ahead of them as they went. As fast as the traveller approached, the margin line receded. It felt very empty and stern in the wintry Sarozek, freezing in its windswept whiteness.

The young, but fast camel bore him in the saddle well, setting out boldly across the virgin soil. But for Yedigei this was neither the ride nor the speed that he was used to. Now if it had been Karanar, it would have been different. His breathing was stronger and his stride was incomparable. The old verses were not composed for nothing:

> *In what way is this horse better than that?*
> *In its superior movement.*
> *In what way is this marauder better than that?*
> *In his superior mind.*

He had a long way to go, and all the while he would be on his own. Yedigei would have been worn out if it had not been for the scarf given to him by Zaripa. All the way he felt the pressure of this modest gift. He had lived all these years, yet he had never known that such an unimportant thing could so warm the heart when it was a gift from a woman whom you loved. He cherished this thought all the way. Putting his hand inside his coat, he stroked the scarf and smiled with pleasure. But then came another thought. What was he to do? How was he to arrange his life in the future? There seemed to be an insurmountable obstacle ahead. What could he do about it? A man has to live with some aim before him, and also have a way to achieve it. But in this case he had neither.

And then a miserable fog clouded Burannyi Yedigei's vision, just like those silent Sarozek prospects in their frosty mist. Finding no answer to his dilemma, he was overwhelmed, suffered and became downhearted and tried once more to raise his hopes with hopeless dreams . . .

Suddenly he experienced real fear in this silence and loneliness. Why did he lead such a life? Why had he ended up in the Sarozek? Why had this unhappy, luckless family, harried by Fate, arrived at Boranly-Burannyi? If it had not been for them, he would be suffering no such pangs and would have led a quiet and comfortable life. But now his soul was irresponsible and wanted the unattainable . . . And what was more, there was Karanar with his insane behaviour, who was also a load on his back, also a punishment from God, and who brought him no luck. No, indeed, he had had no luck in his life.

Yedigei arrived at Ak-Moinak when it was almost evening. The camel was exhausted. It had been a long journey and in difficult conditions.

Ak-Moinak was just another junction like Boranly-Burannyi, except that it had its own well for water. Otherwise there was no difference; just the same Sarozek all around.

As he approached, Yedigei asked someone where he could find Kospan and was told that Kospan was still on duty on the railway. So Burannyi Yedigei went along to the duty hut. When he got there and was about to dismount, a brisk-looking, grinning man of average height, wearing a sheepskin jacket that obviously belonged to someone else, came out on to the porch. His *valenki* were patched and he was wearing an old three-flapped hat at a jaunty angle.

'Ah, Yedigei-aga! Our beloved Boranly-aga!' He recognized Yedigei straight away and ran from the porch. 'So you've come! We were waiting, wondering if you'd come or not.'

'You have to come,' laughed Yedigei, 'when you're sent such a threatening letter!'

'Indeed! But the letter is only half the trouble, Yedigei-aga. A letter is but a piece of paper. But here there are such goings-on! You must free us quickly from the scourge of your Karanar, for we're blockaded! We can't go out into the steppe. If he sees anyone in the distance, he runs up like mad, ready to maim. What a monster! It's terrifying to have such an *atan* (male camel) around.' He stopped talking and looked at Yedigei. 'Tell me – how will you cope with him with just your bare hands?'

'What do you mean, bare hands?' Yedigei took out his whip, with the thong wound around the stock, from one of his saddle-bags.

'You'll use that little lash, eh?'

'What do you want me to use, a cannon? He's only a camel.'

'We don't use rifles. I don't know – perhaps he'll recognize you as his master, then . . . Only his eyesight seems a bit clouded.'

'Well, we'll see,' answered Yedigei. 'But don't let's waste time. You must be Kospan. If so, then take me and show me where he is, and leave the rest to me.'

'He's some way off,' said Kospan, looking around and then at his watch. 'Look, Yedigei-aga, it's late. By the time we get there, it'll be well into the evening. You'll never catch him in the middle of the night. No, that's not on. We don't often get people like you passing through. Be our dear guest, and tomorrow morning you can do as you please.'

Yedigei had not expected this. He had calculated that if he succeeded in catching Karanar, then tonight he would go back to Kumbel' and spend the night with friends near the station, and at dawn he would set off home as early as possible.

Seeing that Yedigei wanted to go, Kospan protested. 'No, Yedigei-aga, that's no good at all. Forgive me for the letter, but there was no other way. Things had become impossible. But I won't let you go now. If – which God forbid – something should happen to you out in the empty steppe at night, I don't want to be held responsible all over the Sary-Ozeki. Stay with us and in the morning, do as you wish. There's my house at the end of the village. I have to work for another hour and a half. Make yourself at home. Do as you like. Put your camel in the enclosure; there'll be fodder there now. We have water – take as much as you like.'

It soon got dark that winter day. Kospan and his family turned out to be wonderful people. There was the old mother, his wife, a boy of about five (the elder child, their daughter was at the Kumbel' boarding school), and everyone, including Kospan, did all they could to make their guest feel at ease. The house was very warm and the household was lively. In the kitchen some of the winter-killed meat was on the boil. Meanwhile they drank tea. The old mother filled his *piala* with tea and all the while asked Yedigei about his family, children, life, the weather, where he had come from, what tribe; then she in her turn told him when and how they had come to Ak-Moinak junction. Yedigei answered her questions readily and praised the yellow melted butter which he spread on pieces of flatcakes and put into his mouth. Cows' butter was rare in the Sarozek. Sheep, goat or camel butter was not bad, but cows' butter was more tasty. Their relations sent it to them from the Ural. Yedigei ate heartily of the buttered cakes and told them that he could even smell the meadow grass, which completely won the heart of the old woman, who then began to tell about her native land – about the Ural river lands, or rather the Yaitski river lands as she called them, about the grass, forests and rivers . . .

Meanwhile, Erlepes arrived, the man in charge at this junction, who had been invited by Kospan to meet Burannyi Yedigei. With Erlepes' arrival the men began to talk about their work, transport matters and snowdrifts on the lines. Yedigei knew Erlepes slightly from a previous meeting – he had worked a long time on the railway, and now they had the chance to get to know one another better. Erlepes was older than Yedigei and had been in charge at Ak-Moinak from the end of the war and Yedigei could see that he was respected by the people working there.

Already night had fallen. As at Boranly-Burannyi, every now and then the trains went noisily past, rattling the windows, and the wind whistled in the shutters. Nevertheless, although on the same Sarozek railway line, it seemed a totally different place, and Yedigei was aware of being among a quite different set of people. Here, although he had come because of the mad behaviour of Karanar, he was being given the welcome appropriate for a guest. With Erlepes' arrival, Yedigei felt even more at home. Erlepes was a good person to talk with and knew the Kazakh history well. The conversation turned to the past, famous people and famous stories.

That evening, Yedigei got very close to his new Ak-Moinak friends. This was due not only to the conversation, but also the hospitable host and hostess, and in no small degree to the good food and drink. There was vodka. Straight in from the frost, Yedigei drank a half glass and ate some *orkoch* with it – the hump fat of a young camel, which was one of the *zakuski* dishes. At once a warm wave went through him, giving him a feeling of well-being and calming his soul. Burannyi Yedigei became slightly tipsy and, with this, revitalized. He smiled. Erlepes had a drink in honour of the guest, and also felt in good form. He asked Kospan, 'For God's sake, Kospan, go to my house and bring me my *dombra*.'

'That's a fine idea,' Yedigei approved. 'From a child, I've always envied those who play the *dombra*.'

'I can't promise anything extraordinary,' said Erlepes, as he took off his jacket and rolled up his sleeves.

Compared with the garrulous, busy Kospan, Erlepes was more reserved. He was a large man with a handsome face which exuded confidence. When he picked up the *dombra* and concentrated on the business of playing, he seemed to detach himself from everyday life, as often happens when a person becomes absorbed in his precious art.

Having tuned the instrument, Erlepes looked at Yedigei with a long, wise look, and in his large black eyes a gleam of light appeared, as if reflected from the sea. Then he touched the strings, running his long fingers up and down over the high neck of the *dombra* and along its whole length and width, producing a whole gamut of sounds and at the same time drawing out new clusters of sounds which he would bring out richly from the strings as he developed the theme.

As he listened, Burannyi Yedigei realized that he was not going to find the music easy or simple to interpret. At first he had felt relaxed and comfortable in his role of guest, but the first sounds from the *dombra* returned him into himself and again threw him head-first into an abyss of grief and troubled thoughts. Why? It seemed that the people who had composed this music so long ago had somehow known what was going to happen to Burannyi Yedigei, what strains and tortures were to be his from birth. Otherwise, how could they have expressed it so perfectly in the music which Erlepes was playing? Yedigei's soul was aroused, it rose and groaned, and at once all the doors to his private world of joy, sadness, thoughts, vague desires and doubts were thrown open . . .

Erlepes was a superb *dombra* player. The long-dead feelings of ancient peoples lived again in the strings, re-kindled like dry wood in a blaze. Now and again Yedigei felt the scarf hidden in the inner pocket of his jacket, and remembered that there was on the earth a woman whom he loved. The very thought of her was both a delight and a torture; he could not live without her, and therefore he would love her always. The *dombra* in Erlepes' hands rang out, then was silent, then roused again, telling of this once more. One tune was followed by others, one melody flowed into the next, and Yedigei's soul floated on the music like a boat over the waves. Once more he felt that he was back on the Aral' Sea. He remembered the invisible currents by the shore, their movements only shown by the long, thick strands of seaweed like a woman's hair, rippled by the current, but staying in one and the same place. Once upon a time Ukubala's hair had been like that, reaching to below her knees. When she swam, her hair flowed over to

261

one side, like those seaweeds in the current. And she laughed happily and was dark and beautiful.

Burannyi Yedigei opened up a little, and was moved. It was so pleasant to hear the *dombra* again. It had been worth making the journey over the winter Sarozek just to hear it. 'How fortunate that Karanar came here!' thought Yedigei. 'For he brought me after him – I simply had to come. And my heart is enjoying the *dombra* once again. What a fine fellow Erlepes is! And what an excellent player! I had no idea . . .'

Listening to Erlepes' playing, Yedigei was busy with his thoughts; he tried to look at his life from above, to rise beyond it like a kite flying high, high up over the steppe and soaring all on its own on outstretched, straight wings on the rising air currents, gazing down on what was below. A vast picture of the wintry Sarozek rose up before his eyes, and there, on a scarcely noticeable curve of the railway line was a group of several buildings and lights: Boranly-Burannyi junction. In one of those houses were Ukubala and the children. No doubt they were already asleep, though Ukubala probably was still awake, lying there thinking, listening to the murmurings of her heart. And in the other house were Zaripa and her boys. Most certainly she would not be asleep, for she was suffering. And ahead of her lay still more grief, for the boys did not yet know about their father. No matter where you went, you could not escape from the truth . . .

He imagined the trains racing through the night with their great noise, their lights blazing, sending up clouds of powdery snow. Yet what a still and endless night lay all around! Not far from that place where he was now a guest, listening to the *dombra*, in the darkness of the steppe, swept by snow and wind, roamed Karanar. No sleep for him, no peace for him. All year he had been building up his strength. Day in and day out, he had been ceaselessly chewing away with his powerful jaws. That was why his stomach was arranged as it was. Chewing the cud – that was what camels were designed for. They chewed the cud while they walked, even while they slept – and all in order to concentrate force in the humps. For the more powerful, full and strong the humps were, so much thicker was the fat and so much more powerful was the male camel for the winter rut. Then the snow and cold meant nothing to him, nor did his master and still less anybody else. Then, he was wild, drunk with his untamed strength. Then he was a Tsar and a ruler, and he felt no weariness, no fear. Nothing else on earth mattered to him – food, drink, nothing existed except the need to satisfy his vast and uncontrolled passion. He had been living the whole year through for this end, and for this purpose he had been storing up energy from day to day. And while Burannyi Yedigei sat as a guest in the warm, well fed and enjoying listening to the music, somewhere nearby Burannyi Karanar was raging and running about, true to the call of his blood, jealously guarding his she-camels from all intruders, not allowing beast or even bird to come near them, roaring and shaking his black mane and terrifying beard . . .

So Yedigei was thinking as he listened to the sounds of the *dombra*.

The music took his thoughts from the past into the present, and back to the ordeal which awaited him tomorrow. There was a strange desire arising within him to hide, to protect from danger all that was dear to him, the whole world. He imagined it freed from suffering. And a vague feeling that in some degree he was to blame before everyone who was connected with his life, roused in him a secret regret . . .

'Forgive me,' said Erlepes, smiling thoughtfully as he came to the end of the latest piece and lightly working on the strings, 'you must be tired from the journey. You need rest, but here am I playing away on the *dombra*.'

'Not at all, Erleke!' Yedigei was surprised and placed his hands on his chest. 'On the contrary I've not enjoyed myself so much for a long time. So long as you're not tired, please continue – you're giving me so much pleasure. Do play some more.'

'And what would you like?'

'You know best, Erleke. The artist himself knows what he has to play. Of course, I prefer the old things, they're dearer to me. I don't know why, but they touch the heart and feed one's thoughts.'

Erlepes nodded with understanding. He laughed as he looked at the unusually quiet Kospan. 'Our Kospan – when he hears the *dombra*, he sort of melts, becomes a different person. Isn't that so, Kospan? But today we have a guest. Don't forget that. Pour us out a little more!'

Kospan woke up a bit and poured fresh drinks into their glasses. They drank and had something more to eat. After a while Erlepes again picked up the *dombra* and again checked that the instrument was in tune by strumming the strings.

'Since you prefer the old pieces,' he said, turning to Yedigei, 'I shall remind you of one story, Yedike. Many old men know it and you know it, too. Incidentally, your Kazangap tells it well, but he just recites it; I play and sing it as well – a whole theatrical production. So, in your honour, Yedike, "The words of Raimaly-aga to his brother Abdil'khan".'

Yedigei nodded his thanks and Erlepes started playing, preparing for the main tale with the well-known overture on the *dombra*. Again Yedigei's heart groaned, because all that was in this story was brought out again in him, this time with special feeling and understanding.

The *dombra* sounded, accompanying Erlepes, who sang in a thick, deep voice, very suitable for the tale of the tragic fate of the famous steppe-bard, Raimaly-aga. Raimaly-aga was over sixty when he fell in love with a young girl, the nineteen-year-old singer Begimai; she shone like a star on his journey. To be precise, she fell in love with him. But Begimai was free, she had her own desires and could do as she pleased. People talked about and criticized Raimaly-aga. Their love story had always had its supporters and detractors. No one could be unaffected by it. Some could not accept it and repudiated the actions of Raimaly-aga and demanded that his name be forgotten; others felt sympathy with him, suffered with him and continued to tell this bitter, sad story of a man in love, handing it down from one generation to the next. That was how this tale of Raimaly-aga had lived on.

Yedigei remembered that evening how abusive and malicious

Hawkeye had been when he found among Abutalip Kuttybaev's papers his manuscript of 'The words of Raimaly-aga to
his brother Abdil'khan.' Abutalip, however, had had a very
high opinion of this story, which he described as a poem about
a Goethe of the steppes – for apparently the Germans also had
a great and wise old man who fell in love with a young girl.
Abutalip wrote down the words of the story of Raimaly-aga as
it was told by Kazangap, in the hope that his sons would read
it when they grew up. He said that there were certain
happenings, events, certain stories which became the property
of many because their value was so great; that the story
contained in itself so much that although it was experienced
by one person originally, it could as it were be distributed to
and shared by all living at that time, and even to those who
came long afterwards . . .

Before him sat Erlepes, singing and playing with inspiration
on the *dombra*. This man was in charge of the junction, and his
first task was to look after a certain stretch of railway track. It
might be asked, why should he have preserved within him this
harrowing story of the distant past, the story of the unhappy
Raimaly-aga? Why should he choose to suffer as if he himself
was in Raimaly-aga's place? This was the message of all real
singing and music, thought Yedigei; they said, die and be born
again and be ready for that moment . . . Oh, if only that light
could always illuminate soul, that light by which a man sees
clearly and freely thinks about himself in the very best way . . .

As he was in a strange place, Yedigei did not fall asleep at
once, although he had gone outside for a breath of fresh air
before going to bed and although his hosts had prepared for
him a comfortable, warm bed with clean sheets, as are kept in
every house for such an occasion. He lay there near the window
and listened to the wind tearing past and whistling, hearing
the trains go past in either direction, waiting for the dawn,
when he would have to bring the unruly Karanar to heel. After
that, he would set off on the return journey as early as possible
and hurry home to Boranly-Burannyi where his children in
both houses were waiting for him, because he loved them all

265

equally and because he lived on this earth in order that all should be well with them.

He was thinking how best to calm down Karanar. That was a problem which other people certainly did not share, for he must surely own the wildest, most obstinate camel in the world. People were frightened of the sight of him and now were even ready to shoot him. He did not just come here of his own accord; Nature had arranged it thus. Karanar was big and strong and recognized no barriers; he would crush whomsoever got in his way. So how was he to deal with Karanar and take him in hand? He would have to put chains on him and keep him shut in for the whole of the winter; it was either that, or off with his wild head – otherwise Kospan or someone else would shoot him. There was nothing else which could be done . . .

As he was dropping off to sleep, he remembered once more Erlepes' singing, how he had played the *dombra* and how he had spent the whole evening with him. The sufferings of Raimaly-aga long ago, whose love had led to his downfall, had been resurrected through the *dombra* and had entered Yedigei's heart. And although there was nothing exactly comparable in their predicament, Yedigei did feel that there was some distant accord, some similarity in their pain. That which Raimaly-aga had suffered some hundred years ago, was now, like an echo, sounding in Burannyi Yedigei, living in the Sarozek desert. Yedigei sighed deeply and turned over in bed. He was sad and miserable from all this confusion and uncertainty. Where should he go? What would become of him? What should he say to Zaripa, and what should be his answer to Ukubala? No, he could not find a way out. He had strayed; he had got caught up . . .

As he went to sleep, he was suddenly out on the Aral' Sea again. His head was spinning from the unbearable blue light and the wind, and, as before in childhood, he was dashing towards the sea, imagining that he was a seagull, freely soaring over the waves. Joyfully he soared on over the broad expanse of the sea, hearing the *dombra* sound ring out all the while, as Erlepes sang of the unhappy love of Raimaly-aga . . . Then he dreamed that he was once more releasing the golden sturgeon back into the sea. The sturgeon was supple but heavy, and when he carried it to the water, he felt the living flesh of the fish quite clearly as it struggled to return to its element. He waded into the surf, the sea coming towards him, and he laughed at the wind and then opened his arms. The golden sturgeon, its rainbow hues shining in the thick blue light, seemed to slide endlessly towards the water . . . And all the while the music was coming to him from somewhere, and someone was weeping and bemoaning their fate.

That night an icy, squally wind blew over the steppe. It was getting much colder. The herd of four she-camels, beloved and protected by Burannyi Karanar, stood in a sheltered spot in a hollow beside a small hill. They were brushed on their undersides by the snow and they huddled close together to keep each other warm, heads on one another's necks. But their insatiable, shaggy lord, Karanar, gave them no peace. The whole time he was moving around, snorting angrily, jealously guarding them. Perhaps he was even jealous of the moon which shone down through the scudding cloud. Karanar could not settle down. He stamped on the snow-dusted snowcrust, a black beast with two humps, a long neck and a bellowing, unkempt head. How mighty he was! All the time he wanted to continue with his love-making, annoying and badgering first one, then another of his she-camels, biting them hard on the gaskins or thighs, pushing them away from one another. All this was unbearable to them – they had had enough of that during the day, when they had willingly submitted to him, but at night they wanted some peace. They also were shrieking angrily as they fought off his unwanted attentions, and had no intention of letting him have his way. At night they wanted some peace.

Nearer dawn Burannyi Karanar calmed down a bit and became quiet. He stood beside the she-camels, occasionally bellowing as if half-awake and looking around wildly. Then the four she-camels, all of them, lay down on the snow, close together, stretched out their necks and lowered their heads to doze a bit. They were dreaming of little baby camels, those

they had already borne and those whom they were to bear
from this black male who had come from heaven knows where
and who had won them in battle with the other males. And
they were dreaming of summer; of the smell of wormwood,
the gentle touch of the sucklings on their udders. Their udders
ached a little, with a pain that came from the dark depths,
foretelling the milk to come . . . And Burannyi Karanar stood
there, as always on guard, with the wind whistling in his
shaggy hair.

Meanwhile the earth continued on its orbit round the sun,
bathed in the upper winds; and at last morning came over the
Sarozek. Suddenly Burannyi Karanar saw that two men were
approaching, riding on a camel. They were Yedigei and
Kospan; and Kospan had a gun with him.

Burannyi Karanar was furious; he shook, yelled and boiled
with rage. How dare people come into his territory? How dare
they approach his harem? What right had they to interrupt his
rut? He shrieked in loud protest and shaking his head on his
long neck, bared his teeth like a dragon, opening wide his
fearsome, yawning maw. His breath poured like smoke from
his hot mouth out into the cold air and settled on his black,
shaggy locks as a white hoarfrost. In his excitement he began
to piss, standing there and sending forth a stream into the
wind so that the air stank of it and icy drops fell on Yedigei's
face.

Yedigei jumped down, and threw his sheepskin coat on the
snow so that he would be free to move in his light sleeveless
jacket and padded trousers. He unwound his whip from
around its handle.

'Look, Yedike, if anything goes wrong, I'll let him have it!'
Kospan was preparing his gun.

'No, not on any account. Don't worry about me. I'm his
master, I'll take what's coming. Keep the gun for your own
protection. If he attacks you, that's quite different.'

'Right!' said Kospan, remaining up on the camel.

Cracking the whip sharply with a sound like gunshots,
Yedigei approached his Karanar. Karanar, observing this, got
more and more enraged, bellowing and spitting, and slowly

268

approached Yedigei. Meanwhile the she-camels got up from their hollow and also began to move around anxiously.

Still cracking the whip – the one with which he used to urge on the camels when clearing snowdrifts – Yedigei walked over the snow, shouting loudly the while to Karanar, hoping that the animal would recognize his voice.

'Ai, ai, Karanar! Don't play the fool! Don't play the fool! It's me! What, are you blind? I'm telling you, it's me!'

But Karanar did not react to his voice, and Yedigei was horrified to see that the shaggy, angry-looking camel was starting to run at him, a vast black mass with his humps shaking on his back. Pushing down his *malakhai* hat, Yedigei immediately went into action with the whip. It was a long one, some seven metres of it, plaited from heavy, oiled leather. The camel yelled, advancing on Yedigei, trying to seize him with his teeth and force him down so that he could trample him. But Yedigei did not let him near, striking with the whip with all his strength. He turned, retreated and advanced again, all the while shouting at the animal, hoping that he would come to his senses and recognize him. So they fought each other, as each knew best and each, in his way, with right on his side. Yedigei was astonished by the indomitable, unabated fervour of the male; his rock-like determination to hold on to his freedom. He knew that he had to take that happiness away from him, but there was no other way out. Yedigei was only worried about one thing: he must not take out Karanar's eyes – anything else did not matter.

Yedigei's determination at last broke down the will of the camel. Whipping and shouting, advancing on the camel, he managed to get close and threw himself at the animal, seizing him by the upper lip – he grabbed it with such force he nearly tore it – and then, with a cunning move, put on the prepared twitch he was carrying. Karanar shrieked and groaned from the unbearable pain which the tightening twitch caused him. In the animal's dilated, unblinking eyes, Yedigei saw a sharp reflection of himself, as if in a mirror, and almost recoiled, amazed by his own appearance. An inhuman expression was distorting his angry, sweating face, and there was the snow churned up all around – he saw all this in a single fleeting moment in Karanar's maddened pupils. At that moment he wanted to throw everything to the devil, to run away rather than to torture the blameless beast; but at once he had second thoughts. They were waiting for him at Boranly-Burannyi, and he could not return without Karanar and leave him to be shot by the Ak-Moinak men. He conquered himself. In his triumph he shouted and began to threaten the camel, forcing him to lie down on the ground. Now he had to be saddled. Burannyi Karanar was still struggling, shrieking and snorting, covering his master with his damp breath, but Yedigei would not give way. He forced the camel to calm down.

'Kospan, throw that saddle over here and drive those she-camels away behind the hillock so that he can't see them!' Yedigei shouted.

Kospan at once tossed over the saddle and ran off to chase away Karanar's herd. Meanwhile all was done: Yedigei had quickly saddled Karanar, and when Kospan returned, running up with Yedigei's sheepskin coat which he had thrown off, Yedigei was able to put it on and with no more delay mounted the saddled Karanar.

The infuriated camel made one more attempt to get back to his she-camels; he even made an attempt to get at his master with his teeth, throwing his head to one side. But in spite of the grunts and angry shrieks and the enraged, unending whining, Yedigei drove him relentlessly over the snowy steppe, all the time trying to talk some sense back into the camel.

'Stop it! Enough!' he said. 'Shut up! You can't go back, you addle-headed beast! Do you think I wish you harm? If it hadn't been for me, you'd have been shot by now as a dangerous, mad animal. What do you say to that? You certainly were mad, that's a fact. Otherwise you wouldn't have come all this way. Hadn't you enough she-camels at home? Listen, when we get home, that'll be the end of your excursions and wanderings around the other herds. I'll put you on a chain and you won't have one more step of freedom, now you've shown yourself for what you are!'

Burannyi Yedigei made these threats mainly to justify

himself in his own eyes. He had taken Karanar by force away from his Ak-Moinak she-camels, which was really unfair. If he had been a more passive animal, like the one he had ridden on to Ak-Moinak, things would have been different. Yedigei had left the riding camel with Kospan, who had promised that he would bring her over to Boranly-Burannyi when there was an opportunity – that would be no problem. But with this other wretched beast, there was only trouble.

After a time, Burannyi Karanar became resigned to the fact that he was once more saddled and under his master's control. He cried out less and settled into an even, quickened pace. Soon he reached his best speed and ran at a trot, sweeping over the Sarozek as if he were run by clockwork. Yedigei also calmed down and sat more confidently between the two humps, wrapped up against the wind, his *malakhai* hat well tied down. Now he was itching to reach the neighbourhood of Boranly-Burannyi.

But he was still fairly far from home, but it was a reasonable day, a bit windy, a bit cloudy. It was possible there would be no snow showers for the next few hours, although at night there would probably be a blizzard. As he returned, Yedigei felt satisfied that he had managed to catch and harness Karanar, and he was especially glad that he had spent yesterday evening with Kospan, Erlepes' *dombra* and his singing.

But then Yedigei returned unwillingly to thoughts of his difficult life. Here there was trouble indeed! How was he to act so that no one suffered? Supposing he did not hide his pain, but said directly to Zaripa, 'Well, it's like this, Zaripa: I love you!' Perhaps if Abutalip's children could not get on in life with their father's name, and Zaripa was agreeable, they could be given his, Yedigei's, name. He would be only too happy to give his surname to Daul and Ermek. Then they would have no difficulties, meet no barriers in their lives. They could achieve success by their own efforts and ability. But perhaps they would be sorry to give up their father's name for this? Such were the thoughts which came to Burannyi Yedigei as he rode along.

Already the day was coming towards its end. The tireless

271

the parable of the mankind

Karanar, though still enraged, bore his master conscientiously now that he was saddled. Ahead were the long hills near Boranly, the familiar hillocks now covered with snowdrifts; now there was the main line of hills and, in front of them on the bend of the railway, the buildings of Boranly-Burannyi junction. There was smoke rising above the chimney pots. How were his beloved families? Although he had only been away one day, the concern he felt was such that he might have been a whole year away from them. He had missed them, especially the children. Seeing the settlement ahead, Karanar began to increase speed. He was sweating and heated, his legs were stretched wide and his breath came from his mouth in clouds. As Yedigei came up to the house, two goods trains met and parted at the junction, one going west, the other east . . .

Yedigei stopped behind the house, so as to put Karanar into the pen straight away. He dismounted, picked up the thick chain buried and anchored in the ground and attached it to the camel's foreleg. Then he left him alone. 'Let him cool down, then I'll unsaddle him,' he decided. He himself was in a great hurry. Straightening his back and legs, Yedigei was just coming out of the enclosure, when his elder daughter, Saule, ran up to him.

Moving with difficulty in his sheepskin coat, Yedigei hurried up to her and kissed her.

'You'll get cold,' he said, for she had run out wearing only light clothes. 'Run home, I'm just coming in.'

'Papa,' said Saule, clinging to her father, 'Daul and Ermek have gone away.'

'Where have they gone?'

'They've gone right away. With their Mama. They got into a train and off they went.'

'They've *gone*? When?' Unable to take in what she had said, he repeated his question, looking into his daughter's eyes.

'This morning.'

'So that's it!' Yedigei exclaimed, his voice quavering. 'You run home.' He let go of her. 'I'll come along soon, soon. Off you go, off you go at once!'

Saule disappeared. And Yedigei, not even bothering to shut

the gate of the enclosure, went just as he was in his sheepskin coat to Zaripa's barrack home. As he went, he still could not believe what he had heard. The child must have been mistaken. Such a thing just could not be.

All around the entrance to the house, the snow was covered in footprints. Yedigei threw open the door and entered. He saw the long, cold, abandoned room with various unwanted things lying around. There was no sign of the children, no sign of Zaripa!

'How? *Why?*' Yedigei whispered into the emptiness, still not wishing to comprehend what had happened. 'Can they really have gone?' But even as he said the words he knew that it was true.

He felt shattered, more shattered than he had ever been before in his whole life. He stood there in his coat in the middle of the room, by the cold stove, not knowing what to do, what to expect now, or how to stop the grief, the sense of injury and loss from bursting out of him. On the window sill lay the fortune-telling pebbles that Ermek had forgotten to take with him – those same forty-one pebbles with which they had hoped to find out when their dead father would return, the pebbles of hope and of love. Yedigei groped into the pile of stones, pressing them in his hand. That was all that was left.

He had no more strength. He turned towards the wall and pressed his hot, grief-stricken face to the cold boards and sobbed painfully, inconsolably. While he wept, from his hands the pebbles fell to the floor, one after the other. He tried feverishly to hold them in his shaking hands, but it was no good; they slipped out and fell to the floor, each with a dull thud, rolling into various corners of the empty home . . .

Then he turned, crawled along the wall, and went down on his haunches, squatting there in his sheepskin coat, with his *malakhai* hat pulled down over his eyes and his back pressed against the wall. Weeping bitterly, he took from his pocket the scarf given to him by Zaripa the day before, and wiped away his tears with it.

For some time he sat there in the deserted home and tried to make out what had happened. It seemed that Zaripa had

273

purposely left with the children while he had been away. Perhaps she had been afraid that he would not have let her go. If so, she was right: he would not have let them go for anything. Whatever might have been the outcome, if he had been there, he would never have let them go. But now it was too late to guess how and what might have happened. They were not there. Zaripa was not there! The boys were not there! He had lost them! Zaripa must have realized that it was better to leave while he was away. It had made her departure easier; but she had never given him a thought, never stopped to think how terrible it would be for him to find the hut empty.

And someone must have stopped the train for her! It was clear who that had been – Kazangap! Who else? Only, of course, he had not been able to pull the emergency brake as Yedigei had done on the day of Stalin's death, but had asked the chief of the junction to stop a passing train. And no doubt Ukubala had helped to get them away as quickly as possible, too!

A hunger for revenge, suppressed and black, boiled in his brain. Now all he wanted was to gather his strength and destroy everything in this God-forsaken junction called Boranly-Burannyi, to destroy it utterly so that not one tiny bit remained. Then he would mount Karanar and ride far out into the Sarozek and die there alone from hunger and cold! As he sat there, in that deserted building, he felt utterly powerless, wasted and devastated by what had happened. Yet still there remained just that shadow of a doubt. Why had she gone? Where had she gone?

At last he went home. Ukubala took his sheepskin coat and hat without a word and put his *valenki* in a corner. Looking at Burannyi Yedigei's face, cold and grey as stone, it was difficult to tell what he was thinking about or what he intended to do. His eyes seemed sightless, expressionless, as if he were making a superhuman effort to restrain himself. Ukubala had put on the samovar several times while waiting for him. Now, full of smouldering charcoal, it was boiling away.

'Hot tea,' she said, 'straight from the fire.'

Yedigei looked at her without a word, and continued to

drink the scalding liquid, barely noticing how hot it was. Both were waiting intently for something to be said.

'Zaripa and the children have left here.' Ukubala spoke at last.

'I know that!' Yedigei blurted the words out, not lifting his head up from the tea. And after a short silence, still not lifting his head, he asked, 'Where has she gone to?'

'She didn't tell us,' Ukubala answered.

Silence again. Yedigei's only thought was how to avoid exploding with rage, tearing the place apart, frightening the children and bringing disaster on them all.

Finishing his tea, he again prepared to go outside and put on his *valenki*, coat and hat.

'Where are you going?' asked his wife.

'I'm going to look at the animal,' he called from the door.

By now the short winter day was over, and the air was visibly darkening all around. The frost was hardening, the ground wind was moving, twisting and writhing in eddies. Yedigei walked gloomily into the enclosure and as he entered with angry eyes, he began to shout at Karanar, who was trying to break free from his chain.

'You're always yelling! You can't keep away from it! Just you wait, you scum! We'll have a short talk now. I don't care what I do to you now.'

In fury, Yedigei struck Karanar's side, swore angrily, heaved off the saddle and threw it to one side, and then undid the chain on the camel's leg. Then in one hand he took the halter, in the other hand he held his whip wound round the handle, and went out into the steppe, leading the yelling, howling camel after him. Several times Yedigei looked round, threatening and waving his arms, pulling at Burannyi Karanar as if hoping he would stop groaning, but all this had no effect, so instead he spat, and paying no more attention, walked on, sullenly and patiently suffering the camel's yelling. On and on he walked through the deep snow, through the wind, over the dusk-covered field, which was darkening now and gradually losing its outline. He was breathing heavily, but he walked on without stopping. He walked for a long time, his head bowed

275

in grim determination. Finally, when he was far from the junction, behind the hills, he stopped Karanar and then prepared for his cruel revenge. He threw down his coat and tied the halter to the belt of his quilted coat so that the animal could not run away and so that he would have both hands free. Then, seizing the whip handle with both hands, he began to beat the camel with the whip, pouring on to the animal all his revenge for all his sorrow. Angrily, mercilessly, he beat Burannyi Karanar, raining down blow after blow, yelling and pouring out oaths and curses.

'That's for you! That! Foul beast! All of this is your fault! You're to blame for everything! In a minute I'm going to let you run away wherever you damn well want to, but first I'm going to maim you! Take that! And that! You greedy animal! Still you'd not had enough, you had to run elsewhere! Meanwhile, she went away with the children! You never gave a damn about me! How can I live now? How can I live without her? If you don't care, then neither do I! So take that and that, you dog!'

Karanar yelled and tried to break away, throwing himself about under the blows of the whip; mad with fear and pain, he knocked his master down and started to run off, dragging him over the snow. With a wild, monstrous strength, he dragged him along like a log, wanting only to get away from him, to get free and to run back to the place from which he had been taken by force.

'Stop! Stop!' Yedigei shouted, choking as he was plunged into the snow over which the camel was dragging him. Off went his hat; he was beaten hot and cold by the snowdrifts, in the head, face and in the belly; the snow got down his neck and on to his chest, the whip was all tangled up in his hands and there was nothing he could do to stop the animal until he could undo the halter from his belt. In panic, the camel dragged him on seeing escape as his sole salvation. No one could say how all this would have ended, had not Yedigei by some miracle succeeded in undoing the strap, pulling on the harness and thus saving himself. Otherwise he would almost certainly have died in the snowdrifts. After he had got hold of the halter properly, he was dragged several metres further before the camel came to a standstill, held by his master's last reserve of strength. At last Yedigei came to himself. Burnt by the snow, trying to recover his wind and unsteady on his feet, he bellowed, 'So that's it, is it! Well take that, beast! And get out of my sight, go! Run off, you damned animal, and never let me clap eyes on you again! Disappear without trace for ever! Rot! Away with you! Let them shoot you! Let them exterminate you like a mad dog! You're the cause of all this! Die out there in the steppe!'

Karanar ran off, yelping, towards Ak-Moinak with Yedigei still running after him, beating him with the whip, keeping up with him and then at last dismissing him, sending him on his way with a rich stream of obscenities. The time for settling accounts and for parting had come.

'Get lost, you devilish animal! Run away! Die there, you insatiable beast! And I hope you get a bullet in your forehead!'

Karanar ran further and further away over the dusky-darkening land and soon disappeared in the snowy mist, his trumpet-like roar fading in the distance, no doubt heading straight through the blizzard and back to the Ak-Moinak she-camels.

'To hell with you!' Yedigei screamed and turned to walk back home along the wide track ploughed by his own body in the snow. Without his hat, without his sheepskin coat, and with the skin on his face and hands burning, he walked along in the darkness, shaking the whip and all of a sudden feeling an utter emptiness and helplessness. Falling on his knees in the snow, he clasped his head tight and wept soundlessly. Completely alone on his knees in the middle of the Sarozek, all he could hear was the wind racing over the steppe, whistling, whirling, whipping up the snow with the ground wind – that, and the sound of even more snow coming down. And each of the millions of snowflakes quietly rustling through the air seemed to be telling him that there was no way to lighten the burden of parting; that there was no point in living without the one he loved; without those boys to whom he was bound, like no other father to his sons. He wanted to die there and be covered with the snow.

'There's no God! He doesn't understand a damned thing about life! What can you expect from others? There's no God, he doesn't exist!'

That was what he told himself, in the bitter loneliness of the Sarozek that night. He had never said such words aloud before. Even when Yelizarov, who was often talking about God, had been trying to convince him that from the scientific point of view God does not exist, he had not believed him. Now he believed . . .

And the earth continued on its orbit, bathed by the upper winds. On it went on its journey round the sun, turning on its axis, carrying on it a man, bowed on his knees in the snow, lost amid the snow-covered desert. No king, no emperor, no ruler, had fallen on his knees in such despair at the loss of his domain and power, as did Burannyi Yedigei on the day when he was parted from the woman whom he loved. And yet the earth spun on.

Three days later, Kazangap stopped Yedigei at the store, where they were receiving spikes and chairs to go under the rails which they were repairing.

'Why are you so unsociable, Yedigei?' he asked matter-of-factly, as he put a bag of metal fittings on to his barrow. 'You're avoiding me. It must be for a reason.'

Yedigei looked sharply and angrily at Kazangap. 'If we began to talk, then I'd strangle you on the spot! And you know that!'

'I've no doubt. But why are you so angry?'

'It was you who forced her to go away!' said Yedigei, for the first time voicing the emotions which had been torturing him and giving him no peace all these days.

'Well, now.' Kazangap shook his head and his face became red, either from anger or shame. 'If that's the idea you've got in your head, then that means that you not only think badly about us, but about her, too. You should be thankful that that woman had greater wisdom, far greater than you've got. Did you ever think how all this might have ended? No? Well, she did, and she decided to go away before it was too late. And I helped her to go, when she asked me. I didn't ask her where she was going with her children and she didn't say. Let Fate take care of that, and no one else. Do you understand? She went away leaving her own dignity and that of your wife intact. And they said goodbye like real people. You should bow before them both, and thank them for saving you from disaster. You'll never find another wife like Ukubala. Any other in her place would have raised such a scene that you'd have had to run away to the edge of the world, even further than your Karanar . . .'

Yedigei said not a word in reply – what could he say? In general, Kazangap was speaking nothing but truth. And yet . . . Kazangap could not understand; it was something that was beyond his experience. So Yedigei was downright rude to him.

'All right,' he said, spitting scornfully on one side. 'I've listened to you, oh, wise one; but you've been stuck here for twenty-three years without a break, without so much as a ripple in your calm life. How could you know a thing about my situation? I've had enough! I've no time to listen to this sort of stuff!'

And off he went, cutting short the discussion.

After this exchange, Yedigei thought seriously of going away from the now hateful Boranly-Burannyi junction. He could not find within himself the strength to forget; he could find no peace, and he could not overcome the pining that gnawed away in his heart. Without Zaripa, without her boys, everything around was faded, empty and dull. So in order to get free himself from these tortures, Yedigei Zhangel'din decided to make an official application to the man in charge of the junction, asking for himself and his family to be sent as far away as possible. He just could not remain there. After all, why should he be tied eternally to this God-forsaken junction? Most people lived in other sorts of places – in towns and villages; they would not have lived in a place like this for even one hour. Why should he pine his life away in the Sarozek?

For what sins was he stuck here? No, he had had enough; he was going away, back to the Aral' Sea or to Karaganda or to Alma-Ata. There were plenty of places on the earth. He was a good worker; his health was satisfactory; he still had a head on his shoulders; he would spit on it all and go away.

Yedigei was just beginning to consider how he would bring the matter up with Ukubala, how to convince her – for once that was done, there would be no problems. But a week passed while he waited for a good moment to broach the subject, and then suddenly Burannyi Karanar, thrown out to freedom by his master, reappeared on the scene.

Yedigei had noticed that the dog was barking behind the house; clearly he was worried by something, because he kept on running around, barking, and then running back to the house again. So Yedigei stepped outside to see what was happening, and saw, not far from the enclosure, an unknown animal. It was a camel, but a very strange camel, standing there motionless. It was only when Yedigei went right up to it that he recognized his Karanar.

'So it's you, is it? Just look at you! You're a wreck! You've worn yourself right out this time!'

The former Burannyi Karanar was now all skin and bone. His huge head was sad and drooping; his neck was scraggy; his shaggy fur looked more like a wig, attached as some form of joke, hanging below his knees; and his humps, which once had risen like two black towers, now drooped to one side like an old woman's pendulous breasts. The once proud male camel was so weak that he could barely reach the fence. He stopped to rest. He had expended his all, down to the last blood corpuscle, to the last cell. Now he had crawled home like an empty sack.

'Ai, ai, ai!' Yedigei was surprised but not without malice, as he looked Karanar over from all sides. 'So this is what you've come to! The dog didn't even recognize you! And you, who used to be such a fine upstanding male! Well, well! So you've come back? No shame, no conscience? Your balls are still there, are they? You didn't lose them on the way? What a

280

stink! Your legs are covered in muck! Look how it's frozen on your backside! You wreck! You've really done it now!'

Karanar stood there, unable to move. He had none of his former strength, none of his former majesty. Sad and pitiable, he just shook his head and tried to stand firm, stay up on his feet. Suddenly Yedigei felt sorry for the animal. He went back to the house and returned with a full dish of special wheat grains, which he had salted with a half handful of salt.

'Come on, eat this up!' He put the food in front of the camel. 'Perhaps this'll cheer you up! Then I'll take you into the enclosure. Have a lie-down there and you'll feel better.'

That day Yedigei went round to Kazangap's house.

'I've come to see you about a certain matter. Don't be surprised; yesterday I didn't want to talk and would have said things I'd regret, but today it's different. It's a serious matter. I want to return Karanar to you. A long time ago you gave him to me as a suckling. Thank you. He's served me very well. Not long ago, I drove him off – my patience was exhausted. Today he staggered home again. He could hardly drag his legs behind him. Now he's lying in the enclosure, but in two weeks he'll be back in his usual old state, strong and healthy. Just now he needs feeding up . . .'

'Wait,' Kazangap interrupted him. 'Just what are you driving at? Why have you suddenly decided to return Karanar to me? Did I ask you to?'

Then Yedigei told him about everything that he wanted to do. How he was thinking of leaving with his family; how he had had enough of the Sarozek and thought it was time to move on somewhere else, where perhaps things would be better.

Kazangap listened to him attentively and then said, 'Look, this is your business. But it seems to me that you don't know what you *do* want. All right, let's suppose you go away; but you won't leave yourself behind. Wherever you go, you won't get away from your troubles; they'll be with you always. No, Yedigei, if you're a *dzhigit*, you'll try to master yourself here. To go away – there's no bravery in that. Any fool can run away. But not everyone can master himself.'

281

Yedigei did not agree with him, but he did not argue; he simply sat there, and pondered, sighing deeply. He thought: 'Perhaps if I *did* go away, went somewhere else, could I forget? What about her? Where is she now with her boys? Those poor boys – too young to know what's happening. And is there someone around to understand and help if anything goes wrong? It's been hard for Ukubala – she's had to put up with my strange behaviour, my gloom . . . She hasn't uttered a word. And for what purpose?'

Kazangap understood how Burannyi Yedigei felt and in a bid to ease the situation, said, with a cough to attract his attention, 'What's the point of my trying to convince you, Yedigei? It's not as if I want to make something out of it. You can work it out for yourself. You're not Raimaly-aga and I'm not Abdil'khan, and there's not a single birch tree for a hundred *verst* to which I could tie you. You're free; do as you like. Only have a good think about it all before you leave here.'

Those words of Kazangap remained for a long time in Yedigei's memory.

CHAPTER TEN

Raimaly-aga was a very famous singer in his day. He achieved fame when quite a young man. By God's mercy he was a *zhirau*, a steppe bard, who combined in himself the three main talents needed by such a man – he was a poet, a composer of his own songs, and a player and singer of high ability, with great powers of breath control. Raimaly-aga astonished his contemporaries. He had only to touch the strings and there flowed a song, composed there in the presence of the audience. And the next day this song would already be on everybody's lips because having heard the melody from Raimaly, each of his listeners carried it with him to the surrounding *auls* and the nomad herds. The *dzhigits* of that time used to sing this song:

The heated horse recognizes the taste of cold water
When he comes down to the stream, falling from the
* mountains.*
And when I ride to you, to reach down to your lips, from the
* saddle,*
I recognize the delight of living on the earth.

Raimaly-aga dressed well, in bright clothes – God himself told him to do this. He was especially fond of wearing rich hats trimmed with the finest furs, different ones for winter, summer and spring. And he had a horse who was inseparable from him – a famous golden skewbald, an *akhaltekinets*: Sarala, given to him by some Turkmens at a great feast. People praised Sarala no less than his owner. Those who knew about such things particularly admired his movement, which was brilliant and magnificent. The witty would say that Raimaly's whole fortune and wealth lay in the sound of his *dombra* and the movement of Sarala.

So it was. Raimaly-aga spent all his time in the saddle, with the *dombra* in his hands. But in spite of his fame, he was not particularly rich. He lived like a nightingale in May, spending all his time at feasts and celebrations, and everywhere he received honour and kindness and his horse was fed.

However, there were other powerful men of substance who did not like him. They said that he lived a feckless, useless life, like the wind in the field. And they said this behind his back.

But when Raimaly-aga appeared at some lavish feast, then with the first notes from his *dombra* and his songs, everyone went quiet; everyone was bewitched, watching his hands, his eyes and his face – even those who disapproved of his way of life. They watched his hands, because there were no feelings of the human heart which these hands could not find on the strings and express in music; they looked at his eyes, because all the power of thought and spirit burned in those eyes, continually changing their expression; they looked at his face, because he was handsome and inspired. When he was singing, his face changed like that of the sea on a windy day . . .

His wives left him in despair, their patience exhausted; but many other women wept secretly at night, dreaming about him.

So his life went by, from song to song, from wedding to wedding, from feast to feast, and, unnoticed, age crept up on him. At first a little greyness appeared in his whiskers; then it spread to his beard. Even Sarala was not the same: his body drooped, his tail and mane thinned; and only by his movement was it possible to see that this had once been a wonderful horse.

Raimaly-aga was entering the winter of his life, like a tall, pointed poplar drying out in proud solitude. But he had no family, no home, no herds or other riches. His younger brother, Abdil'khan, gave him somewhere to live, although to a private circle of kinsmen he declared his displeasure and resentment at having to do so. Nevertheless he arranged for him a separate *yurta*, gave him food and arranged for the washing of his clothes . . .

Raimaly-aga now began to sing about old age and to think about death. Great and sad songs were composed by him in those days, for now his turn had come to try to comprehend, as he rested, the basic problem of thinkers: why is man born on this earth? Now he did not travel about as much as before to feasts and weddings; he spent more and more time at home, playing sad melodies on his *dombra*; he lived with his memories and more and more sat with the older men, talking about the transitory nature of the world . . .

And, God be his witness, Raimaly-aga would have lived out his days peacefully, if there had not taken place an event which shook him in his declining years.

One day, Raimaly-aga could stand this quiet life no longer. He saddled his old Sarala and went to a big wedding to relieve his boredom, taking with him his *dombra*, just in case. Some much-respected people had begged him to come to the wedding, if not to sing, then at least as a guest. With this in mind, Raimaly-aga set off with a light heart and with the intention of returning home fairly quickly.

When he arrived he was greeted with great honours and invited into the best white-domed *yurta*, where he sat in a circle of notable people, drinking *kumys* and carrying on most respectable conversations. He even made a speech of good wishes.

In the *aul*, a massive celebration was in progress, and from all sides came sounds of song, laughter, young voices, games and amusements. Raimaly-aga could hear people preparing for the horse races in honour of the newly wedded couple; the cooks busying themselves by the fires; the herds of horses running free; the dogs happily playing around; the wind blowing in from the steppe, bearing the smells of flowering grasses . . . But above all, and with envy, Raimaly-aga heard the sound of music and singing in the nearby *yurtas* and the laughter of girls . . .

The soul of the old singer was weary, and he pined.

Although his face revealed nothing, Raimaly-aga was back in the past, back in those days when he had been young and handsome, when he had galloped along the roads on the young and ardent Sarala, crushing the grass under his hooves; when the sun, on hearing his song, came out to meet him; when the wind did not affect his chest, when the blood in the hearts of his listeners grew hot, when rich sounds came from his *dombra*, when every word that he sang was full of passion, when he knew how to suffer, when he knew how to love, to blame himself and to weep as he said farewell from the stirrup . . . For what purpose had all this been? In order that he could fade away in old age, like the glimmer of flame under the grey ashes?

Raimaly-aga was sad. He became more and more silent and retreated into himself. Then suddenly he heard footsteps approaching the *yurta*; voices, and the ringing of necklaces and the familiar swishing of dresses caught his ear. Someone lifted up high the embroidered covering over the entrance into the *yurta*, and there on the threshold appeared a girl, with a *dombra* pressed against her breasts. Her face was honest, open, with a mischievous but proud look, with eyebrows tight as bowstrings. Everything about this black-haired beauty showed her very determined character; it was as if she had been so moulded by skilful hands. She stood in the entrance and bowed, together with her escort of girls and several young men, asking the indulgence of the famous people. But no one managed to open his mouth before the girl confidently struck the strings of her *dombra* and, turning to Raimaly-aga, began a song of greeting.

'Like a caravan traveller, coming from afar to a spring to quench his thirst, I have come to you, famous singer Raimaly-aga, and have spoken my words of greeting. Do not condemn me for entering in a noisy crowd – there's a feast here and happiness is king at a wedding. Do not be surprised by my boldness, Raimaly-aga, in daring to come before you with a song, with trembling and secret fear, as if I wished to declare my love. Forgive me, Raimaly-aga. I am charged with boldness, like a cherished gun filled with powder. Although I live free at feasts and weddings, I have prepared for this meeting all my life, like a bee which collects honey in droplets. I have prepared like a flower in a bud which will burst out at the fated, due time. And now this time has come . . .'

Raimaly-aga longed to ask who she was, but did not dare interrupt her song in the middle. However, he was drawn to her in surprise and delight. His heart was confused within him; his flesh was filled with hot blood, and if at that time people had possessed particular powers of vision, they would have seen that he was roused, as if he were spreading his wings, like a golden eagle taking flight. His eyes became alive and were shining, and he was alert as if he had heard a longed-for call in the sky. And Raimaly-aga lifted his head, forgetting his years . . .

Meanwhile the girl continued her song:

'. . . Listen to my tale, great bard, and learn how early I embarked on this course. From my youth I have loved you, singer sent from God, Raimaly-aga. I have followed you wherever you have sung, wherever you have gone. Do not blame me; my dream is to become a poet such as you, as you are still, great master of song, Raimaly-aga. And I have followed you like an unseen shadow, not letting pass one of your words, repeating your songs like prayers, learning all your verses like incantations, by heart. I have dreamed. I have begged God to send down to me the gift of great power, so that one happy day I could greet you and confess my love, in a long, lasting act of worship; I have begged for the power to sing songs, to compose them in your presence, and even – let God forgive my boldness – to vie with you, great master in the art, even if in that contest I should be conquered. Oh, Raimaly-aga, I have dreamed about this day, as other girls might dream about their wedding. But I was small and you so great, so beloved of all, surrounded by so much glory and honour. It was foolish to dream so, for you might not notice me, a small girl in the crowd; you might not pick me out at a feast. Yet still I filled myself, drinking deep of your songs, and burning with modesty, I dreamed secretly about you, longing to become a woman as soon as possible in order to come to you and tell you boldly. I made a vow to myself to become acquainted with the art of the word, to learn so deeply the nature of music and to learn to sing like you, my teacher, so that I could come before you without fearing a punishing gaze, to make my greeting, to confess my love and to throw down my challenge. Here I am! I am here before you, and wait your judgement. Time has passed so slowly while I longed to become a woman, yet at last, this spring, I reached the age of nineteen. And you, Raimaly-aga, in my girlish world, are the same, still the same one – even if just a little greyed. But this is no barrier to loving you, just as one cannot help loving those who are not yet greying. Now please tell me decisively and clearly; you are free to turn me away as a young girl, but as a singer you cannot, since I have come to vie with you in the art of eloquence. I throw down my challenge, master. Now you must speak!'

'But who are you? Where have you come from?' Raimaly-aga exclaimed, rising from his seat. 'What is your name?'

'My name is Begimai.'

'Begimai? Then where were you before this? Where have you come from?' The words sprang unintentionally to the lips of Raimaly-aga, and he bowed his head, his face darkened.

'As I have said, Raimaly-aga, I was small. I have been growing up.'

'I realize that,' he answered, 'but one thing I do not understand – that is my Fate. Why did you grow up to be so beautiful – and towards the sunset of my winter days? Why? In order to render meaningless all that came before? To prove to me that I have lived in vain on this earth, not knowing that I would have such a recompense from heaven as the delightful torture of knowing, hearing, contemplating you? Why is Fate so cruel?'

'You judge so bitterly without cause, Raimaly-aga,' said Begimai. 'For even if Fate has appeared in the form of my face, do not doubt me, Raimaly-aga. Nothing will be dearer to me than to know that I can bring you joy with my young girl's

288

caresses, with songs and with wholehearted love. Do not doubt me, Raimaly-aga. But if you cannot overcome your doubt, even if you close the door to yourself in front of me, loving you so much, I will count it a special honour to engage in a contest of skill with you. I am ready for any tests.'

'What are you talking about? A test of eloquence, Begimai? What is the use of a contest of skill, when there is a test more passionate – that of a love which is frowned on by the society in which we live. No, Begimai, I do not propose to vie with you in eloquence. Not because I have not the strength, not because the power of the word has died within me, not because my voice has faded. Not because of these. But because I can only be delighted with you, Begimai. I can only love you to my cost, Begimai, and only make contest with you in love, Begimai!'

With these words Raimaly-aga took up his *dombra*, tuned it to a new key and began to sing a new song; he sang as he did in days gone by, now like the wind in the grass scarcely to be heard, now like a storm roaring with thunderclaps in the white and blue sky. That song has remained on earth, to this day – the song, *Begimai*.

'If you have come from afar to drink water from a spring, I will run like the wind towards you and fall at your feet, Begimai. And even if this day is the very last given to my by Fate, then today I shall not die, Begimai. And through the centuries I shall not die, Begimai, but arise and live again, Begimai, so as to be with you, Begimai! For to be without you is like being without eyes, Begimai!'

That day remained for a long time in people's memories. Many disputes arose straight away concerning Raimaly-aga and Begimai. As they brought the bride to her husband among the white *yurtas* set up for the feast, thronged with riders and rejoicing crowds, Raimaly-aga and Begimai pranced at the head of the procession, singing songs of good wishes. They rode side by side, stirrup to stirrup, matched in beauty; they turned to God and the forces of good and they wished the newly married pair happiness; they played on their *dombras*, they played on their pipes and they sang their songs, first he, then she, then he, then she . . .

And the people around were amazed at the songs they were hearing. The grasses around were laughing and the birds flew around, the boys were happy riding around on their two-year-olds. People barely recognized the old singer, Raimaly-aga. Once again his voice rang out as it used to; he was once more supple and skilful, as he had been, and his eyes were like two lamps in a white *yurta* in a green meadow. Even his horse, Sarala, stretched out his neck and was proud again.

But not everyone was pleased to see this. There were those in the crowd who spat as they looked at Raimaly-aga. His kinsmen, his fellow tribesmen were shocked at him – these were the Barakbai, as the tribe was called. Those Barakbai at the wedding were enraged. What good would come of this? they asked. Raimaly-aga had gone off his head in his old age. They began to talk to his brother, Abdil'khan.

'How will we be able to appoint you as *volost'* chief? Others will taunt us at the election if the old dog Raimaly puts us to shame. Listen to what he's singing! He's laughing like a young colt. And she, this girl, listen how she is answering, what she is saying. Shame and filth! Before everyone's eyes. No good can come of this. Why should he be taking up with this slip of a girl? He must be taken in hand, so that bad rumours do not float around the *auls*.'

Abdil'khan had long been angry about his brother, whom he considered dissolute and who, in his view, had lived an aimless life. He thought at first that he had grown old and settled down, but look – now he was bringing down shame on to the whole Barakbai tribe.

So Abdil'khan spurred his horse and broke through the crowd towards his brother and shouted, threatening with his whip, 'Pull yourself together! Go home!'

But his elder brother did not hear or see him – he was too immersed in his sweet-sounding songs. His admirers, who were crowded thickly around the mounted singers, hanging on their every word, immediately pushed Abdil'khan away and even succeeded in striking him on the neck with lashes. Abdil'khan rode away in a fury.

On went the singing. In that moment a new song was born.

When the maral buck in love calls to his doe in the morning,
The walls of the ravine repeat his call as an echo.

This was Raimaly-aga's song.

When the cob-swan has been parted from his white pen-swan,
And looks at the sun in the morning, he sees only a black
  circle.

This was Begimai's answer. So they sang in honour of the young married people, now he, now she; now he, now she.

Raimaly-aga, so engrossed at that time, was not to know with what rage boiling in his heart his young brother, Abdil'khan, was riding away; nor that all his kinsmen of the Barakbai tribe had followed after him with anger and thoughts of revenge in their heart. He did not know what a punishment they had agreed to prepare for him. On and on went the songs, now he, now she; now he, now she . . .

Abdil'khan, crouched low over the saddle, rode on like a black cloud. To the *aul*! Home! His kinsmen raced beside him like a pack of wolves, shouting, 'Your brother is mad! He's gone out of his mind! It's a disaster! He must be brought to heel!'

Yet on went the songs, now he, now she; now he, now she . . .

So they accompanied the wedding procession with songs to the appropriate place. Here they once more sang songs of good wishes and of farewell. And turning to the people, Raimaly-aga said that he was happy to have lived to see the blessed day when Fate had sent him as a reward a poet-bard who was his equal, the young Begimai. He said that just as only flint striking flint can make a spark, so only by vying in the art of the word, can poets achieve perfection. But most of all, he was happy because at last, as if at sunset, when the sun shines with all the power contained in it since the creation of the world, he had found love, such a strength of heart which he had not known since birth.

'Raimaly-aga!' Begimai spoke in reply. 'My dream is fulfilled! I will follow you. Wherever you wish, I will appear at once with my *dombra*, so that song can join with song, in order to love you and be loved by you. To that fate I will dedicate my life without a second thought!'

So the songs were sung. Here in front of all the people of the steppe, they agreed to meet two days later at a big fair where they would sing for everyone.

Those who returned home from the wedding carried the news throughout the district that Raimaly-aga and Begimai would be coming to sing at the fair. So the news was spread.

'To the fair!'

'Saddle the horses and off to the fair!'

'Come to hear the singers at the fair!'

'There'll be a real party!'

'There'll be delights in store!'

'What shame!'

'Shamelessness, that's what it is!'

Before they rode away, Raimaly-aga and Begimai said farewell.

'Until the day of the fair, dearest Begimai!'

'Until then, Raimaly-aga!'

The day was nearly over. The great steppe was peacefully sinking into the white dusk of the steppe summer. The grasses had ripened and were just starting to give off that faint smell of withering; after the rains in the mountains there was a fresh coolness in the air; the kites flew low and unhurriedly before the sunset, small birds chirruped, glorifying the peaceful evening . . .

'What silence, what bliss!' said Raimaly-aga, stroking his horse's mane, 'Oh, Sarala, my old fellow, my famous horse, is not life beautiful? To think that even in one's final days one can love so much . . .'

Sarala moved along at a walking pace, whinnying. He wanted to get home, to rest his legs. He had been saddled and travelling all day long; now he wanted to drink from the stream and then go out to pasture in the moonlight.

Soon they reached the *aul* by the bend in the river and saw the *yurtas*, and the cheerful smoke from the fires. Raimaly-aga dismounted and left the horse tethered by its halter at the tethering point. He did not go at once into the *yurta*, but sat down to rest awhile at the outside fire. But there a neighbour's son came up to him.

'Raimaly-aga, there are people asking for you to come into your *yurta*.'

'What people are they?'

'They're all your kinsmen – Barakbai, all of them.'

As he entered, Raimaly-aga saw the elders of the tribe sitting in a tight half-circle, and among them, a bit to one side, his brother, Abdil'khan, looking very glum. He did not lift his eyes, as if he was trying to hide from his brother's gaze.

'Peace to you!' Raimaly-aga greeted his kinsmen. 'Surely there's not been some misfortune?'

'We've been waiting for you!' the head of the family spoke.

'And here I am,' answered Raimaly-aga, 'and I'll take my place in the circle.'

'Stop there! Stay by the entrance! And get down on your knees!'

Raimaly-aga was startled. 'What is the meaning of this? Am I not still master in this *yurta*?'

'No, you're no longer the master! An old man who has gone off his head cannot be the master!'

'What are you talking about?'

'About this – that you will give a solemn promise never to sing again, never to wander from feast to feast, and, what is more, to drive out of your head that girl with whom you sang those obscene songs today. Your behaviour was shameless! You disgraced both our honour and your own! Swear to it! Swear that you will never appear before her eyes again!'

'You're wasting your breath! The day after tomorrow, I am going to sing with her before the people!'

Then the shouting started.

'He covers us with shame!'.

'Renounce her before it's too late!'

'He's out of his mind!'

'Quiet! Silence!' The chief brought them to order. 'Well, Raimaly, have you said all that you wish to say?'

'I've said all.'

'Descendants of the Barakbai tribe, have you heard what our kinsman, the most unworthy Raimaly, has said?'

'We have heard.'

'Then listen to what I shall say to you, unhappy Raimaly. You've spent your life in one-horse poverty, wandering from feast to feast, playing your *dombra*. You've been a clown in a mask. You've used your life to entertain others. We forgave your worthlessness when you were young. Now that you're old and just a figure of fun, we despise you. It's time for you to think about death, resign yourself to it. But instead you've been running around with this girl and giving cause for scandal in strange villages. Like a giddy goat, you've scorned the customary laws of behaviour and now you blatantly disregard our counsel. Well, may God punish you, you yourself are to blame. Now for the second point. Stand up, Abdil'khan! You're his brother of the same blood, of the same mother and father and you are our prop and hope. We wanted to see you as *volost'* chief in the name of all Barakbai. But your brother has gone off his head at last; he doesn't know what he's doing and he could harm your chances. Therefore you've the right to proceed with him and take whatever steps are needed to prevent him from shaming us before other people. No one should spit in our eyes – and no one should mock the Barakbai!'

'No one can be a prophet or judge me,' said Raimaly, speaking before Abdil'khan could answer. 'I'm sorry for you sitting here, and for those who are not here. You've made a gross error – you're pronouncing judgement on matters that should not be discussed at such a general gathering. Don't you know where truth lies, where happiness is in this world? Is it really shameful to sing, when it is right to sing? Is it shameful to love when love comes to you, that which is sent down by God to last for ever? Is it not the greatest happiness on earth to be glad for those in love? Yet you consider me mad because I am singing for love. Love has come to me late in life, I don't deny that, but I am happy with her – and so I am leaving you. I'll go away – the world is large enough. I'll mount Sarala and go away to her, or we'll travel to some faraway country, so as not to disturb you with my songs or my behaviour.'

'No, you won't go away!' Abdil'khan, who had been silent until now, shouted in a threatening croak. 'You'll never leave here. You won't be going to any fair. We'll force you to come to your senses!'

And with these words the brother snatched the *dombra* from the hands of the bard.

'There!' He threw it to the ground and trampled the fragile instrument as a mad bull tramples a herdsman. 'Now you'll forget how to sing! You there, bring in that nag Sarala!' He made a sign.

Those who were standing ready outside quickly brought Sarala in from where he had been tethered.

'Tear off the saddle! Throw it over here!' Abdil'khan commanded, and snatched up a hidden axe. With this, he cut up the saddle into small pieces.

'Now you'll never go! You'll never go to any fair!'

In his rage he cut the bridle and the stirrup straps into little pieces and threw the stirrups into the bushes.

Sarala, meanwhile, was rearing up in fright, then squatting back on his hooves, champing at the bit as if he knew the fate that awaited him.

'So you intended to ride to the fair? Riding Sarala, eh? Then watch this!'

Abdil'khan was completely beside himself in his rage. In seconds, the kinsmen dragged Sarala down and tied the horse securely with a hair lassoo, and Abdil'khan, thrusting five fingers into the animal's nostrils, stretched back Sarala's head and brought a knife across the defenceless throat.

With all his strength, Raimaly-aga broke loose from those who were holding him.

'Stop! Don't kill my horse!'

But his plea came too late. Blood poured out in a hot stream from under the knife, spurting into his eyes like darkness at midday. All covered with the steaming blood of Sarala, Raimaly-aga staggered up from the ground, shouting, 'In vain! I'll go on foot! I'll crawl there on my knees!' and wiped his face with his garment.

'No, you won't!' Abdil'khan got up from where he had been bending over the slaughtered Sarala, his face set in a snarl. 'You won't take one step away from here!' He added this quietly, and then yelled, 'Seize him! Look at him, he's mad! Bind him or he'll kill someone!'

There were shouts. Everyone milled around, colliding with each other.

'Pass that cord over!'

'Tie his hands behind his back!'

'Twist it tighter!'

'He's mad! That's what God's done to him!'

'Look at his eyes! He's completely insane! Ai, ai!'

'Take him over there, to the birch!'

Already the moon was high overhead and the sky and the earth had fallen silent. Some wizards came, scattered the fire, and in a wild dance drove off the spirits which had darkened the mind of the great bard.

But still Raimaly-aga stood there, bound to the birch tree, his hands tied tight behind his back.

Then came a mullah. He read out prayers from the Koran. The mullah told him the error of his ways and showed him the right way.

Turning to his brother, Abdil'khan, Raimaly-aga began to sing:

'Taking the last of the darkness with it, night goes away; and the new day comes again with the morning. But for me there is no light. You have taken the sun from me, my miserable brother, Abdil'khan. You rejoice, you triumph sullenly, because you have separated me from my love, sent to me by God in my old age. You do not know what happiness I have, while I still breathe, while my heart is not yet stilled. You have bound me up, you

296

have twisted me with ropes to this tree, but I am no longer here now, my miserable brother, Abdil'khan. Here there is only my body; but my soul, like the wind, covers the distance between us; like the rain which is joined to the earth, I am not for one moment separated from her. I am like her own hair, like her own breathing. When she wakes at dawn, like a wild goat I will run down from the mountain to her and will wait on the stony rock until she comes from her *yurta* in the morning. When she lights the fire, I will be like the sweet smoke and will be all around her. When she rides her horse and crosses the stream, then I will be in the splashes that fly up from under the hooves of her horse. I will be the drops on her face and hands. When she sings, I shall be her song . . .'

Above his head, the branches were rustling in the morning light. Day had come. Hearing that Raimaly-aga had lost his reason, the neighbours came from curiosity to see. They did not dismount from their horses, but gathered in a crowd far off.

He stood there in his torn clothes, tied to the birch tree, his hands tied tight behind his back. And he sang that song which later on was to become so famous:

When the nomads come down from the black mountains,
Untie my hands, my brother, Abdil'khan,
When the nomads come down from the blue mountains,
Give me freedom, my brother, Abdil'khan.
I did not guess, did not think that you would bind me,
Hand and foot.

When the nomads come down from the black mountains,
When the nomads come down from the blue mountains,
Untie my hands, my brother, Abdil'khan,
Of my own free will I will go up to heaven . . .

When the nomads come down from the black mountains,
I will not be at the fair, Begimai.
When the nomads come down from the blue mountains,
Do not wait for me at the fair, Begimai.
You and I will not sing at the fair, my horse cannot bring me,
I will not be there.

When the nomads come down from the black mountains,
When the nomads come down from the blue mountains,
Do not wait for me at the fair, Begimai,
Of my own free will, I will go up to heaven . . .

That, then, was what this story was about.

And as he went on his way to Ana-Beiit, accompanying Kazangap on his last journey, Yedigei spent most of the time recalling that story.

CHAPTER ELEVEN

Trains in these parts went from East to West, and from West to East.

On either side of the railway lines in these parts lay the great wide spaces – Sary-Ozeki, the Middle lands of the yellow steppes . . .

In these parts any distance was measured in relation to the railway, as if from the Greenwich meridian . . .

And the trains went from East to West, and from West to East . . .

Now they had made the long journey along the red sand precipice of Malakumdychap where once Naiman-Ana had wandered in search of her *mankurt* son, and they were getting close to Ana-Beiit. Continually checking, first his watch, then the position of the sun above the Sarozek, Burannyi Yedigei estimated that all was going according to plan. After the burial they would have plenty of time to get home in order to gather together and hold the wake for Kazangap. Of course, it would be in the evening, but the important thing was to have it on the same day as the burial. Life – what a life! Kazangap would already be lying at rest at Ana-Beiit and they would be at home and once again remembering him with kind words.

They were still travelling in the same order: first Yedigei on Karanar, all got up with his cloth with the tassels; behind came the tractor and the trailer, and behind the trailer the *Belarus'* digger. They were now leaving Malakumdychap behind and were crossing the plain of Ana-Beitt, and still the rusty-coloured dog Zholbars ran along beside them, his tongue hanging out carelessly.

It was here, as they left Malakumdychap, that they came upon the first obstacle. They ran up against a barrier, a barbed wire fence.

Yedigei stopped first. 'What about that!' He stood up in the stirrups and looked to the right and to the left. As far as the eye could see, up and down over the steppe, twisted that impenetrable prickly wire; there were several rows of it, all fixed to four-sided concrete posts set into the earth every five metres. The fence was strong and firm. You could not tell where it started or finished. Perhaps it ran for ever! There seemed no way round it. What was to be done? How could they go on further?

Meanwhile the tractors stopped behind him. First Sabitzhan jumped from the cabin and then Tall Edil'bai.

'What's all this?' Sabitzhan waved his hand towards the fence. 'Are you sure we've come to the right place?' he asked Yedigei.

'Of course we have! Only someone's put up this wretched wire fence, the devil take it!'

'Wasn't it there before?'

'It certainly wasn't!'

'Now what? How can we go on?'

Yedigei said nothing. He had no idea what to do.

'Hi, you! Stop that engine! That's enough of that damned noise!' Sabitzhan shouted this angrily at Kalibek, who was leaning out of the cab of the tractor. He stopped the engine, and then the digger stopped too. All was quiet, completely quiet.

Burannyi Yedigei sat gloomily on his camel, Sabitzhan and Tall Edil'bai stood nearby, while the drivers Kalibek and Zhumagali remained in their cabs; the dead body of Kazangap in its white sheet lay in the trailer and beside it sat his alcoholic son-in-law, the husband of Aizada; the rusty-coloured dog Zholbars taking advantage of the break in the journey, went up to the wheel and lifted his leg.

The great Sarozek stretched out under the sky from one end of the earth to the other, but there was no way through to Ana-

Beiit. They all stood there, puzzled, before the barbed wire fence.

The first to break the silence was Tall Edil'bai.

'Well, Yedike, so this wasn't here before?'

'Never! It's the first time I've seen it.'

'Probably they've put it up especially, because of the launching site,' Tall Edil'bai suggested.

'That must be it. Why else should anyone put up a fence in the middle of the steppe. They think of something and go ahead and do it, the devil take them!' Yedigei swore.

'No use calling on the devil! It would have been better if you'd found out about this before setting off on such a long journey,' offered Sabitzhan gloomily.

There was an uneasy pause. Burannyi Yedigei looked down at Sabitzhan angrily. 'Have a bit of patience. Don't get so worked up!' He spoke as calmly as he could. 'There wasn't any wire here before. How was I to know?'

Sabitzhan gave an angry snort and turned away.

Once more a heavy silence reigned. Tall Edil'bai had an idea.

'What now, Yedige? What shall we do? Is there any other track which leads to the cemetery?'

'There should be. Yes, there's a track five kilometres away in that direction, off to the right,' answered Yedigei, looking around. 'Let's go there; there can't be just no track at all.

'So that's it; you're sure there is such a track?' Sabitzhan asked, wanting to get things clear. 'You're sure it won't have disappeared?'

'There is, there is,' Yedigei assured him. 'Let's get moving. Don't let's waste time.'

So off they went again, the tractors clattering behind, following the line of the wire fence. Yedigei was upset. He was very discouraged by all this. He was disappointed in his heart that they had shut off access to the area and had left no sign to show the way to the cemetery. However, he had some hope that there would be a way through and on this south side, too.

So it turned out. They soon came to a barrier across the track. They approached it. Yedigei noted the permanency, the strength of the control point. Large concrete blocks were alongside, and right beside the edge of the entrance road there was a brick building, with windows all round to give a good view. On the roof were two searchlights to light up the road at night. A tarmac road stretched away into the distance. Yedigei was worried to see such a set-up.

At their approach, a youthful-looking fair-haired soldier, little more than a boy, with an automatic weapon on his shoulder, barrel downwards, came out of the post. He pushed down his tunic and adjusted his cap self-importantly as he walked across. He stopped in the centre of the barrier with a forbidding expression. But he returned Yedigei's greeting as the latter walked up to the barrier across the road.

'Good day.' The guard saluted and looked at Yedigei with his bright-blue, boyish eyes. 'Who are you? And where are you going?'

'We're local people, soldier,' said Yedigei, smiling at the boyish sternness of the sentry. 'We're taking one of our elders to be buried at the cemetery.'

'You're not allowed in without a pass.' The young soldier shook his head from side to side – slightly nervously, since he was trying to lean back from Karanar's maw as the camel busily chewed the cud. 'This is a protected area,' he added in explanation.

'I understand that, but we're on our way to the cemetery. It's not far from here. What's wrong with that? We'll bury him and then come back. We'll waste no time.'

'I can't authorize that. I haven't the authority,' said the sentry.

'Listen, my dear boy,' Yedigei bent down from the saddle so that his military decorations and medals were more visible, 'we're not just a bunch of strangers. We're from the Boranly-Burannyi junction. You've heard of it, of course? We have to bury him. We're only going to the cemetery and back.'

'Yes, I understand that.' The guard began to shrug his shoulders, but at that moment, unfortunately, up came Sabitzhan with the affected, hurrying look of an important man of affairs.

'What's all the trouble about? Why the delay? I'm from the Oblast' Trades Union Council,' he announced. 'What's the reason for holding us up?'

'Because it's not permitted.'

'I'm telling you, comrade sentry, I'm from the Oblast' Trades Union Council!'

'I don't care where you're from!'

'What's that?' Sabitzhan was taken aback.

'This is a protected zone.'

'Then what's the discussion about?' Sabitzhan was very angry.

'Who's discussing? I'm explaining the situation for the benefit of the person on the camel, not for you. So that he can understand the reason. In general, I have no right to engage in conversation with other people when I'm on duty.'

'So there's no access to the cemetery from here?'

'That's right. Not only to the cemetery. There's no entry here for any unauthorized person.'

'So that's it, is it!' Sabitzhan was furious. 'I knew it!' He turned on Yedigei. 'I knew some nonsense would come out of this! I knew there was no point in going there! Ana-Beiit! Ana-Beiit! That's Ana-Beiit for you!' With these words he walked off, spitting with fury and irritation.

Yedigei was embarrassed as he stood before the young guard.

'Forgive me, my son.' He spoke like a father. 'It's clear you're on duty. But what about this dead man? He's not just a log to be thrown away and left.'

'I understand that. But what can I do? As I'm ordered, so I have to act. I'm not in charge here.'

'Yes . . . I realize that,' Yedigei said, drawing the words out. 'And where do you come from?'

'Vologda, Papasha,' the guard said, emphasizing the long 'o'. He seemed a bit embarrassed, but at the same time pleased, like a child; he smiled and did not hide the fact that he liked answering such questions.

'And at home at Vologda, is it the same – are there guards at the cemetery?'

'Papasha! What an idea! At home you can go to the cemetery when you like and as often as you like. But that's not the point. This is a prohibited zone. I can see that you, Papasha, have served in the army and fought; you know how things are – duty is duty. Whether I agree with it or not, I have my orders, and you can't get away from that.'

'Indeed, that's so,' Yedigei agreed. 'But where shall we take the dead man?'

They were silent. Having thought hard, the young sentry shook his white-eyebrowed, bright-eyed head with regret.

'No, Papasha, I can't allow it! It's not within my powers.'

'Well, then.' Yedigei paused, very upset. It was hard for him now to have to turn and face his friends, because Sabitzhan was getting more and more worked up. He was now going up to Tall Edil'bai and Yedigei could hear furious words being spoken over by the digger:

'Didn't I say so? I said there was no need to drag him such a long way! What difference is there where you dump a corpse? But no, Ana-Beiit it had to be! And you also said we'll take him without me. Well, go on, bury him now!'

Tall Edil'bai walked away from him without a word.

'Listen, friend,' he said to the sentry as he came up to him at the barrier, 'I've also served in the army and I know the form. Have you a telephone?'

'Yes, of course.'

'Then do this – ring up the guard commander. Report to him that some local people are asking to be allowed to go to the Ana-Beiit cemetery!'

'What's it called? What? Ana-Beiit?' asked the sentry.

'Yes, Ana-Beiit. That's the name of the cemetery. Give him a call, my friend, there's no other way out. Let him make the decision for us in person. As for us, you can be sure that except for the cemetery, we have no other interest.'

The guard thought, shifting his weight from one foot to the other, and frowned.

'Don't worry, it's all according to the drill. Some strangers have come up to the post. So you report to the guard commander. That's standard procedure – it's exactly what should be done. You have to report.'

'Very well,' nodded the sentry, 'I'll ring at once. The only snag is that the guard commander is doing his rounds of the posts the whole time. He has a big area to cover.'

'Perhaps you'll allow me to be with you in the post while you're telephoning; then, if necessary, I could add something?'

'Come on, then,' said the sentry to Tall Edil'bai.

They disappeared into the building. The door was left open and Yedigei could hear all that was being said by the guard. He rang someone, asked for the guard commander, but apparently the commander could not be found.

'. . . No, I must speak personally to the commander . . . No . . . It's important.'

Yedigei was worried. Where had this guard commander got to? They were out of luck, out of luck indeed. At last he was found.

'Comrade Lieutenant! Comrade Lieutenant!' The sentry spoke loudly with a ringing, excited voice and reported that some local inhabitants had come to bury a man at the old cemetery. What should he do? Yedigei was alert, waiting for the lieutenant to say, 'Let them in!' Then that would be that. Good for Tall Edil'bai! He knew the score . . . However, the conversation was continuing. Now the guard was answering questions.

'Yes . . . How many? Six. And with the corpse, seven. It's some elder who's died. The chief man of the party is on a camel. Then there's a tractor with a trailer and behind that, a digger, an excavator . . . Yes, they need that – it's for digging the grave. What? What shall I say? The answer's no? It's not permitted? Very good, I'll carry out the order!'

Then the voice of Tall Edil'bai could be heard. He had obviously taken over the telephone.

'. . . Comrade Lieutenant! Can you see our situation? Comrade Lieutenant, we've come from Boranly-Burannyi junction. Where can we go now? Please try to understand our position. We'll just bury the man and return at once. Yes? What? Of course! Well, come, come and see for yourself. We have here

305

our elder; he served at the front, he fought there. Explain to him, when you come.'

Tall Edil'bai came out of the building, looking worried, bringing the news that the lieutenant was coming and would decide on the spot. Then out came the sentry and said the same. The sentry was now feeling relieved, since the guard commander himself had taken responsibility for the decision. He began marching to and fro by the striped barrier.

Burannyi Yedigei mused. Who could have thought there would be such a turn of events? They sat and waited for the lieutenant. Meanwhile Yedigei dismounted, led the camel to the excavator and tied him to its bucket, then turned back towards the barrier. The tractor drivers, Kalibek and Zhuma-gali, were chatting quietly together and smoking. Sabitzhan was walking nervously to and fro, on his own, apart from the rest. But Kazangap's son-in-law, Aizada's husband, was still sitting there in the trailer beside the body.

'Well, Yedike, how are things? Will they let us through?'

'They should do so. The man in charge, the lieutenant, is coming. How could they not let us through? What are we? Spies? You should get down and stretch your legs a bit.'

It was already three o'clock and they still had not reached Ana-Beiit, although there was not far left to go.

Yedigei went back to the sentry.

'Son, will we have to wait long for your commander?'

'Oh, no. He'll be here soon in his vehicle. Just ten or fifteen minutes.'

'All right, then, we'll wait. Was this barbed wire put up long ago?'

'A fair time now. We put it up. I've been here a year already. It must be six months since we did the job.'

'So that's it. I didn't know it was here. That's why all this happened. It seems I'm to blame, because I insisted on coming here to bury my old friend. This is our ancient cemetery, you see, Ana-Beiit. This man Kazangap was a very good man. He and I worked thirty years together at the junction. We wanted the best for him.'

The soldier seemed to have some sympathy for Burannyi Yedigei.

'Listen, Papasha,' he said in a business-like way, 'our guard commander, Lieutenant Tansykbaev, will come; you can tell him what it's all about. He's only human. Let him report to higher authority, then perhaps they'll give permission.'

'Thank you for your kind help. What else can we do? What did you say his name was – Tansykbaev? Is that his surname?'

'Yes. He's not been with us very long. You think you may know him? Perhaps he's from these parts. Perhaps he's even a relation of yours.'

'Oh, no,' Yedigei laughed, 'we have as many Tansykbaevs as you have Ivanovs. It's just that I remember one particular man with that name.'

Then the telephone rang in the building and the sentry hurried to answer it. Yedigei was left on his own. His brows were furrowed. Gloomily looking around to see if the vehicle was in sight beyond the barrier, he shook his head. 'And supposing this one *is* the son of that Hawkeye fellow?' Then he swore at himself. 'What am I up to – there must be dozens with that name! It couldn't be the same. I'd got even with that particular Tansykbaev completely, later on . . . All the same, there is truth on earth! There is! And whatever happens, truth will always be there . . .'

He went to one side, got out his handkerchief and carefully polished his decorations, medals and shock worker badges; they had to shine for Lieutenant Tansykbaev.

CHAPTER TWELVE

As for Hawkeye Tansykbaev, his life had turned out as follows:

In 1956, at the end of the spring, there was a large meeting arranged at the Kumbel' depot; everyone available was called in for it, and workers came from all the neighbouring stations and junctions. Only those who were on essential duties on the lines were left.

Burannyi Yedigei had attended many meetings in his life, but this one he never forgot. They held it in the engine repair shop. It was crammed with people; some had even climbed right up under the roof and were sitting on the beams. But most of all he remembered the nature of the speeches being made. Everything about Beria was explained down to the last detail. That accursed executioner was well named, there were no regrets. People spoke strongly until late in the evening; the depot workers themselves came up to the tribune to speak and not one man left the meeting early. They seemed glued to their seats. Their voices rang out like noises in a forest under the arches of the repair shop.

He remembered how someone near him in the crowd remarked on the sound in a purely Russian expression: 'It's just like the sea before a storm!' So it was. His heart was beating strongly in his chest, as it used to during the war before an attack, and he badly wanted a drink of water. But how could you get a drink with such a lot of people around? You had not a chance of getting to a tap. In the interval Yedigei forced his way through the crowd to the depot party organizer, Chernov, the former station master, who was standing on the platform.

'Listen, Andrei Petrovich, perhaps I might speak?'

'Do so, if you want to.'

'I want to do so, very much in fact. Do you remember a man, Kuttybaev, whom we had working at the junction? Abutalip Kuttybaev. Well, an inspector came and wrote a report saying that he was writing his memoirs about Yugoslavia. Abutalip had fought there with the partisans. And that same inspector wrote all kinds of other things. The upshot was that these Beria boys came and took him away. He died because of that – he perished because of them! Do you remember?'

'Yes, I do remember. His wife came to collect the document about him.'

'That's it! And then the family went away. Well, I was listening just now to the speeches, and I thought: we're friends with Yugoslavia now – there are no disagreements. Why should blameless people suffer? The little children of Abutalip have grown up, they're already at school. We must bring up that case again. No one should go on poking them in the eye. Those children have suffered. They were left without a father.'

'One moment, Yedigei. You want to speak about this matter, this case?'

'Yes.'

'What's the name of the inspector?'

'We could find out. It's true I haven't seen him since.'

'From whom could you find out? And is there documentary evidence that it was he who gave the information?'

'Who else could it have been?'

'My dear Burannyi, we need factual proof. And suppose that it suddenly turns out not to have been so. Then there'll be trouble. Listen, Yedigei, listen to my advice. Write a letter about all of this case to Alma-Ata. Write down all that happened, the whole story, and send it to the Central Committee of the Party of the Kazakh Republic. They'll look into it there. There'll be no delay. The Party has got its teeth into this sort of case. You'll see.'

Together with everyone at this meeting, Burannyi Yedigei shouted loudly and firmly, 'Glory to the Party! We approve the line taken by the Party!' And then at the end of the meeting, someone at the back started to sing the Internationale. Several voices at once joined him and within a minute the whole crowd was singing as one, under the arches of the roof of the depot, this great hymn of all people who have ever been oppressed. Never before had Yedigei sung in such a mass of people. The triumphant, proud and at the same time bitter realization of his unity with those who represented the salt and sweat of the earth lifted him up as if on a wave and carried him along. The hymn of the communists all the while swelled, lifted up his spirits, rousing in his heart bravery and the wish to defend and confirm the rights of the many for the happiness of the many. As so often happened with Yedigei when he was strongly moved, he once more seemed to be back on the Aral' Sea. And there his spirit, like that of a seagull flying free, soared above the white-capped waves, above the *alabashi*.

With this feeling of exultation he returned home. As they sat drinking tea, he told Ukubala in lively detail all that had happened at the meeting. He told how he had wanted to get up and speak, and what the present Party organizer, Chernov, had advised. Ukubala listened to her husband, pouring out *piala* after *piala* of tea, and still he went on drinking.

'Heavens,' she said, 'you've emptied the whole samovar!'

'I almost died of thirst at the meeting. I was so excited, but how could I move with so many people? When I left I was still thirsty and then I saw a train about to leave in our direction. I went to see the driver. He turned out to be one of my mates, Zhandos from Togrek-Tam. On the journey he gave me a drink of water. But it was not enough!'

'So I see,' said Ukubala, pouring him out another *piala* full of fresh tea. Then she said, 'It's good, Yedigei, that you thought about them, about Abutalip's boys. Now that times have changed there shouldn't be pressures on those orphans. I'm pleased that you're doing something to speed things along. A letter is a good idea, but while you're writing it, while it's getting there, while they're reading it, while they're thinking it over, weeks may pass – it'd be better if you went yourself to Alma-Ata. Then you can tell them directly everything that happened.'

'So you think I should go to Alma-Ata? Right to the top?'

'And why not? It's important. Your friend, Yelizarov, has often called you on the phone and not been able to speak to you. He leaves his address each time. I can't go. How can I leave this home and the children? Don't put it off. Take some leave. How much leave have you earned and not taken here over the years. Take a bit now, and go and tell the top people about it all.'

Yedigei was surprised by the wisdom of his wife.

'Well, my wife, you talk sense. I'll think about it.'

'Don't think for too long. That'd be wrong. The earlier you get on with it, the better. Afanasii Ivanovich will help you and tell you where to go; he'll know best.'

'That's good advice.'

'Well, I've given it. Don't put it off. And you can get something for the house at the same time. Our girls are growing up; Saule will be going to school in the autumn. Have you thought about that? Shall we send her to the boarding school or what? Have you thought about that?'

'Of course I've been thinking about that,' Yedigei stammered, trying to hide his surprise that his elder daughter had grown up so quickly and was starting school so soon.

'Well, if you've been thinking,' continued Ukubala, 'then off you go and tell the people there what we went through in those years. Let them help those orphans to clear their father's name. You'll also have time to walk around, look for some things that would be suitable for the girls and for me. I'm getting on in life now,' she said with a heavy sigh.

Yedigei looked at his wife. It was strange that you could be together the whole time and not notice the onset of age, until suddenly it came to you in a flash. Of course she was no longer young, but she was still a long way off old age. All the same, he felt that there was something new, unfamiliar about her. Then he understood: he could now see the effect of life's experience in the way his wife looked. For the first time he had noticed three or four white hairs, no more than that, on her brow while they had been talking about what they had seen and lived through.

311

Two days later Yedigei arrived at Kumbel' as a passenger. He had had to go back several stations from Boranly-Burannyi in order to be able to board the Alma-Ata train, but he did not mind this. In any event, he had first to send a telegram to Yelizarov announcing his arrival. This could only be sent from a mainline station such as Kumbel'. After that, the Moscow to Alma-Ata train came in; he was to join this and then travel back through his own Boranly-Burannyi junction. Having found a place on the upper shelf in a compartmented carriage he stowed his things and at once went out into the corridor to stand by the window, so as not to miss the chance of looking at his junction from the train, as a passenger passing through. After that he climbed up into his bunk and had a sleep. At first he was pleased to have two days of travel ahead before getting to Alma-Ata. He was not to know that by the second day, he would be wondering what on earth to do with himself while the journey dragged on. He was astonished, as he looked at the other passengers stretched out in the carriage, to see that they were doing nothing but eat and sleep.

However during the first day, particularly during the first hours, he had a festive feeling in his heart, mingled with concern at leaving his family for such a time. He stood there at the window, excited, holding himself erect. He had on a new hat bought at the station shop for just such an occasion; he was also wearing a clean shirt and a partly undone tunic, carefully preserved by Kazangap since the war. Kazangap had lent him this; indeed he had thrusted it upon him, saying he would look better in it, especially with his decorations on his chest. Finally he was wearing breeches and chrome leather boots of good officer's-type box-calf leather. These boots were a source of great pleasure to Burannyi Yedigei, although he did not often have occasion to wear them. Yedigei considered that in order to make a good impression, a man should always wear good boots and a new hat. Today he had both.

So there he was standing by the window. Those passing through the carriage walked respectfully around him and looked back at him. In his appearance Burannyi Yedigei stood

312

out well, helped no doubt by the expression of self-respect and concern on his face.

The train went on its way at full speed across the open spaces of the springtime Sarozek, as if racing to catch up with the sharp border of the horizon. In this world there seemed only two elements – the sky and the open steppe. They touched in a bright line in the distance, and it was thither the express train was racing.

Now Boranly was coming towards them. Every fold of the landscape, every stone here was an old friend. With the appearance of Boranly-Burannyi, Yedigei moved smartly to the window, smiling under his whiskers as if years had passed since he was last here. Here came the junction! The signal flashed by, then the houses, the various buildings, the pile of rails and sleepers by the warehouse . . . At the speed they were going, all of this appeared to be close beside the line amid the vast desert all around. Yedigei even managed to see his little daughters. Naturally they were out there, looking out for all the passenger trains going from west to east. They were waving their hands and jumping up and down to attract his attention, smiling with delight at the carriage windows racing past them. Their plaits were comically stretched out and their eyes were shining. Yedigei instinctively pressed against the window, waving to them and saying some loving words – but either they did not catch sight of him or they did not recognize him. All the same he was delighted that his daughters had been waiting there to see him pass through. None of his fellow passengers guessed that his children, his house and his junction had just been left behind! Even less could they have known that in the herd of camels out in the steppe beyond the junction his famous Karanar had been walking. Yedigei had recognized him at once in the distance, and a warm look had come into his eyes.

After they had passed through several stations, Yedigei dozed off. He slept for a long time, a sweet sleep, to the peaceful sound of the wheels and the quiet chat of the other passengers.

The next day in the afternoon the Ala-Tau mountains

approached, stretching from Chimkent through the whole Semirech'ye, the land of the Seven Rivers. These were real mountains – and what a fine sight! Burannyi Yedigei gazed in wonder at the magnificent panorama of snow-covered ranges, stretching along the railway as far as Alma-Ata itself; he could not take his eyes off them. For him, a man of the Sarozek steppe, the view was a wonderful mirror of eternity. The Ala-Tau not only inspired in him delight at their magnificence, but also a need to think as he looked at them.

He loved to think in silence when there were mountains in view. In his thoughts he was preparing himself for his meeting with those, as yet unknown, people in authority. They had said that the mistakes of the past must never occur again, and that was why he wanted to tell them the bitter story of Abutalip's family. Let them investigate; let them now decide how to make amends. Abutalip himself could not be brought back to life, but they could ensure that no one would dare to insult his children and that every avenue would be opened to them. The elder boy, Daul, would be going to school this autumn – let him fear nothing and hide nothing. If only he knew where they were now. How were they getting on? And how was Zaripa?

He felt a cold, heavy weight fall on his heart when he remembered this. It was time for the past to be forgotten, to fade away. Indeed, she had gone away so as to put an end to his fond thoughts of her. But only God knows what can be forgotten and what cannot! Burannyi Yedigei was saddened; his heart sank as he yielded to Fate. Whom could he tell about this, who would understand? Perhaps those snow-capped mountains, holding up the sky? But with their great height they surely had no interest in the earth-bound troubles of Mankind. That was why they are the great Ala-Tau – for mortals could come and go, but they remained for ever. Many people might look at them and think, but the mountains themselves were indestructible and silent . . .

Yedigei remembered how after Abutalip had written down 'The words of Raimaly-aga to his brother Abdil'khan,' he had thought a great deal about the legend he had put to paper.

314

Once, in a talk with Yedigei, he had expressed the thought that such people as Raimaly-aga and Begimai, who had met on life's way, brought each other as much happiness as grief. One had led the other into a situation of insoluble tragedy, a state in which a man cannot escape the judgement of other people. Therefore those close to a person act as they think best for his own good, just as Raimaly-aga's kinsmen did for him.

At that time, for Yedigei, these wise words had been just wise words, until he himself realized just how true they were – until he himself had suffered. Zaripa and he had been as far away from the situation of Raimaly-aga and Begimai as stars are from the earth, for nothing had happened between them; but all the same he had thought about her and loved her very much. In the end Zaripa had taken the first blow on herself, in order to get away from her state of indecision. Of her own accord she decided to cut away at once. However, in so doing, she had not given a thought to him, she had not realized what her decision would do to him. It was fortunate that he was still alive. For now such a longing came upon him that he was ready to go to the ends of the earth just to see her, just to hear her voice once again . . .

Yedigei also remembered, laughing to himself, how strange it had been to hear from Abutalip that apparently there had been a very famous person in Germany, the great poet Goethe. His name did not sound very beautiful in the Kazakh pronunciation, but that was not the point. Everyone had a name set for him by Fate. This old man Goethe, already over seventy, also fell in love with a young girl, and she loved him with all her heart. Everyone everywhere knew about this, but no one bound Goethe hand and foot, nor did they pronounce him mad. Yet look how they had treated Raimaly-aga! They had humiliated him, destroyed him . . . and all they had wanted was to do the right thing for him. Zaripa, too, had wanted in her way to do what was best for him, and had acted as her conscience had told her. Therefore he could not be angry with her. Who could be angry with the person they loved? You would sooner accuse yourself, consider yourself to blame. Let everything be worse for you, but not for her . . . And if you could, after she had left you, you still wished to remember her and love her . . .

With these thoughts, Yedigei travelled on, remembering and loving her, remembering about Abutalip and his orphaned children . . .

They were approaching Alma-Ata when Yedigei had the sudden thought – what if Yelizarov was not at home? That would be something! For some reason he had not thought of that before he had left, and neither had it occurred to Ukubala. They had considered the matter only from their viewpoint. If you lived in the Sarozek, you went nowhere and you assumed that everyone everywhere else did the same. It was indeed very likely that Afanasii Ivanovich would not be at home. He worked at the Academy; people all over the place expected him to visit them; such a scientist had many commitments, visits to make. He might have had to go somewhere on a long attachment and be away from home a long time. 'That would be awful,' thought Yedigei, and was worried. But then he thought that if this were so, he would have to consult the editorial staff of the Kazakh language newspaper which he read – the address was in every issue. They would tell him what to do and where to go. Who better than people working on a newspaper to know such things? When he had been at home, it had all seemed so simple; just pack and go. Now as he approached his destination, Burannyi Yedigei began to feel very worried. It was truly said that a bad hunter dreamed about the hunt when he was sitting at home. That was what he had been doing. But, of course, he was counting on Yelizarov. Yelizarov was his friend, a friend of long standing, who had often visited him at the junction; moreover, he knew about the case of Abutalip Kuttybaev. He would understand at once. How could he tell people who did not know, whom he did not know how to address – give evidence to them, as if in court, make a statement? How do you do that? Would they listen to him? And what would they say in reply? 'And who are you, that you should want to whitewash Abutalip Kuttybaev? What connection have you with this matter? Are you his brother, brother-in-law or father-in-law? . . .'

Meanwhile the train was already passing through the suburbs of Alma-Ata. The passengers had collected their baggage together and were out in the corridor waiting for the train to come to a stop. Yedigei was also ready. Now he could see the station – it was at the end of the line. There were masses of people on the platforms, people meeting trains or preparing to catch trains. The train was gradually slowing down to a halt. Suddenly Burannyi Yedigei saw Yelizarov through the window, as one of the faces going past; he was wildly glad, like a child. Yelizarov politely waved his hat at him and walked alongside the train. That was a bit of luck! Yedigei had not dreamed that Yelizarov would come to meet his train.

They had not met for some time – not since last autumn. Afanasii Ivanovich had not changed much, although he was getting on in years. But he was still the same active, lean person. Kazangap had once called him an *argamak*, or thoroughbred. This was high praise indeed – *argamak* Afanasii! Yelizarov knew about this and goodnaturedly agreed to the nickname. But he added – an old *argamak*, but all the same an *argamak*! Usually he came out to the Sarozek in his working gear, in rough leather boots and an old cap which had seen much service in its time, but here he was, dressed in a good, dark-grey suit and even wearing a tie. The suit was well-cut to his figure and went with the colour of his hair, which was already half grey.

As the train came to a standstill, Afanasii Ivanovich walked alongside, half-facing Yedigei and smiling at him. Yelizarov's grey eyes with their bright eyebrows were alight with real pleasure at their meeting. This made Yedigei feel warm, and his worries of a short while ago vanished. 'It's a good beginning!' he thought, delighted. 'God grant that this journey will be successful!'

'So you've come at last! Once in a blue moon! Good day, Yedigei! Good day, Burannyi!' said Yelizarov as they met.

They embraced warmly. Yedigei was a bit confused by the crowds of people, and also from sheer pleasure at the reunion. While they were walking to the square in front of the station, Yelizarov bombarded him with questions. He asked after everyone. How was Kazangap? Ukubala? Bukei? The children? Who was now in charge? He even remembered to ask about Karanar. 'And how's your Burannyi Karanar?' he asked with interest, having laughed at something just before his question. 'Just the same, is he – a roaring lion?'

'He's still on his feet. Whatever happens to him, he roars,' answered Yedigei. 'He's got the freedom of the Sarozek; what more could he want?'

Near the station there was a large black car, shining and polished. It was the first such car that Yedigei had seen. It was a ZIM, the best car of the Fifties.

'This is *my* Karanar,' joked Yelizarov. 'Get inside, Yedigei!' He opened the door as he spoke. 'We'll get on our way.'

'Who's going to drive?' Yedigei asked.

'I am,' said Yelizarov, as he sat behind the wheel. 'I've learnt in my old age. Mustn't lag behind the Americans!'

Yelizarov confidently started the engine. But before he drove off, he looked questioningly at his visitor, smiling.

'Well, you've come, at last. Tell me, for how long?'

'I'm here on business, Afanasii Ivanovich. I'll be here as long as it takes to get it done. But first of all I want your advice.'

'I thought as much. Nothing else would have dragged you out of the Sarozek! Well, let's do this – we'll go first to my house. You can stay there. No, I insist! No hotels for you. You're a special guest. As I stay with you in the Sarozek, so you'll stay with me here. As they say in Kazakh, mutual respect.'

'Yes, that's what it is!' Yedigei confirmed.

'So that's decided, then. Besides, it'll be very pleasant for me. My Yulya has gone to Moscow to visit my son. Our second grandson has just been born, so she's hurried off to share the excitement with the young people.'

'Second grandson, eh? Congratulations!' said Yedigei.

'Yes, the second already,' said Yelizarov, raising his shoulders. 'When you're a grandfather, you'll understand how I feel! Though you've got some time to go yet. At your age I could still feel the wind in my hair. What's funny is that you

318

and I understand each other in spite of the difference in our ages. Shall we get going? We have to go across the town and up higher. See the snow-capped mountains over there? We're going there, among the mountains, to Medeo. I've told you, I think, that our home's out in the suburbs, almost in a village.'

'I remember, Afanasii Ivanovich. You said it was right by a river. You can always hear the sound of water.'

'Soon you'll hear it for yourself. Off we go. While it's light, we'll take a look at the town. It's lovely now. Spring and flowers everywhere.'

From the station the road was straight and seemingly endless, as they crossed the town; then gradually they were climbing upwards among poplars and parks. Yelizarov drove without hurry. As he went, he pointed out the landmarks – all the large buildings, shops, blocks of flats. In the very centre of the town in a square, open on all sides, stood a building which Yedigei recognized at once from a picture he had seen – the Republic's House of Government.

'This is where the Central Committee works.'

They drove past, not thinking that the next day they would be in there on business. Burannyi Yedigei recognized another building as they forked to the left off the straight street – it was the Kazakh Opera House. Two blocks later on, they made a further turn towards the mountains and took the Medeo road. Now the centre of the town was behind them. They went along a long street between houses, gardens, irrigation ditches brimfull of mountain water; past gardens full of flowers.

'It's beautiful!' said Yedigei.

'I'm glad that you've come just now,' answered Yelizarov, 'Alma-Ata couldn't be looking better. It's beautiful in winter, but now it makes your heart sing.'

'So you're feeling good?'

Yedigei was glad to see Yelizarov in this mood. Yelizarov, looking at him with his grey, somewhat protruding eyes, nodded and then looked serious. For a moment he frowned, but then once more the lines around his eyes wrinkled into a smile.

'This is a special spring, Yedigei. There are changes. Even

though we're getting old, it's interesting to be alive now. People have changed their minds and are looking at things anew. Have you ever been ill and then recovered, with a new taste for life?'

'I don't remember,' Yedigei answered ingenuously, 'perhaps after my shellshock, though . . .'

'Oh, you're as healthy as an ox now!' Yelizarov laughed. 'But I'm not talking about health; that was by-the-by, meta-phorically . . . No, more this way. The Party said the first word. I'm very pleased about it, although as far as I'm personally concerned, I've no special reason to be affected. But I feel glad in my heart, and I feel hopeful, as I did when I was young. Or is this because I'm getting old, eh?'

'Afanasii Ivanovich, I've come here on just such a matter.'

'What is it then?' Yelizarov did not quite understand.

'Perhaps you'll remember – I told you once about Abutalip Kuttybaev.'

'Oh, yes, of course, indeed I do! I remember well now. So that's it – and now you're getting to the bottom of the matter. Good for you! You've certainly wasted no time.'

'I'm not the one to be praised. Ukubala had the idea of my coming in person. Only how can I begin? Where should I go?'

'How to begin? We must consider that. Let's get home, have some tea and consider the matter at leisure.' Yelizarov was silent for a moment, then he added in a tone full of meaning, 'Times are changing. Three years ago one would never have thought about raising such a matter. Now there's nothing to be afraid of. That's how it should be, in principle. We must, all of us, all as one, hold on to this view of justice. And there must be no exceptional rights for anyone. That's how I understand it.'

'Things are clearer for you as a scientist,' said Yedigei. 'They spoke about that at the meeting at the depot, too. Then at once I thought about Abutalip. The memory of what had happened to him gave me pain deep down inside for a long time. In fact, I wanted to raise it at the meeting. But the point is not only about justice. Abutalip left his children behind; they're growing up now, and the elder boy will be starting school this autumn.'

'Where are they now, this family?'

'I don't know, Afanasii Ivanovich, and it'll soon be three years since they went away. We just don't know.'

'That doesn't present any difficulties. We can find out; they can be traced. The main thing now, as the lawyers would say, is to reopen the case of Abutalip.'

'That's it! You've found exactly the right expression. That's why I've come to you.'

'And I don't think you've come in vain.'

As he knew it would, so it turned out. Very soon, exactly three weeks after Yedigei had got home, a document arrived from Alma-Ata in which it was stated in black and white that the former worker at Boranly-Burannyi junction, Abutalip Kutty-baev, who had died during an investigation, had been fully rehabilitated, and that there was no evidence that he had committed any crime. The document had been sent with the intention that it should be brought publicly to the attention of all in the collective in which the victim had been working at the time.

Almost at the same time as this document, there arrived a letter from Afanasii Ivanovich Yelizarov. It was a wonderful letter. Yedigei kept this letter all his life among his most important documents – his birth certificate, war decorations' citations, his papers about his war wounds and his work testimonials.

In that long letter, Afanasii Ivanovich said that first of all, he was delighted with the speed with which Abutalip's case had been reviewed and about his rehabilitation. This very fact was a good sign of the times. As he expressed it, it represented a great victory over ourselves. this too appears often

He wrote further that, after Yedigei had left, he had gone again to the offices which he had visited with Yedigei, and had found out other important facts. First the investigator Tansyk-baev had been relieved of his post, his awards had been taken from him and he had been required to answer for his actions

321

in that matter. Secondly, he had been told that the family of Abutalip Kuttybaev were now living in Pavlodar. (So that was how far away they had gone!) Zaripa was once more working as a school teacher and she had married again. This was the news which had come from the place where she was now living. Furthermore, he wrote, 'Your suspicions, Yedigei, about that inspector were proved right during the review of the case. It seems it was he who had informed on Abutalip Kuttybaev. Why had he done this? What drove him to such an evil act? I have thought a lot about this, remembering what I know about similar cases and what you told me, Yedigei. Having considered all of this, I tried to understand what prompted him. But still it was hard to explain. What could have inspired such hatred in him towards a person whom he did not know? Perhaps this was a certain disease, an epidemic, which infected people in that period of our history? Perhaps there was a pernicious, envious streak in people that gradually made them heartless and led them to acts of cruelty? But what sort of jealousy could the person of Abutalip Kuttybaev arouse? This remains a mystery to me. As for the method used, it was as old as the world itself. Once, you had only to denounce someone as a heretic and he would be stoned to death in the bazaars of Bukhara, or in Europe, burnt at the stake. We spoke a lot about this when you were here, Yedigei. After the facts had been revealed in the review of Abutalip's case, I was once more convinced that it will take a long time more for people to rid themselves of this disease, this hatred of a person's personality. How long, it's hard to say. But against all this I revel in the knowledge that justice cannot be destroyed on this earth. Here once again it has triumphed. It may have been at a high price, but it has triumphed! And that will always be so, as long as the world lasts. So I am pleased, Yedigei, that you achieved justice in this case, particularly as you were not directly involved.'

Yedigei spent several days under the influence of this letter, and was surprised to find that somehow he had changed; something had been added and had become clear within him. And for the first time he began to think that the moment had

322

come to prepare for old age which was not so far away across the mountains and was advancing towards him . . .

This letter from Yelizarov was for him a milestone; there was life before the letter, and life after the letter had come. All that had been before the letter had gone away, was covered in a haze, like the shore as seen from out at sea; all that happened after the letter flowed quickly by from day to day, reminding him that it would last long, but not for ever.

But the most important thing that he had learned from the letter was that Zaripa had married again. This news caused him to live once more through some very hard and oppressive minutes. He consoled himself with the fact that he had known, that in some way he had *felt* that she had remarried, even though he did not know where she was, how the children were, or how she was getting on in her new surroundings. He felt all this especially strongly when he had been returning home from Alma-Ata in the train. It was hard to say why such a feeling had come into his head, but it had not been because he was feeling down. On the contrary, Yedigei had left Alma-Ata feeling good and with his heart uplifted. Everywhere he had been with Yelizarov, they had been received with understanding and goodwill. This clearly increased his confidence in the correctness of his chosen course and his hopes for a successful conclusion.

This is what had happened on the day that Yedigei had left Alma-Ata. Yelizarov had taken him to lunch at the station restaurant. There had been plenty of time before the train left, and they had sat there enjoying a drink and having a heart-to-heart talk before they parted. In that talk, Afanasii Ivanovich had stated what Yedigei now realized was his most precious thought. He, a former Moscow Young Communist League member, had come to the Turkestan Krai in the Twenties, to fight against the Basmachi rebels; afterwards, he had settled there for the rest of his life, working as a geologist. It was his view that the world had not staked its hopes on the October Revolution in vain. However heavily they had had to pay for mistakes and omissions, the movement along the way had not stopped – this was a fact of history. He went on to say that now that movement would progress with new strength, helped on by the current cleansing of society. 'Once we can talk to each other, ourselves, about this, that means we have strength for the future!' stressed Yelizarov. Yes, they had had a good discussion that lunchtime.

It was with that confident feeling that Burannyi Yedigei had set off back to his home in the Sarozek.

Once again the blue, snow-covered Ala-tau appeared before his eyes and he gazed upon the distant thick-set range stretching across the Semirech'ye. Then, as he thought back over his stay in Alma-Ata, he realized that some inner voice was telling him that Zaripa had married again.

Looking at the mountains, looking at the spring view, Yedigei thanked God that there were on earth people reliable in word and deed such as Yelizarov. Without them, a man's life on earth would be much more difficult.

After the completion of all the visits concerning Abutalip's case, he had thought about the ironies of history, of living in a time of rapid change. If Abutalip had lived, not died, they would have annulled the false accusations and, perhaps, he would again have had happiness and a life of peace with his children. If he had remained alive! Those words said it all. If he had remained alive, then of course Zaripa would have waited for him until the very last day. That was a fact. A woman like her would wait for her husband whatever happened. But if there was no person to wait for, then there was no reason for a young woman to continue to live on her own. If that was so and if she met someone who was suitable, she would remarry – and why not? Yedigei was upset by these thoughts. He tried to direct his attention to something else, tried not to think at all, tried not to give his imagination rein. But it was no good. To take his mind off them, he went along to the restaurant car.

Here there were few people and it was still clean and fresh so soon after the start of the journey. Yedigei sat down by the window and he ordered a bottle of beer so as to have something to pass the time. The large windows of the restaurant car enabled him to see, at one and the same time, mountains, steppe and the sky above them. This green expanse, with occasional masses of poppy colour on the one side and the magnificent snow-clad range on the other, lifted up his soul to unattainable desires, and led to bitter disillusionment. Suddenly he felt a need for something bitter to match his mood, so he ordered some vodka. Having downed several small glasses, he felt as though he had drunk nothing at all. Then he ordered more beer and sat there deep in thought. The day was drawing to its end. In the clarity of the spring evening, the countryside was racing past. Villages flashed by, gardens, roads, bridges and herds – but all this hardly touched Yedigei, because a tedious longing had come upon him with fresh fire, saddening and oppressing his soul, bringing with it dim premonitions.

So there he sat until it got dark, when crowds of people came into the restaurant car and it became hard to breathe because of tobacco smoke. Yedigei could not understand why these people seemed so unconcerned. Why did unimportant conversations arouse them so? And why did they find pleasure in vodka and tobacco? The women accompanying the men were especially irritating to him; their laughter was unbearable. He got up, staggering a bit as he got to his feet, found a waitress puffing away with her tray and, having paid his bill, started on his way back to his carriage. He had to go through several others before reaching his. While he walked, rocking with the train's motion, he felt more and more weighed down by a feeling of his complete isolation and alienation.

Why should he go on living? Why should he go on travelling?

Now he no longer cared where or why he was travelling, where the express was hurrying through the night. At one corridor end he stopped and pressed his hot forehead to the cold glass pane of the door and stood there, neither looking out, nor paying any attention to other passengers pushing past him.

The train went rushing on its way. He could open the door – for Yedigei, like all railway workers, carried with him a pass key – open the door and take that step out . . .

In some deserted spot, Yedigei made out in the distance two far-off beckoning lights. They took a long time to disappear.

Were they the lights from the windows of some lonely house, or were they two small fires? What people would he find by those lights? Who were they? Why were they there? Ah, if only Zaripa were there with the children! He would have jumped from the train, run to her, run to her without stopping, fallen at her feet and wept unashamedly, wept away all the pent-up pain and longing . . .

Burannyi Yedigei groaned under the weight of this thought as he looked at those lights out in the steppe; already they were almost out of sight. He stood there by the window, sobbing noiselessly and not turning round, nor paying attention to the noise of passengers walking along the train. His face was wet with tears. He could still open the door and take that step out . . .

The train went rocking on its way.

Trains in these parts went from East to West, and from West to East.

On either side of the railway lines in these parts lay the vast empty spaces of the desert – Sary-Ozeki, the Middle lands of the yellow steppes.

In these parts any distance is measured in relation to the railway, as if from the Greenwich meridian.

And the trains went from East to West, and from West to East.

Rising up from its nest on the Malakumdychap precipice, the big bird of prey, the white-tailed eagle, flew out on an inspection of the district around. He flew around his territory twice daily, once before midday and once in the afternoon, carefully watching the surface of the steppe, noting everything that moved below him, even crawling beetles and bright lizards. The bird flew silently over the Sarozek, occasionally flapping its wings, gradually gaining height in order to see further into the steppe beyond, and at the same time moving in smooth circles towards his favourite hunting ground, the prohibited zone. Since this large area had been fenced in, the number of small animals and various sorts of birds had increased, because the foxes and other roaming predatory animals did not dare to try to get through the new obstacle. But the fence did not bother the eagle. On the contrary, it was a positive advantage to him.

However, this was not always the case. For three days now he had seen from above a small leveret; but when once he had swooped like a stone, the leveret had managed to run under the wire, and the bird had almost crashed headlong on to the barbs. He only just managed to turn, banking away, climbing steeply, and went angrily upwards, having lost some of his feathers in the sharp barbs. Some down from his breast later came loose in the air and flew away on the wind. Since this incident the bird had tried to keep well away from this dangerous fence.

So there he was, flying like the ruler he was; with dignity, not hurrying, without any unnecessary wing movement, so as not to attract the attention of his prey down below. On his first flight in the morning and now on the second flight, he noticed great activity among the people and vehicles on the broad, concreted area of the launching site. The vehicles were hurrying to and fro and were especially active around the rocket launching pads. These rockets, pointing skywards, had been in place for some time and the bird had long got used to them, but today something unusual was going on around them. There were too many vehicles, too many people, too much movement . . .

Neither had the small procession on the steppe, consisting of a man on a camel, two rattling tractors and a rusty-coloured, furry dog, escaped the notice of the bird. Now they were at a standstill by the barbed wire, as if unable to go further. The rusty-coloured dog annoyed the bird with its idle appearance and its way of circling round near the people; but he did not show any real concern with the creature – he would not demean himself that far. He simply circled over the spot, observing intently what would happen next, what this dog, wagging its tail as it busied around the people, intended to do . . .

Yedigei lifted his bearded face and saw the soaring, white-tailed bird. 'A big one.' And he thought, 'If only I were that bird, nobody would be able to stop me – I would fly off at once and go and land on the tombstones of Ana-Beiit!'

Just then an approaching vehicle could be heard. 'He's coming!' Burannyi Yedigei was glad. 'Please God, all will now be arranged.'

The *Gazik* drove up quickly to the barrier and stopped sharply to one side of the doors of the building. The sentry was waiting for the vehicle. At once he sprang to attention and saluted the guard commander, Lieutenant Tansykbaev, as the latter got out of the GAZ-67. He began his report.

'Comrade Lieutenant, I am reporting . . .'

But the guard commander stopped him with a sign and as soon as the sentry had lowered his hand quickly from the peak of his cap, turned to the people standing on the other side of the barrier.

'Who are you, you strangers? Who is waiting to speak to me? Is it you?' he asked, turning to Burannyi Yedigei.

'It is, it is, my son. They won't let us through to the Ana-Beiit cemetery. Please do something to help us, my son.' Yedigei spoke in Kazakh, trying to ensure that his medals caught the eye of the young officer.

But this effort had not the slightest effect on Lieutenant Tansykbaev; he simply coughed, and when the old man tried to continue, stopped him coldly.

'Comrade stranger, speak to me in Russian. I am on duty,' he snapped, his black eyebrows in a frown over his slanted eyes.

Burannyi Yedigei was very upset.

'Oh, excuse me, excuse me. If I've done wrong, excuse me.' He was now so confused that he had lost all power of speech and forgotten what he wanted to say.

'Comrade Lieutenant, permit me to state our request.' Tall Edil'bai spoke up to help the old man.

'State it. Only be brief!' the guard commander warned.

'One moment. Let the son of the dead man take part in this.' Tall Edil'bai turned towards Sabitzhan. 'Sabitzhan, Sabitzhan, come over here.'

But Sabitzhan, walking about some distance away, just waved angrily. 'You do the talking.'

Tall Edil'bai blushed. 'Excuse me, Comrade Lieutenant. He is upset about what has happened. He is the son of the dead man, our old Kazangap. And this is his son-in-law here in the trailer.'

Thinking that he was needed, the son-in-law began to climb out of the trailer.

'These details do not interest me. Get to the point,' said the guard commander.

'Very well.'

'Briefly and in sequence.'

'Very well, then, briefly and in sequence.'

Tall Edil'bai began to tell everything – who they were, where they had come from, their purpose and why they were there. While he was talking Yedigei watched the face of Lieutenant Tansykbaev and realized that they would get little joy from him. He was standing there on the other side of the barrier; he was just going through the motions of hearing their request. Yedigei understood what that meant, and his soul seemed to go dark inside. All the circumstances of Kazangap's death, all the preparations for the journey, all that he had done to get the younger men to agree to bury the dead man at Ana-Beiit, all his thoughts and all that he had seen, the vital thread connecting the dead man with the history of the Sarozek – all this had, in a moment, come to nought; all this was useless, for it meant absolutely nothing to Tansykbaev. All those good intentions and feelings were despised. Yedigei was both amused and enraged to tears at the cowardly Sabitzhan, who only yesterday had been knocking back the vodka and *shubat* and sounding off about ancient gods, about radio-controlled people, trying to impress the people of Boranly with his knowledge, and who now did not want to open his mouth. He was amused and enraged, too, by the absurdly got-up Burannyi Karanar, with his carpet cloth with the tassels – what use was this to anyone now? This Lieutenant Tansykbaev, who either did not wish or was simply afraid to speak in his native Kazakh tongue – how could he possibly appreciate the significance of

Karanar's trappings? He was amused and enraged, too, by the unhappy alcoholic son-in-law of Kazangap, who had not let a drop of spirits pass his lips and had travelled in the shaking trailer so as to be beside the body, but who had now come up and was standing beside them, still apparently hoping that they would be allowed to go through to the cemetery. Even the dog, the rusty-coloured Zholbars, amused and enraged Burannyi Yedigei. Why had he joined them of his own accord? And why was he waiting patiently for them to go further? Why should he be concerned, this dog? But perhaps the dog had foreseen that things would turn out badly for his master and had joined them so as to be with him at this time? In the cabins sat the young men, the tractor drivers Kalibek and Zhumagali. What could he say to them, and what would they think after all this?

Yet although he was humiliated and upset, Yedigei still felt a wave of revolt arising inside him; he felt the blood racing hot and angrily from his heart. Knowing how dangerous it was for him to give way to anger, he tried to stifle it with a great effort of willpower. No, he had no right to lose his temper because the dead man was still lying there, unburied, and in the trailer. It was not seemly for an old man to become angry and raise his voice. As he thought about all this, he clenched his teeth and tensed his jaw muscles so as not to show by word or gesture what was going on inside him.

As Yedigei had anticipated, the discussion between Tall Edil'bai and the guard commander had at once become hopeless.

'I cannot help. Entry on to the territory is categorically prohibited to unauthorized persons,' said the lieutenant, after hearing Tall Edil'bai.

'We didn't know about this, Comrade Lieutenant, otherwise we wouldn't have come here. Now we're here, please ask your superiors to allow us to bury the man. We can't just take him back home.'

'I've already made a report in the course of my duties. And I have received instructions not to admit anyone on any pretext whatsoever.'

'What do you mean "pretext", Comrade Lieutenant?' Tall Edil'bai was dumbfounded. 'Would we resort to "pretext"? Why should we? Would we have seen anything, there, in your zone? If we weren't intending to bury this corpse, we'd hardly have embarked on the journey.'

'I'm telling you once more, Comrade Stranger, no one is allowed to enter here.'

'What's all this talk about "strangers"?' All of a sudden the alcoholic son-in-law, silent until then, spoke up. 'Who's a stranger here? Are we?' As he said this, his flabby drink-sodden face turned bright red.

'He's right. Since when are we strangers?' Tall Elil'bai said, supporting him.

Anxious not to overstep the mark, the alcoholic son-in-law did not raise his voice but just said quietly, for he knew he spoke Russian badly, stopping and correcting the words as he spoke. 'This is our, our Sarozek country. And we are, we are the people of the Sarozek. We have the right to bury our dead here. When they buried Naiman-Ana here long ago, no one knew that there'd be a prohibited zone here.'

'I don't intend to enter into the argument with you,' announced Lieutenant Tansykbaev. 'As guard commander at the present time, I inform you once more: there can be and will be no access here to the territory of the zone, for any reason whatsoever.'

There was a silence. 'If only I can control myself,' thought Yedigei. 'If only I can avoid swearing and cursing at him!' Taking a firm grip of himself, he glanced up into the sky and again saw that great bird, circling in the distance. Once again he envied the calm, powerful eagle. He decided that they should not tempt Fate any more; they should leave and not try to force their way into the area. Looking up at the bird once more, Yedigei said, 'Comrade Lieutenant, we are going away. But you can tell those your superiors, be they generals or higher, that this should not have been so. Speaking as an old soldier, I say this is unreasonable.'

'Unreasonable or not, I have no right to question an order from my superiors. Furthermore, so that you will know for the future, I have been instructed to inform you that the Ana-Beiit cemetery is to be done away with and levelled.'

'Ana-Beiit?' Tall Edil'bai was astonished.

'Yes, if that's what it's called.'

'But why? Is this cemetery getting in anyone's way?' Tall Edil'bai was most upset.

'There's to be a new microraion, a new township, there.'

'That's rich!' Tall Edil'bai waved his hand. 'Haven't you anywhere else to put it? No space?'

'This is the planned site.'

'Listen, who's your father?' Burannyi Yedigei asked Tansykbaev suddenly.

The man was amazed.

'What's this now? What business is it of yours?'

'You have no right to talk to us like that. You should be telling the facts to the people in there, the ones who've taken the decision to destroy our cemetery. Didn't your fathers die? Aren't you going to die one day?'

'That has no bearing on the matter.'

'Good, then I'll tell you something that does. Comrade Lieutenant, I demand to speak to your highest superior, let him listen to me – I demand that I should be allowed to make a complaint to the chief man in charge in there. Tell him that war veteran and Sarozek inhabitant Yedigei Zhangel'din wants to say a couple of words to him!'

'I cannot do that. I've been told how to act in this matter.'

'What on earth *can* you do?' In came the alcoholic son-in-law again in despair. 'Even the Militia at the bazaar can do better than this!'

'Stop making this scene!' The guard commander turned pale and drew himself up. 'Stop it! Leave this barrier immediately and clear these tractors off the road!'

Yedigei and Tall Edil'bai took hold of the alcoholic son-in-law and pulled him away towards the tractors, but he continued to shout – in Kazakh now: 'You'll never have enough roads! You'll never have enough land! I spit on you!'

Sabitzhan, who had been silent all this time and had been

walking gloomily around some way off, now decided to show himself and walked to meet them.

'Well? Turned back at the gates! So it should be! Now you're having to run away! Ana-Beiit! Nothing else was good enough for you! Now you're running away like beaten dogs!'

'Who's a beaten dog?' The alcoholic son-in-law was now really angry. 'If there's a dog among us, then it's you, you scum! What's the difference between that one standing there and you? And you boast "I'm a government man"! You're no sort of man at all!'

'You drunkard, hold your big tongue!' Sabitzhan shouted, and threatened him, making sure that his words could be heard at the control point. 'If I was in their shoes, I'd have taken you in and sent you off somewhere, so that there was no trace of your stink nearby! What value are you to society? People like you should be destroyed!'

With these words Sabitzhan turned his back on them, as if to say 'I spit on you and on those with you!' and then, suddenly displaying signs of his managerial ability, began to organize and give orders to the tractor drivers.

'What are you doing there with your mouths wide open? Start up your tractors, we'll go back the same way as we came! To the devil's mother! Turn round! Enough of this! I've been caught up with fools! Now I'm taking charge.'

Kalibek started his tractor and began to turn round and to leave; meanwhile the alcoholic son-in-law took up his position beside the corpse. Zhumagali was waiting until Yedigei untied Karanar from the bucket of the digger. Seeing this, however, Sabitzhan did not wait, but continued to hurry him on.

'Why aren't you starting up? Come on! That doesn't matter! Turn round! That is what's called burying him! I was against it from the start! Now I've had enough! Let's get home!'

While Burannyi Yedigei mounted his camel – he first had to get it to lie down, then clamber into the saddle and then get it up on to its feet again – the tractors started off on the homeward journey, making their way back along their own tracks. They did not even wait for Yedigei, because Sabitzhan, sitting in the first tractor, was already urging them on.

In the sky, that same white-tailed eagle was circling, looking down from on high at the rusty-coloured dog, which for some reason infuriated the bird beyond reason with its pointless behaviour. The eagle watched the dog's every move. He could not understand why the dog did not start running in front with the tractors when they moved off, but remained near the man and the camel, waiting for him to mount and then following behind him.

The people on the tractors, the camel rider behind them and the rusty-coloured dog behind him, running and trotting, were once again moving across the Sarozek in the direction of the Malakumdychap precipice, where, on an outcrop in one of the quiet gullies, was the eagle's eyrie. At any other time, the bird would have become alarmed, giving warning calls, keeping at a distance but not taking his eyes off the intruders; flying fast, he would then have called to his mate, hunting nearby over her part of territory, summoning her to join him in case they had to defend the nest. But the bird was not worried now – the young eaglets had long since fledged and left the eyrie. Their wings were getting stronger every day and with their amber-yellow eyes, the hook-beaked young birds were already independent, each with its own territory in the Sarozek. In fact they turned quite hostile if they saw their parent taking a quick look over their territories.

The bird followed the people closely on their return journey. He was accustomed to keeping an eye on everything which went on in his territory. His curiosity was still partly aroused by the rusty-coloured hairy dog which was in the party. What was the connection between dog and people? Why did it not hunt on its own? It ran along, wagging its tail, all the time they were busy with their affairs. Why ever did it want to lead such a life? But the bird's attention was also drawn to some flashing objects on the chest of the man on the camel. Suddenly the bird noticed that the man on the camel following the tractor had turned to one side and was crossing a dried-up tract of land, while the vehicles made a detour around it. He was urging the camel to go faster and faster, waving his whip, while the shining objects on his chest jumped up and down with a

334

ringing sound; the camel was running fast, throwing its legs out in a wide, long stride, while the rusty-coloured dog scurried along after him.

This went on for some time, until the man on the camel drew level with the tractor in front and then stopped across its track at the entrance to the Malakumdychap gorge. The tractor also stopped.

'What's this? What's up now?' Sabitzhan asked, looking out of the cab.

'Nothing. Stop that motor!' Yedigei shouted, 'I want to say something.'

'What have you to say? Don't hold us up, we've done enough riding around already.'

'You must stop, because we're going to have the burial here.'

'Enough of this joking!' Sabitzhan was in a burning rage, pulling even harder at his tie, which was now in shreds. 'I'll bury him myself at the junction and there'll be no more talk! Enough!'

'Listen, Sabitzhan, no one is disputing that it's your father whom we've set out to bury. But you're not the only person in the world. Listen, you saw and heard what went on at the control point. None of us was to blame for that. But think – when has a dead man ever come back home from his burial journey? It's just not done. There would be shame upon our heads. Nothing like that has happened over the centuries.'

'And I spit on it all!' Sabitzhan snapped.

'You may be spitting now. In the heat of the moment you can say anything – but tomorrow you'll feel ashamed. Think about it – you'll never live down that shame. He who has been taken out of his house for burial should not come back.'

At that moment Tall Edil'bai climbed from the cab of the digger, while the alcoholic son-in-law and the excavator driver Zhumagali also came along to find out what was going on. Burannyi Yedigei, still mounted up on Karanar, stopped them.

'Listen, dzhigits,' he said, 'don't go against Man's customs, don't go against nature. It's never been that people have brought a corpse back home from the cemetery. He who has

335

gone out to be buried, must be buried. That's the custom. Here is the Malakumdychap precipice. This is also part of our Sarozek land! Here on Malakumdychap, Naiman-Ana wept. Listen to me, the old man Yedigei – let Kazangap's grave be here! And let my grave be here, too. With God's mercy you'll bury me here, too. I beg of you to do that. And now it's not too late, there is time. Over there, by the edge of the precipice, we will commit the dead man to the earth.'

Tall Edil'bai looked at the place Yedigei had indicated.

'Well, Zhumagali, will your excavator get there?' he asked.

'Oh, yes, it'll get there. Why not?'

'Wait – what's all this?' Sabitzhan interrupted. 'You'll ask *me* in future!'

'And we are asking,' answered Zhumagali. 'You heard what he said? What more do you want?'

'I say that there's been enough mucking about! This is an outrage! Let's go home to the junction!'

'Well, if that's your plan, then there really *will* be outrage when you bring the body back!' Zhumagali said. 'Think about that!'

Everyone was silent.

'You do as you like,' said Zhumagali, 'but I'm off to dig the grave. It's my job to dig it and as deep as possible; there's time to do it now. But when it gets dark, we won't be able to do a thing. You can do as you like!'

And Zhumagali went over to his *Belarus'* digger. Wasting no time, he started it up, drove on to the edge of the track and went past them up on to the hill and from there to the top of the Malakumdychap precipice. After him followed Tall Edil'bai on foot, and Burannyi Yedigei on his Karanar.

The alcoholic son-in-law said to the tractor driver, Kalibek, 'If you don't go up there' – he pointed up to the precipice top – 'then I'll lie under the tractor. That'd cost me nothing.' And with these words he stood up in front of the driver.

'No need for that. Shall we go?' Kalibek asked Sabitzhan.

'All around me are scum, all around are dogs,' swore Sabitzhan. 'Don't sit there, start up and go after them.'

The white-tailed eagle up in the sky was now watching what

the people were doing on the precipice. One of the machines started to shake as it dug into the ground, depositing a pile of earth to one side, just like a marmot near its burrow. Meanwhile up crawled the tractor with the trailer. In the trailer sat one person, and in front of him a strangely motionless object wound round with white cloth and placed in the middle of the trailer. The rusty-coloured shaggy dog was still fussing around among the people, but spent most of the time near the camel. It lay down by the camel's feet.

The bird realized that these people would be staying for some time on the precipice, digging into the ground. He glided off smoothly to one side and, making wide circles over the steppe, flew towards the enclosed zone, intending to hunt on the way and also to see what was going on at the launching site.

For two days running there had been activity on the various parts of the launch-site; work had been going on non-stop, day and night; at night the whole launch-site area with all its special services and zones had been lit brightly by powerful floodlights. On the ground it was brighter than by day. Tens of heavy, light and special vehicles and teams of scientists and engineers were busy preparing to carry out *Operation Hoop*.

The anti-satellite rockets designed to destroy other space-craft had been standing by for a long time, ready to lift off from the special launch pads. But under the terms of OSV–7 (Salt–7) they had been 'frozen' by a special clause, as were similar rockets on the American side. Now they were to be used in connection with the setting in train of *Operation Hoop*. Similar controlled rockets had been prepared for launch in the same operation over at the American Nevada launching site.

The time for blast-off in the latitude of Sarozek was 20.00 hours. Exactly at that time the rockets were to be launched. In a sequence, with an interval between launches of one and a half minutes, eight anti-satellite rockets were to be launched into deep space from the Sarozek, their task being to form in the West-East plane a permanent hoop around the globe, as protection against the penetration of the earth's atmosphere by vehicles from other planets. The Nevada rockets were to form the North-South plane of the hoop.

Exactly at three o'clock in the afternoon at the Sary-Ozek-1 launching site, the 'Five Minutes' system came into operation. Every five minutes on all screens and displays and on all channels, reminders came over, together with the voice announcement 'Four hours fifty-five minutes to lift-off! . . . Four hours fifty minutes to lift-off!' At three hours before lift-off, the 'Minute' system took over.

Meanwhile the *Parity* orbital station had had its parameters changed and, simultaneously, the on-board radio channels were reallocated and recoded in order to exclude any possibility of communication with parity-cosmonauts 1–2 and 2–1.

All the while, completely in vain, truly like a voice crying in the wilderness, from out in the far galaxy came an uninterrupted stream of signals from parity-cosmonauts 1–2 and 2–1. In despair they begged that contact with them should not be broken off. They were not disputing the decision of *Obtsenupr*, but were simply proposing again and again that study of the problem of possible contacts with the Lesnaya Grud' civilization should be continued, in the interests of peoples upon earth. They were not insisting on their own rehabilitation; they were prepared to do anything in order that their stay on the planet Lesnaya Grud' should serve the people of both solar systems.

However, they did protest against *Operation Hoop* and against the isolation which would result. In their opinion, this would lead inescapably to the continuation of the historical and technologically hide-bound nature of Man's society and set back human progress by thousands of years. Yet no one on earth could hear them, and no one either thought or knew that their voices were still calling out in peaceful space, in the midst of silence.

By then at Sary-Ozek-1 the 'Minute' system had been put into effect, irrevocably bringing nearer the launch of the 'Hoop' system.

As the white-tailed bird made its next circuit, it again came over the Malakumdychap precipice. The people were busy –

338

they were now wielding spades. The excavator had dug out a large pile of earth and was now lowering its bucket deep into the ground, bringing out the last loads of soil. Soon it ceased to work and moved away to one side, while the people continued their work at the bottom of the hole. The camel was still in the same place, but now the rusty-coloured dog was nowhere to be seen. Where had it gone? The bird came in closer and circled over the precipice, wheeling left and right, and finally it saw that the rusty-coloured dog was lying under the trailer, stretched out by the wheels. It had slumped down to rest, probably dozing and it was certainly quite unconcerned about the bird. How many times had he flown over the dog, and it had not once even looked up into the sky? A marmot, even when it was frozen in its tracks, would first look all round and upwards to see if there was any danger threatening. Obviously the dog had got used to living near people and was afraid of nothing – just look how it had lain down there! The bird hovered for a moment, strained, and sent a hot, green-and-white stream down towards the dog. *That's what I think of you, then!*

Something splattered from above on to Burannyi Yedigei's sleeve. Birdshit! Where had that come from? Yedigei shook it off and looked upwards. 'That white-tailed eagle again, the same one; trust him to be just above my head! Wonder what he did that for? He's having a high old time. Just floats around in the air.' Just then the voice of Tall Edil'bai from the bottom of the hole broke into his thoughts.

'Have a look now, Yedigei! Is that enough or shall we dig out some more?'

Yedigei bent gloomily over the edge of the grave.

'Go into that corner,' he told Tall Edil'bai, 'and you, Kalibek, hop out for a moment. Thank you. Yes, the depth is about right now. But, Edil'bai, the chamber must be a bit wider, it needs to be a bit more roomy.'

Having given this advice, Burannyi Yedigei took a small can of water and going behind the digger, carried out the ablutions, as was the custom before prayer. Now although they had not succeeded in burying Kazangap at Ana-Beiit, his soul was

339

more or less settled. At least they were avoiding the disgrace of having to drag the dead man home unburied. If he had not been as firm, that would have been unavoidable. Now they had to get finished in time so that by dusk they would be back at Boranly-Burannyi. Of course, those left behind at home would be waiting and worrying, wondering why they were late getting back. They had promised to be back not later than six, the time the wake was supposed to start. Now it was already half-past four. There was still the burial to complete, and then the journey home. Even at a fast pace that would take some two hours. However, to hurry, to cut short the burial ceremony would not be right. At least they would be remembering him late that same evening. There was nothing to be done about it.

After the ablutions, Yedigei felt easier and ready to perform the final ritual. Twisting the cork back into the can, he appeared from behind the excavator with a serious expression on his face, smoothing out his beard and whiskers.

'Sabitzhan, the son of the departed servant of God, stand on my left side, and you four, bring the body to the edge of the grave, laying the head towards the West,' he pronounced, in an exultant voice. When that had been done, he said, 'Now we shall all turn towards Mecca, towards the holy Kaaba. Open your hands before you, think about God, so that our words and thoughts can be heard by Him at this time.'

Odd as it might seem, Yedigei heard no sniggers or talk behind his back. And he was pleased, for he had been afraid they might say, 'Stop it, bossing us about, the devil take you! What sort of a mullah are you? It'd be better to dig him in quickly and get off home!'

Yedigei had decided to be so bold as to say the prayers of burial standing up and not sitting, because he had heard from those who knew, that in Arab countries from where this religion had come, they prayed in the cemeteries standing upright. Whether that was so or not, Yedigei wanted to have his head as close as possible to heaven.

Before he started the ritual, Yedigei bowed to the right and to the left, towards the earth and the sky, bowing to the Creator of the world, into which Man came by chance and then vanished with the unchanging cycle of day and night. As he did so, Yedigei saw once more the white-tailed raptor in front of him. It was gliding along, just moving its wings and gradually gaining height in a wheeling, spiralling motion. The bird did not disturb his inner composure, on the contrary, it helped him concentrate on higher thoughts. Before them, on the edge of the gaping hole, there lay on the stretcher the body of the dead Kazangap, wound in a white cloth. As he intoned in a low voice the words of the burial prayers, prayers intended for all time until the end of the world, Yedigei repeated words in which has been told from time immemorial Man's inevitable destiny. These words held the same meaning for all men, whatever age they might have lived in, and they applied equally to those yet to be born. In pronouncing these all-embracing canons for life, made by and handed down from the prophets, Burannyi Yedigei also tried to enhance them with his own thoughts from deep in his soul and personal experience. A man had not lived in this world for nothing.

'If you hear well, Oh God, the prayers which I repeat after the forefathers from the books of wisdom, then hear me also. I think that the one will not hinder the other.

'Here we are, standing on the Malakumdychap precipice, by the grave of Kazangap, in an uninhabited and wild place, because we were unable to bury him at the cemetery where he had asked to have his grave. And that bird up in the sky looks down at us, seeing us standing here with open palms and saying farewell to Kazangap. You, oh great one, if You exist, forgive us and in your mercy accept the burial of your Kazangap and, if he deserved it, grant his soul everlasting peace. All that we have had to do, we have done. Now the rest is up to You!

'And now, now that I have spoken to You at such a time, listen to me while I am still alive and have the power of thought. It's clear that people only know how to ask You for pity, help, protection. They expect too much from You – and on all occasions, whether they're right or wrong. Even a murderer wants in his heart that You should defend him. And You are silent the whole time. What can we say? We are but

341

people; it seems to us, especially when things are difficult, that You are only there in heaven for the purpose of giving help. It must be hard for You, that I can understand; there's no end to our prayers. And You are God alone. But I will ask nothing. I'll just say now what I think.

'I was shattered that our cherished cemetery, where Naiman-Ana lies buried, is now no longer accessible to us. And therefore I wish that my fate should be to lie here in this place on Malakumdychap, where she once walked. Grant that I may lie here beside Kazangap whom we are about to commit to the earth. And if it's true that after death the soul is transferred to some other creature, then why should I be an ant? I would like to be transferred to a white-tailed eagle, so that I could fly over the Sarozek like that one up there, and look down as much as I want from a great height over my land.

'That is all.

'And now concerning my testament, I shall now speak to these young men who have come here with me. I give to them the task of burying me here. Only I don't see who will say the prayers over me. They don't believe in God and know no prayers at all. No one knows, and no one *will* ever know, if there is a God. Some say there is, others say there isn't. I want to believe that You exist, and You are in my thoughts, when I come to you with my prayers. In fact I speak through You to myself, and at such times I am given the gift of thinking. It is as if You, Creator, had Yourself thought these thoughts of mine. In this lies the heart of the matter. But these young men do not think about this, and they despise prayer. But what will they have to say for themselves and for others at the great hour of death? I am sorry for them. How can they appreciate their innermost, secret humanity, if they have no way in which to rise up in their thoughts as if each of them should seem to be a god?

'Forgive me this blasphemy.

'Not one of them could become a god, for otherwise you would cease to exist. If a man cannot imagine himself in secret as a god, fighting for others, as you would have to fight for

342

people, then You, God, would also cease to exist . . . And I do not wish that You should disappear.

'That is my importunity and my sorrow speaking. Forgive me, however, if it's not like this. I am just one man. I think as best as I can. Now I will finish by saying the last words from the holy books and we will complete the burial. Bless us for this work . . .

'. . . Amen.' Burannyi Yedigei finished the prayer and once again looked up in silence at the bird of prey with a deep longing; then he turned round to face the young men standing beside him, about whom he had just given his opinion to God Himself. The talk with God was now over. Before him stood the same five men with whom he had come there and with whom he now, at last, had to finish the long-drawn-out burial.

'That's it,' he said. 'What had to be said in the prayers, I've said on your behalf. Now let's get on!'

Putting his jacket with the medals to one side, Burannyi Yedigei went down into the hole. Tall Edil'bai helped him. Sabitzhan, as the son of the dead man, stood aside, showing his sorrow by bowing his head. The other three – Kalibek, Zhumagali and the alcoholic son-in-law – took from the stretcher the felt bag with the body inside and lowered it into the grave, into the hands of Yedigei and Tall Edil'bai.

'So the hour of parting has come,' thought Burannyi Yedigei, as he lowered Kazangap on to his last eternal resting place on the burial shelf in the depths of the earth. 'Forgive us that for such a long time we were unable to find a resting place for you. We've been going to and fro for a whole day. That's how it turned out. It wasn't our fault that we didn't bury you at Ana-Beiit. But don't think I'll leave things at that. I'll go wherever it's necessary. So long as I'm alive, I won't keep silent. I'll tell them! And you can lie peacefully in your grave. The earth is vast and unbounded, but as you can see, your place six foot down turned out to be here. But you won't be alone here. Soon I'll come along here, too, Kazangap! Wait awhile for me. Don't have any doubts. Unless something untoward happens, if I die as I should, I'll come here and we'll be together again. And we'll turn into Sarozek soil together. Only we won't know about that. People only know about such things when they're alive. Therefore I'm talking as if to you, but really to myself. That which was you is now no more. So we go away from reality into nothing. And the trains will run on over the Sarozek, and other people will come to take our places . . .'

At this point old Yedigei could control himself no longer. He burst into tears. All that had taken place in many years of life at Boranly-Burannyi junction, all this great strain over a long time, all the troubles, difficulties and joys he had lived through – all this had to be expressed in a few words of farewell in the few minutes of laying to rest. How much, yet how little, is given to a man!

'You hear, Edil'bai?' said Yedigei, as their shoulders touched in the confined space. 'You are to bury me here, so that I can be beside him. And lay me down here with your hands, and set it all up as we've done it today, so that I shall be at rest. Do you give me your word?'

'Stop it, Yedike, we'll talk about that later. Now climb out into God's good light. I'll finish things down here. Calm down, Yedike, climb out! Don't wear yourself out!'

With his wet face smeared with mud, Burannyi Yedigei clambered out of the grave. The others stretched him a hand and he climbed out, weeping and mumbling a few compassionate words. Kalibek brought over a can of water so that the old man could wash.

Then they walked down along the edge of the pile of earth and began to fill in the grave from the upwind side. At first they used spades, and then Zhumagali got behind the wheel and moved the earth over using the bulldozer blade of the digger. Finally they took up their spades again to make the mound over the grave.

The white-tailed eagle still soared above them, observing the cloud of dust below. Clearly this party of people were doing something very strange on the Malakumdychap precipice. He noticed some special activity among them when, on the site of the hole, there began to grow up a fresh heap of earth. Now the rusty-coloured dog, stretched and got up from its place under the trailer and was now moving around among the people. What did it want? Only the old camel, decorated with the rug-like cloth with tassels, sat there unmoved, chewing the cud, continually moving its jaws . . .

It looked as though the people were now preparing to leave. But not yet – one of them, the owner of the camel, passed his hands before his face and all the others did the same.

Time was not on their side. Burannyi Yedigei looked around them all with an intent gaze, and said, 'That is all. Was Kazangap a good man?'

'He was good,' they answered.

'Does he owe anyone anything? Here is his son, let him take over his father's debts.'

No one answered at first, then Kalibek spoke for all of them, 'No, he left no debts.'

'In that case, what have you to say, Sabitzhan, son of Kazangap?' Yedigei addressed the words directly to him.

'Thank you all.' The answer was brief.

'If that's the lot, then let's get off home!' said Zhumagali.

'One moment. There's just one more word to be said.' Burannyi Yedigei stopped him. 'I am the oldest here among you. I have a request to you all. If anything happens, bury me here, side by side with Kazangap. You've heard that? That is my wish, you must understand that!'

'No one knows how things will turn out, Yedike. Why think about it beforehand?' Kalibek was doubtful.

'All the same,' Yedigei was adamant, 'I want to say that and you must hear me out. When such needs to be done, then remember that I expressed that wish.'

'Will there be any other great wishes? Let's have them all now!' Tall Edil'bai joked, hoping to ease the tension.

'Don't laugh,' Yedigei said, upset, 'I'm quite serious.'

'We'll remember, Yedike,' Tall Edil'bai said soothingly. 'If anything happens, we'll do as you wish. Don't doubt that!'

'That's the word of a *dzhigit*!' Yedigei said, and there was satisfaction in his tone.

Now the tractors began to turn round and leave the precipice. Leading Karanar by the halter, Burannyi Yedigei walked down beside Sabitzhan while the tractors got to the level ground below. He wanted a word with him alone about something that greatly worried him.

'Listen, Sabitzhan, our hands are now free again, but there is one subject I want to talk about. What are we do to about our cemetery, about Ana-Beiit?'

'What can be done now? No need to worry your head,' answered Sabitzhan, 'the plan is the plan. They'll do away with it, level it, all according to the plan. That's all that can be said.'

'I don't mean that exactly. One can wash one's hands of anything in that way. Now, you were born and grew up here. Your father brought you up here. And now we've buried him. But his grave is in open country – the only consolation is that it's his own country. You're an educated man, you work at the oblast' centre; you can talk to anyone there. You've read many books . . .'

'What of it?' asked Sabitzhan.

'The point is, that you could help me in talking to people. Perhaps we could go together, before it's too late, tomorrow, to see the local commander – if there's anybody there who's sufficiently high up. It must not be permitted that Ana-Beiit be levelled. That's the point.'

'But these are all old legends, Yedike. At this place, at the cosmodrome, global, *universal* problems are being decided, and here we come complaining about some old cemetery! Who cares about that? For them it's just so much nonsense. And in any event they won't let us inside.'

'If we don't try, then of course they won't let us in. But if we demand, then they will; if not, then at least the man in charge could come out and meet us. He's not some mountain that he can't get up and walk.'

Sabitzhan gave Yedigei a look full of irritation. 'Leave it alone, old man, it's pointless to try. Don't count on my help. I'm not concerned at all.'

'That's just what you would say! End of conversation! Just legends!'

'What do you think? That I should run around as you suggest? And for what? I have a family, children, work. Why should I piss against the wind? Just so that they can phone my boss and tell him to give me a kick up the arse? No, thank you!'

'You can stuff your "thank you"!' blurted out Burannyi Yedigei, and added angrily, 'A kick up the arse! It's just about what you deserve!'

'It's easy for you – who are you? A nobody! But we have to look after Number One – that sweet things drop into our mouths! You can say what you like, but don't go looking for any help from me.'

'Don't worry, I won't. That's all I have to say. We'll have the wake and then, please God, we'll never meet again!'

'Then that's how it'll be!' Sabitzhan made a wry face.

On that sour note, they parted. While Burannyi Yedigei was mounting his camel, the tractor drivers waited for them, their engines running. But he told them not to wait for him, but to go on ahead as fast as they could, for people were waiting for the wake to begin. He would return alone, by his own route – he could go anywhere on the camel.

After the tractors had rattled off, Yedigei stayed a long time there, deciding what he should do next.

Now he was alone, in complete isolation amid the Sarozek – that is if you didn't count the faithful dog, Zholbars, who had, at first, run off after the departing tractors, but then, realizing that his master was not going with them, had run back to him. But Yedigei paid no attention to him. If the dog had run home, he still would not have noticed it; he was too concerned about other things. The world was unkind. In no way could he quench the burning pain in his heart after the conversation with Sabitzhan, or relieve the oppressive, threatening emptiness that had resulted. This continuous pain inside him felt like a great hollow, a ravine in which there was only cold and mist. Burannyi Yedigei now very much regretted that he had started that conversation. It had been a complete waste of breath. Had Sabitzhan ever been a person to whom it was worth turning to for help and advice? He had hoped that he might have been; he was an educated man, after all; he would have found it easier to talk with people in authority.

347

But look at the results of all that study on all those courses and at all those institutes! Perhaps that was why he had turned out as he had? Perhaps somewhere, some sharp-minded person, like the devil, had expended much effort on Sabitzhan, so that Sabitzhan became the Sabitzhan that he was now and not some other, more civilized sort of person? Him and his nonsense about radio-controlled people! These times are coming, he had said! Indeed! And what if that unseen and all-powerful man was *already* controlling them by radio?

The more the old man Yedigei thought about all this, the more upset and inconsolable he became.

'You're a *mankurt*! A genuine *mankurt*!' he whispered in his heart, hating and pitying Sabitzhan.

However he did not intend to take all this lying down. He knew that he had to do something, to take some action and not just be meekly obedient. Burannyi Yedigei was aware that if he gave up now, he would regard this in his own eyes as a defeat. Although he could see that he had to do something against this fact that had emerged during the day, he could not yet see exactly what his course of action should be – where he should begin, how he could ensure that his concern for the future of Ana-Beiit came to the attention of those who really had the power to countermand the order. Would these thoughts of his reach, convince and effectively change their minds?

In this state of deep thought Yedigei, mounted on Karanar, looked around him. All around was the silent steppe. The early evening shadows were already creeping over the red sand cliffs of Malakumdychap. The tractors had long since disappeared in the distance and could no longer be heard. The young men had clattered off. The last of those who knew, the last to keep in his heart the history of the Sarozek, the old man Kazangap, was now lying up on the precipice under the freshly piled up mound of his lonely grave amid the vast steppe. Yedigei imagined to himself how this mound would gradually settle, become eroded and finally merge with the wormwood colour of the Sarozek. Soon it would become difficult, impossible, to make out the grave's position. No one could outlive the earth, no one escape it . . .

348

The sun was going down, sinking heavily towards the end of the day, its great mass slowly slipping closer and closer down to the horizon. The light of the setting sun was changing from minute to minute. In the belly of the sunset, darkness was imperceptibly being born, a pouring together of the blue of the evening light into the gold of the brightly lit sky.

Thinking over and further considering his position, Burannyi Yedigei decided to return to the barrier at the entrance to the zone. He could think of no other way to act. Now that the burial was over and he was unhampered by anyone else and could therefore rely fully on his own strength – such strength as had been left to him by nature and experience – now he could act on his own responsibility and do what he considered necessary. His first aim was to achieve the following – to make the guards take such action as would mean that he would be taken, under guard if it were necessary, to the senior man on the spot; or, if that was impossible, to make that senior commander come to the barrier and listen to him, Burannyi Yedigei. Then he would say all that he had to say directly to that man's face . . .

He had thought out all this plan and decided to put it into effect without delay, using as direct grounds for a complaint the most painful episode connected with the burial of Kazangap. He had decided to be firm and persistent at the barrier, to demand entry and a meeting, and to make it clear to the guard that he would go on trying to achieve his aim until the highest-ranking officer there had heard him out – a senior officer, and not just some Tansykbaev . . .

This last thought strengthened his resolve. *'Taubakel!* If the dog has a master, then the wolf has God!' Thus he encouraged himself and, beating Karanar with new confidence, he set off for the barrier.

Meanwhile the sun had set, and it began to get dark quickly. There now remained about half a kilometre to go to the barrier and ahead he could already see the lights around the post. Yedigei decided to dismount before he got near the guards. He climbed down from the saddle. He would be better off without the camel; the animal would only get in the way. Some senior officer might come along and, not wishing to discuss the matter, could say, 'Get away from here, you and your camel! Where have you sprung from? No one can receive you!' And he would refuse to even let him enter the office. But the chief reason for leaving the camel was that Yedigei had no idea how long his enterprise would take, how long he might have to wait for the outcome. It would be better to arrive on foot and to leave Karanar, meanwhile, hobbled out on the steppe where he could graze.

'You wait here awhile, and I'll go and see what I can achieve.' Although he addressed this remark to Karanar, it was mainly for his own benefit. First he had to get the camel down on to the ground, because he had to get the hobbles out from the saddle bag and prepare them.

While Yedigei was busy in the dark with the hobbles, it was so quiet all around, there was such an immeasurably deep silence, that he could hear his own breathing and the squeaking and buzzing of some insect up in the air. Overhead a vast multitude of stars were shining – it seemed as though they had suddenly appeared in the clear skies. It was silent, just as if something was about to happen . . .

Even Zholbars, who was used to the quiet of the Sarozek, was very restless and was whining for some reason. What could be worrying him in this silence?

'What are you doing, getting under my feet?' His master spoke angrily. Then he thought: what should he do about the dog? For some time he considered this point as he checked the camel fetters in his hands. What should he do with the dog? It was obvious the dog would not leave him; if he chased him off, he would only come back. To appear with the dog would not be very appropriate when one was making a complaint and request. Even if nothing was said, they would laugh to themselves and think, 'The old man's come to defend his rights and there's no one with him but his dog!' It would be better not to have Zholbars with him. So Yedigei decided to tie him on the long halter to the camel's harness. Let dog and camel be on the one halter while he was away. He called to the dog, 'Zholbars! Zholbars, come here!' He bent down to tie the halter around the animal's neck.

At this moment, something happened in the air. There was a growing, volcano-like roar. Quite close, somewhere very close at hand, within the launching site area, a great burst of terrifying flame was rising up like a column into the sky. Burannyi Yedigei recoiled in alarm and the camel jumped to its feet with a cry. The dog ran in fear towards his master's feet.

It was the first of the automated operational rockets for the trans-space defensive system *Hoop*, lifting off. In the Sarozek it was exactly eight o'clock in the evening, 20.00 hours. After that first rocket, up climbed a second; after that, the third, and then yet another and yet another . . . The rockets soared up into deep space to form around the earth a continuously active barrier so that nothing should change on the earth, so that everything should stay as it was . . .

The sky seemed to be falling about their heads, opening up in swishing clouds of flame and smoke . . . The man, the camel, the dog, those three most simple creatures, ran off, terrified out of their wits. Seized by fear, they ran together, fearing to be separated from each other. Across the steppe they ran, their frantic progress lit up by the pitiless, gigantic, terrifying flames.

But however far they ran, it was like running on the spot, for each new explosion covered them from head to foot in a fiery, piercing light and all around them was a shattering cacophony.

So they ran – man, camel and dog – running without looking back. And suddenly it seemed to Yedigei that out of nowhere, on one side of them, there appeared that white bird which, once upon a time, had formed from Naiman-Ana's white scarf when she fell from the saddle, pierced by the arrow fired by her *mankurt* son. The white bird was flying fast beside them, calling to him amidst all the maelstrom of noise and light:

'Whose son are you? What is your name? Remember your name! Your father is Donenbai, Donenbai, Donenbai, Donenbai, Donenbai, Donenbai . . . !'

And its voice could be heard for a long time yet as the darkness closed in around them . . .

Some days later, both of Yedigei's daughters, Saule and Sharapat, came from Kzyl-Orda to Boranly-Burannyi with their husbands and children, having received a telegram notifying them of the death of the Sarozek's grand old man, Kazangap.

They had come to remember, to express their sorrow and, at the same time, to spend a day or two with their parents. There was nothing bad, without some compensating good.

When they had all got out of the train in a procession and had appeared at Yedigei's door, they found their father was not at home, but Ukubala came hurrying out to meet them, crying, hugging and kissing the children, doting as she did on her daughters and grandchildren.

'Many thanks be to God! Here you all are, at the right time! Your father will be so pleased! How excellent it is that you have come! And you've all come together! You met up together and came! Your father will be so pleased!'

'Where is father?' asked Sharapat.

'He'll be back this evening. He went this morning to Letter Box, to see the man in charge there. It's all about some business of his! I'll tell you about it later. But what are you all standing there for? This is your home, my children!'

Trains in these parts went on running from West to East, and from East to West.

And on either side of the railway lines in these parts lay the great wide spaces of the desert – Sary-Ozeki, the Middle lands of the yellow steppes.

Cholpon-Ata,
December 1979 – March 1980